Fostering Sustainable Growth in Ukraine

Stephan von Cramon-Taubadel
Iryna Akimova
Editors

Fostering Sustainable Growth in Ukraine

With 72 Figures
and 56 Tables

Physica-Verlag
A Springer-Verlag Company

Prof. Dr. Stephan von Cramon-Taubadel
Georg-August-University Göttingen
Department of Agricultural Economics
Platz der Göttinger Sieben 5
37073 Göttingen
Germany

Prof. Dr. Iryna Akimova
Institute for Economic Research
and Policy Consulting
Reytarskaya uliza 8/5-A
01034 Kiev

ISBN 3-7908-1464-4 Physica-Verlag Heidelberg New York

Cataleging-in-Publication Data applied for
Die Deutsche Bibliothek – CIP-Kurztitelaufnahme
Fostering Sustainable Growth in Ukraine / Stephan von Cramon-Taubadel; Iryna Akimova (Eds.). – Heidelberg: Physica-Verl., 2002
ISBN 3-7908-1464-4

Physica-Verlag Heidelberg New York
a member of BertelsmannSpringer Science+Business Media GmbH

Printed in Germany

Cover design: Erich Kirchner, Heidelberg

SPIN 10862315 88/2202-5 4 3 2 1 0 – Printed on acid-free paper

Preface

by Anatoliy Kinakh, Prime Minister of Ukraine

After a deep and long-lasting recession, the Ukrainian economy has for the past two years demonstrated some very positive dynamics in its quantitative development indicators. This is essentially the result of reforms, which still require to be consolidated in order to engage the factors and mechanisms capable of ensuring long-term qualitative and sustainable development in our economy. How do we ensure sustainable growth, and realise the improvements in the main macroeconomic indicators together with serious and complex improvements at the micro-level, which would allow us to achieve the urgently needed shifts in the social sphere? These actual problems are the main priorities of macroeconomic policy. Furthermore, the search for solutions to these problems of our transitional economy requires profound scientific analysis. The following presentations made at the Conference on "Factors of Economic Growth in Ukraine" are serious scientific contributions by prominent economists in this field.

Today the Government of Ukraine carries out a pragmatic social and economic policy, which is based on the principal constitutional program document: The Annual Message of the President of Ukraine to the Supreme Rada. This policy is above all centred on the two main priorities of the national interest, including their precise comprehension and sustainability, which are to eliminate poverty and to develop a civil society. A strategic issue of governmental policy is to engage the factors and mechanisms of qualitative changes in the development of the real economy. This will stimulate domestic demand and, at the end of the day, will improve the living standard of the people. Here, we speak about some real positive gains in the structure of material production, the development of innovations and of human potential. The main goal of our society today is to gain certainty that there are prospects for development, and that these positive changes are sustainable and irreversible. It is therefore necessary to closely analyse the influences of certain short-term and long-term factors on economic growth. All economic and political risks and their possible destabilising influences must be taken into account, to consolidate the positive tendencies of increased savings and of investments in all sectors of the economy. We have to start profound structural reforms and lay the foundations for an innovative model of long-term development.

The factors of growth, considered in this book, have a systemic character and are extremely important for providing qualitative changes and development for the Ukrainian economy. Most conclusions by the authors of this collection of articles are useful and interesting for the realisation of an economic growth policy. The practical implementation of these important measures for sustainable development - such as a systematic reduction of taxes, a gradual phasing out of the regulatory and fiscal factors sustaining the shadow economy, a comprehensive reform of the system of public finance, an active structural and investment policy - certainly is a very important strategic priority aimed at increasing the efficiency of the economic activities in all sectors of the Ukrainian economy. This book will certainly be useful as a guide for the broad issues which the economists and practitioners concerned with economic development problems in Ukraine deal with on a daily basis.

In particular I would like to underline the important contribution to the preparation and realisation of this book by the TRANSFORM-Program, which made possible the realisation of many projects related to facilitating the development of mutual relations between Ukraine and Germany.

With the best regards,

Preface

by Dr. Werner Müller, Federal Minister of Economics and Technology, Federal Republic of Germany

This year Ukraine celebrates the tenth anniversary of its independence. Its move towards becoming a democratic and market-oriented state in Europe went along with a drastic decrease in economic performance for many years. Only towards the end of 1999 was it possible to put the Ukrainian economy back onto a growth path. In the years 2000 and 2001, Ukraine realised impressively high growth rates.

Strengthening democracy and market economy is necessary for Ukraine to make economic growth a lasting and sustainable feature. Detailed analyses of factors responsible for creating and sustaining such growth are therefore of greatest importance for Ukraine. It is helpful for analytical purposes of this kind to include into the discussion and decision-making processes the experience of experts from international organisations and of internationally renowned scientists. This book is meant to contribute to an intensive discussion about the best approaches.

The Federal Republic of Germany has actively helped Ukraine along this path from the date of its independence. Both sides attach high priority to bilateral relations. Regular intergovernmental consultations between Chancellor Schröder and President Kutchma as well as the German - Ukrainian Co-operation Council bear witness to close contacts at both the political and economic levels.

The TRANSFORM programme provides the framework for German advice to the Ukrainian Government and Ukrainian business. The German Advisory Group on Economic Reform has been successful through ist activities in Ukraine since 1994. To place these activities on an sustainable basis, Ukrainian reform-oriented politicians and the Advisory Group joined hands to set up the Institute for Economic Research and Policy Consulting in Kyiv. This book reflects the co-operation of reputed scientists, of members of the Advispry Group, and of young Ukrainian researchers from the Institute.

The authors of the book have reached the conclusion that sustainable economic growth in Ukraine is only attainable through persistent efforts for continuing reform policies.

The Government of the Federal Republic of Germany wishes to encourage the Ukrainian Government to continue and to intensify its reform efforts for democracy, social market economy and the creation of a civil society.

The Federal Republic of Germany is determined to continue its support to this process in Ukraine also in future.

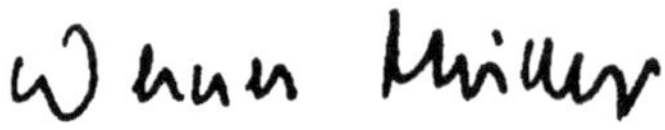

Contents

Introduction

Stephan von Cramon-Taubadel and Iryna Akimova

1 Background

Ukraine has recorded impressive economic growth since late 1999. After falling in every year since independence, real Ukrainian GDP increased by 5.8% in 2000. And in 2001 a real cumulative GDP increase of 10.5% was recorded through to the end of July. Growth is a very welcome economic development for Ukraine. But this does not mean that there are no questions associated with the recent turnaround in economic performance. The most important of these questions, of course, regards cause: What factors, exogenous and endogenous, have triggered Ukraine's ongoing economic growth?

Explaining growth is a fascinating academic challenge that has occupied some of the best minds in the field of economics over the centuries. However, our interest is less academic than practical. The *German Advisory Group on Economic Reforms with the Ukrainian Government* has been advising the Government, Presidential Administration, National Bank, and Parliament of Ukraine on economic policy since 1994. As applied economists working closely with policy makers, we are not interested in growth for its own sake but rather as a means of increasing material standards of living that have fallen dramatically since independence for the majority of the Ukrainian population. The impressive progress that has been made in recent years notwithstanding, Ukraine remains in desperate need of continued growth. If recent growth is to continue in Ukraine, it is important to understand the factors that have contributed to it. In particular, we must attempt to understand the actual and potential contribution of those factors that can be influenced by policy makers.

Economic growth is a complex phenomenon. In empirical studies employing cross-section data on various subsets of the countries of the world, economists have identified many factors that influence growth. In one such study using panel data for 25 transition countries, Havrylyshyn et al. (1999) find, for example, that rates of inflation above the range of 20-30 % have a significant negative impact on growth. However, such results, while interesting, must be treated with caution; they may apply on average to a large group of countries, but there is usually considerable variation about this average. Even in the most refined studies, a large share of the variation in economic performance between countries remains unexplained, and the complex interactions between the different factors that influence growth remain largely hidden from view.

What factors are among those suspected of having contributed to Ukraine's recent economic growth? During the first months of growth in late 1999 and early 2000, some analysts argued that the low statistical base remaining after years of economic contraction was largely responsible. However, as growth continued and strengthened, it became clear that this explanation is insufficient, and the search for other factors intensified.

The real devaluation of the Hryvnia that followed in the wake of the financial crisis in 1998 is certainly a prime suspect. This devaluation increased the competitiveness of Ukrainian tradable goods production, providing a major boost to both export goods (e.g. metallurgy) and import substitutes (e.g. many processed food products). However, there remain a number of open questions regarding the lags that characterise the relationship between devaluation and growth in Ukraine – i.e. how long does it take for the effect of a devaluation to be felt – and the relative contribution of the different components of this devaluation *vis a vis* Ukraine's major trading partners in Russia, Europe and North America.

A positive international climate for economic growth – strong economic growth world-wide and especially in Ukraine's most important trading partner Russia – has certainly played a role as well. The greater this role, the more Ukrainian policy makers must be concerned by recent indications that the world economy could enter a recessive phase. Recent growth in Ukraine is also at least partly due to some formerly unofficial economic activity moving 'out of the shadows'. While this phenomenon cannot represent a source of sustained growth, reducing the size of the shadow economy does have important implications for both government revenues and the overall 'governability' of the economy.

Beside and sometimes interacting with these exogenous factors, the endogenous factor 'reform' is often mentioned as a cause of economic growth in Ukraine. Important market-oriented reforms were announced and implemented following the Presidential elections and the instalment of the new Government lead by Victor Yushchenko in late 1999. While it is unlikely that these reforms would have triggered almost instantaneous growth in late 1999 and early 2000, it is reasonable to believe that they have contributed to continued growth since then. The combination of emerging growth and a new pro-reform government certainly contributed to a new climate of optimism in Ukraine, with attendant effects on the supply and the demand sides of the economy. Reform is especially important because of all the factors listed above it is the one that policy makers in Ukraine can influence directly. While exogenous factors will determine the range of possible economic outcomes in coming years, the pace of reform will determine what actual outcomes from within this range are realised. Sustainable growth without the continued implementation of economic reform is inconceivable.

In June 2001, the *German Advisory Group* hosted a conference in Kyiv as a forum for the exchange of ideas and evidence on explaining and sustaining economic growth in Ukraine. Ukrainian and international experts representing a wide variety of different countries and institutions were invited to present their views on how to foster sustainable growth in Ukraine. This book is a compilation of the presentations made at that conference. In it, many of the causes of growth discussed above are subjected to detailed scrutiny, using the best data and methods that can be brought to bear. We are especially pleased that many of the chapters in this book, and all of those in Part IV, have been contributed by young researchers who work at the *Institute for Economic Reform and Policy Consulting* (IERPC) in Kyiv. The IERPC works closely with the *German Advisory Group*, and after a little more than one year of existence is producing insightful and policy-relevant research.

2 The structure of this book

Part I of this book is comprised of four papers that focus on the International Environment and Growth. In Achievements or Missed Opportunities: Factors of Economic Growth in Russia – What Lessons are Relevant to Ukraine?, EVGENY GAVRILENKOV discusses the factors that have influenced growth in Russia since 1999. Along with the devaluation of the Rouble, he stresses the role played by high world market prices for oil that led to considerable inflows of currency into Russia. At the same time, he points out that much of the value added generated by the Russian economy continues to go offshore. Foreshadowing a later chapter in this book (chapter 4 by Thorvaldur Gylfason), he alludes to the fact that resource rich countries tend to under-perform in international comparison, and that they tend to suffer from permanent capital outflows, something which has also been true of Russia. Referring to Korea's vertically integrated *chaebols*, he also discusses what he terms "chaebolisation" of the Russian economy, which could lead to the bulk of the country's assets being controlled by perhaps 15-20 large conglomerate enterprises.

In Economic Growth in Bulgaria and Romania, GÁBOR HUNYA & RUMEN DOBRINSKY contrast the course of economic reforms and growth in these two Black Sea neighbours of Ukraine. Like Ukraine, both of these countries made only half-hearted transition efforts in the first half of the 1990s. Their paths diverged significantly in 1997, when Bulgaria accelerated reforms and introduced a currency board, while Romania continued, as the authors put it, a policy of "muddling through". As a result, the Bulgarian economy has grown in each year since 1998, while Romania only began to experience growth in 2000. These experiences highlight the importance of economic reform in initiating growth; experience in both countries reminds us that growth episodes (Romania in 1993-95 and Bulgaria in 1994-95) can be short-lived if not shored up by reform.

YILMAZ AKYUZ, in the chapter entitled Trade, Capital Flows and Economic Growth in Developing Countries, discusses the impact of conventional

'Washington consensus' reforms that were implemented in the aftermath of the debt crisis in the early 1980s. Drawing on research undertaken by UNCTAD, AKYUZ derives a number of controversial conclusions. In particular, he concludes that the "empirical record has been at odds with the promises" that were made in connection with trade and liberalisation policies. AKYUZ argues that after over 10 years of liberal reforms, payments disorders in developing countries "remain as acute as ever". He questions whether the impact of FDI on developing economies has been as unambiguously positive as is often implied, pointing out that FDI flows can engender instability and that if China is excluded, almost three quarters of FDI flows to developing countries between 1992 and 1997 went to mergers and acquisitions rather than greenfield investments. AKYUZ concludes with a call for reform of the "global financial architecture" and for increasing the power of developing countries to manage capital in- and outflows.

In Natural Resources and Economic Growth: What is the Connection?, THORVALDUR GYLFASON addresses an issue that has been the focus of considerable research – the impact of resource wealth on economic growth. GYLFASON suggests a number of mechanisms by which resource wealth can negatively influence growth, including the well-known Dutch disease phenomenon as well as the rents and rent seeking behaviour associated with natural resources. According to GYLFASON the common denominator is that natural capital can engender a false sense of security that leads to the neglect of other forms of capital that are prerequisites for sustained growth, such as human, foreign, social and physical capital. Should Russia also 'suffer' from its resource wealth in this manner, this would have negative implications for the sustainability and stability of growth in Ukraine for as long as the Ukrainian economy remains highly dependant on trade with Russia.

In Part II entitled Sustaining Growth of the Ukrainian Economy, five chapters deal specifically with the factors influencing economic growth in Ukraine. MAREK DABROWSKI begins with Is the Economic Growth in Ukraine Sustainable?, in which he presents a short history of economic decline and growth in Ukraine since Independence and then proceeds to discuss hypotheses concerning the sources and sustainability of recent growth. DABROWSKI distinguishes between 'windfall' factors such as the 1998-99 devaluation and longer term structural effects brought about by privatisation and restructuring. While the latter effects have contributed to growth, DABROWSKI expresses concerns about the sustainability of this growth. The Ukrainian economy has huge potential productivity reserves and current macroeconomic stability. However, these will not suffice to guarantee sustainable growth without continued structural reform.

In Is there any Economic Growth in Ukraine?, VALERIY HEYETS argues that while Ukraine has assumed many characteristics of a market economy, much remains to be done. He points out that a lack of functioning labour and stock markets, for example, has a detrimental impact on growth. Using statistics on the input-output structure of the Ukrainian economy, he demonstrates that recent growth has taken place mainly in industries that are characterised by relatively low value added and/or high energy intensity. HEYETS concludes that current growth can continue for the next one to two, and at most three years, but that sustainable growth will depend on Ukraine's ability to mobilise resources for scientific and technical innovation.

OLEH HAVRYLYSHYN, BOGDAN LISSOVOLIK & MOHAMMAD SHADMAN-VALAVI provide us with a counterfactual experiment in Economic Growth in Ukraine: What if Reforms and Economic Recovery Had Started Earlier? Using the performance of Poland and other Central and Eastern European Countries as benchmarks, they estimate where Ukraine would be today if comprehensive reforms had begun in 1992 or 1994. While acknowledging the limitations of their method, the authors argue that it demonstrates that the economic costs of delayed reforms in Ukraine have been very high. Had comprehensive reforms begun in 1994, Ukraine's real GDP would have been between 25% and 50% higher in 1999 than was actually the case. Not surprisingly, the authors conclude that implementing and accelerating market reform is the key to avoiding similar growth deficits in the future.

JOACHIM JAHNKE begins his contribution on Finance and Growth in Ukraine with the reminder that "private investment, entrepreneurship and innovation that drive growth cannot be sustained without well-functioning credit institutions and markets". JAHNKE points out that Ukraine's internal market for long-term finance is severely underdeveloped. For example, stock market capitalisation in Ukraine amounts to roughly 6% of GDP, much less than in countries such as Poland and Hungary. Inflows of external finance are also very small and heavily dependent on international financial institutions and other official lenders. Reform of the banking sector and the pursuit of privatisation, especially in the energy and utilities sectors, would increase the availability of finance in Ukraine.

It is often argued that some of Ukraine's recent growth is due to economic activity moving 'out of the shadows' and into the official sphere. Using a currency demand function, IRYNA MEL'OTA & ULRICH THIESSEN analyse the causes and size of the shadow economy in Ukraine. In Fiscal and Regulatory Causes of Ukraine's Shadow Economy they also attempt to measure the impact of specific reforms on the size of the shadow economy. The authors demonstrate that the direct tax burden, the regulatory burden and the complexity of the tax system influence the size of the shadow economy. Their estimates also indicate that the size of the shadow economy in Ukraine has been falling in recent years and was roughly 7% smaller in 2000 than at its peak in 1997.

Part III of this book is entitled Institutions, Competition and Growth. It begins with an analysis of Enterprise Restructuring and Economic Growth in the Byelorussian Republic by PAVEL DANEYKO & SERGEY PUKOVICH. There has been very little market-oriented reform in Belarus, financial markets remain undeveloped and foreign investment is almost non-existent. Nevertheless, the

Byelorussian Economy has been growing in recent years. Based on a survey of over 200 managers of former socialist enterprises and 300 CEOs of new private companies, the authors demonstrate that enterprises have been restructuring and adapting to changes in the domestic and international environment, making changes that have led to improvements in productivity.

In Performance of Small and Medium Sized Manufacturing Firms in Ukraine: Does the Quality of Governance Matter?, IRYNA AKIMOVA studies the importance of the business climate for the performance of small and medium enterprises (SMEs) in Ukraine. AKIMOVA argues that not only the average state of the business climate (corruption, regulatory burden etc.) but also its variation between firms can have an important impact on performance and growth. Using survey data on 265 Ukrainian SMEs, AKIMOVA demonstrates that Ukraine has failed to establish equal conditions for SMEs as regards the security of property rights, the enforceability of contracts and the tax burden. The resulting 'uneven playing field' creates powerful incentives for managers to bribe officials and evade taxes, leading to resource waste and reduced growth.

Part III closes with two chapters on the investment environment. The first is The Investment Environment in Russia and Ukraine: Common Weaknesses in the Institutional and Policy Framework by EVA THIEL. THIEL discusses the importance of foreign direct investment (FDI) as an engine of growth and the components of an "enabling framework" for FDI. She contrasts Ukraine's record of attracting FDI with that of other countries, and discusses recent OECD studies that analyse why Ukraine's record is relatively poor. In Ukraine: "A Miracle in Waiting" – Challenges and Reforms for an Improved Foreign Investment Environment, MEHMET ÖGÜTÇÜ also analyses Ukraine's ability to attract FDI, and proposes policy measures that could help the Government of Ukraine reach its stated objective of increasing FDI inflows. Like THIEL, ÖGÜTÇÜ stresses the importance of competition and transparency in the form of institutions such as provisions for international arbitration of disputes and the adoption of international accounting and auditing standards.

Part IV is dedicated to Empirical Studies of the Determinants of Growth in Ukraine. It begins with an analysis of Reserve Requirements and Implicit Taxation of Commercial Banks in Ukraine by IGOR EREMENKO. EREMENKO analyses the high reserve requirements of the National Bank of Ukraine as a form of implicit taxation of financial institutions that inflates the interest rate spread. The effects of high reserve requirements – such as lower deposit rates, higher loan rates and reduced intermediation – can negatively influence aggregate investment and lead to output decline. EREMENKO estimates the costs of this implicit taxation for the Ukrainian banking sector to be about UAH 1 bn /year and discusses options for a gradual decrease in reserve requirements in Ukraine.

Many studies have identified efficient infrastructure as a prerequisite for economic growth. However, quantifying something as heterogeneous as infrastructure – a factor which has both physical and institutional components – is difficult. In Efficient Infrastructure Supply as a Condition for Economic Development: The Case of Ukraine, BORIS DODONOV, CHRISTIAN VON HIRSCHHAUSEN, PETRA OPITZ & PAVLO SUGOLOV propose a methodology for infrastructure monitoring which extends the existing EBRD methodology by allowing for both indicator disaggregation and the incorporation of legislation implementation issues and key performance indicators such as the existence of payment arrears and mutual settlements. The authors apply their methodology to policy reforms in six key infrastructure sectors in Ukraine: power, gas, water, telecommunication, railways, and roads. They discuss the need for the deregulation of the infrastructure sector in Ukraine, stressing that it should be carried out simultaneously with commercialisation and tariff reform.

Agriculture is one of the most important sectors in Ukraine, employing a very large share of the population, helping to absorb the shock of restructuring in other sectors and, potentially, serving as an engine of export driven growth. In A Regional Agricultural Trade Model for Ukraine: The Case of Wheat and Sunflower, ALEXANDER KOBZEV argues that excessive marketing costs and ineffective instruments of state agricultural policy implicitly tax domestic agricultural production and reduce total social welfare. Using simulations based on a quadratic programming model, KOBZEV estimates the regional welfare effects of different agricultural policy measures. For example, he shows that in 2001/2002, the reduction of excessive wheat marketing costs would increase total social welfare by USD 64.5 m. KOBZEV stresses the necessity to abolish regional restrictions on the movement of agricultural commodities in order to increase the efficiency of regional and ultimately international agricultural trade in Ukraine.

Government interventions tend to create dead-weight losses. Thus, interventionist government policies should be designed and implemented only after thorough analysis of public benefits and costs. NINA LEGEIDA begins her contribution on Economic Implications of Government Support to the Steel Industry with a description of the direct and indirect subsidies that have been granted by the Ukrainian government to steel producers within the framework of an "economic experiment" in the ore-mining and metallurgical sectors. LEGEIDA applies a partial equilibrium analysis to study the effects of an ad-valorem subsidy in the form of foregone budget revenues (that results from a tax break for metallurgical enterprises) under small- and large-country assumptions. In the short-run, this subsidy seems to foster growth in the supply of ferrous metals as well as in budget and inter-enterprise payments. However, its long-run effect might be negative, especially when the internal market for steel is underdeveloped and dependence on external markets is preserved. The author underlines the distortionary and welfare-reducing nature of the tax subsidy and stresses the importance of a tax reform for economic growth as a whole.

In The Relationship between Foreign Direct Investment and Trade Flows in A Transition Economy: The Case of Ukraine, NADIYA MANKOWSKA & JAMES DEAN analyse the relationship between FDI and trade flows in Ukraine. They provide empirical evidence that the relationship between FDI and trade flows depends on the extent of similarities between investing and recipient countries. MANKOWSKA and DEAN analyse the relationships between FDI and trade in primary and secondary industries, and show that FDI from the European Union (EU) into primary industries is mostly export-oriented and thus complements trade, whereas FDI into secondary, manufacturing industries tend to substitute for trade. By contrast, FDI from the countries of the former Council for Mutual Economic Assistance (CMEA) complements trade in secondary products. The differences in FDI motives and trade patterns between the EU countries and former CMEA members have important implications for the design of policies for enhancing FDI and trade with these two groups of countries.

In The Debt Structure of Ukrainian Firms MARTA OLEKSIV analyses 1999 data to demonstrate that the allocation of credits to firms in different industries in Ukraine is inefficient. Bank loans play a minor role in enterprise financing and are mainly directed towards export-oriented industries (non-ferrous metallurgy, chemical and textile industries) and unprofitable firms. Ukrainian enterprises use payables as a short-term source of finance; while profitable enterprises tend to accumulate tax arrears, financially distressed firms turn to the accumulation of wage arrears. OLEKSIV shows empirically that the distribution of credits was significantly skewed: firms in a few select industries absorbed the majority of bank loans and accumulated the largest volumes of payables and receivables, regardless of their financial situation. This indicates that the allocation of credits is led by sector-specific government priorities rather than economic rationality.

The development of market structures that provide for the optimal allocation of resources is crucial for restructuring former state-owned enterprises. ALEXANDER SCHERBAKOV in his paper on the Restructuring Trap in Transitional Economies: Where Does It Lead? argues that initial conditions (in terms of excessive market concentration inherited from Soviet times) are at least of the same importance for enterprise restructuring as correct settings of market-oriented incentives. SCHERBAKOV shows that in a transition economy large and inefficient incumbent firms can resist competition by using their status of being ‘too big to fail’. As a result, the outcome of restructuring can be negative due to increased monopolisation. Following Sutton’s tradition, this may be interpreted as the endogenisation of exogenous sunk costs previously funded by the government.

Part IV closes with a chapter on the Feasibility of Monetary Targeting in Ukraine by VADIM VOLOSOVYCH who studies monetary targeting as an instrument to assure price stability, influence inflationary expectations, and increase the transparency of monetary policy. The results of VOLOSOVYCH’s empirical analysis confirm the validity of the monetary approach and show that of the available aggregates, M2 is best suited as an intermediate target of a monetary policy aimed at curbing inflation. VOLOSOVYCH stresses that this conclusion depends on the predictability of exchange rate behaviour. In the case of unstable exchange rates priority may be given to the narrower aggregate M1.

3 Outlook and acknowledgements

Fostering sustainable growth in Ukraine: The chapters in this book discuss the factors that have contributed to past and present growth in Ukraine, as well as the prospects for future growth. Of course it is not possible to provide a definitive quantitative decomposition of recent growth in Ukraine into its component parts; the time series at our disposal are too short and many key factors defy measurement. However, it is clear that along with a number of important exogenous 'windfall' factors, endogenous or 'home-made' policy reform in Ukraine has made a significant contribution. And regardless of its exact quantitative contribution, policy reform has the most important influence on growth from a pragmatic perspective because it is the one factor that policy makers can determine. As some exogenous factors, such as the global economic climate, threaten to turn against Ukraine, the need to make the most of those factors that Ukrainian policy makers can influence grows. Recent experience in Ukraine has demonstrated that market-oriented reforms, for example in agriculture, can have a powerful positive impact on economic growth. At the same time, recent growth has enhanced macroeconomic stability, contributing to considerably improved internal and external balances. Hence, the need for continued and decisive structural reform as a means of fostering sustainable growth in Ukraine is clear, and the conditions for such reform are given.

As the editors of this book we would like to express our thanks first and foremost to the Government, President's Office, Parliament and National Bank of Ukraine. In over 6 years of open, constructive dialog, we have built a relationship based on trust that serves as a constant source of motivation. This trust and dialog is a prerequisite for the mutual exchange of questions and answers without which the work we do in Ukraine would be in vain.

We would also like to thank the authors who have contributed to this book and who travelled to Kyiv from many corners of the world to present, debate and discuss their thoughts with policy makers, colleagues and students.

The work of the *German Advisory Group* and the IERPC in Kyiv would not be possible without the support of the German government's TRANSFORM-Program, funded through the German Ministry of Economy and co-ordinated by the Kreditanstalt für Wiederaufbau. On the Ukrainian side, the Ministry of Economy of Ukraine has been a most supportive project partner, not only helping us with the inevitable administrative details but also providing us with questions, advice, information and inspiration. Svitlana Shchokina, Inna Morgun and Kyryl

Savin (in Kyiv) and Harald von Cramon (Montréal) have assisted Lars Handrich (Kyiv and Berlin) with the 'nuts and bolts' of compiling this book. Without their hard work and Lars' co-ordination, this book would not have been possible, and we are correspondingly grateful.

References

Havrylyshyn, O.; I. Izvorski, and R. van Rooden (1999): Growth in Transition Economies 1990-1997: An Econometric Analysis. In: Siedenberg, A. and L. Hoffmann (1999): *Ukraine at the Crossroads – Economic Reforms in International Perspective with Application to Ukraine*, Phyisica-Verlag, Heidelberg.

Part I

THE INTERNATIONAL ENVIRONMENT AND GROWTH

1

Achievements or Missed Opportunities: Factors of Economic Growth in Russia. What Lessons are Relevant to Ukraine?

Evgeny Gavrilenkov

1 Some empirical facts about the economic performance during 1999 and 2000

As shown by the most recently published data of the Russian Central Committee on Statistics (Goskomstat), the country's GDP increased by 14.1% and industrial output increased by more than 24% over the period of 1999 and 2000. In 2000, GDP grew 8.3%. Thus, at the end of 2000 the seasonally adjusted GDP slightly exceeded the level in early 1994 (see Graph 1.1). Industrial output grew over 10% in 2000, and fixed investments grew over 17%. The rapid growth of investment was one of the most impressive results of the fast recovery. Consumption also grew steadily in 2000; thus retail sales expanded 8.9%, well behind the growth of real disposable income, which increased 9.1% in 2000 over 1999.

The major factors contributing to the high growth rates after the August 1998 crisis seem to be well-known. They are: devaluation resulting in import substitution, low domestic energy prices that were not allowed to grow as fast as inflation, and high world market oil prices that contributed to substantial currency inflows into Russia. The 1998 devaluation contributed to a substantial decrease of household incomes, while increasing corporate incomes. This in turn resulted in high investment growth rates.

It should be stressed that the corporate sector did not fully use this opportunity to invest: the Russian economy delivered high growth rates even against the background of continuous capital outflows that roughly accounted for nearly one tenth of the GDP in both 1999 and 2000. This may prove that the rapid crisis recovery taking place in Russia in 1999-2000 occurred mostly due to natural reasons, such as the above mentioned devaluation and/or the world market oil prices, but not as a result of any government strategy.[1] Most likely the high investment growth rate was not a result of an improved business climate, but it arose out of high corporate profits generated mostly in export-oriented sectors. As a matter of fact, many other indicators show that the business climate in Russia was far from perfect. Thus in 2000, foreign direct investments in Russia (USD 2.7 bn) decreased relative to the already low level of 1999. In contrast Russian legal direct investments abroad (USD 3.1 bn) grew substantially in 2000 and for the first time exceeded foreign direct investment inflows into Russia. In fact, Russia became a net exporter of legal direct investments.

Official statistics also show that in 2000 the number of small and medium size businesses decreased in Russia (by roughly 1.3% relative to 1999). The output share produced by small and medium size businesses correspondingly decreased as a percentage of GDP.

Graph 1.1
Quarterly real GDP from 1993 to 2001 (RUR bn)

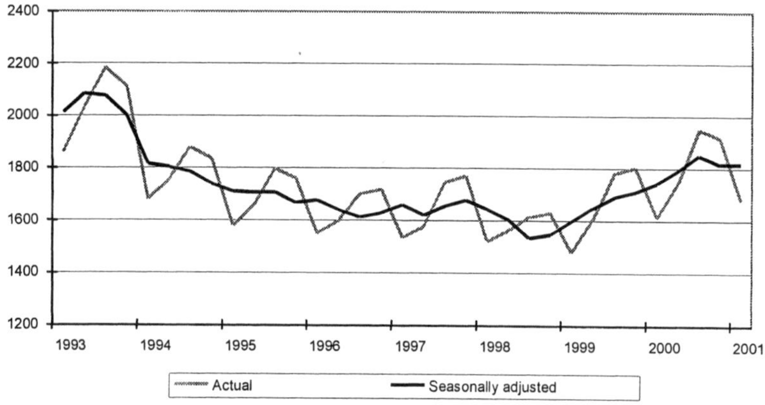

Furthermore, growth rates slowed during the second half of 2000, first in industry, and then in the overall GDP as well (see Graph 1.1 and 1.2). Some indications of industrial output contraction could already be seen starting in September 2000. Although – according to official statistics – the output contraction stopped in early 2001, there are no clear indications yet that the economy had started growing again as rapidly as before. According to preliminary estimates by the Ministry of Economic Development and Trade, GDP increased roughly 4.2% (year-on-year basis) during the first quarter of 2001, mostly as a result of a much lower base in 2000.

---

1 Even despite the announcement of such a strategy by the government during the middle of 2000. In fact, it looks as if the strategy's implementation lagged well behind its publication.

It should also be noted that investment growth rates decreased substantially at the beginning of 2001. From January to May 2001 they increased by only 4.2% compared to the same period of 2000. At the same time household incomes and consumption were growing much more rapidly. This means that the causes for growth in early 2001 must have changed substantially. In 2000 investment was a major catalyst for economic growth, while in early 2001 growth was driven mostly by household consumption, a consumption fuelled by rapidly growing imports.

Graph 1.2
Industrial output from 1993 to 2001 (in %, December 1992=100)

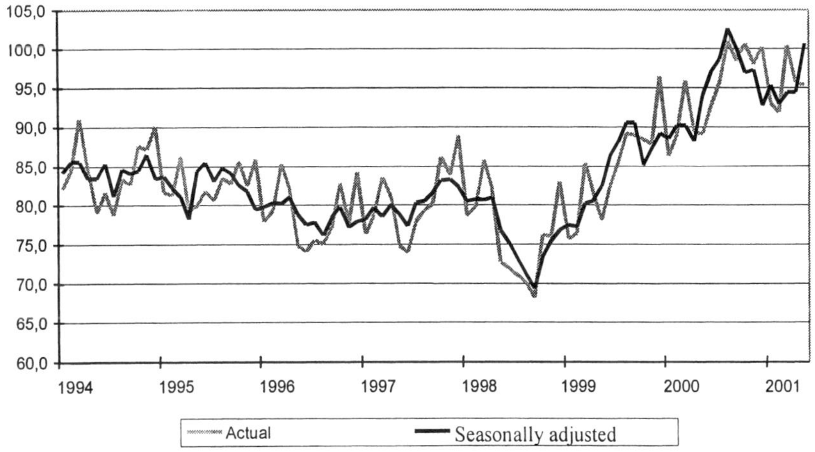

The above analysis of the changes in the growth mechanisms would be incomplete if the sectoral allocation of the investments would not be taken into account. Thus, as proven by the official statistics, though investments in 2000 increased substantially, this rapid growth was primarily caused by an increased investment activity in the oil-and-gas sector and in transportation.[2] These two sectors absorbed nearly one half of the total fixed investment. If these two sectors are subtracted, it then becomes evident that the investment in the economy had not increased at all, but had even contracted (by 0.2%). In some industries, such as machine building and food, investment had contracted dramatically in 2000. Also, as seen in Graph 1.3, seasonally adjusted total investment actually began to fall during the second half of 2000.

2 This includes pipeline transportation.

Graph 1.3
Investments in fixed capital from 1994 to 2001 (December 1998 prices, RUR bn)

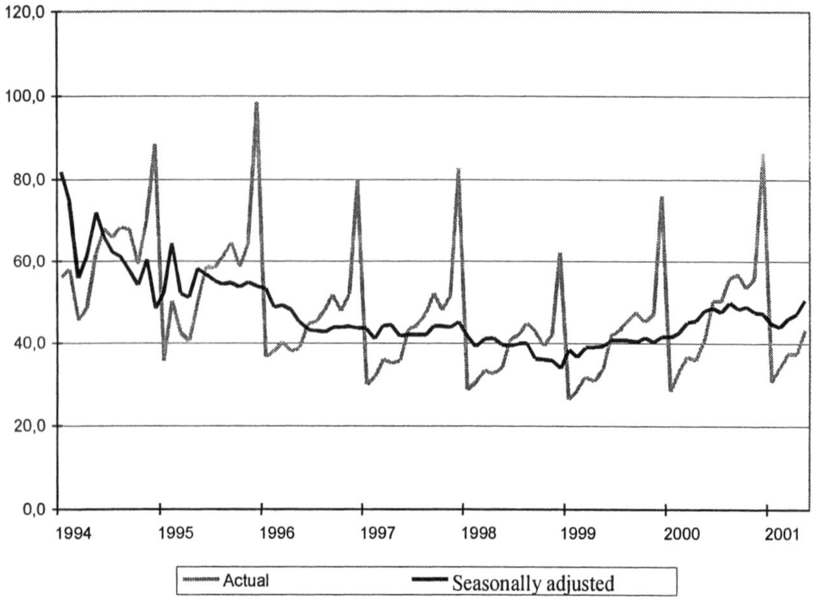

The situation looked a little different in the first quarter of 2001. Although overall investment was not growing as rapidly as during the preceding year, there was some increase in investment (3.7%) in that aggregated part of the economy that excludes oil-and-gas and transportation. In fact, seasonally adjusted overall investment grew again in February and March 2001. It is quite possible that the increased investment activity in manufacturing resulted from the fact that exporters, who had earned high profits during the previous year, now began actively to acquire assets in Russia – in addition to exporting capital. There are indications that Gazprom was acquiring significant amounts of agricultural land in southern Russia, that aluminium producers were buying machine-building enterprises, and that oil companies were also taking control of the manufacturing sector of the Russian economy. Due to high levels of export earnings, certain sectors were able to accumulate "excess" financial resources, some of which were used to buy property inside Russia.

2 Growth, institutions, and the exchange rate policy dilemma

One of the major conclusions to be derived from the revised growth figures is that growth acceleration in 2000 was not as rapid as was thought before. In fact, the difference between 8.3% and 5.4% for the revised growth rates in 2000 and 1999 respectively is less significant than that between 7.7% and 3.2% for the old data. Which means that the impact of high oil prices on economic performance was probably overestimated initially. It may be that the rapid growth in 2000 originated not primarily from external factors, but was largely due to internal reasons, among them especially institutional changes.

The need to reallocate the "excess" financial resources generated by the export-oriented sectors to the rest of the economy is one of the key problems for Russia. Exporters are able to accumulate "excess" profits largely due to some still existing enormous relative price distortions, including an undervalued Rouble.[3] Since institutions in Russia are still unable to "process" all the value added generated by the Russian economy, substantial parts of this money goes offshore. Weak institutions, such as the lack of financial intermediation, poor property rights guarantees, frequent violations of minority shareholders' rights, high barriers to entry into the market, etc. are not attracting investors. Although the government is attempting to solve these problems, this is likely to take a long time. Until then investor confidence will remain low and investment risks will remain high in Russia. In this sense, the poor institutional framework and the frequent changes in the "rules of the game" were the major impediments to growth in the 1990s. This is likely to be the same in Ukraine, given that – according to the balance of payment – foreign direct investment (total or per capita) remains at a low level.

Although the official data show that at present more than 70% of the GDP is generated within the private sector in Russia, this does not mean that a real market system already exists in the country. Privatisation quickly created the private sector, thereby helping to solve the well-known political problems of the early 1990s. But that was not the same as establishing a functioning market system. The establishment of new companies is still very complicated and associated with corruption. It is evident that capital would rather move to countries where the barriers to entry are lower and the "rules of the game" more stable.

Thus, for instance, the US economy which is less regulated than many other economies remains attractive to investors (and to human capital as well) despite all of the problems it faces. Capital inflows to the US economy exceed USD 1.0 bn per day, which of course causes many other problems, but it clearly demonstrates that the matter of confidence is a key issue for investors.

---

3 The undervalued Rouble can also be considered as a price distortion.

The slow down of investment activities in Russia during the second half of 2000 was to some extent the investors' reaction to the widening gap between the government's good intentions and reality. However, the investment slow down did by no means contribute to the production slow down.

The production slow down must also be attributed to the real appreciation of the Rouble. In the fall of 2000, imports began growing against the background of a real appreciation of the Rouble, while a production slow down started concurrently. Graph 1.4 shows that production began growing rapidly immediately after the August 1998 crisis, and that a weak Rouble prevented massive imports till about mid-2000. Increased inflation in mid-2000 caused an accelerated rate of Rouble appreciation and imports began to grow rapidly. Deflated by the CPI, the Rouble appreciated by some 15%; while deflated by the PPI, the Rouble appreciated by some 21%.

Graph 1.4
Seasonally adjusted industrial output and imports from 1994 to 2001

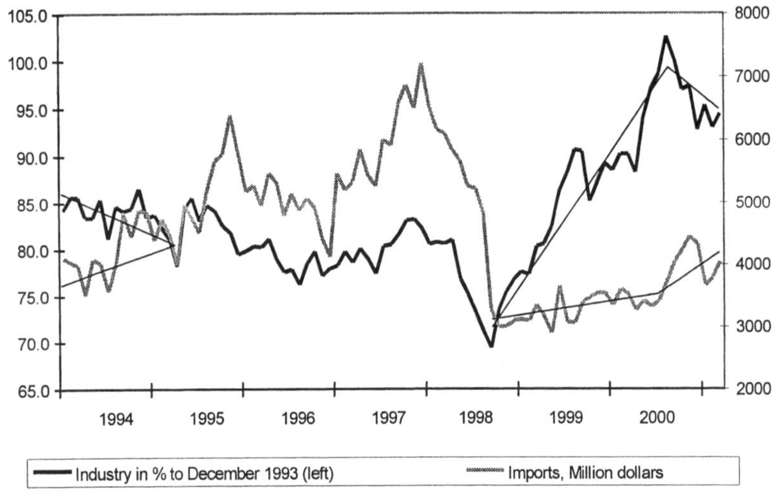

Therefore it was only natural that the gap between slowing production and growing consumption was filled by increased imports. Thus, imports during the fourth quarter of 2000 were 21% higher than during the fourth quarter of 1999. Most important however, was that imports from the CIS increased much faster than imports from the rest of the world. For the whole year, imports from the CIS grew by nearly 30% relative to 1999, while imports from the non-CIS countries increased by 7.8% only. Total imports grew by nearly 13.5% in 2000.

The growth of imports from the CIS appears to indicate that some sort of restoration of the former Soviet Union (in the sense of economic relations) was taking place. In 2000 while Russia benefited from increased export earnings generated mostly by the energy sector, other CIS countries also benefited from the increased trade with Russia. Russia imported from the CIS both finished and intermediate goods. That means the country continues to be an energy exporter to the rest of the world and an importer of higher valued added products from its CIS neighbours. In this way, Russia in 2000 "shared" to some extent with other CIS countries the advantages obtained from high oil prices through stimulating production in those states. Whenever Russia imported intermediate products from CIS countries, this could be considered as increasing the co-operation between Russian and CIS firms. Yet growing imports of finished goods were definitely not in favour of Russian producers facing strong competition from CIS producers. For example, the food industry output during the first quarter of 2001 already started shrinking with Russian products becoming less competitive relative to CIS products.

It should be noted that already in early 2001, the continuous real appreciation of the Rouble caused imports from non-CIS countries to grow faster (17.9% in 1Q 2001 on a year-on-year basis) than from CIS countries (7.1%). This means that given a price-quality choice, CIS products are becoming less competitive on the Russian market than European or Asian products. A further appreciation of the Rouble may well result in a further contraction of CIS imports; on the other hand, it might stimulate more efficient production within the CIS.

Graph 1.5
Real exchange rate and seasonally adjusted imports from 1994 to 2001

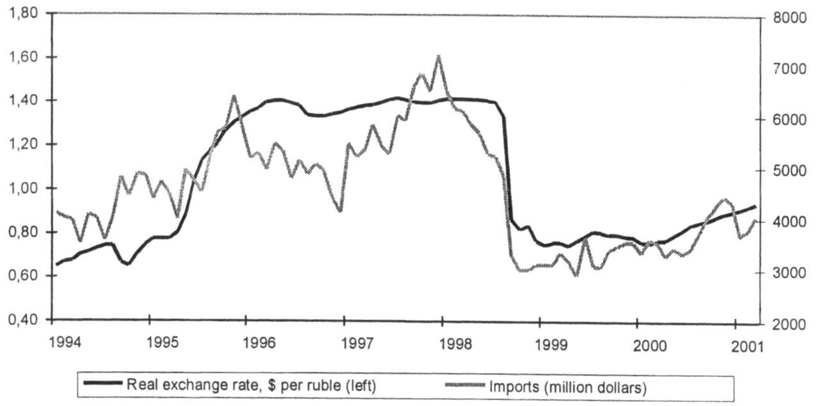

In any case, this problem of CIS and non-CIS trade exchange rate policy remains a key issue for the Russian government and its monetary authorities. Graph 1.5 actually confirms the high correlation between imports and the real exchange rate in Russia. On the one hand, a weaker Rouble is somewhat more preferable for the economy as it protects domestic producers from competition. On the other hand the need to solve the foreign debt problem requires a stronger Rouble. Hence some balance must be found. As shown on Graph 1.5, in real terms the Rouble is now at about the level of mid-1995 with enough remaining for its further appreciation. Finding a rate of appreciation that would not critically undermine the competitiveness of the economy thus remains a major concern.

Evidently, in the long run the exchange rate policy should not be considered only as a tool of macroeconomic policy. It can also be used as an indicator of whether policy implementations were successful or not. Given the substantially undervalued national currencies in the CIS countries, their real appreciation over the long run is quite likely, provided domestic policies are reasonable. An improvement of the business climate will inevitably reduce capital outflows in some cases (namely Russia) and increase foreign capital inflows in others. This in turn will inevitably make the local currencies stronger. It therefore makes sense to advocate a stronger Rouble once real success with structural and institutional reforms has been achieved. At that time the stronger currency would allow increasing the import of technologies, machines, and equipment, and not only of consumer goods as it happened in the 1990s and to some extent now. A weak Rouble can be seen as a real constraint to modernisation of the economy. And is associated with a growing economy reproducing its obsolete and inefficient energy and resource intensive structure.

Due to high world oil prices Russia's exports in 2000 were as high as never before in the 1990s. In fact they reached USD 105.7 bn while imports accounted for USD 44.9 bn. This huge trade surplus allowed the monetary authorities to increase the international reserves (excluding gold) by USD 15.8 bn, or by 2.9 times, during the year. By the end of 2000 the total international reserves (including gold) had reached USD 28 bn, the highest level ever. In this environment a real Rouble appreciation was quite natural.

Building up the reserves was followed by a rapid money supply expansion. The money supply in Rouble increased by 62.4% in 2000 while inflation was only 20%. This rapid monetisation of the economy obviously stimulated production and substantially reduced the seriousness of the problem of arrears and other non-monetary transactions. Thus, in some sense the Rouble liquidity was sterilised by a growing economy.

The fiscal surplus was another means of sterilising the excessive Rouble liquidity. Along with a strong balance of payments the budget execution in 2000 was also as strong as never before. The total surplus of the federal budget reached RUR 173.5 bn or 2.5% of GDP. Federal revenues (tax plus non-tax revenues) reached 16.2% of GDP, revenues of the consolidated budget (federal plus local) reached 29.9% of GDP. That was higher than a year ago.

Taxes on foreign trade (mostly import and export duties) contributed nearly a quarter of the total tax revenues and were higher than the profit tax collections. By introducing and raising export duties for oil the government was able to improve its fiscal situation substantially. In 1999 the export duties on oil were relatively low: EUR 5 per ton of oil. In the fall of 1999 the government raised the rate to EUR 7.5 and again in December 1999 to EUR 15 per ton. Following further oil price increases in 2000, the export duty was raised to EUR 34. On 1 January 2001 the export duty was raised to EUR 48 for a short time, but then, given the decrease in world oil prices, the government returned the export duty to the previous lower level. Calculations show that corporate gross profits in the oil sector had increased roughly 3.3 times in 2000 relative to 1999. At the same time the collected export duties increased nearly 5 times. In any case, it is quite obvious that despite increased export duties the oil companies benefited a lot in 2000 (which was partially reflected in increased investments and in capital flight).

The export duties collected in 2000 (RUR 164.3 bn) reached 2.4% of GDP, practically equalling the fiscal surplus. Given that the oil companies paid other taxes too, one can state that the oil sector was the principal contributor to macroeconomic stability. But this fact also proves that the financial stabilisation in 2000 was rather fragile since the Russian budget still depended too much on external conditions.

During this period, the value-added tax remained the major source of federal revenues contributing to more than half of the total revenues of the federal budget. The excise tax was another major source of federal budget revenues contributing 13.3% to total tax revenues.

In contrast to the fiscal authorities the monetary authorities were not able to carry out active sterilisation policies in 2000. The role of the financial markets remained negligible in the economy. Thus the excessive Rouble liquidity increased inflationary expectations so that in early 2001 inflation was close to 2% per month. This may result in total inflation in 2001 being substantially higher than projected in the budget.

Early in 2001 the Central Bank's policy became tougher. The monetary base decreased in January and then was growing more slowly than before. Since inflationary expectations in early 2001 were high, the commercial banks attempted to increase their hard currency reserves. In February the money markets experienced some lack of Rouble liquidity, however the banks were not willing to sell US Dollars. On some days in February one could observe substantial fluctuations of the overnight interest rate (up to 100% and shortly after back to the regular 10-20% per annum) indicating that the markets were very nervous, which confirms that the government was still unable to fully restore confidence.

3 Growth and structural changes

As pointed out in the part 1 of this paper nearly half of the total investment in 2000 was attracted to the energy sector and to transportation – quite naturally so, since profits in these two sectors were high. The energy sector benefited from high world market prices and transportation benefited mostly from transporting exports (at higher rates than for transporting non-tradables). In preceding years the share of the energy sector and of transportation in total investment had also been high, but lower than in 2000 (see Graph 1.6). This graph also shows that their share has constantly increased throughout the 1990s. It should be noted that according to the official statistics transportation and the energy sector produce less than 20% of the GDP (at domestic prices).[4] Thus, at present the remaining 80% of the economy, which includes manufacturing, services, agriculture, and many other sectors receive only half of the total investment.

Graph 1.6
Fixed investment in the energy sector and in transportation as a percentage of total fixed investment from 1992 to 2000

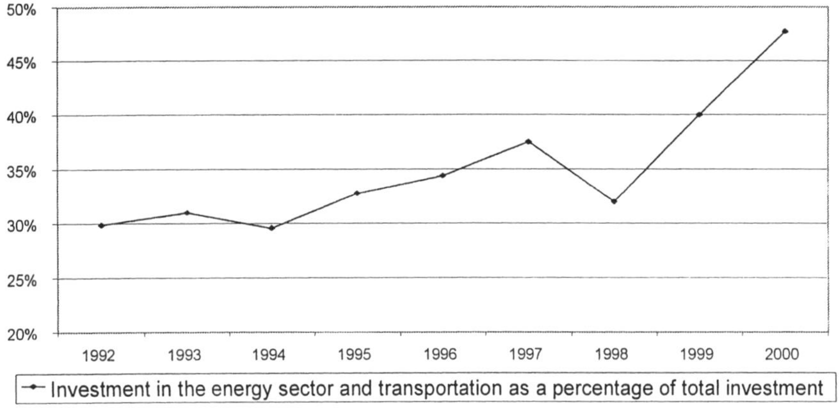

Several studies[5] have shown that resource-poor countries performed much better during the post-war era than resource-rich ones. It was the resource-poor countries that developed new economic sectors (e.g. telecommunications, information technologies, etc.), while the resource-rich countries were mostly extracting resources and transporting them. Also resource-rich countries saw most of their export earnings going offshore rather than coming back since owners of mining

4 This share would be higher if calculated at world market prices, but obviously would still be much less than half of GDP.

5 See for instance M. Auty "The Political Economy of Resource-Driven Growth", Sachs and Werner "The Case of Natural Resources" (Russia was not examined in these papers) and the chapter by Gylfason in this book.

companies were primarily interested in developing their main businesses and paid little attention to the local economy. For obvious reasons the political elites in most of these countries were quite supportive of domestic exporters. Thus, the resource-rich economies suffered from permanent capital outflows. This is obviously true for Russia as well.

It is instructive to have a brief look backwards and to realise that Russian history demonstrates that the growth rates of the Soviet (or Russian) economy during the second half of 20th century slowed down after new deposits of oil and gas were discovered. This happened against the background of growing investments in the energy sector and in transportation (mostly pipeline transportation.). Soviet planners allocated more and more investment to resource extraction while other sectors that could have potentially produced higher value-added products suffered from under-financing (see Graph 1.7). Hence, the present growth of investment in the energy sector in Russia should be considered not only as a positive sign, but also as a warning signal with respect to long-term perspectives.

Graph 1.7
Output growth rates (in %, left-hand scale) and the share of fixed investment allocated to the energy sector and to transportation in total fixed investment (right-hand scale)

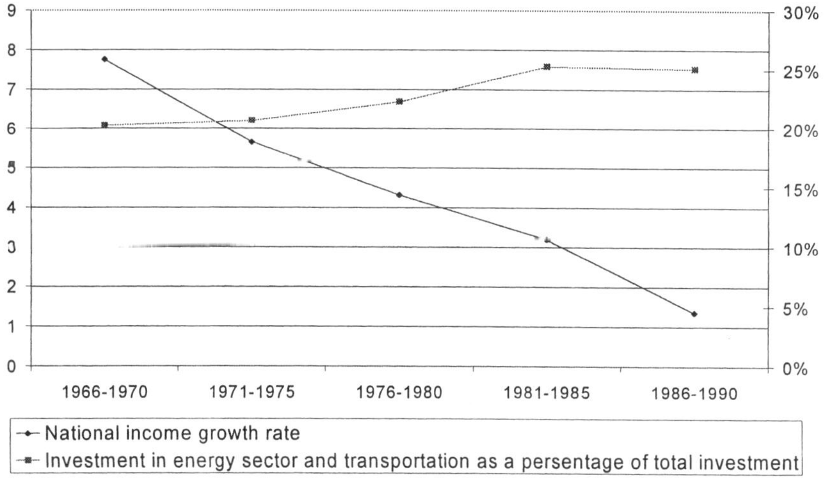

The high growth rates targeted in the above mentioned long-term government strategy require a different structure of the economy. The present economic structure is not able to deliver sustainable high growth rates since it is highly dependent on exports of energy and semi-finished products. Sectors with low value-added products dominate the Russian economy. Investment in economic restructuring and in the renovation of capital stock is crucial. This evaluation, too, comes to the conclusion that both radical improvement of the business climate and proper institutions are essential.

Graphs 1.8-1.10 demonstrate that only investment correlates well with output in the 1990s in Russia. Thus, one should not rely on stimulating growth through non-interest spending by the government. As seen in Graph 1.8 public consumption in Russia was growing despite some fluctuations between 1994 and 2000, even when the GDP was contracting during some time of that period. Thus, no one can guarantee that the economy will resume sustainable growth when the government is stimulating demand.

Graph 1.9 shows that growing private consumption as it was the case in 1996 and 1997 cannot be a reliable guarantee for sustainable growth either, if not supported by other policy measures. Finally, Graph 1.10 shows that there was a much closer correlation between investment and output trends in Russia.[6] Thus, unlocking the investment activity is most likely to lead to a resumption of sustainable growth. Since the growth potential in Russia is very high, given the substantial amounts of under-utilised financial resources, this mean that investment growth should occur at the expense of falling capital flight. Only in this case will consumption be expanding as it has done in 1999 and 2000.

Graph 1.8
Seasonally adjusted GDP and public consumption in real terms

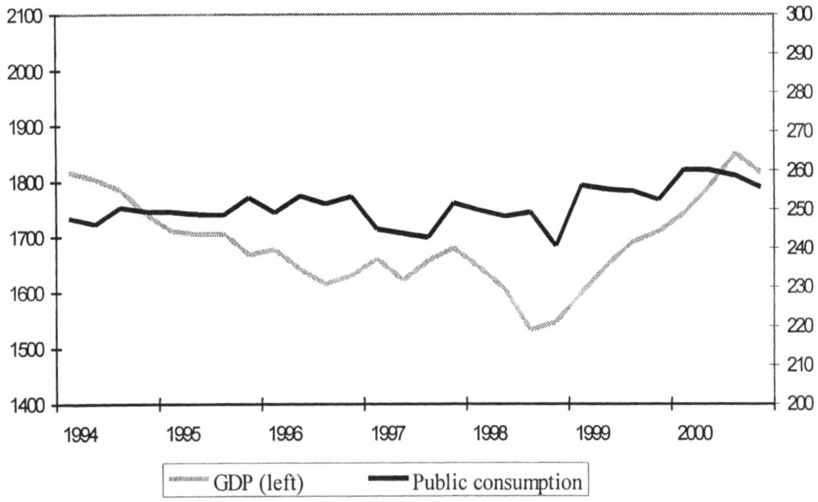

---

6 The GDP figures in Graph 1.8 to 1.10 are based on average prices in the year 2000.

Graph 1.9
Seasonally adjusted GDP and private consumption

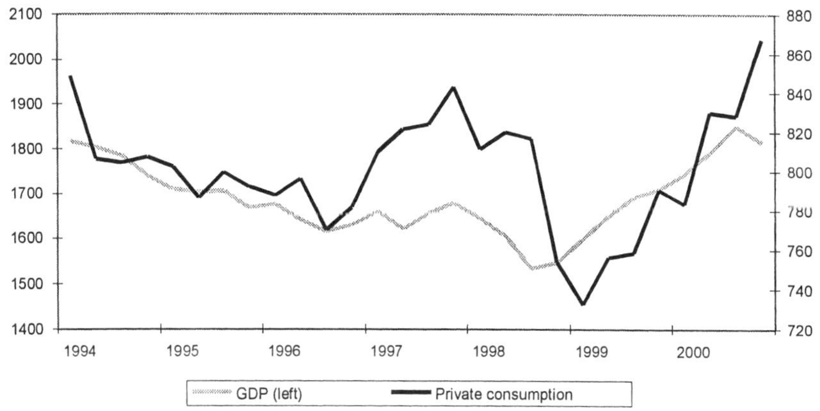

Graph 1.10
Seasonally adjusted GDP and gross investments

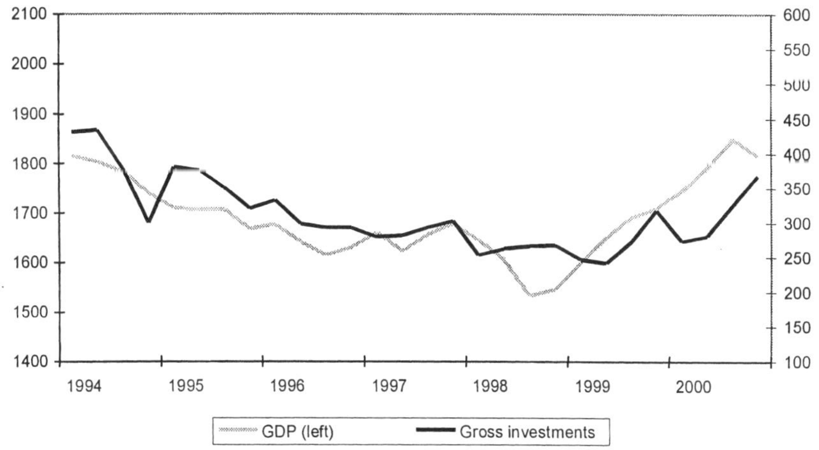

As noted earlier, one has to realise that improving the business climate and restoring confidence may require quite a lot of time. Until governmental strategies have created a better institutional system, the economic system could evolve in different ways. In the mean time, the problem of allocating the excess value received from exports to the rest of the economy should somehow be addressed.

A simple administrative reallocation through higher taxation of the exporters could be considered as one possible approach. To some extent this had already taken place in past years, when the government collected more taxes through higher export duties. This approach had in fact been used for decades, thus the low efficiency of this mechanism is well known. Another result was that the more taxes the government was able to collect, the more it spent on financing the domestic economy. High inflation in early 2001 was one result of this administrative reallocation. The illusion persisted that the more pensioners and public sector employees are paid (of course, regardless of the economic situation), the better this will be for the economy. Yet, the too rapid increase in public spending during a period of stagnating economy resulted mostly in a higher than expected inflation.

Another way of reallocating value-added profits can be to reallocate property, such as described in part 1, where the exporters began to invest broadly across the economy. In the short and medium term such an evolution of the economic system should contribute to a substantial improvement of the macro indicators. High growth rates are achievable, both due to investment and to consumption at the expense of shrinking net exports. To some extent this evolution will be in the direction of the Asian type of economy, for instance the South Korean one. This could end up with an economy divided into 15 to 20 big Russian *"chaebols"* controlling the bulk of the country's assets. Such a system exists not only in Korea, but also in the Philippines, or in Indonesia where 15 of the richest families control between 60% and 70% of the country's assets. It looks as if the Russian economic system might somehow evolve into this type of organisational structure.

Too many close ties with the government is one of the major drawbacks of such a system, resulting in a lack of transparency in decision making, lessened competition, corruption, etc.. Such a system is not dissimilar from the administrative type system, wherein both the political and business elites have a joint interest and co-operate closely. The system does not need a developed banking sector, or more generally speaking financial markets, since the reallocation of financial resources can be arranged within the vertically integrated *chaebols*. In particular, it would be rather difficult to accumulate private savings or to carry out pension reform as intended by the government. Furthermore, international experience has proven that corporate governance of such systems is not perfect; there are many cross-subsidisation cases and many other flaws. Though it may appear that in the short run such a system can deliver rapid success, it will also give birth to various illusions.

A third way of reallocating the value-added profits from a limited number of exporters to the rest of the economy is associated with institutional and structural reforms. Given that this is a long-term process, it is likely that in the Russian case the evolution towards the Asian type of economic system is the most likely. It is very important that the authorities are fully aware of the long-term problems associated with such a system. Success of the third way depends above all on an adjustment of relative prices. A distorted relative price structure allows some sectors to be in fact subsidised by others. For example, the non-ferrous metals industry was heavily subsidised by the power industry. Electricity tariffs set at too low a level (1.5 Cents per kWh as an average for 2000) permit several energy intensive industries to enjoy low costs within Russia and high profits outside. In fact, cheap energy is a competitive advantage for some chosen sectors of the economy, but it is a disadvantage for the economy as a whole.

A rise in energy tariffs[7] would force exporters of energy intensive goods to start thinking about energy savings, cost reduction, modernisation, etc.. This would mean that the value added (or at least some part of it) which is now generated by the exporters would be reallocated to manufacturing more along market principles, namely through an increasing domestic demand for more efficient technologies, machines and equipment.

Actually the Russian government adopted restructuring plans for some natural monopolies, for RAO UES in particular, which assumed gradual relative price adjustments at the initial stage. It can be demonstrated that a rise in the electricity (and correspondingly the gas) prices will inevitably require further structural reforms, particularly in the transportation sector.[8] A reform of the housing sector was also announced as a top priority on the government's agenda. Housing reform will require solving several technical problems, such as how to create a mechanism for targeting subsidies to the poorest parts of population, but such questions are solvable. The present illogical system, whereby the richest part of population, which has the bigger apartments and consumes more heat and electricity, benefits more from state subsidies through low energy prices should be abolished. This system is similar to the subsidisation of the metal exporters.

It does appear that the Russian economic system will evolve somewhere in between the three options described above. In the short run *chaebolisation* is the most likely way of its evolution. To further a movement towards a developed market economy the government should urge structural reforms.

---

7 We do not argue for an immediate rise of domestic energy pieces up to international levels.

8 From a macroeconomic point of view the elimination of cross-subsidisation in the transportation sector is necessary in order to achieve the needed gap between electricity prices and the rest of them. If a rise in electricity tariffs results in a corresponding rise in cargo transportation tariffs, then the inflation chain reaction will somehow spread across other sectors finally resulting in higher consumer prices for most products. This has been the usual case in Russia over the past years. Rising passenger transportation tariffs will allow transportation companies to keep profits unchanged, and at the same time the cost-push of inflation will not spread across the economy. The same is true for the housing sector. All this will inevitably change the structure of household expenditures, but in the right direction.

2

Economic Growth in Bulgaria and Romania

Gábor Hunya and Rumen Dobrinsky*

1 Introduction

The two south-east European countries share the last places among the EU accession countries concerning economic development, structural change and institutional reform. At the same time they are more advanced in these respects than many other south-east European or CIS countries. At the first glance, the two country have a similar track of economic development: first a deep transitional recession in 1990-1992/93, then a modest recovery which proved unsustainable and called for a second stabilisation effort which incurred recession. Both of them inherited highly distorted economic structures from the communist regime and introduced only half-hearted transformation measures in the first half of the 1990s. But economic policies since 1997 have made the two countries radically different from each other. The Bulgarian shock therapy compares with the Romanian muddling through policy. Bulgaria gets better notes from international organisation for its transformation policy than Romania which has a notorious credibility problem. Currently both countries are on a recovery path from earlier setbacks, but the structure of output changes only very slowly, foreign financial constraints are severe and the investment rate is low. These features question the sustainability of the current medium-high GDP growth rates in both countries.

2 Comparative overview

Bulgaria and Romania are compared in this section with Ukraine as well as with two more advanced CEECs of similar sizes, Hungary and Poland. The latter are used only as a virtual point of reference and will be not discussed in detail.

---

* The views expressed are those of the author and not of the organization he is affiliated with.

In Bulgaria the crisis in the mid-1990s was deeper as it went hand in hand with a foreign debt crisis. The banking system collapsed and the introduction of a currency board regime was thought to be the only solution to restore stability and confidence. As a result, economic growth has been positive and inflation low since 1998. Fiscal and monetary policies are prudent, the fixed exchange rate system is sustainable. The country has successfully finished a three year stand-by agreement with the IMF and enjoys wide recognition for its stabilisation policy.

In Romania the second transformational crisis was thought to be less severe but triggered a more prolonged decline in the second half of the 1990s. Romania has, despite recognizable progress, a somewhat intransparent fiscal policy, medium high inflation, an unpredictable floating exchange rate. Subsequent governments have had a serious credibility problem as all five accords signed with the IMF in the last eight years have been aborted due to under-performance in the field of restructuring.

Despite all these differences, the relative per capita GDP at purchasing power parity of the two countries has not changed between 1990 and 2000: the Romanian lead is 10% and both countries are at about one quarter of the EU average.

Both Romania and Bulgaria spend about 70% of their GDP on private consumption while the share of capital accumulation is only about 15%. The low investment rate signals that the present economic growth is mainly based on the utilisation of existing capacities and that it will not be sustainable without massive new investments.

As to international financing, the two countries started transformation from two opposite positions. Bulgaria was highly indebted and practically insolvent in the first half of the nineties until an international debt relief agreement came into force. Capital inflows have been mostly from multilateral sources, the Eurobond market has not been tested yet. Romania on the other hand started transformation debt-free but in a few years it accumulated a sum equal to one year's exports. When most of the Eurobonds matured in 1999 the country came under substantial financial strain. Foreign public debt was converted into domestic debt with interest payments amounting to 30% of central government budget expenditures. In 2001 both Eurobonds issues and EU financing will have a growing role.

Foreign direct investment was low in both countries for most of the 1990s, but picked up in the last three years when privatisation by sales started. This is true especially for Bulgaria which has taken a more radical approach to the state-owned industry than Romania. The share of the foreign sector in manufacturing is about 15% in Romania, and 30% in Bulgaria. In banking assets the foreign share amounts to some 40% in Romania and 60% in Bulgaria.

Inflation in Bulgaria was generally high in the first half of the 1990s and exploded in the beginning of 1997. Currency board was introduced in July 1997 and the depreciated currency was pegged to the Deutsche Mark. Since then, inflation is under hard constraints. Romania has had medium high inflation all through the decade except for some years with price-controls which suppressed inflation and years of liberalisation with a onetime price-shock. Today inflation is driven by expectations and the monetisation of quasi-fiscal deficits.

Both countries rely heavily on cheap labour as comparative advantage in international trade. Underemployment and unemployment are more explicit in these countries than in Ukraine. Due to stepped-up restructuring and hardening budget constraints, the Bulgarian unemployment rate is now the highest among the EU accession countries. Romania has been slower with reforms not allowing the unemployment rate to grow much above 10%; however the participation rate declined more than in Bulgaria.

The export sectors of both countries have suffered a lot due to the loss of traditional markets and the decline of traditional industries. The reorientation of trade to the EU is more complete in the case of Romania, while for Bulgaria the CIS countries are still important partners also on the export side (one quarter). Both countries specialise in low value added low tech products in their exports. For Romania the primary commodities are clothing, shoes, and furniture, for Bulgaria chemical products. Steel products are important for both countries. Romania is increasingly becoming the "tailor of Europe" due to wage contracts (outward processing trade) of Italian and German companies. Bulgaria has not been able to go this ways due to the effects of the Yugoslav wars which had cut the countries main transport routes to the West.

Both countries are able to afford a modest foreign trade deficit. Unfortunately most of the deficit is not due to technology imports but to imports of semi-finished and consumer goods.

In sum, both countries are undergoing an economic recovery which is based on the utilisation of existing capacities. In part it is driven by the high EU demand in 2000 and the first half of 2001, in part by a recovery of private consumption. Growth has little foundation in capital accumulation and is meagrely supported by the inflow of foreign capital. With more rapid restructuring, Bulgaria may attain higher average growth-rates in 2001-2002 than Romania which is running the risk of exploding current account deficits which may curtail its growth prospects for next year.

3 Main current features of economic growth in Bulgaria

The Bulgarian economic scene has changed completely since the major economic and financial crisis of 1996-1997. In accordance with the currency board arrangement introduced in July 1997, the Bulgarian Lev was pegged to the Deutsche Mark (and was formally re-pegged to the Euro in 1999) for an indefinite period of time. Under this regime, the convertibility of base money is unlimited as the level of base money cannot exceed the level of the foreign reserves held by the central bank. The Bulgarian National Bank does not perform open market operations and cannot extend credit to the government or to refinance commercial banks; accordingly, interest rates should in principle be entirely market determined. The only policy instrument available to the government is fiscal policy; however, if long-term fiscal solvency and the macroeconomic regime are to be sustained, the degrees of freedom in taking a fiscal stance are constrained. (See Table 2.1 in the Appendix for all major economic indicators.).

The introduction of the currency board in July 1997 helped to restore macroeconomic and financial stability as well as fiscal and financial discipline. Economic activity started to recover and Bulgaria has seen three consecutive years of positive GDP growth between 1998 and 2000. Annual CPI inflation was brought down to single-digit numbers and real incomes have been rising. Public finances are in relatively good health, on the one hand, thanks to the successful effort by the government to raise more revenue and to collect its receivables more efficiently and, on the other hand, due to the closing of the chronic fiscal gap and the greater concern about long-term fiscal sustainability. On the negative side, unemployment has soared despite the revival in economic activity and the external balance has been weakening due to the widening of the trade and current account deficits.

Another negative implication of the currency board is the greater vulnerability to external shocks due to the limited powers of government to take an active policy stance and undertake offsetting policy measures. This weakness of the Bulgarian macroeconomic regime surfaced in the aftermath of the Russian crisis in August 1998 whose economic repercussions were later reinforced by the implications of the Kosovo crisis in 1999. These events were equivalent to a strong external demand shock causing a further plunge in Bulgarian manufacturing. It was thus only in 2000 that industrial output started to recover, after three subsequent years of decline.

As the external demand shock impacted negatively on exports, only domestic demand could drive the economic recovery in 1998 and 1999. This was indeed the case: private consumption and retail sales were growing at high rates throughout most of this period while the surge in gross fixed capital formation allowed to offset the large drop in fixed investment recorded in 1996-1997. Economic policy did play an active – though limited – role for the recovery in domestic demand. Especially in 1999 a certain loosening of the fiscal allowed a recovery in final domestic demand. Real incomes grew strongly in 1999, partly due to the lower than expected inflation. In addition, the government initiated a number of publicly financed infrastructural projects which boosted investment activity and aggregate output.

Final demand changed to the reverse in 2000: the strong rebound in western European demand and the end of the Kosovo war gave a strong boost to Bulgarian exports which led the recovery in that year together with the surge in services (in the first place, tourism). By contrast, final consumer demand weakened, due to the stagnation of real incomes caused by the resurgence of higher inflation in 2000 and the rise in unemployment. In addition, public investment was scaled down in the second half of the year, leading to slower growth in fixed investment compared to the previous two years.

The currency board provides a robust nominal anchor for the economy. With the nominal exchange rate fixed, no independent monetary policy, and practically balanced broad public finances, the domestic monetary sources of inflation are reduced to a minimum. Given that the economy is small and open, an assumption of perfect markets and instantaneous adjustment would imply that the domestic prices of tradable goods are borrowed from the international markets, whereas the domestic prices of non-tradable goods depend on the productivity differential (and the differential between the growth in productivity) in the tradable sector vis-à-vis the main external trading partners (the Balassa-Samuelson effect).

The price dynamics of the years after the introduction of the currency board largely reflect this type of pricing mechanism. Since the economy has not experienced a period of fast growth and productivity catch up, imported inflation has been the dominant factor for domestic price formation. Consequently, when world commodity and energy prices were falling in 1998-1999, there was a period of fast disinflation. In contrast, the upsurge in world commodity and energy prices in 2000 triggered a reversal in this process and lead to higher domestic inflation.

The situation on the labour market has been continuously deteriorating since the beginning of reforms and especially after 1996. Since 1996 there was net job creation only in the sector of agriculture and some service industries. In 2000, the rate of unemployment reached its highest level since the start of economic transformation, hitting 19%. Both total employment and employment in manufacturing have been shrinking. Thus the total number of employed persons in 2000 was 11% lower than in 1996 and 33% below the level of 1989. During the 1990s, employment in industry dropped by one million persons, from 1,646,000 in 1989 to 624,000 persons in 2000. The restructuring and liquidation of loss-making state-owned enterprises has resulted in massive layoffs both in 1999 and 2000 and in numbers this is more than offset the newly created jobs in this period. There are no visible signs of improvement on the labour market and the escalating social tension due to the rising unemployment has been an important factor on the political scene.

Over the 1990s, the direction of Bulgarian trade has changed radically, with a massive re-orientation of the trade flows from the CIS and Eastern Europe towards the European Union which is now Bulgaria's main trading partner. The re-direction of trade flows were also accompanied by substantial changes in their composition. It should be noted however, that the most dramatic changes both in direction and in composition took place in the period 1990-1992; in the years thereafter, the dynamics of trade has evolved in a more evolutionary manner.

The product structure of Bulgaria's exports (dominated by low value added and resource-intensive goods), make it rather vulnerable to changes in external demand and in world commodity prices. Thus a reversal in the favourable trends that prevailed in 2000 may have a strong negative impact on Bulgarian exporters.

The current economic situation in Bulgaria is generally favourable with positive economic growth for three consecutive years coupled with a stable macroeconomic environment. The negative sides of this picture are the persistent high unemployment rate and the widening external imbalance. Despite the seemingly benign situation at present, the combination of a high external debt and high current account deficit pose certain threats for macroeconomic stability in the medium term. The key to resolving the deadlock with the external imbalance is in competitiveness. But achieving competitive gains under the present macroeconomic regime is a major policy challenge which may face serious political constraints. Different policy approaches may lead to widely divergent outcomes for macroeconomic performance in the medium term.

The only policy option to effectuate the needed macroeconomic adjustment which is available under the current macroeconomic arrangement is to pursue an improvement in cost competitiveness through a reduction in relative unit labour costs. This is by far not a trivial and, certainly, not a short-run policy task. First of all, it implies fast growth of output and productivity in the manufacturing sector. Given the appalling record of the past decade and the dire massive decapitalisation of the manufacturing sector in this period, fast progress in this sphere is difficult to imagine. If this goal is to be realised, it will require to mobilise massive new investment in the manufacturing sector, including the attraction of large-scale greenfield FDI. This in itself is a daunting policy challenge and no Bulgarian government so far has a good record in this area. Secondly, achieving competitive gains through a relative restraint in unit labour costs is a policy that is difficult to implement in practice due to its social implications. Basically it comes to the fact that wages have to grow more slowly than productivity for a sufficiently long period of time.

4 Main current features of economic growth in Romania

Among the ten EU accession countries, Romania recorded up to 2000 the slowest economic growth and the highest rate of inflation. In the four years of the centre-right coalition, GDP shrunk by 16%. Inflation could not be brought down below

40% p.a. and the national currency lost value in line with inflation. The assessment of the EU does not consider Romania as a functioning market economy and cannot see much progress happening.

Romania has undergone a stop-go transformation process with a major setback in 1996, which led to an economic depression in 1997-1999. (See Table 2.2 in the Appendix for all major economic indicators).

The post-socialist history of Romania reflects both the significance of inherited obstacles to a fast and successful transformation and the impact of policy mistakes aggravating the problems. The governments up to late 1996 lacked a clear commitment to creating a market economy. The centre-right coalition which came to power following the November 1996 elections introduced some change in this respect. But political commitment faded during 1997 and a government crisis further delayed action. The government dealt more with short-term problems to avoid financial collapse in 1999.

Yet, there are reasons to believe that the economic situation may improve. In early 1997 it was obvious that previous growth rates had been achieved by means of short-term borrowing and that the adjustment necessary to avoid runaway inflation and to eliminate the fiscal and quasi-fiscal leakage would lead to a decline in GDP. Price liberalisation, some progress in privatisation and improving budget discipline were major achievements. By early 2000 the decline in GDP was stopped.

The Romanian economy has been on a growth path since early last year. In the first quarter of 2001 economic growth accelerated to 4.8% over the same pre-year period. While in the first half of last year net exports were the main demand factor behind the upswing, this year it is domestic consumption. Household consumption increased by 7.2% fuelled by increasing real wages (8.1%). Gross fixed capital formation went up also by 7% albeit from a very low level. Government consumption remained modest, because until the adoption of this years budget only in April expenditures were constrained.

The annual average inflation was almost 46% in both 1999 and 2000. In this respect, government and National Bank of Romania forecasts grossly failed to attained pre-set targets in both years. Attempts to control inflation by managing the devaluation of the national currency failed repeatedly during the last eight years in the absence of adequate reserves and real sector improvement. A neutral exchange rate policy seems to be the best the National Bank of Romania can currently achieve.

Romania has interconnected problems with restructuring, arrears and inflation. The inefficient public sector is responsible for excessive fiscal arrears, close to 7% of GDP at the end of 2000. This quasi-fiscal spending is financed by money creation which causes high inflation. Overcoming this set of problems is essential for alleviating future social hardship. Yet there is no sign that this lesson drawn by leading economists in the country can have an impact on policy making. Slow action on restructuring means further accumulation of fiscal and inter-enterprise arrears and continuing high inflation. The interest of the government in fighting inflation is tempered by the fact that fiscal policy gains by high inflation as revenues increase nominally while expenditures are kept flat.

Employment in the Romanian economy has been shrinking since the outset of transformation. Industrial employment declined more rapidly since 1997 when restructuring got some momentum. Following a surge in 1998, the unemployment rate keeps more or less constant at 10-11%. Agriculture is the main buffer for unemployment. Following the 1990-1992 land reform, 86% of the agricultural land became the property of 4.2 million households. Subsistence farming provides the basic staple for almost half of the population.

Romania shows relatively small trade volumes, less than 50% of GDP. Exports to the EU increased and reached 65% of the export sales. Exports to crisis-hit destinations such as Russia and Asia shrank. Romanian exports performance depends to a large extent on EU demand for light industry consumer goods. The structural change of exports in the recent years has been very slow and the vulnerability to changes on the EU market is substantial. Low-wage Romania is a frequent target of outward processing trade (OPT) for Italian and German firms. The current real appreciation of the local currency against the EUR can hit the financial soundness of the firms involved in OPT, but they may still be competitive compared with other CEECs. The recent privatisation and restructuring steps may improve the export possibilities of other industrial products such as cars as well as non-electric machinery and components in the future.

2000 was the first year with substantial export growth pulled by widening European demand. This trend continues in 2001 as well. High rates of exports growth (19.6%) were achieved in the first quarter of 2001 together with an even higher increase of imports (36.6%). The three-months deficit stood at USD 820 m, over four times higher than a year earlier. Imports usually increase at least at the speed of exports as the value added in wage-contracts is low. In addition, both the investment and private consumption boom triggered high imports. With a continuing trend, the annual trade deficit would be well above USD 3 bn or two times of last year's. If so, several related questions emerge. Will also the current account come into a deficit which would be almost impossible to finance? Will the government have to make stabilisation measures to curtail the deficit?

As to the first issue, during the last few years the current account deficit has become lower than the trade deficit. In the year 2000, service and income deficits were shrinking while the surplus on current transfers increased. The transfers of Romanians living abroad have become a major new income source for the country. Both temporary and permanent outmigration has been high over the last few years affecting mainly young graduates. Remittances doubled in five years to over USD 1 bn last year compensating in part for the trade deficit. In the first quarter of 2001 the current account deficit reached USD 455 m, five times of the same pre-year period. The major item was the expanding trade deficit, but the service deficit was lower and the tourism deficit somewhat higher than in the first quarter of 2000. Incomes deficit, mainly interest payments halved (USD 41 m) while the positive net revenues from current transfers remained approximately at the pre-year level (USD 172 m). It is mostly this latter item which allows to predict that the annual current account deficit will not exceed USD 2.5 bn. This corresponds to some 6.5% of GDP which is in a dangerous zone for a country with very narrow financial flows and limited access to international financial markets.

Appendix

Table 2.1
Bulgaria: Selected economic indicators

	1996	1997	1998	1999	2000 [1]
Population, th pers., end of period	8.340,9	8.283,2	8.230,4	8.190,9	8.149,5
Gross domestic product, BGN m, nom.	1.748,7	17.055,2	21.577,0	22.776,4	25.453,6
annual change in % (real)	-10,1	-7,0	3,5	2,4	5,8
GDP/capita (USD at exchange rate)	1.189	1.224	1.484	1.510	1.459
GDP/capita (USD at PPP - WIIW)	4.990	4.770	4.980	5.210	5.600
Gross industrial production					
annual change in % (real)	5,1	-5,4	-7,9	-9,3	5,8
Gross agricultural production					
annual change in % (real)	-11,5	12,4	0,2	-0,6	-16
Goods transport, public, m t-km	79.850	86.543	76.039	79.446	84.767
annual change in %	-8,4	8,4	-12,1	4,5	6,7
Gross fixed capital form., BGN m, nom.	238,5	1.841,0	2.850,8	3.632,2	4.111,3
annual change in % (real)	-21,2	-23,9	32,9	25,3	8,2
Construction output total					
annual change in % (real)	-14,0	-4,4	-0,2	8,0	-16,8
Dwellings completed, units	8.099,0	7.452,0	4.942,0	9.824,0	8.795,0
annual change in %	18,8	-8,0	-33,7	98,8	-10,5
Employment total, th pers., average	3.285,9	3.157,4	3.152,6	3.087,8	2.943,4
annual change in %	0,1	-3,9	-0,2	-2,1	-4,7
Employees in industry, th pers., average [2]	728,1	838,7	802,5	722,5	624,3
annual change in % [2]	-5,5	-2,7	-4,3	-10,0	-13,6
Unemployed reg., th, end of period	478,5	523,5	465,2	610,6	682,8
Unemployment rate in %, end of period	12,5	13,7	12,2	16,0	17,9
Average gross monthly wages, BGN [2]	14,0	127,9	183,3	201,0	238,0
annual change in % (real, gross) [2]	-17,6	-18,3	17,2	9,4	7,7
Retail trade turnover, BGN m	723,7	5.469,3	7.214,2	8.023,0	8.746,0
annual change in % (real)	-7,6	-36,4	18,5	12,3	0,7
Consumer prices, % p.a. [3]	121,6	1.058,4	18,7	2,6	10,3
Producer prices in industry, % p.a.	130,0	971,1	16,5	3,1	17,2
Central government budget, BGN m [4]					
Revenues	350,0	2.983,3	4.245,6	4.543,5	6.120,9
Expenditures	540,8	3.650,0	3.930,8	4.132,0	6.304,8
Deficit (-) / surplus (+)	-190,9	-666,7	314,7	411,6	-183,8
Deficit (-) / surplus (+), % of GDP	-10,9	-3,9	1,5	1,8	-0,7
Money supply, BGN m, end of period					
M1, Money	236,6	2.266,9	2.755,6	2.996,6	3.632,2
Broad money	1.310,3	6.018,6	6.597,2	7.351,1	9.290,7
Base rate of NB % p.a., end of period	342,1	6,8	5,2	4,5	4,7

Table 2.1 (cont.)
Bulgaria: Selected economic indicators

	1996	1997	1998	1999	2000 [1]
Current account, USD m	163,7	1.046,3	-61,4	-651,7	-701,4
Gross reserves of NB excl. gold, USD m	483,4	2.121,0	2.679,4	2.892,0	3.154,9
Gross external debt, convert. curr.,USD m	9.601,6	9.760,2	10.274,3	10.204,3	10.364,3
Exports total, fob, USD m [5]	4.890,2	4.939,7	4.297,0	4.006,4	4.812,3
annual change in %	-8,7	1,0	-13,0	-4,5	20,1
Imports total, cif, USD m [5]	5.073,9	4.932,0	5.031,3	5.515,1	6.493,9
annual change in %	-10,3	-2,8	2,0	11,3	17,7
Average exchange rate BGN/USD	0,176	1,677	1,760	1,836	2,123
Average exchange rate BGN/EUR (ECU)	0,192	1,896	1,972	1,956	1,956
Average exchange rate BGN/DEM	0,118	0,968	1,000	1,000	1,000
Purchasing power parity BGN/USD, WIIW	0,042	0,435	0,525	0,532	0,557

1) Preliminary. - 2) Up to 1996 public sector only. - 3) Revised data according to Eurostat methodology. - 4) From 2000 including some extrabudgetary funds and accounts. - 5) From 1999 new methodology.

Source: WIIW Database incorporating national statistics; WIIW forecasts

Table 2.2
Romania: Selected economic indicators

	1996	1997	1998	1999	2000 [1)]
Population, th pers., mid-year	22.607,6	22.545,9	22.502,8	22.458,0	22.442,8
Gross domestic product, ROL bn, nom.	108.920	252.926	368.261	521.736	796.534
annual change in % (real)	3,9	-6,1	-5,4	-3,2	1,6
GDP/capita (USD at exchange rate)	1.563	1.565	1.844	1.515	1.636
GDP/capita (USD at PPP - WIIW)	6.630	6.310	6.050	5.970	6.200
Gross industrial production					
annual change in % (real)	6,3	-7,2	-13,8	-8,0	8,2
Gross agricultural production					
annual change in % (real)	1,3	3,4	-7,5	5,5	-14,1
Goods transport, m t-km [2)]	106.758	87.590	62.365	45.989	42.131
annual change in %	-15,8	-18,0	.	-26,3	-8,4
Gross fixed investment, ROL bn, nom.	20.945,3	44.134,7	60.515,2	70.571,8	106.728,3
annual change in % (real)	3,1	-5,4	-18,6	-12,3	5,0
Construction output total					
annual change in % (real)	3,7	-24,4	-0,5	-12,2	5,4
Dwellings completed, units	29.460	29.921	29.692	29.517	26.127
annual change in %	-17,8	1,6	-0,8	-0,6	-11,5
Employment total, th pers., end of period	9.379,0	9.022,7	8.812,6	.	.
annual change in %	-1,2	-3,8	-2,3	.	.
Employees in industry, th pers., average	2.586,0	2.443,0	2.272,0	1.999,9	1.887,9
annual change in %	-1,1	-5,5	-7,0	-12,0	-5,6
Unemployed reg., th, end of period	657,6	881,4	1.025,1	1.130,3	1.007,1
Unemployment rate in %, end of period	6,6	8,9	10,4	11,8	10,5
Average gross monthly wages, ROL	426.610	846.450	1.357.132	1.957.731	2.876.645
annual change in % (real, net)	9,3	-22,6	3,4	-0,7	-4,0
Retail trade turnover, ROL bn [3)]	35.316	83.035	125.513	.	.
annual change in % (real) [3)]	15,3	-12,1	20,6	5,0	3,8
Consumer prices, % p.a.	38,8	154,8	59,1	45,8	45,7
Producer prices in industry, % p.a.	49,9	152,7	33,2	42,2	53,4
Central government budget, ROL bn					
Revenues	18.373	43.835	67.216	93.230	120.342
Expenditures	23.732	52.897	77.617	106.887	149.169
Deficit (-) / surplus (+)	-5.359	-9.062	-10.401	-13.656	-28.827
Deficit (-) / surplus (+), % GDP	-4,9	-3,6	-2,8	-2,6	-3,6
Money supply, ROL bn, end of period					
M1, Money	11.173	18.731	22.110	29.669	46.331
M2, money + quasi money	30.335	62.150	92.530	134.123	185.060
Discount rate, % p.a., end of period	35,0	40,0	35,0	35,0	35,0
Current account, USD m	-2.571	-2.137	-2.968	-1.296	-1.400
Gross reserves of NB excl. gold, USD m	545,8	2.193,5	1.374,8	1.526,3	2.469,7
Gross external debt, USD m [4)]	7.208,9	8.584,3	9.308,1	8.709,5	9.842,9

Table 2.2 (cont.)
Romania: Selected economic indicators

	1996	1997	1998	1999	2000 [1)]
Exports total, fob, USD m	8.084,5	8.431,1	8.302,0	8.503,0	10.366,5
annual change in %	2,2	4,3	-1,5	2,4	21,9
Imports total, cif, USD m	11.435,3	11.279,7	11.837,8	10.395,3	13.054,5
annual change in %	11,3	-1,4	4,9	-12,2	25,6
Average exchange rate ROL/USD	3.082,6	7.167,9	8.874,8	15.332,9	21.692,7
Average exchange rate ROL/EUR (ECU)	3.862,9	8.090,9	9.988,4	1.6295,3	19.955,8
Average exchange rate ROL/DEM	2.048,6	4.133,6	5.043,5	8.331,6	10.187,0
Purchasing power parity ROL/USD, WIIW	726,9	1.779,3	2.703,5	3.890,5	5.721,5
Purchasing power parity ROL/EUR, WIIW	788,2	1.939,2	2.934,8	4.203,8	6.225,0

1) Preliminary. - 2) From 1998 new methodology in road transport. - 3) From 1998 new methodology. - 4) Medium and long-term.

Source: WIIW Database incorporating national statistics; WIIW forecasts

3

Trade, Capital Flows, and Economic Growth in Developing Countries*

Yilmaz Akyuz

1 Liberalisation, external constraints, and growth

In recent years developing countries have striven hard, and often at considerable cost, to integrate more closely into the world economy. But, in the face of deep-seated imbalances in economic power and biases in the international trading and financial systems, their expectations of the gains from such integration in terms of faster growth, greater employment opportunities and reduced levels of poverty have been disappointed. A clear example is the extravagant predictions made regarding the gains they could reap from the Uruguay Round. By contrast, the downside risks have proved far greater than was generally expected, as recently demonstrated by the experience of East Asia and Latin America. The humbling of the Asian tigers since 1997 has revealed the vulnerability of even the strongest developing economies to the powerful forces unleashed by globalisation. There is now a growing sense of unease about the policy advice that was proffered in the past decade.

Much of that advice was fashioned in response to the debt crisis of the early 1980s, when a reorientation of policies in the industrial countries led to considerable macroeconomic distress in many developing countries and a sharp fall in their growth rates. Severe balance-of-payments crises revealed the extent to which rapid growth in the South had come to depend on steadily rising export earnings and capital inflows and just how disruptive an interruption to these sources of foreign exchange could be. For many, the crisis was final proof that inward-oriented growth strategies and interventionist policies could not extract developing countries from the mire of poverty and underdevelopment. Thus, in the second half of the decade, a powerful consensus was forged around "getting prices

---

* This chapter is based, in large part, on the work done for *Trade and Development Report 1999*, UNCTAD.

right". Close integration with the world economy through rapid liberalisation of trade, finance and investment was believed to be the recipe for preventing setbacks to development caused by recurrent payments crises. Trade liberalisation would ensure the best allocation of resources according to comparative advantage, securing the export revenues needed to import key ingredients of faster growth. Financial liberalisation would attract foreign capital seeking high returns in these capital-scarce countries, allowing them to invest more than they save without running into a payments constraint. A bigger flow of foreign direct investment would further accelerate growth not only by supplementing domestic resources for capital accumulation, but also through transfer of technology and organisational skills.

Fast integration into the world economy thus seemed to promise an alternative to stop-go growth and development through export expansion and inflows of private foreign capital, providing the inspiration for widespread reform and encouraging "big bang" liberalisation. Indeed, the growth of world trade and, perhaps even more decisively, the recovery of financial flows to developing countries in the 1990s were taken as confirmation that a new era of prosperity was beginning to unfold and that it would include a growing number of developing countries.

However, few attempts have been made to examine what rapid integration has actually meant for developing countries. The research undertaken in UNCTAD shows that the empirical record has been at odds with the promises.[1] Inevitably, the discussion involves "nuts and bolts" economics of a technical nature, but the conclusion is a simple and striking one. It is that, after more than a decade of liberal reforms in developing countries, their payments disorders, which had earlier ushered in a rethinking of policies, remain as acute as ever, and their economies depend even more on external financial resources for the achievement of growth rates sufficient to tackle the deep-rooted problems of poverty and underdevelopment:

- Growth in developing countries generally recovered in the 1990s from the levels of the 1980s, but it remained well below the average of 5.7% achieved during the 1970s. This recovery has been accompanied by a significant worsening of external deficits. For developing countries as a whole (excluding China), the average trade deficit in the 1990s was higher than in the 1970s by almost 3 percentage points of GDP, while the average growth rate was lower by 2% per annum.
- Low prices of oil are only part of the story. In the non-oil-exporting developing countries the trade deficit in the 1990s stood at approximately the same proportion of GDP as in the 1970s, while the average growth rate was lower by 2% per annum.

---

[1] See, in particular, *Trade and Development Report* 1997, 1998 and 1999.

- The pattern is broadly similar in all developing regions. In Latin America the average growth rate is lower by 3% per annum in the 1990s than in the 1970s, while trade deficits as a proportion of GDP are much the same. In sub-Saharan Africa growth fell, but deficits rose. The Asian countries managed to grow faster in the 1980s, while reducing their payments deficits, but in the 1990s they ran greater deficits without achieving faster growth.

- In almost half of the developing countries examined, which include exporters not only of commodities but also of manufactures, the trend is one of widening trade deficits, with falling or stagnant growth rates. Where trade balances have improved, there has generally been a slowdown in economic growth and imports. Among the countries which succeeded in achieving faster growth, the majority experienced a deterioration in their trade balances, financed by inflows of private capital. However, such inflows could not always be sustained and eventually led to currency crises, economic contraction and massive import cuts. Only a very small number of countries, notably China and Chile, have been able to buck this general trend by combining faster growth with improved trade performance.

The reasons why trade deficits have been increasing faster than income in developing countries are undoubtedly complex. However, the evidence shows that a combination of declining terms of trade, slow growth in industrial countries and "big bang" liberalisation of trade and of the capital account in developing countries has been a decisive factor.

For developing countries as a whole the terms of trade fell by more than 5% per annum during the 1980s. The more favourable trend around the mid-1990s due to a recovery in oil and non-oil commodity prices has been more than offset by large losses since 1996, when these prices declined by about 16% and 34%, respectively. For non-oil developing countries, the decline in the terms of trade has been steady, at about 1.5% per annum, since the early 1980s. Terms-of-trade losses are no longer confined to commodity exporters. Many manufactures exported by developing countries are now beginning to behave more like primary commodities as a growing number of countries simultaneously attempt to raise their exports in the relatively stagnant and protected markets of industrial countries. For example, the prices of manufactures exported by developing countries fell relative to those exported by the European Union by 2.2% per annum from 1979 to 1994. Similarly the manufacturing terms of trade of developing countries with the United States declined by 15.6%, or by almost 1.1% per annum between 1981 and 1997.

The slower growth in industrial countries during the past two decades than in the 1970s may have added to trade deficits of developing countries perhaps by as much as 1% of GDP. Rapid trade liberalisation in the latter countries has further added to their deficits; it led to a sharp increase in their import propensity, but exports failed to keep pace, particularly where liberalisation was a response to the failure to establish competitive industries behind high barriers. With the notable exception of China, liberalisation has resulted in a general widening of the gap between the annual growth of imports and exports in the 1990s, but the impact was particularly severe in Latin America, where the gap averaged about 4 percentage points.

Liberalisation of capital flows, often prompted by the need to finance growing external deficits, has actually made matters worse. It has led to currency appreciations and instability, thereby undermining trade performance. Despite greater exposure to foreign competition, there have been serious shortcomings in exchange-rate management, even compared to the interventionist regimes of the 1970s and 1980s. An examination of exchange-rate movements in 58 developing countries shows that, after persistent appreciations, 8 of them resorted to real devaluations in the 1970s of 25% or more but that there were as many as 24 in the 1980s. From 1990 until 1997, before the more recent turmoils in East Asia or Latin America, 19 countries experienced comparable reversals.

2 Private capital flows: solution or problem?

With today's globalised financial markets, access to foreign private capital is generally expected to greatly alleviate the external constraint on growth. Certainly, the 1990s witnessed a rapid expansion of private capital inflows into developing countries, registering a sevenfold increase over the average for the 1970s. Portfolio flows and foreign direct investment (FDI) have shown the strongest growth, accounting for more than two thirds of total private inflows.

While such figures have received increased attention in the financial press, and seem to have had a mesmerising effect on many policy makers in the South, a sense of proportion is called for:

- The upsurge in the 1990s represents no more than a return to trend after the blighted years of the 1980s. The annual capital inflow in the 1990s was around 5% of GNP, which was roughly the level prevailing in 1975–1982. If China is excluded, the ratio is actually lower than in the earlier period by one percentage point.
- Not all trends are rising. Official development assistance has steadily declined throughout the present decade, falling in real terms in 1998 to its lowest level for many years. The share of official financing in total capital inflows fell from over 50% in the 1980s to 20% in the 1990s.
- As official financing took a back seat, capital inflows have increasingly been concentrated in a small group of 20 or so emerging markets which received over 90% of total inflows of capital in the 1990s, compared to some 50%

before the outbreak of the debt crisis. As regards FDI, China, Brazil and Mexico together accounted for almost one half of the total inflow; their per capita inflow, in the range of USD 20-80, and an inflow of as much as USD 223 per capita in Malaysia, stand in stark contrast to under USD 5 in many countries in sub-Saharan Africa.

- An important part of private capital inflows, notably liquid capital seeking arbitrage profits, is highly unstable and hence constitutes an unreliable source of development finance. This is particularly true for short-term loans and portfolio equity, which together reached USD 100 bn by the middle of the decade (about 40% of all private inflows into developing countries) but fell to a mere USD 15 bn after the financial crises in East Asia and Russia.

Moreover, a growing proportion of net private capital inflows is absorbed by activities which add little to productive capacity in those emerging markets fortunate enough to receive them: of every dollar brought in by non-residents 24 Cents were taken out by residents, compared to 14 Cents in the 1980s. No less disturbing is that more than 20 Cents of every dollar of net capital inflow are put aside for the accumulation of foreign-exchange reserves, notwithstanding policy reforms designed to ensure greater exchange-rate flexibility and increased access to global capital markets. Developing countries have increasingly been advised to cover their short-term liabilities by reserves as a safeguard against speculative attacks on the currency and reversal of capital flows; the increase in reserves from 1990 to 1998 amounted to a staggering 60% of the increase in their import bill during the same period.

The cost has been high, since reserves are borrowed at much higher rates than they can earn in international financial markets. The net cumulative cost over 1990-1997 may have been as much as USD 50 bn. The tendency to build up excessive reserves as a safeguard against a rapid exit of short-term capital increased after the recent bouts of crisis in emerging markets. Moreover, short-term capital inflows have a high rate of leakage. In the 1990s, for every dollar of short-term capital brought in by non-residents, 56 Cents were taken out by residents for investment in short-term assets abroad. Thus, such capital flows provide little for current-account financing, while provoking significant instability. There is consequently an urgent need to reconsider the case for their liberalisation.

Even the strong growth of FDI flows to developing countries in the 1990s should not be allowed to hide the simple fact that it largely reflects mergers and acquisitions (rather than greenfield investment), which accounted for well over half of the total FDI inflow in 1992–1997 and for almost three quarters if China is excluded. Much of this merger activity was in service sectors, and has the potential to add to payments difficulties. Attempts to meet foreign-exchange deficits of TNC-related activities by encouraging new inflows of the same kind would be self-defeating. In any case, it is not clear whether the recent momentum of FDI attracted by acquisition of existing assets can be maintained over the longer term, since there are limits to the stock of assets for sale, particularly in the public sector.

Although an important part of recent capital inflows into developing countries has allegedly been "non-debt-creating", external indebtedness is again on the rise, in both absolute and relative terms. In Latin America, for instance, for the first time in the 1990s, the ratio of debt to exports increased in 1998, reaching 203%, from 191% in 1997, and there was likewise an increase in the ratio of interest payments to exports. In a number of the so-called Baker-15 countries that suffered from the debt crisis of the 1980s (Algeria, Brazil, Colombia, Peru and Venezuela), debt service as a percentage of exports was higher in the late 1990s than in the mid-1980s. Higher interest payments add to the difficulties caused by widening trade deficits and run the risk of incurring an unsustainable debt burden. Developing countries should not heed the doctrine, popularised by the more exuberant exponents of liberal orthodoxy, that rising current-account deficits and external indebtedness generated by the private (as opposed to the public) sector are immune to the dangers that proved so destructive in the early 1980s.

In any case, on recent trends, the level and composition of net capital flows received by many developing countries are inadequate to meet their existing external financing requirements.

Certainly faster growth in industrial countries, better market access for the exports of developing countries and improved terms of trade would go a long way in reducing the resource gap in the South. But there is also a need to reduce excessive dependence of developing countries on private foreign capital. In most East Asian countries where the domestic saving rates exceed 30% of GDP, heavy reliance on foreign capital would not be necessary to attain rapid growth (UNCTAD, 2001). Many middle-income countries in Latin America need to increase domestic savings and nourish a dynamic entrepreneur class with a high propensity to save and invest. For low-income countries, private capital inflows do not promise much in the way of narrowing their savings gap, and their external resource requirements should be met by multilateral financial institutions as well as bilateral flows.

This does not mean that the developing countries should not tap international financial markets to promote trade, investment and growth. Indeed, in the past many East Asian countries, notably the Republic of Korea, drew successfully on borrowing in international financial markets to supplement their domestic savings for faster accumulation without running into the kind of difficulties they experienced in the 1990s. This was in large part because of existence of a judicious control over private borrowing abroad and restrictions over capital transactions. Again China has received large amounts of FDI without adopting a hands off approach to private capital flows. Success in attracting appropriate forms of foreign capital does not require capital account liberalisation and close or full integration into the international financial markets.

It is thus essential that the autonomy of developing countries in managing capital flows and choosing whatever capital-account regime they deem appropriate should not be constrained by international agreements on capital-account convertibility or trade in financial services. Indeed, a basic objective for countries at all levels of development should be to roll back the control that financial capital has established over trade, industry and employment. It should also be recognised that private capital markets have not always been successful in replacing official development finance. Reform of the global financial architecture should focus on these issues, and include a greater role for official financing for the poorest developing countries

Developing countries need to improve the management of their exchange rates if they are to benefit from greater integration into the trading system. The advice they have received in recent years has been at best confusing and at worst misleading. Under free capital mobility, no exchange-rate regime can guarantee stable and competitive rates. Contrary to some perceptions, countries with floating rates are no less vulnerable to financial crises than those with pegged or fixed ones. Differences among pegged, floating and fixed regimes lie not so much in their capacity to prevent damage to the real economy as in the way damage is inflicted in the first place. There now appears to be a growing consensus that developing countries should target real exchange rates in combination with the control and regulation of destabilising capital flows. This offers a viable alternative to free floating or to ceding completely monetary authority to a foreign Central Bank. Successful examples of control over inflows and outflows abound, from Chile to China, India and Malaysia, and provide a rich arsenal of tools for better management of the capital account and exchange rates.

References

UNCTAD: Trade and Development Report (various years).

4

Natural Resources and Economic Growth: What Is the Connection?

Thorvaldur Gylfason

1 Introduction

The structure of recent models of the relationship between natural resource abundance or intensity and economic growth is nearly always the same. An abundance of or heavy dependence on natural resources is taken to influence some variable or mechanism "X" which impedes growth. An important challenge for economic growth theorists and empirical workers in the field is to identify and map these intermediate variables and mechanisms.

To date, four main channels of transmission from natural resource abundance or intensity to slow economic growth have been suggested in the literatur.[1] As we shall see, these channels can be described as crowding out: natural capital, it will be argued, tends to crowd out other types of capital and thereby inhibit economic growth.

2 Channel 1: The Dutch disease and foreign capital

An overvalued currency was the first symptom associated with the Dutch disease following the discovery of natural gas deposits within the jurisdiction of the Netherlands in the North Sea in the late 1950s and early 1960s, but subsequently several other symptoms came to light. Natural resource abundance is, as a rule, accompanied by booms and busts: the prices of raw materials fluctuate a great deal in world markets, and so do supplies. The resulting fluctuations in export earnings trigger exchange rate volatility, perhaps no less so under fixed exchange rates than under floating rates. Unstable exchange rates create uncertainty that can be

---

1 This discussion draws on Gylfason and Zoega (2001).

harmful to exports and other trade, including foreign investment. Further, the Dutch disease can strike even in countries that do not have their own national currency. In this case, the natural-resource-based industry is able to pay higher wages and also higher interest rates than other export and import-competing industries, thus making it difficult for the latter to remain competitive at world market prices. This problem can become particularly acute in countries with centralised wage bargaining (or with oligopolistic banking systems, for that matter) where the natural-resource industries set the tone in nation-wide wage negotiations and dictate wage settlements that other industries can ill afford.

In one or all of these ways, the Dutch disease tends to reduce the level of total exports or bias the composition of exports away from those kinds of manufacturing and service exports that may be particularly good for growth over time. Exports of capital – i.e., inward foreign direct investment – may also suffer in the same way. The mechanism is essentially the same. In other words, natural capital tends to crowd out foreign capital, broadly speaking.

Graph 4.1
Exports of goods and services 1960-1998 (% of GDP)

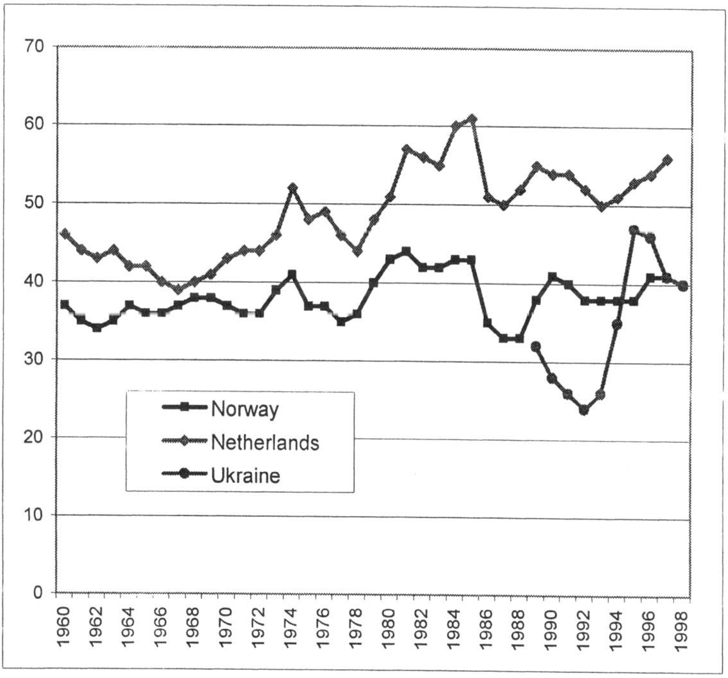

Graph 4.1 presents relevant empirical evidence for two resource-rich European countries, Norway and the Netherlands, as well as for Ukraine for comparison.

Graph 4.2
Foreign direct investment 1975-1998 (% of GDP, ppp)

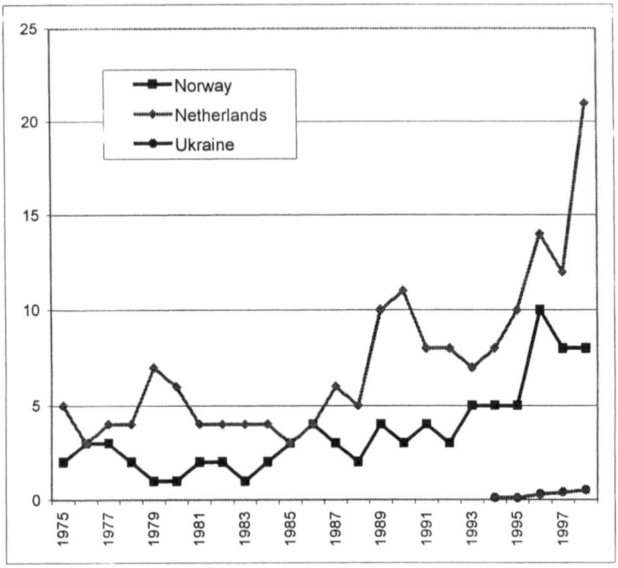

Graph 4.3
Manufacturing exports 1980-1998 (% of total exports)

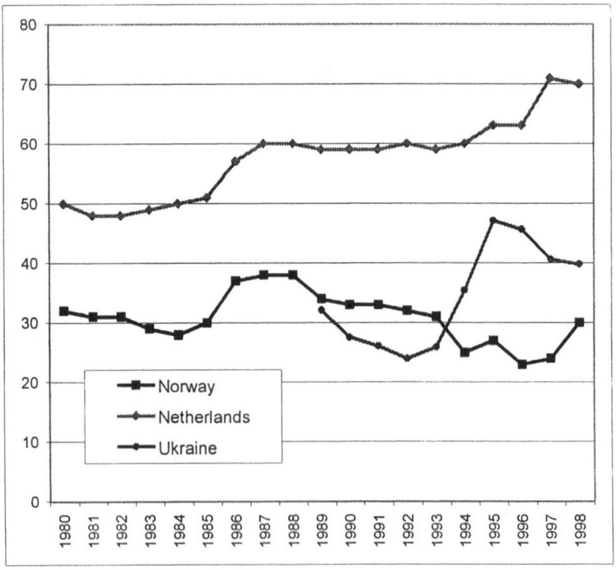

Graph 4.1 shows that the Netherlands recovered quickly from the Dutch disease, having seen a persistent upward trend in their total merchandise exports relative to GDP since the mid-1960s. Meanwhile, Norway's total exports have been stagnant relative to GDP at a level well below that of the Netherlands, even if the Dutch economy is almost three times as large as that of Norway.

Graph 4.2 tells a similar story about foreign direct investment, which has increased relative to GDP in both countries since 1975, but less rapidly in Norway than in the Netherlands. Graph 4.3 shows that the share of manufacturing exports in total exports in the Netherlands increased from 50% in 1980 to 70% in 1998, while the same ratio has hovered around 30% in Norway without showing any tendency to rise over time. These things matter because exports and foreign investment are good for growth (see, for example, Frankel and Romer, 1999). Openness to trade and investment stimulates imports of goods and services, capital, technology, ideas, and know-how. Further, too much primary-export dependence and too little manufacturing may hurt economic growth over the long haul. The upshot is that the Dutch disease is a matter of concern mainly because of its potentially deleterious consequences for economic growth.

What is the empirical evidence? Graph 4.4 shows a scatterplot of natural resource abundance and openness to external trade around the world. Natural resource abundance or intensity, which is measured along the horizontal axis, is measured by the share of natural capital in national wealth in 1994 – i.e., the share of natural capital in total capital, which comprises physical, human, and natural capital (but not social capital; see World Bank, 1997). The natural capital share used here is close to the source: it is intended to come closer to a direct measurement of the intensity of natural resources across countries than the various proxies that have been used in earlier studies, mainly the share of primary (i.e., nonmanufacturing) exports in total exports or in gross domestic product (GDP) and the share of the primary sector in employment or the labor force. Openness on the vertical axis is defined as the difference between the actual average ratio of exports to GDP over the period under review, 1965-1998, and the export ratio predicted by a linear regression of the average export ratio on the logarithm of the average population (in thousands) across countries to adjust for country size. This adjustment is made to reflect the fact that large countries are less dependent on foreign trade than smaller ones that need to extend their home markets beyond their national borders to make up for their small size. This indicator of openness is above zero for countries that are more open to trade than their size predicts, and below zero for countries that are less open to trade than their size predicts. The 91 countries in the sample are represented by one observation each for each variable under study.

The regression line through the scatterplot in Graph 4.4 suggests that an increase of ten percentage points in the natural capital share from one country to another is associated with a decrease in the openness indicator by about four percent of GDP

Graph 4.4
Natural capital and openness 1965-1998

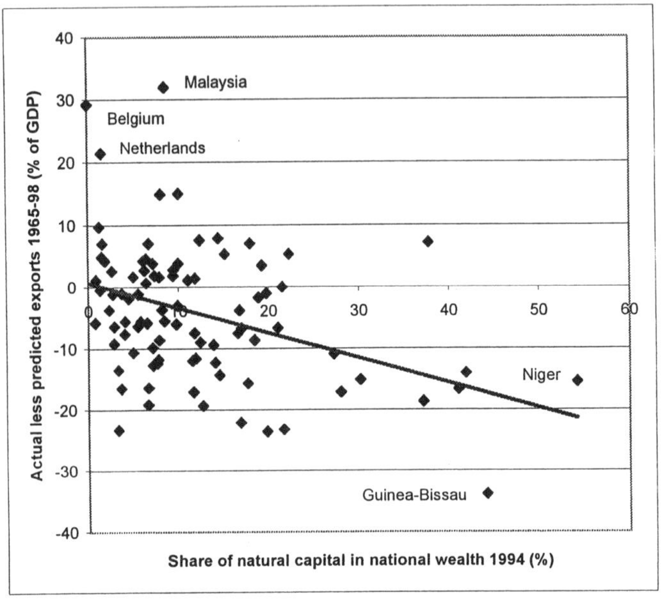

Graph 4.5
Openness and economic growth 1965-1998

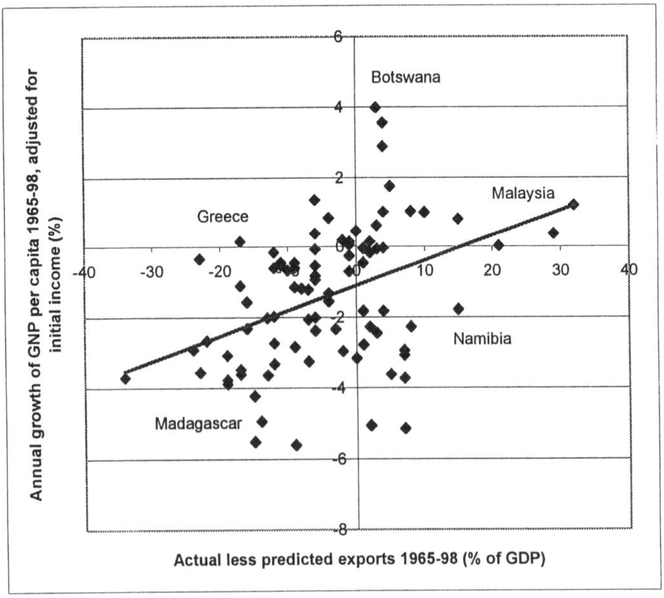

on average. The relationship is economically as well as statistically significant (Spearman's rank correlation is -0.33).[2] Given existing evidence that foreign trade is good for growth, Graph 4.4 suggests that natural resource abundance may hurt growth by harming trade.

It needs to be understood that no conclusions are being drawn here as to cause and effect. Graph 4.4 is only intended to display the data in a way that accords with the results of multivariate regression analyses that can help account for more potential determinants of exports (Gylfason, 1999), and where the attempt was made to distinguish cause from effect. The same disclaimer applies to all the figures that follow. Even so, the study of bivariate cross-sectional relationships has many shortcomings. For one thing, such studies bypass the diversity of individual country experiences. For another, they do not account for economic developments over time, as panel studies are designed to do.

Graph 4.5 shows a scatterplot of openness as defined above and economic growth per capita from 1965 to 1998. The figure covers 87 countries. The growth rate has been adjusted for initial income: the variable on the vertical axis is that part of economic growth that is not explained by the country's initial stage of development, obtained from a regression of growth during 1965-1998 on initial GNP per capita (i.e., in 1965) as well as natural capital. The regression line through the scatterplot in Graph 4.5 suggests that an increase of 14 percentage points in the openness indicator from one country to another is associated with an increase in per capita growth by one percentage point per year on average. The relationship is thus economically as well as statistically significant; Spearman's rank correlation is 0.40. The data thus seem to support the view that openness is good for growth.

Taking Graphs 4.4 and 4.5 together, we see that an increase in the natural capital share by ten percentage points goes along with a four point decrease in the openness index which, in turn, goes hand in hand with a decrease in annual per capita growth by about 0.3 percentage points.

3 Channel 2: Rent seeking and social capital

In second place, huge natural resource rents, especially in conjunction with ill-defined property rights, imperfect or missing markets, and lax legal structures in many developing countries and emerging market economies, may lead to rampant rent-seeking behavior on the part of producers, thus diverting resources away from

---

2 Gylfason (forthcoming) presents corresponding scatterplots of exports and natural capital and of foreign direct investment and natural capital.

more socially fruitful economic activity (Auty, 2001; Gelb, 1988). The combination of abundant natural resources, missing markets, and lax legal structures may have quite destructive consequences. In extreme cases, civil wars break out – such as Africa's diamond wars – which not only divert factors of production from socially productive uses but also destroy societal institutions and the rule of law. In other, less extreme cases, the struggle for huge resource rents may lead to a concentration of economic and political power in the hands of elites that, once in power, use the rent to placate their political supporters and thus secure their hold on power, with stunted or weakened democracy and slow growth as a result (Karl, 1997).

Rent seeking can also take other, more subtle forms. For example, governments may be tempted to thwart markets by granting favored enterprises or individuals privileged access to common-property natural resources or they may offer tariff protection or other favours to producers at public expense, creating competition for such favours among the rent seekers. Extensive rent seeking – i.e., seeking to make money from market distortions – can breed corruption in business and government, thus distorting the allocation of resources and reducing both economic efficiency and social equity. Empirical evidence and economic theory suggest that import protection (which is often extended to foreign capital as well as goods and services), cronyism, and corruption all tend to impede economic efficiency and growth (Bardhan, 1997; Mauro, 1995).

Furthermore, abundant natural resources may imbue people with a false sense of security and lead governments to lose sight of the need for good and growth-friendly economic management, including free trade, bureaucratic efficiency, and institutional quality (Sachs and Warner, 1999). Put differently, abundant natural capital may crowd out social capital, by which is meant the infrastructure and institutions of a society in a broad sense: its culture, cohesion, law, system of justice, rules and customs and so on, including trust (Woolcock, 1998; Paldam and Svendsen, 2000). Incentives to create wealth through good policies and institutions may wane because of the relatively effortless ability to extract wealth from the soil or the sea. Manna from heaven can be a mixed blessing. The argument can be extended to unconditional foreign aid. There are indications that natural-resource-rich countries are more dependent than others on foreign aid, which may actually exacerbate their economic predicament.

Now consider corruption, to take but one aspect of social capital corrosion into account. Insofar as natural resource abundance involves public allocation of access to scarce common-property resources to private parties without payment, thereby essentially leaving the resource rent up for grabs, it is only to be expected that resource-rich countries may be more susceptible to corruption than others. What do the data say?

In Graph 4.6, which covers 60 countries, the share of natural capital in national wealth is plotted along the horizontal axis as before and the corruption perceptions index for the year 2000 along the vertical axis.[3] The corruption perceptions index (from Transparency International, Berlin) is constructed from information obtained from businessmen who are willing to report how often and how forcefully bribes and the like are demanded of them in various countries, and how high these are. The index extends from zero, in countries where corruption is greatest, to ten, where corruption is practically nonexistent (as, for example, in Finland and Denmark). The picture shows a clear and statistically significant relationship: corruption, as measured by this index, increases from one country to the next in accordance with the increase in natural resource abundance or intensity. When the share of natural capital in national wealth goes up by 15 percentage points, the corruption perceptions index drops (i.e., corruption increases) by two points. The rank correlation is -0.52.[4]

Graph 4.6
Corruption and natural capital 1994-2000

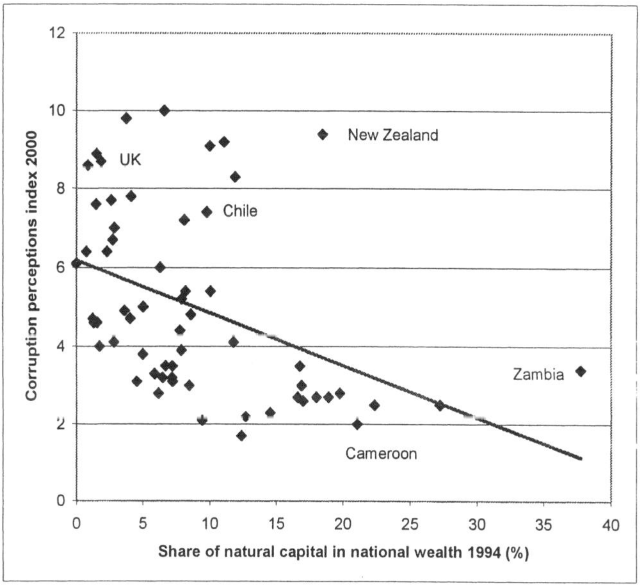

Similar results obtain when natural resource abundance or intensity is instead measured by the share of the primary sector in the labor force, 1965-1990 (Graph 4.7). Now we have data for many more countries, or 88 rather than 60. The correlation is again quite significant; the Spearman rank correlation is -0.67.

---

3 Corruption rankings for earlier years (1995-1999) give similar results.

4 When the corruption index is purged of that part which is caused by initial income, the results remain unchanged.

Graph 4.7
Corruption and employment in primary sector 1965-1990 (% of labour force)

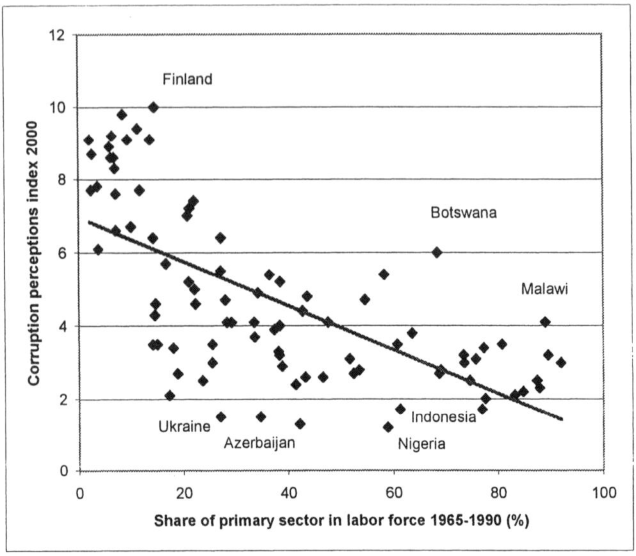

Graph 4.8
Corruption and economic growth 1965-1998

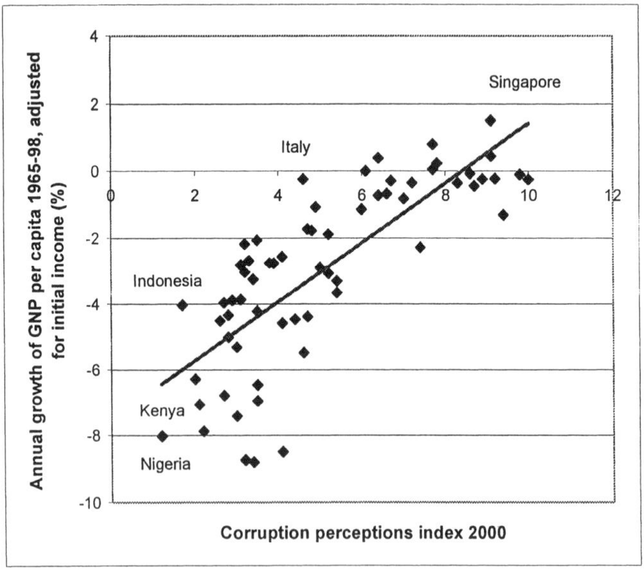

Graph 4.8 shows the cross-sectional relationship between corruption and economic growth. The figure suggests that an increase in the corruption perceptions index (i.e., a decrease in corruption) by one point from one place to another goes along with an increase per capita growth by almost one percentage point per year on the average, for given initial income.[5] This is not a small effect – if it is an effect, that is, as opposed to a mere correlation.[6] The pattern is quite significant; the rank correlation is 0.78. The number of countries is 64.

Taking Graphs 4.7 and 4.8 together, we see that an increase in the primary labor share by 16 percentage points goes hand in hand with a decrease in the corruption perceptions index by one point (Graph 4.7), which in turn goes along with a decrease in per capita growth by one percentage point per year on the average, for given initial income (Graph 4.8). Here we have another possible reason why natural resource abundance or intensity appears to inhibit economic growth across countries.

4 Channel 3: Education and human capital

Third, natural resource abundance or intensity may reduce private and public incentives to accumulate human capital due to a high level of non-wage income – e.g., dividends, social spending, low taxes. Awash in cash, natural-resource-rich nations may be tempted to underestimate the long-run value of education. Of course, the rent stream from abundant natural resources may enable nations to give a high priority to education – as in Botswana, for instance, where government expenditure on education relative to national income is among the highest in the world. Even so, empirical evidence shows that, across countries, school enrolment at all levels is inversely related to natural resource abundance or intensity, as measured by the share of the labor force engaged in primary production (Gylfason, Herbertsson, and Zoega, 1999). There is also evidence that, across countries, public expenditures on education relative to national income, expected years of schooling, and school enrolment are all inversely related to natural resource abundance (Gylfason, 2001; see also Temple, 1999).

---

5 Notice that the growth measures are slightly different in Graph 4.5 and 4.8. The reason is that the adjustment for initial income in the two figures is based on different measures of natural resource abundance, the natural capital share in Graph 4.5 and the primary labor share in Graph 4.8. This difference has no material effect on the patterns displayed in the figures.

6 For comparison, Mauro (1995) presents econometric evidence that suggests that a decrease in the corruption index by one point (i.e., increased corruption) from one country to the next is associated with a reduction in per capita growth of one-quarter a percentage point per year on the average.

Graph 4.9
Education and natural capital 1980-1997

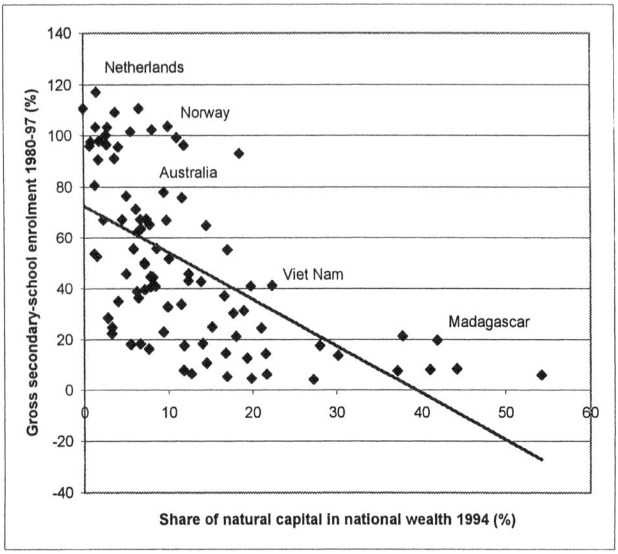

Graph 4.10
Education and economic growth 1965-1998

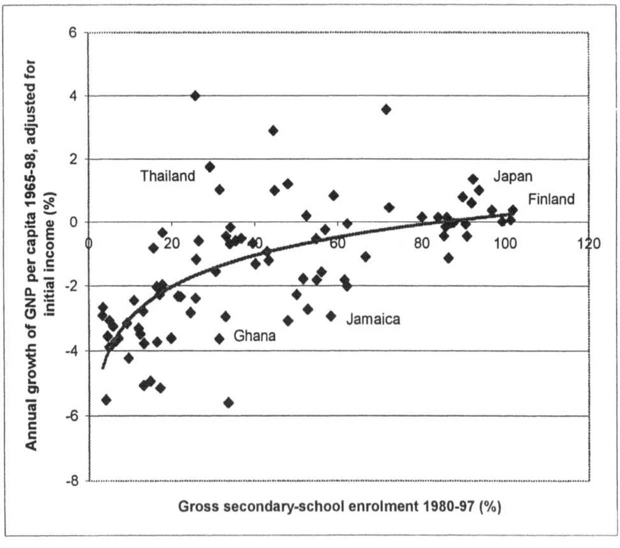

Once again, abundant natural capital appears to crowd out human capital. This matters because more and better education is good for growth.

As far as economic growth is concerned, however, the supply of education may matter less than demand. This is relevant here because public expenditure on education tends to be supply-led and of mediocre quality, and may thus fail to foster efficiency, equality, and growth, in contrast to private expenditure on education, which is generally demand-determined and thus, perhaps, likely to be of a higher quality and more conducive to growth. For this reason, I prefer to use school enrolment rates rather than public expenditures on education as a measure of education in the empirical analysis to follow.

Graph 4.9 shows a scatterplot of secondary-school enrolment as a percentage of each cohort from 1980 to 1997 on the vertical axis and, on the horizontal axis, the natural capital share measured as in Graphs 4.4 and 4.6. Imperfect though it is, secondary-school enrolment is the most commonly used yardstick for education in the empirical growth literature. Even so, other measures of education such as primary-enrolment rates, tertiary-enrolment rates, public expenditures on education, and years of schooling for girls or boys yield similar results (Gylfason, 2001). The regression line through the 91 observations suggests that an increase of ten percentage points in the natural capital share from one country to the next is associated with a decrease in secondary-school enrolment by 18 percentage points. The relationship is also statistically significant: the Spearman rank correlation is -0.66.

Graph 4.10 shows a scatterplot of secondary-school enrolment for both genders from 1980 to 1997 and economic growth. If we fit a straight line through the scatter (not shown), the figure shows that a 25 percentage point increase in secondary-school enrolment goes along with a one percentage point rise in the annual rate of growth of GNP per capita. In fact, the relationship is significantly nonlinear, indicating decreasing returns to education, and it is, moreover, statistically significant (the rank correlation is 0.62). The number of observations is 87. It needs to be emphasized that school enrolment reflects, at best, the quantity of education provided rather than the quality of education received. Public expenditure on education is also positively correlated with economic growth across countries in our sample (not shown), but the correlation is not significant in a statistical sense.

Taking Graphs 4.9 and 4.10 together, we see that, across countries, secondary-school enrolment is inversely related to natural resource abundance and directly related to economic growth. Specifically, an increase in the natural capital share by 25 percentage points goes along with a decrease in secondary-school enrolment by 45 percentage points according to Graph 4.9, which, in turn, goes along with a decrease in economic growth by almost two percentage points by Graph 4.12. Therefore, natural resource abundance seems capable of reducing economic growth significantly, not only through the Dutch disease, rent seeking, and overconfidence that tends to reduce the quality of economic policy and structure, but also by weakening public and private incentives to accumulate human capital. If so, the adverse effects of natural resource abundance on economic growth since the 1960s that have been reported in the literature may in part reflect the effect of education on growth.

How can we interpret these results? Natural-resource-based industries as a rule are less high-skill labor intensive and perhaps also less high-quality capital intensive than other industries, and thus confer relatively few external benefits on other industries (Wood, 1999). Moreover, workers released from primary industries, such as agriculture, fisheries, forestry, or mining, generally have relatively limited general, labor-market relevant education to offer new employers in other industries. There are exceptions, though, such as in modern agriculture and, indeed, in high-tech oil-drilling operations. But insofar as high-skill labor and high-quality capital are less common in primary production than elsewhere, this may help explain why natural resource abundance and the associated preponderance of primary production and primary exports tends to impede learning by doing, technological advance, and economic growth. This linkage reinforces the case for investment in education and training as an engine of growth: more and better education tends to shift comparative advantage away from primary production towards manufacturing and services, and thus to accelerate learning by doing and growth.

5 Channel 4: Saving, investment, and physical capital

Fourth, natural resource abundance may blunt private and public incentives to save and invest and thereby impede economic growth. Specifically, when the share of output that accrues to the owners of natural resources rises, the demand for capital falls, and this leads to lower real interest rates and less rapid growth (Gylfason and Zoega, 2001). Moreover, if mature institutions are conducive to an efficient use of resources, including natural resources, and if poorly developed institutions are not, then natural resource abundance may also retard the development of financial institutions in particular and hence discourage saving, investment, and economic growth through that channel as well. As in the case of education, it is not solely the volume of investment that counts because quality – i.e., efficiency – is also of great importance. Unproductive investments may seem unproblematic to governments or individuals who are flush with cash thanks to nature's bounty.

Graph 4.11 shows a scatterplot of the average ratio of gross domestic investment to GDP in 1965-1998 and natural resource abundance or intensity measured as in Graphs 4.4, 4.6, and 4.9. The regression line through the 87 observations, one per country, suggests that an increase of about ten percentage points in the natural

Graph 4.11
Investment and natural capital 1965-1998

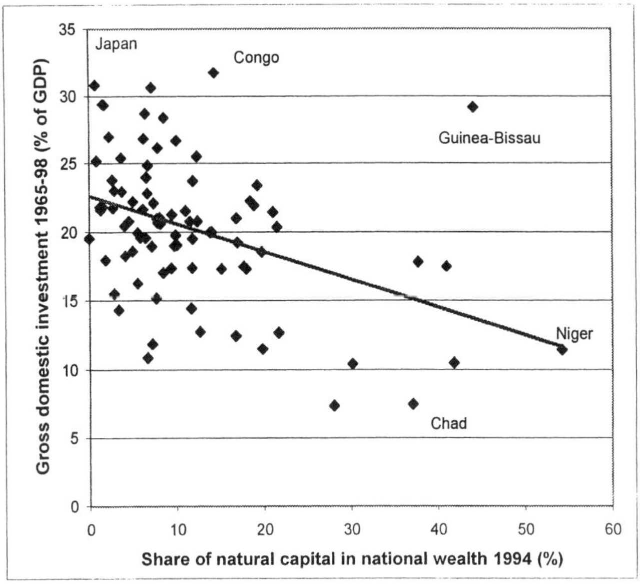

Graph 4.12
Investment and economic growth 1965-1998

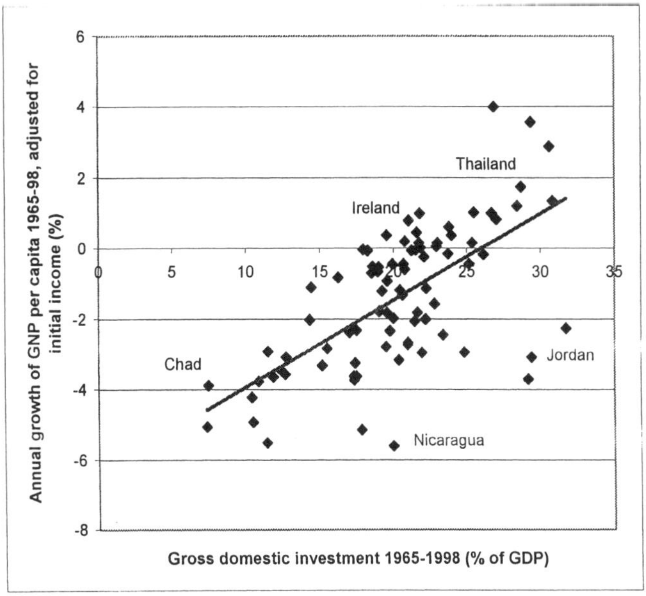

capital share from country to country is associated with a decrease in investment by two percent of GDP. The relationship is statistically significant: the rank correlation -0.37.

Graph 4.12 shows a scatterplot of economic growth as measured in Graphs 4.5, 4.8, and 4.10 and the average investment ratio over the same period, 1965-1998. The regression line through the 85 observations suggests that an increase in the investment ratio by about five percentage points is associated with an increase in annual economic growth by one percentage point. The relationship is highly significant: the rank correlation is 0.65. The slope of the regression line is consistent with the regression coefficients on investment in cross-country growth equations reported in recent literature (Levine and Renelt, 1992).

In sum, an increase in the natural capital share by 25 percentage points goes along with a decrease in the investment ratio by five percentage points by Graph 4.11, which in turn goes along with a decrease in economic growth by one percentage point by Graph 4.12. Thus, empirical evidence seems consistent with the idea that an abundance of or heavy dependence on natural resources may erode or reduce the quality of foreign, social, human, and physical capital, and thus stand in the way of rapid economic growth on a significant scale.[7] It is a matter of taste and classification whether the some or even all the mechanisms reviewed above are regarded as additional symptoms of the Dutch disease or as separate channels of transmission from resource dependence to slow growth.

6 Natural capital and economic growth

To conclude the story, Graph 4.13 shows a scatterplot of economic growth per capita from 1965 to 1998 and natural resource abundance as measured in Graphs 4.4, 4.6, 4.9, and 4.11. The figure covers 85 countries. The growth rate has been adjusted for initial income as before. The regression line through the scatterplot in Graph 4.13 suggests that an increase of about ten percentage points in the natural capital share from one country to another is associated with a decrease in per capita growth by one percentage point per year on average. The relationship is also significant in a statistical sense (Spearman's rank correlation is -0.64), and conforms to the partial correlations that have been reported in multiple regression analyses where other relevant determinants of growth (investment, education, etc., as well as initial income to account for catch-up and convergence) are taken into account. A relationship of this kind has been reported in a number of recent

---

7 There is also evidence that natural capital may crowd out financial capital. See Gylfason and Zoega (2001).

Graph 4.13
Natural capital and economic growth 1965-1998

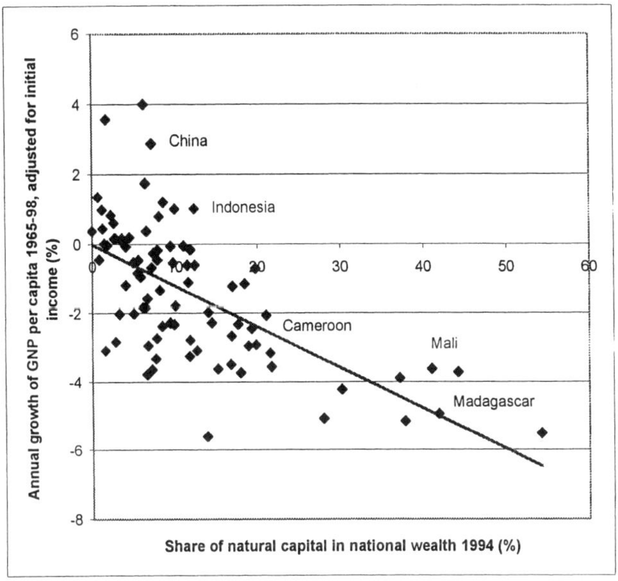

Graph 4.14
Natural resources and economic growth 1965-1998, again

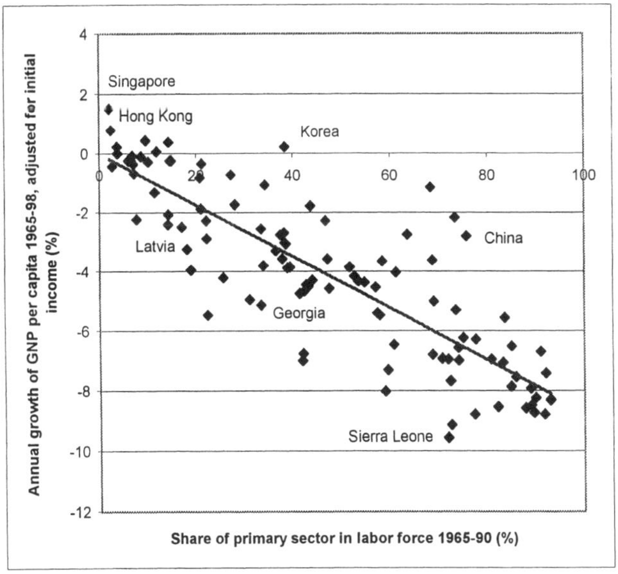

studies (Sachs and Warner, 1995, 1999; Gylfason, Herbertsson, and Zoega, 1999).

At last, Graph 4.14 shows that a similar inverse relationship between natural resources and economic growth emerges when natural resource abundance or intensity is measured by the share of the primary sector in total employment as in Graph 4.7. There are now 105 countries in the sample. The relationship is significant. The rank correlation is -0.85. The adjustment for initial income entails a speed of convergence of about 2% a year (not shown), a common result in empirical growth research. An increase of 11 or 12 percentage points in the primary labor share from one country to the next is associated with a decrease in per capita growth by one percentage point per year on average, for given initial income. A reduction by one percentage point in any country's annual growth rate is a serious matter because the (weighted) average rate of per capita growth in the world economy since 1965 has been about 1.5% per year.

7 Concluding remarks

Natural resources bring risks. One is that too many people become locked in low-skill intensive natural-resource-based industries, including agriculture, and thus fail through no fault of their own to advance their own or their children's education and earning power. Another risk is that the authorities and other inhabitants of resource-rich countries become overconfident and therefore tend to underrate or overlook the need for good economic policies and institutions as well as for good education and good investments. In other words, nations that believe that natural capital is their most important asset may develop a false sense of security and become negligent about the accumulation of foreign, social, human, and physical capital. Indeed, resource-rich nations can live well of their natural resources over extended periods, even with poor economic policies and institutions and a weak commitment to education. Awash in easy cash, they may find that difficult reforms do not pay. Nations without natural resources have a smaller margin for error, and are less likely to make this mistake. In resource-rich countries, awareness of these risks, as well as a conscious effort and ability to contain them, is perhaps the best insurance policy against them.

References

Auty, R. M. (2001) (ed.): Resource Abundance and Economic Development. Oxford University Press, Oxford and New York.

Bardhan, P. (1997): Corruption and Development: A Review of the Issues. Journal of Economic Literature, No. 35, September, pp. 1320-1346.

Frankel, J. A. and D. Romer (1999): Does Trade Cause Growth? American Economic Review, No. 89, June, pp. 379-399.

Gelb, A. (1998): Windfall Gains: Blessing or Curse? Oxford University Press, Oxford and New York.

Gylfason, T. (1999): Exports, Inflation, and Growth. World Development, No. 27, June, pp. 1031-1057.

Gylfason, T. (2001): Natural Resources, Education, and Economic Development. European Economic Review, No. 45, May, pp. 847-859.

Gylfason, T. (forthcoming): Nature, Power, and Growth. Scottish Journal of Political Economy.

Gylfason, T., Tryggvi T. Herbertsson and G. Zoega (1999): A Mixed Blessing: Natural Resources and Economic Growth. Macroeconomic Dynamics, No. 3, June, pp. 204-225.

Gylfason, T. and G. Zoega (2001): Natural Resources and Economic Growth: The Role of Investment. CEPR Discussion Paper, No. 2743, March.

Karl, T. L. (1997): The Perils of the Petro-State: Reflections on the Paradox of Plenty. Journal of International Affairs, No. 53, Fall, pp. 31-48.

Levine, R. and D. Renelt (1992): A Sensitivity Analysis of Cross-Country Growth Regressions. American Economic Review, No. 82, September, pp. 942-963.

Mauro, P. (1995): Corruption and Growth. Quarterly Journal of Economics, No. 110, August, pp. 681-712.

Paldam, M. and G. T. Svendsen (2000): An Essay on Social Capital: Looking at the Fire behind the Smoke. European Journal of Political Economy 16, No. 2, pp. 339-366.

Sachs, J. D. and A. M. Warner (1995, revised 1997, 1999): Natural Resource Abundance and Economic Growth. NBER Working Paper 5398, Cambridge, Massachusetts.

Sachs, J. D. and A. M. Warner (1999): Natural Resource Intensity and Economic Growth. Ch. 2 in Jörg Mayer, Brian Chambers, and Ayisha Farooq (eds.): Development Policies in Natural Resource Economies, Edward Elgar, Cheltenham, UK, and Northampton, Massachusetts.

Temple, J. (1999): A Positive Effect of Human Capital on Growth. Economics Letters 65, pp. 131-134.

Wood, A. J. B. (1999): Natural Resources, Human Resources and Export Composition: a Cross-Country Perspective. Ch. 3 in Jörg Mayer, Brian Chambers, and Ayisha Farooq (eds.): Development Policies in Natural Resource Economies, Edward Elgar, Cheltenham, UK, and Northampton, Massachusetts.

Woolcock, M. (1998): Social Capital and Economic Development: Toward a Theoretical Synthesis and Policy Framework. Theory and Society 27, pp. 151-208.

World Bank (1997): Expanding the Measure of Wealth: Indicators of Environmentally Sustainable Development. Environmentally Sustainable Development Studies and Monographs Series No. 17, World Bank, Washington, D.C.

Part II

SUSTAINING GROWTH OF THE UKRAINIAN ECONOMY

5

Is the Economic Growth in Ukraine Sustainable?[1]

Marek Dabrowski

1 Introduction

Ukraine is just celebrating the 10th anniversary of its independence. Unfortunately, this decade cannot be considered as successful, at least from the economic point of view. Ukraine experienced the longest and one of the deepest declines of GDP among all the transition economies. In addition, the first half of the decade was marked by the extreme macroeconomic instability and hyperinflation (see Dabrowski, 1994). In the second half of the decade progress in disinflation and currency stabilisation was seriously damaged by the 1998 financial crisis caused by the unsustainable fiscal policy. Only in the second half of 1999 the Ukrainian economy entered into a period of growth and relative macroeconomic stability.

This unfavorable course of economic events can be explained both by enormous distortions and instability inherited from the Soviet economy and by the slow and inconsequent path of economic transition to a market system. While the first factor was responsible for the very difficult starting point of the independent Ukraine and

---

[1] In the recent few years most of my work related to Ukrainian economy, including the problem of economic growth was carried out under the USAID funded Ukraine Macroeconomic Policy Program (Award No. 121-A-00-98-00623-00) implemented by the CASE – Center for Social and Economic Research in Warsaw. Author wants to express his gratitude to Anna Myslinska, Magdalena Tomczynska, Mirosław Gronicki, Janusz Szyrmer and other members of the CASE and CASE-Ukraine team for providing me with the recent statistical data and possibility to discuss the issue of growth perspectives in Ukraine what occurred to be very helpful in preparing this chapter. The chapter reflects, however, only my personal opinions and not necessarily those of CASE, CASE Ukraine or the USAID. I accept the sole responsibility for the content and quality of the presented material.

the deep output decline in the beginning of 1990s, insufficient progress in economic reforms significantly delayed an output recovery.

When finally economy started to grow the question about growth sustainability became crucial. The short history of transition in our region includes several growth episodes, which occurred to be short living and replaced soon by the new round of output decline (Romania 1993-1995, Bulgaria 1994-1995, Russia 1997). Many economists are concerned that the same may happen with the current growth in Ukraine.

However, answering the question on growth sustainability in any transition country for a number of reasons is not an easy task. First, we do not have any comprehensive growth theory in transition economies so far. What is available, is a couple of more or less empirically verified hypotheses concerning influence of various macro- and microeconomic factors on growth performance. Second, statistical data series in transition economies are still too short and unstable as result of various methodological changes in statistics itself and structural and institutional changes in the economy. That makes serious econometric analysis risky. This argument is particularly relevant to Ukrainian economy, which entered structural and institutional changes with significant delay compared to other countries, and where the quality of statistics is below the regional average. Third, most of transition economies, including the Ukrainian one, is open enough in terms of trade and financial flows. Hence, they have become dependent on influence of external factors such as growth fluctuations in the world economy as the whole and in major trade partners, changing attitude of financial investors to emerging markets, etc.. As result, even countries considered having strong and sustainable growth potentials can seriously suffer from adverse external shocks as it happened in 1998-1999 with the Baltic countries and Poland after the Russian and Ukrainian financial crises.

Taking into account the above reservations, I am not going to give any definite answer to the question underlined in the title of this chapter. On the contrary, my perception is that we know too little about real sources and driving forces of the current economic growth in Ukraine to risk any hard forecast. In addition, continuation of the growth trend in longer term will strongly depend on further progress in reforming the Ukrainian economy and the latter, in turn, will be determined by the political developments. So any conclusions presented here should be considered as the very preliminary and contributing only to the future more complex research on this topic rather than providing any definite answer.

My analysis starts with the short resume of the history of economic decline/ growth in Ukraine in the last decade (section 2). This is followed by the attempt of decomposition of recent growth figures in components of global demand and individual sectors (section 3). Section 4 deals with hypotheses concerning sources and sustainability of economic growth in the empirical context of experience of other transition countries. Finally, section 5 contains the concluding remarks.

2 Short history of economic decline/growth in Ukraine

All the former communist countries experienced a period of deep output decline during last years of the command economy and in the first years of transition. The size and nature of this decline raised a lot of controversies.

Graph 5.1
Cumulative growth performance, 1991-2000

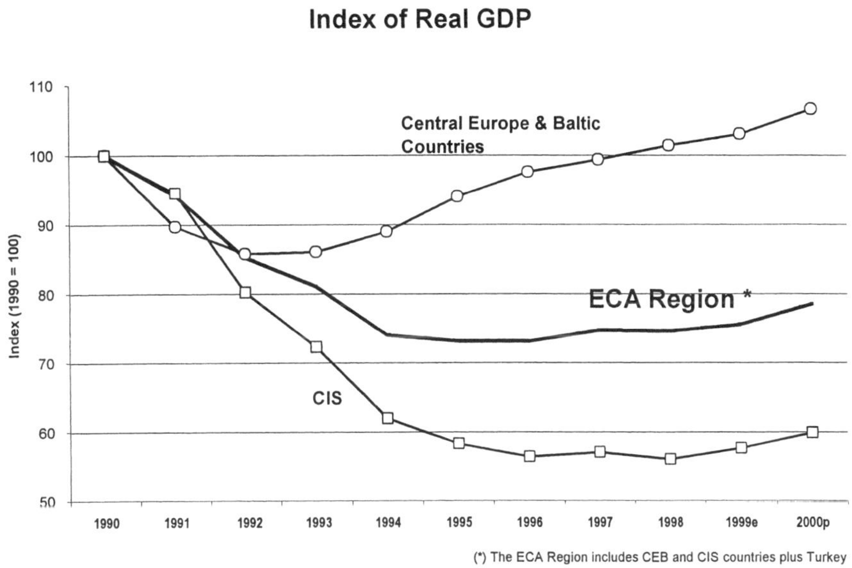

Source: World Bank (2000, Graph 2.1)

Some authors compared the large scale of the official GDP decline with the Great Depression of 1930s (see, for example, Laski, Bhaduri and Levcik, 1993; World Bank, 2000) but this kind of analogy seems to be highly irrelevant from any point of view. Also the opinion that it was transition to market economy and especially its radical variant, which were responsible for a deep transformation recession is wrong.[2] First, output decline started already in the last years of communist regime. Second, countries, which decided to enter the path of radical and fast reforms, suffered smaller cumulative decline and started recovery earlier than the slow reformers. This is illustrated by Graph 5.1 where Central European and Baltic

2 See Joseph Stiglitz (2000) on Russian and Chinese transition and Dabrowski, Gomulka and Rostowski's (2001) discussion thereof.

(CEB) countries following fast transition track present much better growth performance than countries of the Commonwealth of the Independent States (CIS) reforming their economies slower and in much less consistent way.

In both groups of countries (CEB and CIS) the size of the officially recorded GDP decline has been overestimated for a number of reasons (see Bratkowski, 1993; Winiecki, 1990; Aslund, 2001). First, the official GDP level under the centrally planned economy was systematically over-reported (so-called pripiska) by all levels of administration. Second, it did not reflect the poor quality of production, the chronic market shortages, and limited consumer choice. Third, the significant portion of GDP in the former USSR (and other former communist countries) was consumed for military and quasi/military purposes and did not contribute to peoples' living standard. Fourth, after the transition process started over-reporting was replaced by the massive underreporting in order to avoid tax liabilities (or strip profits and assets from the official sector to the informal one). Fifth, the period of high inflation/ hyperinflation also contributed to numerous statistical mistakes related particularly to GDP deflators.

As result, the actual size of GDP decline (not saying about real living standard) was probably much smaller in all transition countries than officially reported. However, it did not change or changed very little in a relative growth performance of individual countries. CIS countries have performed generally much worse than CEB countries, and Ukraine has occurred to be one of outsiders in the CIS group (see Table 5.1).

The phenomenon of the initial transformation recession could be explained by two groups of factors: (i) micro- and macroeconomic distortions inherited from the command economy; (ii) bad economic policies (see World Bank, 2000). Generally speaking, while inherited distortions (extremely large in the case of Ukraine) might be considered as the substantial factor explaining initial output decline, it was the bad economic policy, which made the decline phase so prolonged and severe and brought an economic recovery so late. Even a very rough comparison of the Ukraine's growth trend with that of Baltic countries, particularly of Estonia (see Table 5.1), shows that having the similar starting point in terms of inherited structural and institutional distortions the latter managed to stop output decline and start a sustainable economic growth much earlier than Ukraine did.

Among the main characteristics of bad policies run by the subsequent Ukrainian government one can mention very expansionary monetary and fiscal policies in the beginning of decade (leading to hyperinflation at the end of 1993), late and inconsequent liberalisation and macroeconomic stabilisation, continuous fiscal imbalances in 1995-1998 leading to the currency crisis in September 1998, slow path of insider dominated and non-transparent privatisation, intensive rent-seeking of the oligarchs and widespread corruption, over-regulation of the economy and extremely bad investment climate, and many others.

Table 5.1
Cumulative output decline and recovery in individual transition countries, 1990-1999

Country	Number of consecutive years of output decline	Cumulative output decline	Index of 1999 Real GDP (1990 = 100)
Central and South-Eastern Europe and Baltic States *	*3.8*	*22.6*	*103.1*
Albania	3	33	102
Bulgaria	4	16	78
Croatia	4	36	84
Czech Republic	3	12	97
Estonia	5	35	80
Hungary	4	15	105
Latvia	6	51	58
Lithuania	5	44	66
Poland	2	6	141
Romania	3	21	80
Slovak Republic	4	23	104
Slovenia	3	14	113
Commonwealth of Independent States *	*6.5*	*50.5*	*57.7*
Armenia	4	63	50
Azerbaijan	6	60	53
Belarus	6	35	82
Georgia	5	78	29
Kazakstan	6	41	60
Kyrgyz Republic	6	50	62
Moldova	7	63	34
Russia	7	40	59
Tajikistan	7	50	56
Turkmenistan	8	48	63
Ukraine	10	59	41
Uzbekistan	6	18	93

* simple average, except for the Index of 1990 GDP, which shows population weighted averages.
Source: World Bank (2000, Table 1)

The first signs of output recovery (particularly in industry) were observed in the last quarter of 1997 and first half of 1998 following the similar tendencies in Russia with the approximately 3 quarters lag. However, the financial crisis spiral, which started in November 1997 (see Dabrowski et al., 1999) brought quickly the end of this short episode. Devaluation of Hryvnia and near-default of 1998-1999 was followed by the new wave of the output decline. Finally, from the second half of 1999 Ukrainian economy re-entered the growth path, again with a half a year time lag compared to a similar trend in Russia.

In spite of initial carefulness and some skepticism of many analysts[3], this time growth performance occurred to be longer lasting. Moreover, the growth rate is increasing every quarter what seems to falsify the initial hypotheses about the significant role of some `windfall' factors such as the low statistical base of 1999, high demand for Ukrainian metals on the international markets, and expectations of the gradually declining rate of growth (see UEO, 2000/1). In year 2000, Ukrainian GDP increased by 5.8% placing this country in the group of the highest growing economies in the region (see Graph 5.2)

Graph 5.2
GDP growth rate in transition countries, 2000

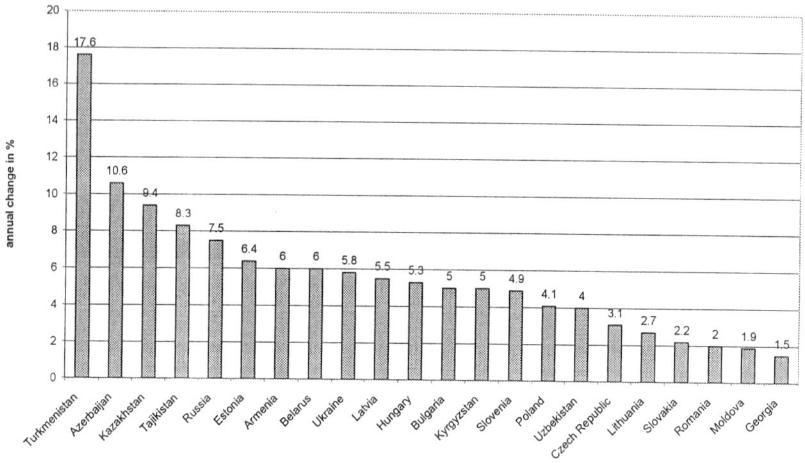

Source: WEO (2001, Table 1.10 and 1.11); CASE database

This leads us to the questions on sources of this growth and its sustainability in the medium to longer-term perspective.

---

3 Including the author of this paper and CASE analytical group – see the subsequent issues of the UEO (2000 and 2001).

3 Decomposition of growth trend by components of global demand and by sectors

As mentioned before the available growth statistics in Ukraine is limited in terms of time series, disaggregation and quality. Looking for factors being able to explain sources of the current growth trend we start from the analysis of components of global demand. Graph 5.3 gives this kind of disaggregation for the period from the beginning of 1998 until the third quarter of 2000 based on the available statistics of national accounts.

Graph 5.3
Components of global demand

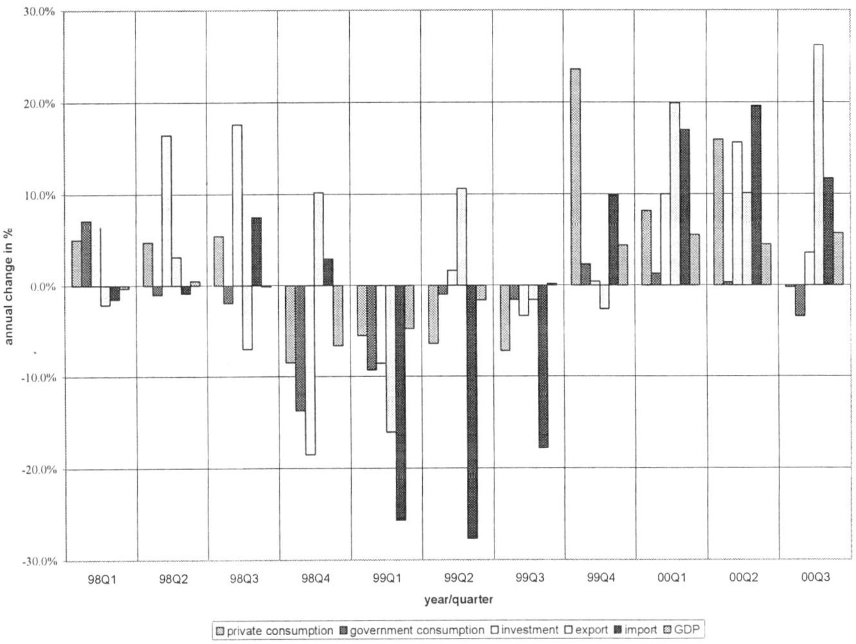

Source: State Statistics Committee of Ukraine; CASE database

Unfortunately, no regularities in terms of demand components determining a growth performance can be observed in this figure, apart from some role of investment demand. The influence of all other major components of global demand – private consumption, government consumption, export and import – fluctuates strongly from one quarter to another. This may be connected, to some extent, with methodological imperfections of the foreign trade statistics (particularly in relation to trade with the CIS and unregistered `shuttle' trade) and with the difficulties to estimate the size of a shadow economy and private consumption financed from unregistered sources of income. On the other hand, the mentioned sources of statistical uncertainty have a long lasting and `regular' nature and can hardly bring so big fluctuations between subsequent quarters. Possibly, longer data series in future will be able to bring more light in respect to the demand sources of the current growth in Ukraine.

Graph 5.4
Value added by sectors

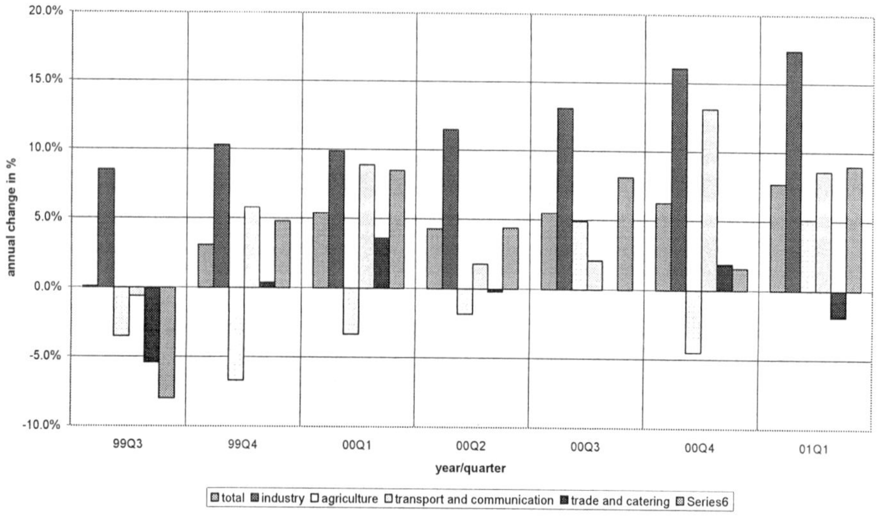

Source: State Statistics Committee of Ukraine; CASE database

Analysing sectoral structure of GDP growth (see Graph 5.4 illustrating value added growth in individual sectors) one can find that industry plays the role of the engine of the recent recovery, followed by transportation and telecommunication, and services. Very recently agriculture started to contribute to economic growth too. This is a new phenomenon because during the second half of 1990s output decline in agriculture was the most severe. The decreasing trend in this sector continued even at the time when industry already presented the first signs of improvement.

Looking at branch decomposition of industrial growth in the year 2000 we can identify ferrous and non-ferrous metallurgy (representing the traditional Ukrainian industries) on the one hand, and some market oriented subsectors such as textile, food, timber, glass and ceramic production, on the other.

Thus, the available sectoral/branch data do not provide so far a clear picture what is the nature of the current growth episode and whether any serious structural changes are behind it.

4 Hypotheses concerning sources and sustainability of economic growth. Experience of other transition countries

Generally speaking, there are two groups of hypotheses concerning sources of the recent economic growth in Ukraine. The first one refers to various temporary factors such as the low statistical base and presence of free production capacities after many years of output decline. Other 'windfall' factor can be connected with effects of 1998-1999 devaluation of Hryvnia, and strong external demand, particularly for the metallurgy products in year 2000. The second approach believes that long-term structural factors such as effects of privatisation and restructuring carried out so far, and moving a part of the shadow sector into the official one created a favorable environment for economic growth. While the latter leads to conclusion that the current growth may be sustainable in longer term the former suggests a gradually decreasing growth trend.

Advocates of each hypothesis can find some empirical evidence in favor of their interpretation. Certainly, many years of continuous output decline have left significant production capacities unused. In these circumstances initial catching up growth can be relatively easy achieved but short lived if not supported by new investments. Substantial real depreciation of Hryvnia during and after 1998 financial crises created a market niche for an import-substituting production, particularly of consumer goods. And the year 2000 was really unique in term of strong international demand and high export prices of Ukrainian metal products. These highly favorable external conditions were additionally strengthened by the so-called tax experiment in metallurgy, meaning, in practice, extensive exemptions in profit tax for this industry (see UEO, 2001/1). Graph 5.5 illustrates the level and dynamics of metallurgy export being closely correlated with the overall GDP dynamics (at least until the end of 2000).

On the other hand, there is evidence of some progress in restructuring of Ukrainian enterprises, particularly those producing consumer goods, which were the first object of privatisation in mid-1990s. And whatever can be said critical about mass voucher privatisation in Ukraine (and in other CIS countries) it finally brought changes in the ownership structure and economic behavior of many firms, particularly those exposed to market competition and not being large enough to rely on effective rent-seeking. Starting recovery in agriculture production can also probably be seen as result of reforms in this sector started in the end of 1999.

Graph 5.5
Changes in metallurgy production exports, (%, yoy) and Ukrainian GDP (USD m), 1998-2001

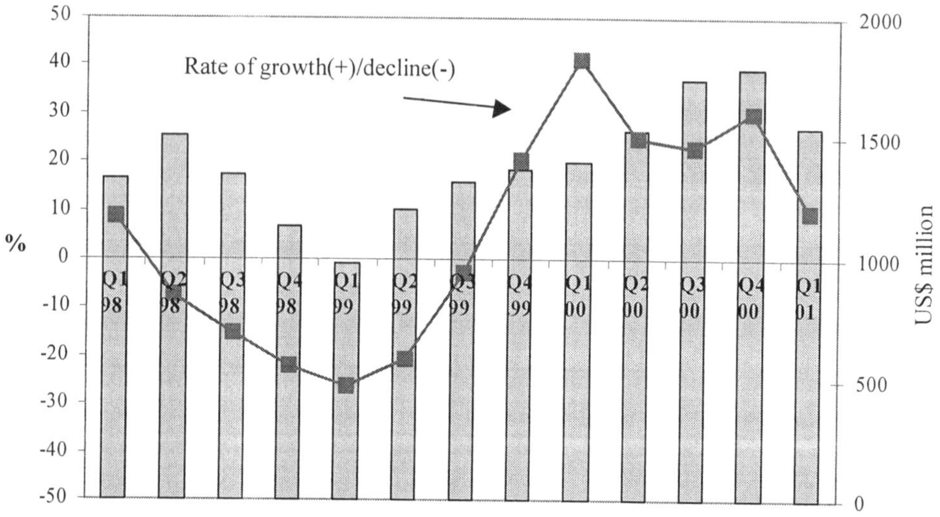

Source: State Statistics Committee of Ukraine; CASE database

Finally, the decrease in imports of energy resources from Russia observed from the beginning of 2001 may be a signal of starting rationalisation in energy production, distribution and consumption as a result of the strong disciplining effort undertaken by the Victor Yushchenko government in 2000-2001. However, it is still too early to proclaim progress in this sphere and a longer observation period for energy imports and consumption is needed in order to formulate harder conclusions.

There is also some evidence that deregulation measures undertaken in 1999-2000, including the simplified tax schemes for small firms pushed part of the informal sector back into the legal sphere. If true, this means that part of recorded growth has one-off and purely statistical character, being in fact a reversal of the opposite trend (moving to shadow economy) observed through most of the previous decade. Nevertheless, this kind of tendency should be very welcomed both from the fiscal point of view (broader revenue basis, more equal market position of firms) and as evidence of improving entrepreneurial and investment climate. It also needs in more detail statistical investigation as very little is known about the scale of this phenomenon so far.

As time goes and high rate of growth continues (in spite of real appreciation of Hryvnia and deteriorating situation in the international markets for metal products), there are more and more arguments in favor of hypothesis that the observed growth trend is not just a temporary, `windfall' phenomenon but probably has deeper roots and creates some hopes for future. However, presenting longer-term forecasts, going beyond the year 2002, seems to be a very risky job as our knowledge about growth sources and determinants is very limited yet.

Although there is not any comprehensive growth theory in transition economies so far the experience of other countries allows to identify some crucial factors. Apart from prudent macroeconomic management reflected in low inflation (below 10%), fiscal equilibrium, and sustainable current account balance, these are solid microeconomic and institutional reforms that determine a medium and long-term path of economic growth. Among many concrete characteristics, one can mention the following crucial policy measures determining long term growth chances:

- liberalisation of business activity allowing easy entry of new private firms and favorable regulatory environment for their development;
- stable and market oriented legal environment, law enforcement, secure property rights, and corporate governance rules and structure;
- transparent privatisation aiming in bringing strategic investors (including foreign investors) to privatised firms;
- hard budget constraints for existing big enterprises (in public and private sector);
- reorientation of foreign trade towards industrialised countries;
- inflow of foreign direct investments;
- effective privatisation of agriculture;
- soundness and market oriented behavior of the financial sector.

Unfortunately, if we compare Ukrainian economy with the most advanced transition economies of Central Europe and Baltic region with respect to any of the above mentioned characteristics the result will be unfavorable for Ukraine.

Graph 5.6
Share of employment in small enterprises (firms with 50 employees or less)

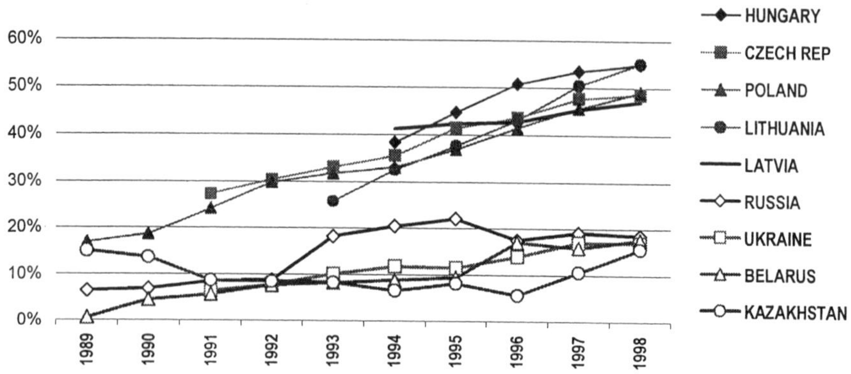

Source: World Bank (2000, Graph 3.4)

Graph 5.7
Share of value added in small enterprises (firms with 50 employees or less)

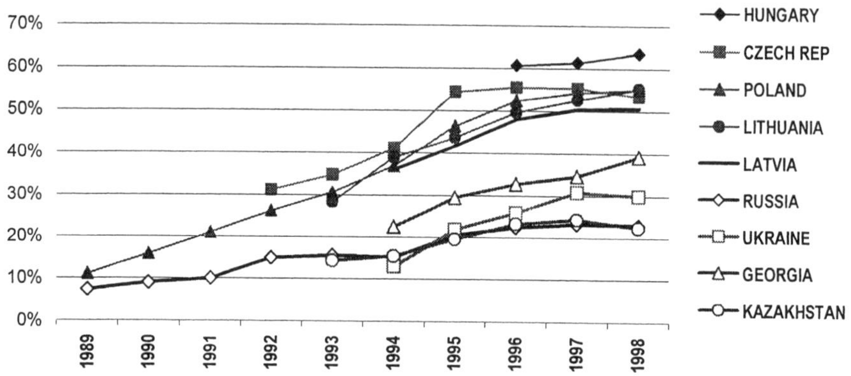

Source: World Bank (2000; Graph 3.5)

Graph 5.6 shows the share of employment in small firms (defined as firms employing 50 people or less) in the total employment. Graph 5.7 presents a similar proportion for value added. In both cases this ratio for Ukraine (and other CIS countries) was more than twice smaller in comparison with the Czech Republic, Hungary, Lithuania and Poland in 1998. Although this gap probably narrowed a bit during the last two years as a result of the above mentioned deregulation measures in Ukraine, it is very unlikely that the basic picture changed fundamentally.

Analysing the share of private sector in GDP in 1999 (see Graph 5.8) we find that Ukraine lagged behind not only leading reformers but also many CIS countries. Again, some progress in privatisation was recorded in 2000-2001 but a large enough share of the Ukrainian economy remains still in state hands. Besides, openness and transparency of the privatisation process are still very far from internationally recommended standards as was confirmed during the privatisation of the steel, aluminium and energy distribution industries in years 2000-2001.

Graph 5.8
Private sector share in GDP, 1999

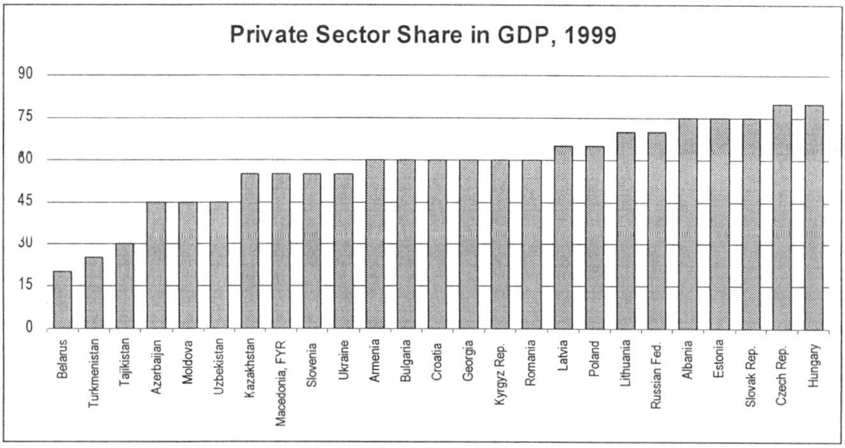

Source: EBRD (1999, Graph 4.6); World Bank (2000, Graph 3.1)

With respect to security of property rights, Ukraine's position is even more dramatic. According to EBRD/World Bank rating Ukraine has the least secure property rights for private investors among 22 analysed countries (see Graph 5.9). As a result, the inflow of foreign investments to Ukraine is one of the smallest among transition countries (in terms of share of GDP and per capita) and represents mainly CIS/offshore origin.

Graph 5.9
Insecurity of property rights in transition countries

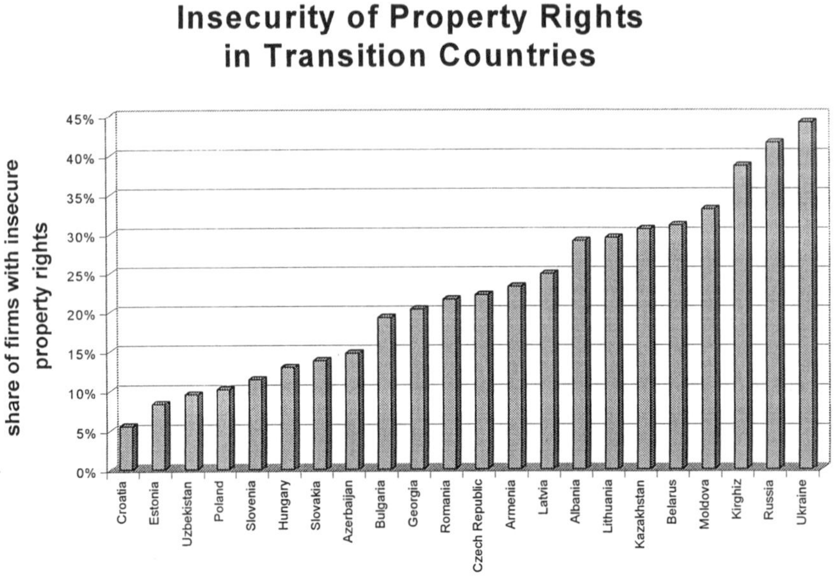

Source: World Bank (2000, Graph 3.13)

Also the geographic structure of the Ukrainian export dramatically differs from that of CEB countries (see Table 5.2). Although during the last three years this structure improved somewhat, most of Ukrainian export flows are still destined for CIS and developing countries. This is indirect evidence of the low international competitiveness of the Ukrainian economy and its technological backwardness.

Looking at other above-mentioned characteristics we will also find a picture, which is not very optimistic. Budget constraints although tightened seriously in year 2000 are still relatively weak in the energy sector, agriculture, and heavy industry. Agriculture reform, while strengthening the group of large rural entrepreneurs (mostly chairmen of the formerly collective farms), has not brought clarification in land ownership structure and has not promoted family farms. The financial sector is underdeveloped and extremely fragile and finds itself on the verge of a serious crisis. So most of the fundamental conditions for sustaining economic growth in the longer term are not in place yet.

Table 5.2
Export growth and destination in selected countries

Country	Exports growth rate (real terms, %) a/	Share of exports to industrial countries (%) b/	
	1993-1998	*1992-1993*	*1998-1999*
Central and South-Eastern Europe and Baltics (ave.)	*8.8*	*35.8*	*67.5*
Albania	22.0	62.9	94.1
Bulgaria	4.3	55.1	59.0
Czech Republic	10.4	29.9	69.3
Estonia	10.8	25.9	71.3
Hungary	11.1	67.4	81.5
Macedonia, FYR	7.3	22.2	65.5
Poland	12.9	71.6	75.5
Romania	8.7	44.3	71.0
Slovak Republic	6.9	15.9	59.2
Slovenia	5.7	33.7	70.7
Comm. Indep. States (ave.)	*3.2*	*28.0*	*29.0*
Armenia	-8.6	9.1	34.9
Azerbaijan *	14.0	4.2	20.0
Belarus	-3.2	15.3	11.0
Georgia *	10.3	2.3	25.9
Kazakhstan	3.4	43.8	29.6
Kyrgyz Republic	-2.4	24.7	44.0
Moldova	4.8	6.2	31.3
Russian Federation	4.7	59.3	49.4
Ukraine	5.8	18.1	23.3

* 1995-1998
Sources: World Bank (2000, Table 4)

5 Concluding remarks

The analysis carried out in this chapter was based both on an investigation of Ukraine's growth trend and its components, and on an assessment of the systemic factors crucial for growth perspectives. In the latter I referred to experience of other transition economies when data relevance and availability allowed for it. However, no definite conclusion can be drawn from this analysis. While a year ago skeptical forecasts of growth sustainability seemed to be justified (and the author of this chapter shared this skepticism), today more arguments support the hypothesis that the current growth episode is not just a temporary phenomenon. The growth trend has gained momentum, and seems to have deeper structural and institutional roots. I have in mind some (although limited) progress in privatisation, deregulation and restructuring. `Windfall' factors such as a real depreciation of Hryvnia or boom in metallurgy export are playing a gradually decreasing role. It appears that growth can continue at least in 2001 and 2002.

However, any forecasts going beyond 2002 would be very risky. Certainly, the Ukrainian economy has huge reserves in terms of potential productivity gains. At the moment, it consumes simple reserves coming from more market-oriented behavior of privatised enterprises, tightening budget constraints, better macroeconomic equilibrium, and relaxing regulatory burden. However, these reserves are limited, unless further substantial progress in structural and institutional reforms will be achieved. The comparative analysis carried out in the previous section (although limited to some factors only) shows how much Ukraine lags behind leading reformers in the Central Europe and the Baltic region. Closing this gap will determine the long-term sustainability of economic growth in Ukraine.

This perspective strongly depends on political developments. While year 2000 gave a ground for limited optimism in this respect, the situation in 2001 looks much more gloomy. The `Kuchmagate' scandal, the decomposition of the parliamentary majority, the vote of non-confidence in the Yushchenko government, a kind of international isolation of Ukraine, and the starting parliamentary election campaign have resulted in a stopping or slowing down of various important reforms and delayed privatisation of the energy and telecommunication sectors. While macroeconomic stability in terms of the inflation rate, exchange rate stability and fiscal and current account balance is much stronger than a few years ago this is not enough to guarantee sustainable economic growth in the longer term without a continuation of microeconomic reforms at a fast pace.

References

Aslund, A. (2001): The Myth of Output Collapse after Communism. Carnegie Endowment for International Peace, 12 January.

Bratkowski, A. (1993): The Shock of Transformation or the Transformation of the Shock?, Communist Economies & Economic Transformation, Vol. 5, No. 1.

Dabrowski, M. (1994): The Ukrainian Way to Hyperinflation. Communist Economies & Economic Transformation, Vol. 6, No. 2.

Dabrowski, M. (ed.), M. Dekhtiarchuk, U. Gorski, P. Kovalev, Y. Kuz'min, and K. Sultan (1999): Ukraine: From Fragile Stabilisation to Financial Crisis, CASE – Center for Social and Economic Research, Warsaw, Studies & Analyzes, No. 158.

Dabrowski M., S. Gomulka, and J. Rostowski (2001): Whence Reform? A Critique of the Stiglitz Perspective. Journal of Policy Reform, Vol 5, No. 1.

EBRD (1999): Transition Report 1999. European Bank for Reconstruction and Development, London.

Laski, K., A. Bhaduri, and F. Levcik (1993): Od gospodarki planowej do systemu rynkowego: co sie nie powiodlo i co teraz trzeba zrobic (From Planned Economy to a Market System: What Failed and What is Necessary to do Now), in: Gospodarka polska 1993: Ocena doswiadczen – postulaty dla polityki gospodarczej (The Polish Economy 1990-1993: Assessment of Experience and Proposals for thc Economic Policy), INE PAN & Semper, Studia i Materialy, No. 43.

Stiglitz, J. (1999): Whither Reform? Ten Years of Transition, Keynote Address presented at the Annual Bank Conference on Development Economics, April, Washington D.C.

UEO (2001 and 2001): Ekonomika Ukrainy. Tendencii, Ocenki, Prognozy (Ukrainian Economic Outlook), CASE – Center for Social and Economic Research, Warsaw & Kyiv, various issues

WEO (2001): World Economic Outlook, International Monetary Fund, April.

Winiecki, J. (1990): Post-Soviet-Type Economies in Transition: What Have We Learned from the Polish Transition Programme in Its First Year, Weltwirtschaftliches Archiv, Band 126, Heft 4.

World Bank (2000): Transition after Decade. Lessons and an Agenda for Policy, First Draft, 2 November, World Bank.

6

Is there Any Economic Growth in Ukraine?

Valeriy Heyets

There are currently two major themes in the discussion. The first is whether there is any economic growth is Ukraine, or whether it is just a statistical slight of hand, that allows the government to justify this or that policy, as opponents of the current economic strategies claim. The second is whether this economic growth is stable and long-term, or simply the result of momentary political pressures, raising doubts about there being a sustained economic policy.

There are certainly reasons at this time to assert that economic growth does exist in Ukraine, and is a result of a changing economic approach. After discarding the old economic system, after some successes and some failures, it has been proven that the new approach works and produces positive results under market principles that regulate supply and demand.

To my mind, there exists another much more profound problem: Has Ukraine created the basis for implementing a long-term development strategy? At this point in time, one can state that several market features are available in Ukraine:

- demand and supply are balancing each other, primarily through pricing mechanisms;
- markets are saturated with goods and services of various quality levels, enabling people to buy what they can afford;
- the money market is functioning, with the exchange rate being defined to some extent. The economy reacts to its fluctuations by promoting or limiting price competitiveness;
- after a period of "aggressive" imports into Ukraine, there is now some import substitution taking place. The domestic market is developing as a consequence of the national currency devaluation which followed the financial crisis, and increased competitiveness between national producers in some industries;
- exports have increased due to foreign demand, which reflects a certain openness of the Ukrainian economy;
- a market-oriented institutional environment also exists.

However, a market economy is as yet far from being fully established. There is still much room for development.

First of all, we do not have a real labour market since this most important resource has not been truly valued so far. This substantially restricts the effective use of labour, especially because other resource prices have reached world levels long ago. This fact is a serious obstacle on the way to economic growth, especially taking into account the present skill level of labour. As a result, the motivation to work efficiently diminishes. Moreover, taxation does not provide incentives; on the contrary, it hinders the economic activity of people, thus limiting long-term economic growth.

All this is aggravated by an extremely slow development of the stock market – a compulsory attribute of any market economy. As far as the state securities market is concerned, it had in fact been frozen for a while after a failed start. The stock market situation is causing a lot of concern, since this extremely important sphere of the market economy does not meet the needs of today, let alone the future. Everywhere in the world, the stock market is a financial instrument which helps to allocate, distribute, and direct investment capital into various spheres of the economy, primarily into the real sector. The Ukrainian stock market has not compensated for the lack of governmental planning and administrative levers. The underdeveloped stock market is impeding the investment processes, thus hampering economic restructuring without which it is impossible to increase competitiveness. There is a lack of transparency and of stock market liquidity; there are high systematic risks. The current system regarding taxation of investment funds and security profits discourages investment. The rights of investors and shareholders (founders, partners) of joint stock companies and other businesses remain unprotected.

A low level of corporate culture, a general legal nihilism, a lack of legislative support for property rights and for the legal vested interests of investors do not facilitate the inflow of investments into the Ukrainian economy, and are limiting the prospects for long-term economic growth.

The process of legalising the shadow economy has had a positive influence on economic growth. The legalised economy seems to demonstrate – or produces the effect of – economic growth. So far it is impossible to be sure about the correlation of this process with the real growth, since the required calculations have never been made, though some indicators suggest that this relationship is real. There will be further reduction of the shadow economy on the economy, but its effect will probably be limited. The shadow economy will likely stabilise at the typical level for transition economies, i.e. at about 30% to 35%, where it is expected to remain for quite a long period of time, retrenching only slowly. To my mind, this question will relatively soon become immaterial, which is why we will not pursue it in the context of this growth policy investigation.

What we are mainly interested in is to what extent recent changes (1999-2001) can be considered as long-term ones. In order to do that, we tried to consider how resources used for production in Ukraine have been created and have been employed. One piece of information, which is contained in the inter-industry input-output balances, enables us to analyse this. Although this method is not often used for analyses now-a-days, we have turned to it because it combines all components – resource creation and product distribution – at the same time, thus enabling us to see many interesting things and arrive at certain conclusions.

If we analyse some structural indicators concerning the distribution of goods and services among industries between 1987 and 1999, we see quite an interesting picture. Intermediate consumption rose from 46.8 to 51.5%, in spite of the fact that during the financial crisis of 1998 it was somewhat lower (as compared to 1995). Another component is affiliated with the final consumption costs, which went down during that period of time from 25.6 to 19.5%. And finally, the gross capital formation reduced by almost one half.

As far as export is concerned, here is some very interesting data, which can be extended into 2000 as well. Industry's contribution rose from 18.5 to 24.9% (Table 6.1). We can also observe that the share of imports in the structure of resource consumption increased to 25% (Table 6.2). This means that the resources of industry, in the part of import component creation went up. Against the background of shrinking accumulation and consumption, intermediate consumption and exports went up. Meanwhile, the share of industry in the general scope of the resources used was 67.6% in 1988, 57.3% in 1993 and 59.9% in 1999. If we compare this with the more or less stable situation of the 1980s, then the role of industry and industrial products in resource formation has in general diminished, which might have some rather unpleasant consequences.

Why I am emphasising this? The 2000 growth took place mainly in those industries which have relatively low value added, that is, in those industries, which are not able to create adequate financial resources for their development. Let's look at the appropriate structural indicators for some industries. In ferrous metallurgy for example, the final consumption expenses remain rather low, gross resource creation is even negative, and the export percentage rose from 34.1% in 1987 to 58.8% in 1999, which at first sight could be treated as a positive trend (Table 6.1).

Table 6.1
Structural indicators of goods and services distribution in different industries, 1987-1999

Industries	Total	Intermediate consumption							Final consumption cost							Gross formation							Export						
	1987-1999	1987	1988	1990	1993	1995	1998	1999	1987	1988	1990	1993	1995	1998	1999	1987	1988	1990	1993	1995	1998	1999	1987	1988	1990	1993	1995	1998	1999
Industry	100-100	46.8	46.6	44.9	57.9	54.6	51.4	51.5	25.6	25.8	31.4	21.9	17.8	21.8	19.5	9.14	9.14	6874	5.8	4.25	6.06	4.11	18.5	18.5	16.8	14.4	23.4	20.7	24.9
Agriculture	100-100	70	75.4	72.1	56.8	48	58.7	57	24.1	24	22.2	24.9	37.3	37.6	37.5	3.83	-2.8	3188	17.9	12.6	-1.62	-1.2	2.1	3.4	2.5	0.4	2.1	5.3	6.7
Transport	100-100	91.7	87.7	89	98.1	57.4	40.1	30.5	8	8	7.1	1.9	11.8	15.8	15.8	0	0	0	0	0	0	0	0.3	4.3	3.9	0	30.8	44.1	53.7
Electric power	100-100	67.1	65.6	66.8	85.5	86.6	86.5	85	23.2	22.7	22.3	12.3	6.48	10.6	12.9	0	0	0	0	1.32	0	0	9.7	11.7	10.9	2.2	5.6	2.9	2.1
Ferrous metallurgy	100-100	66	66.3	65.9	65.5	50.2	49.1	44.5	0.4	0.4	0.4	0.3	0	0.1	0.1	-0.5	-2.3	-0.6	-7.1	-1.3	-1.6	-3.4	34.1	35.6	34.3	41.3	51.1	52.4	58.8
Machine-building and mechanical engineering	100-100	35.3	34.9	33.4	34.1	32.6	34	34	3.9	8.8	13.2	14.9	11.2	7.35	0.1	31.2	32	40.13	32.9	28.4	36	29.8	24.6	24.3	13.3	18.1	27.8	22.6	36.1
Chemical and petrochemical	100-100	59.5	57	55.1	61.3	54.6	52.1	44.8	13.7	13.7	13.9	8.4	9.76	13.9	16.9	4	6.9	9.8	-7.9	0.64	-0.52	0	22.8	22.4	21.2	38.2	35	34.5	38.3
Light industry	100-100	39.7	40.6	39	43.8	27	27.4	33	48.8	48.6	59.5	50.7	68.5	56.9	46.3	2.1	1.4	-5.6	2	-12	-4.92	-5.6	9.4	9.4	7.1	3.5	16.8	20.6	26.3
Food industry	100-100	26.2	27.2	28.3	23.7	21.2	16.5	18.6	57.4	58	60.3	59.2	59.9	65.8	63.7	0.8	-0.4	-1.5	5.9	-1.4	5.41	3.7	15.6	15.2	12.9	11.2	20.3	12.3	14

But the problem lies elsewhere. It is important to assess the appropriate costs and tendencies (respecting their dynamics) at the time when the changes took place. Looking at the coefficients of direct and total costs we see that the total cost of electric power in ferrous metallurgy has been continuously increasing, including in 1999. During that period of time, according to Table 6.2, direct electric power costs in metallurgy increased by 2.9 times, including by almost 3% in 1999. Meanwhile, it is noteworthy, that 1999 was the year in which it was the metallurgical sector and its foreign trade activities which allowed reaching the first positive changes in industry during the last 10 years. As far as ferrous metal production costs are concerned, including those due to increased output in 1999, they rose more than 3 times during the whole period of time, and by 3.5% in 1999. It is clear that the increment in metallurgy in 1999, under such changes in total and direct costs, can in no way be characterised as long-term; it leads to the inefficient use of resources in the whole economy, to the increased use of energy and hence debt dependence of the Ukrainian economy, and to increased inflation and hence to creating the conditions for financial destabilisation of the economy in the medium term.

Table 6.2
Structural indicators of using imported and own resources in production through the industries in 1988-1999

	The share of import in the structure of production resources consumption							The share of certain industries in the total scope of resources used						
	1988	1989	1990	1993	1995	1998	1999	1988	1989	1990	1993	1995	1998	1999
Industry	20	20.6	19.7	1.4	26	24.3	25	67.6	71.2	69.5	57.7	63.8	58.9	59.9
Agriculture	2.6	2.5	2.1	1	1.8	0.6	1.2	17.4	16	17.5	12.5	11.2	12.2	11.1
Transport	0	4.2	3.9	0	6.5	6.7	6.4	3.5	2.9	3.3	5.9	6.5	6.1	6.4
Electric power	2.7	3	3	2.1	6.7	3.5	0.2	2	2	1.7	4.6	5	4.5	5.4
Ferrous metallurgy	12.8	12.8	11.6	3.1	8.6	4.3	5.1	6.9	6.3	6	7.2	9.4	8.2	8.8
Machine-building and mechanical engineering	23.4	23.8	23.5	10.4	30.4	36.4	37.3	19.1	21.2	20.6	10.7	10.8	8.9	8.4
Chemical and petrochemical	30.6	32.2	30.8	16.1	30.5	34.6	33.3	4.3	5.1	5	3.5	5	4.4	4.7
Light industry	28.3	29.8	29.6	5.3	38.7	41.1	41.9	7.6	9.1	8.8	3.4	2.9	2.6	2.5
Food industry	9.6	10	6.6	0.7	6.4	7.4	9.2	14.6	14.1	13.9	10.9	10.2	11.2	11

The changes in direct and total energy costs were of the same nature in the machine-building, chemical and petrochemical industries, based on the data in Table 6.2.

Only in the light and food industries is the growth of the direct and total cost coefficients not present. In all other industries (especially in the electric power sector) these costs have grown continuously. Thus, we were striving for growth, but it was mainly situational, and every unit of growth cost us more and more (especially energy). At the same time, the use of the price competitiveness effect in our economy that appeared after the financial crisis may produce positive effects later on under the effective use of the available financial resources (e.g. by investing in the quick capital turnover sphere).

It should be added, that the share of exports has increased in all sectors of the economy: in agriculture from 2.1 to 6.7%, in transport from 0.3 to 53.7% (Table 6.1).

Looking at the data characterising the resource dynamics' structure which we acquired during the period under consideration, we see a considerable dependence of most industries on their foreign economic activities. On the one hand, the export share rose, and, on the other hand, imports increased as well. This tendency is certainly positive since it implies the integration of the Ukrainian economy into the global one. However:

- most industries contributing to economic growth and having the tendency to grow have a low share of value added;
- Ukraine's import dependence increased and – more important – Ukraine's energy dependence grew, i.e. exports increased against a background of the absence of serious structural changes.

These are all grounds to assert that the economy was growing during 1999 2000, but it was traditional industrial growth typical for the economy in the past, and mainly at the expense of abundant capacities. Meanwhile, the integration into the world community progressed, but it enhanced strategically not very profitable and not very promising sectors of the economy. In fact, the resources for broad production restructuring could not be created, hence the dependence on external factors increased, especially for those imported resources which are required to make the Ukrainian economy function better.

Thus today, the Ukrainian economy functions and attains certain results in a way quite different from the former planning and distribution system. At the same time, the transition towards the new system has not yet enabled Ukraine to solve the issue of the restructuring. This involves primarily industrial restructuring and getting rid of the exterior factor, which was the situation in the USSR when the economy of Ukraine played an organic role within a single economic complex.

Table 6.3
Direct and total output cost coefficients in industries in 1988-1999 (UAH per UAH 1000 of products)

Industries		Electric power						Ferrous metallurgy						Machine building					
		1988	1990	1993	1995	1998	1999	1988	1990	1993	1995	1998	1999	1988	1990	1993	1995	1998	1999
Electric power	Direct	6.5	6.5	87.3	60.3	27.3	29.7	38.2	40.1	91.2	86.9	107.9	111.1	14.1	13.5	47.0	48.3	40.7	54.9
	Total	30.5	31.6	241.1	212.	127.1	127.6	92.0	98.0	283	248.	268.5	277.9	44.9	41.8	163	156.1	121.6	146.4
Ferrous metallurgy	Direct	1.8	1.7	9.45	10.2	13.7	10.9	416	407.6	393.	345.	327.0	319.4	85.0	77.0	120.3	116.7	85.8	82.1
	Total	31.2	28.2	101.3	90.7	80.9	59.7	745.7	718.7	716.	595.	561.3	527.2	233.6	202	285.8	249.7	185.9	173.6
Machine building	Direct	64.2	65.2	86.23	23.5	35.9	35	37.6	39.4	27.4	42.3	55.3	52.2	335.	315.	207.8	162.8	144.3	159.6
	Total	134.0	131.8	198.9	113.	106.	96.4	145.0	147.3	140.	143.	169.6	157.8	541.0	492.	318.8	251.4	224.5	241.6
Chemical and petrochemical	Direct	3.2	3.1	11.1	70.8	26	14.8	10.1	10.2	17.0	21.3	24.9	18.3	35.2	32.6	43.6	34.1	22.8	22.8
	Total	29.0	25.1	64.9	160.8	92.3	62.1	51.5	49.6	79.0	102.	112.6	82.8	94.9	83.7	104.1	98.9	75.7	68
Light industry	Direct	1.3	1.3	0.8	1.2	2.2	1.8	3.4	3.2	4.9	2.1	2.6	2.5	7.6	7.0	4.3	4.9	3.1	2.7
	Total	15.1	13.8	11.2	13.3	11.5	10.6	26.3	25.7	22.0	13.6	15.8	16.7	35.4	31.2	17.0	16.9	14.4	14.2
Food industry	Direct	0.9	0.9	0.1	0.1	0.3	0.3	0.8	0.8	0.1	0.8	0.9	1.0	2.4	2.2	0.7	0.6	1.3	1.6
	Total	5.5	4.8	8.0	19	8.4	8.4	6.6	6.3	7.0	16.3	11.6	13.5	10.2	9.2	7.3	22.5	17.5	14.7

Table 6.4
Direct and total output cost coefficients in industries in 1988-1999 (UAH per UAH 1000 of products)

Industries		Light industry						Food industry						Other industries					
		1988	1990	1993	1995	1998	1999	1988	1990	1993	1995	1998	1999	1988	1990	1993	1995	1998	1999
Electric power	Direct	5.1	4.9	21.5	22.3	12.3	18.5	4.5	4.4	11.4	14.4	11.1	15.5	23.2	21.6	107	113	106	129
	Total	21.3	20.2	97	94.8	60.8	76.6	22.6	22.3	97.1	80.4	60.8	69.7	42.4	41.4	208	203	183	206
Ferrous metallurgy	Direct	0.7	0.6	2.9	2.2	2	1.1	1.9	1.9	2.6	5.8	3.4	3.3	3	3.4	6.4	8.3	39.2	34.4
	Total	14.5	12.1	33.6	33.9	28.3	20.3	22.5	19.4	33.7	40.6	31.5	24.6	24.7	24	57.8	54.3	99.9	81.5
Machine building	Direct	4.7	4.6	4.8	6	3.3	4.4	6.1	6	5.6	7.3	5.5	4.7	13.6	16.4	13.3	19.9	32.2	27.6
	Total	36.1	31.1	47.4	50.9	46.6	39.2	75.8	69.1	54.7	61.9	58.2	47.3	68.8	66.5	81.1	78.5	91.5	79.2
Chemical and petrochemical	Direct	43.4	40.7	39.1	29.8	17.9	27.9	3.9	3.7	7.3	7.4	9.1	8.5	30.5	35.3	21.4	30.8	35.9	26.2
	Total	135	118	106	81.9	62.8	78.1	69	61	41.4	55.9	57.5	47.7	94.4	95.2	65.2	96.8	95	71.8
Light industry	Direct	475	451	384	242	242	354	3	2.9	4.3	1.8	2.7	2.6	47.6	61.4	11.5	6.5	27.2	22.1
	Total	918	835	630	327	334	557	29.1	28.4	15.9	10.3	15.7	13.3	118	143	27.2	17.6	48	44.9
Food industry	Direct	8.7	7.6	0.6	0.7	2.2	2.7	244	241	194	138	107	141	80.2	72	33.3	15.7	19	21.8
	Total	34.2	29.3	15.9	44.1	42.1	26.8	366	369	269	198	155	189	141	131	61	41.1	40.6	38.6

The nature of the dependence has changed in many respects, but it is still not one which is promoting the creation of a new economy, an economy that primarily makes use of Ukraine's resources on the base of a new, innovative system of development.

How might this situation evolve in the future? Here one should distinguish between short-term (1-2 years) and medium-term aspects, since they have different effects on building a rational development strategy.

After the complete 2000 data is available, some indicators will likely show a slightly different tendency, despite all the negative points made above. The indicators will have better relationships than during the earlier periods, 1999 in particular. Preliminary assessments support this, even though this issue is still uncertain. Therefore one should continue to exploit those positive factors which worked well for the Ukrainian economy in 1999-2000, i.e. to keep the situation under control for 1 or 2 years (2000-2002). If so, the economy would have some 4 to 5 years (1999-2002) to create some financial resources in order to change the situation on the supply and not on the demand side. There are necessary prerequisites for this, but it should be born in mind that for this scenario to work, Ukraine must also tackle the problems of government finance and of the debt burden. In addition the government should introduce changes to its investment policy, since the present approach is not satisfactory, primarily because it strongly favours investments into the so-called base industries. In fact, the functional investment structure has drastically changed its character. During USSR times, about 70% of investment went into construction and 25% into new equipment purchases. Today, 70-75% is used for reconstruction, thus the nature of investment activities has significantly changed and cannot but positively influence production competitiveness.

The main task is to support economic growth by all means possible, so that the potential being accumulated can be used for the reconstruction and restructuring of the whole economy. It should be noted that the proportion of equipment 21 years old and older will have reached 75% by 2010. Until then Ukrainian industry will therefore have to reconstruct or replace at least half of all fixed assets in order to preserve employment, to increase competitiveness and to provide for economic growth. We believe that during the next 3 to 5 years the situation in industry will significantly change with respect to supply. However, to reach this goal it will be necessary to promote demand. On the other hand it is likely that the global rates of economic growth during the next few years might be slightly lower, judging by the forecasts of United States economic development. As far as the economies of Europe are concerned, their projected growth is only 2.5%. The economies of the South Asian region also enter or rather already are in a serious structural crisis. This slowdown is expected to continue for 7 to 8 years, leading to reduced rates of world-wide economic growth. For this reason, external demand will not be as strong as the Ukrainian economy would like it to be. This in turn means that promoting domestic market development within Ukraine (and within other transition economies) is issue number one. In addition, the Ukrainian economy, sensing the coming restrictions and having intentionally worked for export in 2000 – mainly into ex-USSR countries – has to some extent re-established the traditional production co-operation of the past, a tendency that deserves support.

The most positive effect of foreign investments in the Ukrainian economy is on management and marketing. Regarding the amount of these investments, however, they cannot solve all existing problems. They will start playing a certain role once Ukraine becomes attractive for investments. Hence, a system of domestic savings – which in turn create investments – should be developed, including savings insurance and guaranties that the saving can be redeemed whenever desired, that they will be efficiently used for simultaneous institutional capacity building, and that the process will be transparent and efficient. Serious reforms in the banking sector are necessary, together with the development of the appropriate stock market instruments. We maybe have two, at most three years to solve these problems.

Regarding the reforms which the government should pursue and which Western visitors especially emphasise so often: One important problem remaining is which businesses should remain in government hands and which should be privatised. The implementation of privatisation will continue for some years yet, since we have not yet succeeded in separating business and state. In fact, if implemented too rapidly, we would in reality be selling the objects of privatisation at prices well below their real value, i.e. the low receipts would not enable us to create the necessary new capacities. Aside from the privatisation effect being negative, it would be illegitimate. In the recent past, e.g. in 2000 and 2001, privatisation was mostly done for the sake of the privatisation to meet political demands and with fiscal benefits in mind. It should rather have investment character with investment obligations.

Another important problem remains production-restructuring reforms. None of the scenarios followed by other countries have been fully employed in Ukraine. A serious approach is required, because restructuring at the expense of investments cannot achieve the necessary results under the circumstances. Thus, the main issue remains to create conditions which will remove government interference from business, but not just concerning restructuring or changing some executive functions within industry. Without separating government and business, all changes will only be partially effective. This is an extremely important and serious issue.

One more aspect is the necessity to proceed with institutional reforms. It seems to me that the key to institutional reform is the creation of an efficient triangle: state, society and economy. We are moving too slowly along this way.

Going back to the components which I discussed under macroeconomic policy changes above, and which enable the economy to achieve growth, I believe that economic growth can be achieved during the next one to two, at most three years. A first step should be to favour import-replacement and to provide incentives for domestic demand and price competitiveness. During this period it should be possible to make some profound changes in investment strategies and other fields. The goal is to create serious long-term economic growth resources which can be used in the medium term, thus eliminating some of the above-mentioned negative tendencies. In the long run, development will depend on what resources Ukraine can free up for scientific and technical purposes. So far this issue has not been treated seriously. It will be necessary to decide whether Ukraine's economy shall be based on technological leadership in certain fields, or on technological adaptations, or on something else.

7

Economic Growth in Ukraine: What if Reforms and Economic Recovery Had Started Earlier?*

Oleh Havrylyshyn, Bogdan Lissovolik, Mohammad Shadman-Valavi

1 Summary

The paper examines Ukraine's hypothetical economic performance over the decade of the 1990s based on assumptions that its market-oriented reforms could have started earlier and been more comprehensive. A simple methodology of superimposing performance of other countries is used, with Poland's performance indicating an optimistic benchmark, and with that of other countries providing intermediate alternatives. Had Ukraine replicated the economic performance of "comparator" countries, its economic position by the year 2000 – when economic growth actually started – would have been much better. In particular, had comprehensive reforms started in 1994, Ukraine's real GDP could have been 25-50% higher than its actual level in 1999. Had such comprehensive reforms started as early as 1992, it is conceivable that Ukraine's 1999 GDP could be more than twice as high by 1999. Similarly, Ukraine would have had more macroeconomic stability and less exchange rate depreciation. With respect to external indicatiors, the picture would also have been more sustainable, but more nuanced, as higher growth of exports would have been matched by higher imports, yielding ambiguous paths with respect to the current account and external debt ratios. Still, it is likely that Ukraine's external position would have been more sustainable because of the larger role of foreign direct investment. Some policy recommendations are suggested.

---

* The views expressed here are those of the authors and do not represent the official position of the IMF, its Board, Management or officers. An earlier version of the paper was presented by Oleh Havrylyshyn at the Conference "Ukrainian Politics in the Twentieth Century" in Yale University, New Haven, Connecticut, on April 9, 2000.

2 Introduction

A decade has passed since the process of economic transition from central planning to the market first began in a few Central European countries about 1990, and soon followed by initial steps in the countries of the former Soviet Union. The opportunity provided by independence and the freedom to establish a market system was expected to result in a blossoming of democracy and economic prosperity. For most of Central Europe and the Baltics, this promise is proving real, even if slower than hoped. For many of the new countries further east, the economic recovery was more limited. In particular, Ukraine's economic recovery did not start until late 1999, making it the last former Soviet country to resume growth.

There has been considerable discussion of the performance gap between the more successful transition economies of Central Europe and Baltics on the one hand, and the lagging economies of CIS on the other. There have also been analyses of the particular reasons for Ukraine's lack of economic growth.[1] The theme of this chapter is slightly different. We develop estimates of potential economic performance in a counterfactual exercise, answering the question: *What might have Ukraine's economy looked like today if the reforms had started earlier than 1994, or been more successful in promoting restructuring investment and new growth?* There is no good methodology in economics to simulate accurately such counterfactuals, and the benchmarks we use (performance in Russia, Central Europe, and Poland) do not, of course, provide perfect analogues of possible better paths in Ukraine. But we believe they can give a reasonable broad-brush picture of what might have happened.

The remainder of the chapter is organized as follows. Section 2 describes briefly the economic performance of Ukraine in comparison with other transition countries. Section 3 outlines the methodology and assumptions underlying the counterfactual calculations. Section 4 presents the numerical results. Section 5 presents some policy recommendations.

1 The performance gap between CIS and other countries is discussed, inter alia, by Havrylyshyn et al. (1999) and Berg et al. (1999). The growth performance in Ukraine was discussed by Havrylyshyn (1999); World Bank (1999) and Pynzenyk (2000).

3 Actual economic performance in transition

The transition process is a unique multui-dimensional historical event that is not easy to analyse.[2] While not intending to take a categorical "economic determinism" view, we would suggest that growth may be a useful simplifying core theme — a common thread tying together the different country experiences of transition. GDP statistics suggest that many transition countries, unlike Ukraine, were experiencing economic growth by 1997 (Table 7.1). Even Russia and the CIS as a whole fared slightly better — at least as measured by economic output indicators such as GDP. This record is described in more detail elsewhere, including IMF (1999-RED), Barisitz (1999), Havrylyshyn (1999).

The recent recovery of Ukrainian economy – which grew by around 6% in 2000 and is expected to continue growing in 2001 – has been a welcome break from the past and has put in evidence the advantages of economic growth. The output growth has been an important factor behind good budget revenue performance, permitting an increase in real wages and repayment of wage arrears without jeopardizing macroeconomic stability. It also helped reverse the continual decline in investment. These developments highlight the opportunity costs of previous delays in growth resumption from the economic and social points of view.

Table 7.1
Comparison of GDP growth

	1999 GDP as % of 1991	Year GDP growth started	Average GDP growth since recovery
Ukraine	41.1	2000	5.8
Poland	147.8	1992	5.0
Central Europe	112.5	1992-95	4.3
Baltics	76.3	1995	4.7
Russia	63.2	1997[1)]	1.0
CIS	58.6	1994–2000[2)]	4.1

Sources: Havrylyshyn, et al. (1999) for data through 1998; updates from IMF estimates

[1)] Russian GDP growth in 1997 was positive but very low (below 1%, a negative -4% in 1998 and then recovered to about 4% in 1999; we approximate the average growth over these years at about 1%.

[2)] Armenia was the first of CIS countries to experience economic recovery in 1994, and by 1997, all but Ukraine and Turkmenistan had begun the recovery process. Many saw an interruption of this trend in 1998, or at least a sharp slowdown as a result of the Russia's financial crisis of August 1998. Most were back to positive growth in 1999.

---

2 For an early overview of transition issues, see Fischer and Gelb (1991) and Clague and Rausser (1992).

The history of delayed growth in Ukraine raises the more deeply interesting question: *why*? Perhaps the central consensus, if there is one, consists of the view that incomplete economic reforms and a still poorly functioning market economy explain the poor economic performance (Odling-Smee (1999), Barisitz (1999)).[3] While we broadly share this view, more complex stories can be told involving matters such as nation-building, power struggles, the burden of the soviet military-industrial complex, energy dependence, the anti-reform attitudes of the "new capitalist" vested interests, and others.[4] We briefly discuss some of these underlying factors of reform below.

4 Methodology of counterfactual simulations

4.1 Economic logic of the counterfactual

Studies of recent performance in transition economies suggest there are three broad categories of explanatory factors: initial conditions; progress on reforming the economy into a market-oriented one; and the degree of development of supporting institutions. The first is a given; for example, Ukraine's greater burden of Soviet period over-industrialisation might preclude it achieving quickly results as strong as Poland's. While recognizing this as a limitation, one should not exaggerate the negative effect, for it is not the sole determinant, and it can, with time, be offset by greater market reform. We hypothesize that the pace of Polish economic performance establishes an upper-bound benchmark for Ukraine's counterfactuals. Even these hypothetical paths are less strong than Poland's – because one cannot imagine circumstances where Ukraine could have started the reform process as early as Poland. The lower-bound benchmark is taken as Russia's performance, which was certainly not stellar, but in terms of economic recovery at least, marginally superior to Ukraine's.

We describe next the type of reform measures that might have been taken to achieve performance better than the actual one. *Progress on reforms towards a functioning market economy is the area where Ukraine lags behind most*, as Table 7.2 demonstrates. The index is an amalgam of various detailed measures or progress prepared by the European Bank for Reconstruction and Development

---

3 Although throughout much of 1990s Ukraine relied on international financial and technical assistance, including from the IMF, many of the reforms that were connected with this assistance were not implemented in a complete and timely fashion.

4 This more variegated story and the (still central) role of economic reforms is told in Havrylyshyn (1999).

(EBRD), and Ukraine scores better on some, worse on others. For 1999, the values were, for illustration purposes, as follows:

- private sector share of GDP (Ukraine 55%; Hungary 80%; Turkmenistan 25%);
- large-scale privatisation (Ukraine scores 3- on a scale of 4+; Hungary and Poland 4+; Belarus 1);
- small-scale privatisation (Ukraine 3+; most of central Europe 4+ except Balkan states with 4-; Belarus and Turkmenistan 2);
- price liberalisation (Ukraine 3; Poland 3+, Uzbekistan, Turkmenistan 2, Belarus 2-).

Table 7.2
Market reforms index 1997 and 1998 (EBRD values, ranges 0–1.0)

	1997	1998
Poland	0.81	0.82
Central Europe and Baltics Average	0.73	n.a.
Russia	0.72	0.61
CIS Average	0.54	n.a.
Ukraine	0.59	0.58

Source: EBRD (1998 and 1999)

- trade and foreign exchange liberalisation (Ukraine 3; most of central Europe 4 to 4+; Belarus 2-, Turkmenistan 1);
- competition policy (Ukraine 2+; central Europe 3; Turkmenistan 1);
- banking sector reform (Ukraine 2; Hungary 4; Belarus, Turkmenistan 1);
- development of securities markets (Ukraine 2; Hungary, Poland 4-; Turkmenistan 1).

On balance — and even accounting for inaccuracies of the EBRD scores[5] — it is clear that Ukraine's progress towards the market is far behind that of central Europe and the Baltics, is probably behind the more "advanced" CIS reformers such as Kazakhstan and Armenia, is perhaps similar to such CIS countries such as Russia, and Azerbaijan. The only countries that are clearly even farther behind are Belarus, Turkmenistan, and Uzbekistan. From this platform, we leap into the counterfactual concept; our *fundamental thesis is that, had Ukraine implemented more effectively and completely the reform process begun in the fall of 1994, or*

[5] In general, an upward bias exists in subjective measures like those of the EBRD, giving too much weight to *de jure* changes in laws, regulations, and too little weight to the de facto implementation of new "freedoms" in the economy.

even better started this process two years earlier, with some lag time, its economic performance would have been much better. Marginally better reforms would result in marginally better performance (the lower-bound Russia path), stronger reforms would have resulted in stronger performance, perhaps analogous to the upper-bound Poland path.

4.2 Technical aspects

Ukraine's counterfactual scenarios are constructed from the actual data of comparator countries or groups of countries. These scenarios are labeled according to the countries (or groups of countries) they refer to, with an addition of the term "proxy." With respect to the *timing of reform*, we posit two basic counterfactual scenarios. As a *"baseline" scenario*, it is assumed that a comprehensive structural reform effort in Ukraine would have started in 1994. This would roughly coincide with the beginning of the Kuchma presidency, when Ukrainian government and society had undergone some, albeit limited, exposure to the workings of a market economy. As an *alternative* – somewhat less plausible – *scenario*, it is assumed that serious reforms would have started fairly quickly after Ukraine gained independence, i.e., in 1992. This latter scenario is admittedly optimistic, in part because it likely underestimates difficulties of generating a credible reform momentum by the post-independence Ukrainian society. Finally, it is assumed that reforms started in a given year would make an impact only starting from the following year.

With respect to *real growth*, actual rates in Poland, Central Europe and Russia are applied to Ukrainian levels of real GDP. A similar lagged relationship between the beginning of reforms and growth is assumed. For example, since growth started in Poland in the second year after the onset of reforms in 1990, the *baseline* scenario assumes that Ukraine's first year of positive growth would have been 1996, two years after the hypothetical reform effort in 1994. For the *alternative* scenario, however, the assumed lag is larger by one year, and – with the assumed start of reforms in 1992 – Ukraine's first year of positive growth would be 1995. The reason for this additional complication concerns the relatively rudimentary nature of markets in Ukraine in 1992, as compared to Poland in 1990, or the very Ukraine in 1994. Under those circumstances, it would have taken somewhat longer for even the boldest market-oriented reforms to make impact on growth.

For *inflation*, comparator country data have been used – similarly to real GDP growth — to generate counterfactuals in the baseline and alternative scenarios. The exchange rate counterfactuals were obtained in two ways. The first approach also simply uses comparator country data. In the second exercise, nominal exchange rate counterfactuals have been obtained by combining actual real appreciations in Ukraine, which broadly repeated the real appreciations of other transition economies, and the hypothetical inflation rate generated in the first exercise.

The *GDP level* counterfactuals have been obtained in two alternative ways. First, the comparator country data for nominal and US Dollar GDP growth rates have been applied to the levels of GDP in Ukraine starting in 1995 for the baseline scenario and 1993 for the alternative scenario. Second, the nominal GDP proxies have been constructed by combining the real growth and inflation counterfactuals as generated above. Similarly, the GDP numbers in terms of US Dollar have been obtained by combining the above counterfactual for nominal GDP with the exchange rate obtained in the second exercise.

With respect to external sector variables, *exports* have been generated using the actual comparator country data for export rates of growth (in dollar value terms). As to *imports*, the projection for the dollar value series is constructed from the counterfactual scenarios for real growth above and a reasonable projection for import elasticity with respect to real GDP. The projection for the *current account* simply takes exports and imports counterfactual scenarios and substitutes those for the actual data observed in Ukraine. The counterfactual of the flow of *foreign direct investment (FDI)* is constructed by adding net additional imports in the above scenario to actual flows of FDI. There are two alternative assumptions: in the first exercise, the FDI is increased by the value of all additional imports, while in the second one (more plausible) only half of the additional imports are assumed to be financed by FDI. The dollar value of *external debt* is calculated by taking the relevant beginning-of-period stock of Ukraine's debt, adding the difference between the counterfactual current account deficit and actual deficit, and subtracting the difference between counterfactual and actual FDI.

5 Results and interpretation

As is shown in Graph 7.1, the level of Ukraine's real GDP in 1999 would have been considerably higher had effective reforms begun earlier. In the baseline scenario, real output in that year would have been about 50% higher if reforms were as successful as in Poland, as indicated by the Poland proxy in the Graph. In the alternative scenario of earlier reforms, real output would have been more than double the 1999 level. As expected, results for the Central Europe proxy are similar to those for the Polish proxy, while those for the Russia proxy are considerably less impressive.

As expected, an earlier reform effort would have made Ukraine's stabilisation quicker and more sustainable, as the experience of comparator countries suggests. With respect to *inflation* stabilisation, the baseline scenario (Graph 7.2) indicates that earlier reforms would have produced a significantly better outcome in 1995, a moderately better outcome in 1996, and a performance that is broadly comparable to that of comparator countries thereafter. This would confirm the consensus among many economists that Ukraine's stabilisation effort was effective in the narrow sense of the term.

The baseline scenarios for the exchange rate in Graph 7.3 show that more effective reforms might have prevented much of the nominal depreciation that occurred in Ukraine. In particular, the exchange rate for the Polish proxy is considerably (about 3 times in US Dollar terms) more appreciated by 1999 (Panel 1). As is shown in Panel 2, an assumption of a constant real exchange rate would imply a significant counterfactual depreciation of the Hryvnia, which is not surprising in view of its considerable real appreciation over 1995–1997. Panel 3 in the same Graph attempts to augment the scenario of Panel 2 by assuming a path of real exchange rate appreciation that occurred in Ukraine.

As follows from Graph 7.4, the level of Ukraine's US Dollar GDP would have been significantly higher with an early start of economic reforms. This reflects both the higher real counterfactual growth and Ukraine's avoidance of the significant depreciation of its currency. If serious reforms started in 1994, Ukraine's GDP could possibly exceed USD 70 bn by 1999, which is more than double Ukraine's actual level. If reforms had started in 1992, Ukraine's US Dollar GDP could have reached USD 100 bn in 1999.

Graph 7.5 shows that Ukraine's exports would have performed significantly better and would have more than doubled in dollar terms had it replicated Poland's export performance, as compared to the relative stagnation over the 1990s. Interestingly, replicating Russia's export performance would not have resulted in a significant improvement for Ukraine. This underscores the fact that – while Russia's performance might have been somewhat better than Ukraine's in some respects – in other crucial areas such as exports the reforms have had a broadly similar effect.

With regard to imports, Graph 7.6 indicates that the Poland proxy (start of reforms in 1994) would have yielded a result similar to that for exports (an approximate doubling compared to the actual outcome by 1999), although with a somewhat different path. Graph 7.7 illustrates what would have happened with the current account given the above projections of exports and imports. Both Poland and Russia proxies show larger current account deficits. The Polish proxy exhibits a sharper deterioration but by 1999 the current account swings into surplus, indicating that the deficit would achieve sustainability after widening during the investment boom. By contrast, the Russia proxy indicates a slower improvement in the current account, perhaps because export performance was little affected by the capital that flowed into Russia in the second half of 1990s.

Graph 7.8 shows the counterfactuals for levels of debt and debt-to-GDP ratios. In terms of nominal debt, both Russian and Polish proxies show considerably higher numbers than Ukraine, which is not surprising given the current account deficits discussed above. Nevertheless, the Poland proxy tends to stabilise in towards the end of the period, while the Russia proxy continues to increase rapidly. Regarding the debt/GDP ratios, the Poland proxy is fairly stable throughout the decade in the baseline scenario (assuming that financing of additional imports is equally split between FDI and debt) and declines to very small levels if it is assumed that additional imports are financed by FDI. By contrast, the Russian debt proxy continues to increase and exceeds 70% of GDP, substantially higher than Ukraine's actual.

In the scenarios for foreign direct investment of Graph 7.9, both Polish and Central European proxies exhibit a steady improvement, with the end-result of almost 10-fold increase in FDI inflows over what actually occurred in Ukraine. Performance of the Russian proxy is intermediate, with about 5-fold improvement. However, FDI flows for the Russia proxy would have peaked in 1997, and started to decline thereafter.

6 Policy recommendations

Our calculations suggest that – subject to the qualifications on accuracy stated at the outset – the economic costs of delayed reforms in Ukraine were very high. In addition, a remark is in order on the interpretation of these results. We believe that these are mostly conservative estimates of the opportunity costs. However, some of these results may reflect optimistic assumptions about Ukraine's capacity to implement reforms and the impact of these reforms on economic growth. In the absence of a well-specified quantitative econometric model of growth (an extremely difficult, if not impossible, exercise for Ukraine at this stage), the direction of our bias is uncertain. Still, in some sense the consistency framework we use offers some cushion for the basic result of this paper for economic growth. For example, if our estimates of nominal and real exchange rate paths have been overly "optimistic" (i.e., appreciated), the more realistic scenario of somewhat greater nominal and real depreciation – and provided that the ambitious structural reforms are pursued – would, ceteris paribus, constitute a more growth-oriented policy mix than the one that prevailed in the countries with which the comparison is made.

Since we have argued along with many others that inadequate reforms are a major cause of slow growth, the most obvious policy recommendation is self-evident: *do more to move forward market reforms*. This conclusion would apply both to the period of output decline and to the current period of economic growth, to make it sustainable. Beyond the standard prescription of macroeconomic prudence, three key areas need attention if Ukraine were to break the current situation and make the recent recovery sustainable.

Ukraine must create an environment that is conducive to economic growth and private investment, perhaps through active pursuit of an EU integration strategy, up to and including membership. While today this seems far-fetched, and the political difficulties are well known, the prize is surely worth considerable effort. The experience of countries that are now on track for EU membership demonstrates that the benefits of this anchor are large and begin well in advance of actual membership. The harmonisation of policies and laws in Ukraine with those in the EU member countries will instill confidence in the direction of economic and political developments, encourage foreign investment, and promote economic growth.

In the interim, Ukraine must forcefully implement the rule of law, insist on transparency of government operations, and make members of government (at state and local levels), parliament and managers of public enterprises accountable under law. Delayed reforms in these areas have allowed many anti-reform interests to develop — or regenerate, as the case may be. Thus, the old Soviet managerial and administrative bureaucracy, now joins hands with the "new capitalists" who, often through insider deals, take over private control of the old state assets, and find it preferable to maintain a quasi-monopolistic market environment and oppose a truly competitive environment. This "capture" of government by anti-reform interests and a freezing of the transition is the biggest cost of the delay. The first thing that must be done is to re-impose an institutional rule of law and break this hold of vested interests on economic policy-making.

Ukraine must also substantially reduce government intervention in economic activity, forcefully promote privatisation (especially small entrepreneurial activity); and impose financial discipline and transparency in public enterprises. A radical simplification and easing of all government relations is necessary to encourage private activity in the formal economy. Deregulation must promote development of new entrepreneurs and small businesses. This should range from making very simple the process of registering and starting a new business, to a lifting of the excessive burden of inspection by tax authorities ("harassment" some have labeled it), building inspectors, fire and health regulators, etc.. Agricultural privatisation should be an important component of this strategy. The number of public enterprises must be reduced dramatically, and those that remain in the public sector must be run efficiently and face hard budget constraints. In addition, the government must create a level playing field for private and public enterprises. The basic goal of this strategy is to ensure that government promotes private activity instead of protecting the interests of a few influential interest groups. If a political catch-phrase is needed to capture this, it might be "capitalism for all."

References

Berg A., E. Borensztein, R. Sahay, and J. Zettlemeyer (1999):The Evolution of Output in Transition Economies: Explaining the Differences. IMF, Working paper 73, May.

Barisitz S. (1999):Ukraine : Macroeconomic Development and Economic Policy in the First Eight Years of Independence. Focus on Transition, 2, pp. 70-80.

Clague C. and G. Rausser (1992): The Emergence of Market Economies in Eastern Europe. Basil Blackwell, Cambridge, MA.

European Bank for Reconstruction and Development (1998-2000): Transition Report. London, UK.

Fischer S. and A. Gelb (1991): Process of Socialist Economic Transformation. Journal of Economic Perspectives, 5, Fall, pp. 91-105.

Havrylyshyn O. (1999): What Makes Ukraine Not Grow?: Political, Economic, and Historical Facts that Hamper Economic Growth. Paper presented at conference "Problems of Development of Ukraine," Toronto, 5-7 November.

Havrylyshyn O., T. Wolf, J. Berengaut, M. Castello-Branco, R. Van Rooden, and V. Mercer-Blackman (1999): Growth Experience in Transition Economies, 1990-1998., IMF Occasional Paper No 184.

IMF (1999): Ukraine – Recent Economic Developments. IMF Staff Country Reports, Washington DC, May.

Odling-Smee J. (1999): Why Resume Lending?: Russia's current economic policies are deserving of IMF support. IMF Survey, 28, pp. 273-274, August.

Pynzenyk V. (2000): Vozmozhen li v Ukraine stabil'nyi ekonomicheskii rost? (in Russian). Mirror Weekly, No 13 and 14 April.

World Bank (1999): Ukraine: Restoring Growth with Equity: A Participatory Economic Memorandum. October, Washington DC.

Appendix

Graph 7.1
Ukraine: Index of real GDP growth under counterfactual scenarios, 1991–99, (1991=100)

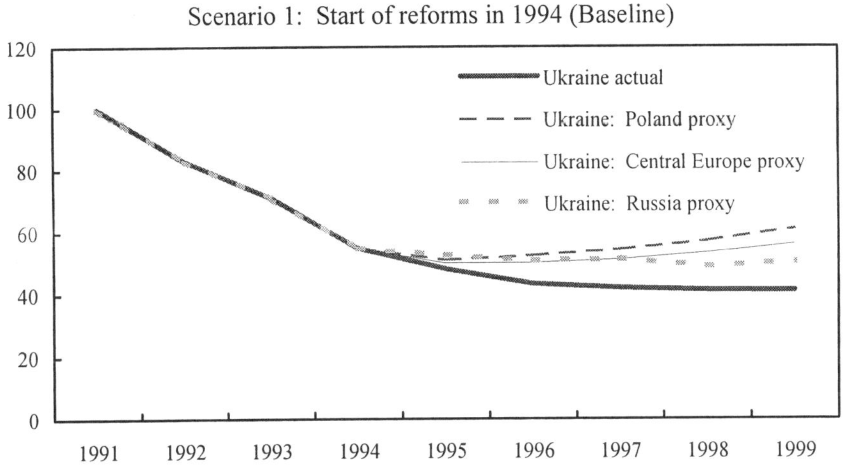

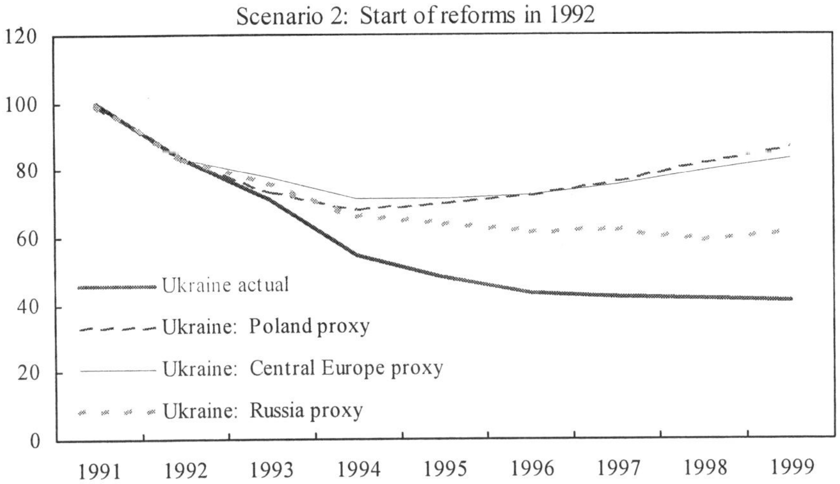

Source: National authorities; own estimates

Graph 7.2
Ukraine: The development of consumer prices between 1992 and 1999 assuming start of reforms in 1994

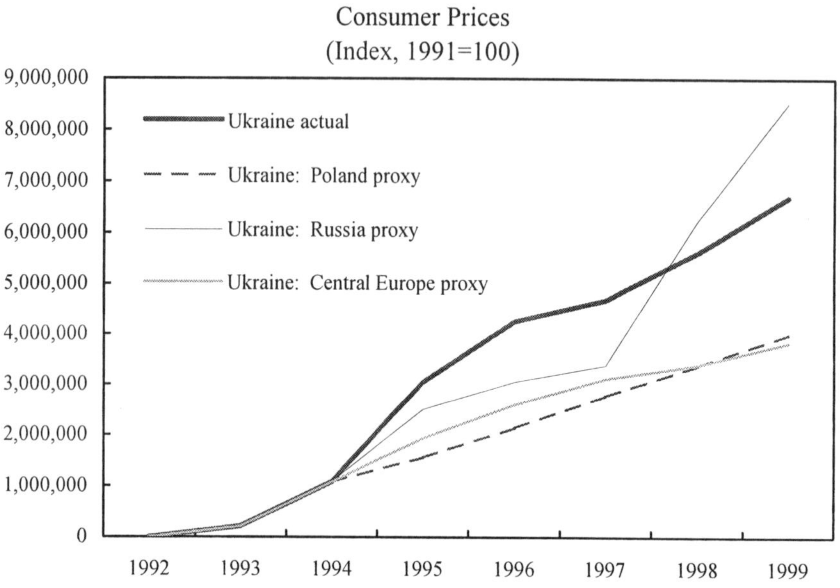

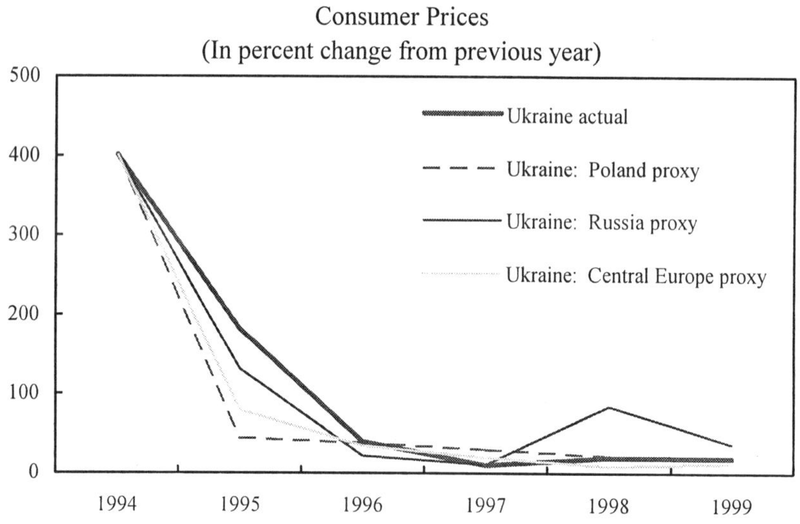

Source: National authorities; own estimates

Graph 7.3

Ukraine: Nominal exchange rates under counterfactual scenarios, 1992-99 (in UAH per USD)

Scenario 1: Start of reforms in 1994 (Baseline)

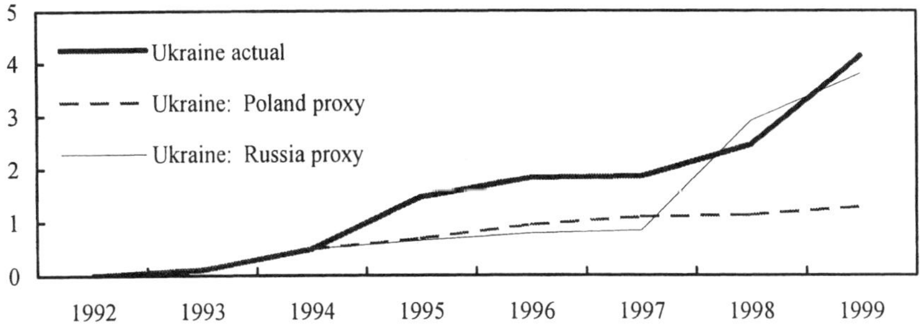

Scenario 2: Start of reforms in 1994, constant real exchange rate

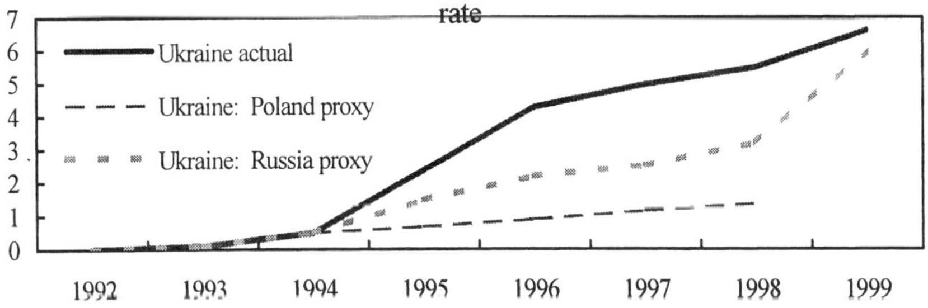

Scenario 3: Start of Reforms in 1994 , transitional real appreciation

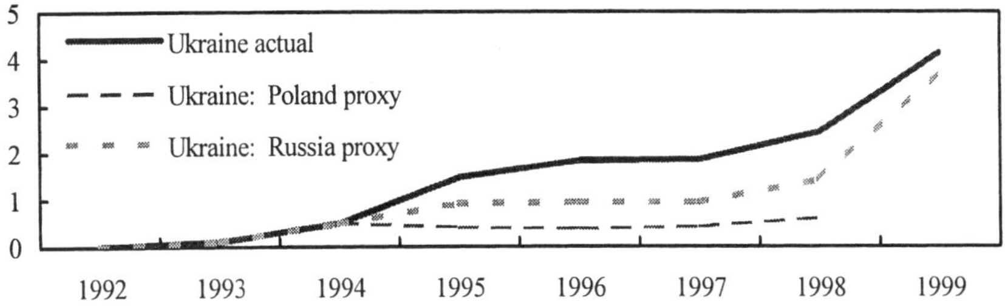

Source: National authorities; own estimates

Graph 7.4
Ukraine: GDP under counterfactual scenarios, 1992-99 (in USD m)

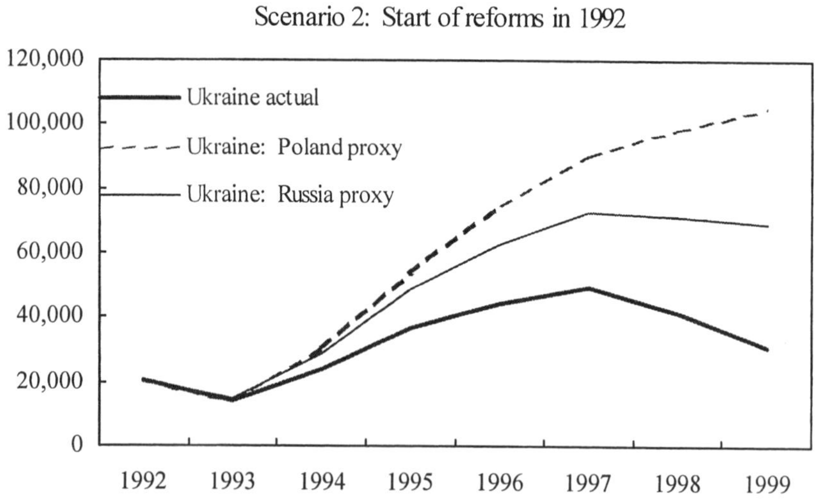

Source: National authorities; own estimates

Graph 7.5
Ukraine: Exports under counterfactual scenarios, 1992-99 (in USD bn)

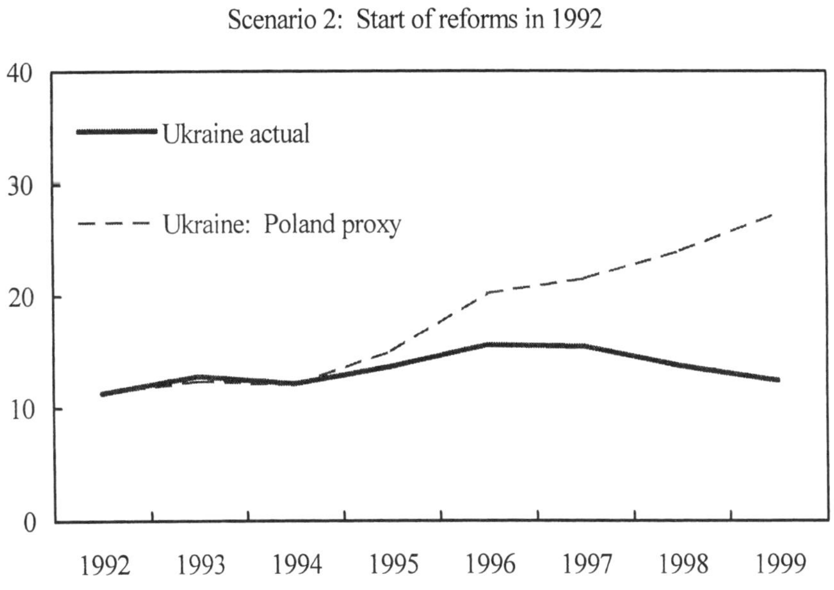

Source: National authorities; own estimates

Graph 7.6
Ukraine: Imports under counterfactual scenarios, 1992-99* (in USD bn)

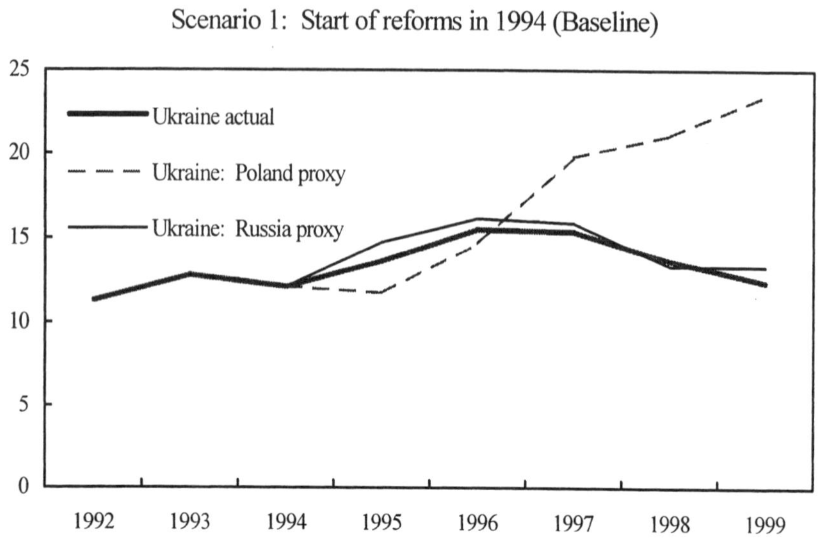

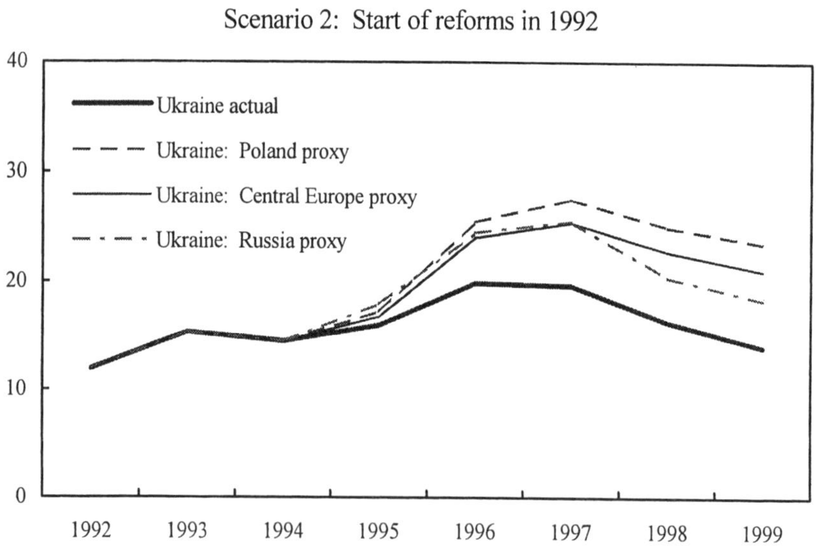

* Assumed elasticity path but adjusted for Ukraine actual

Source: National authorities; own estimates

Graph 7.7
Ukraine: Current account balance assuming start of reforms in 1994 (Baseline), 1992-99*
(in USD bn)

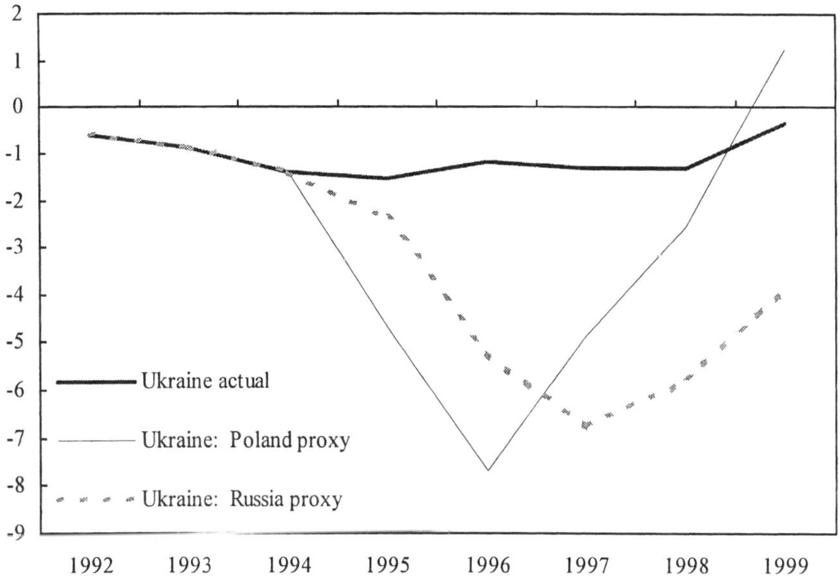

* Assumed elasticity path but adjusted for Ukraine actual

Source: National authorities; own estimates

Graph 7.8
Ukraine: Debt, assuming start of reforms in 1994, 1992-99

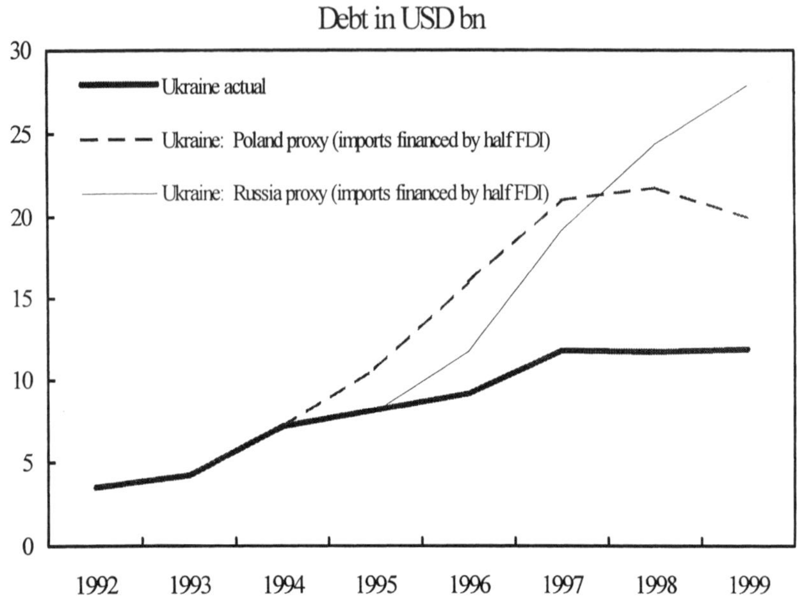

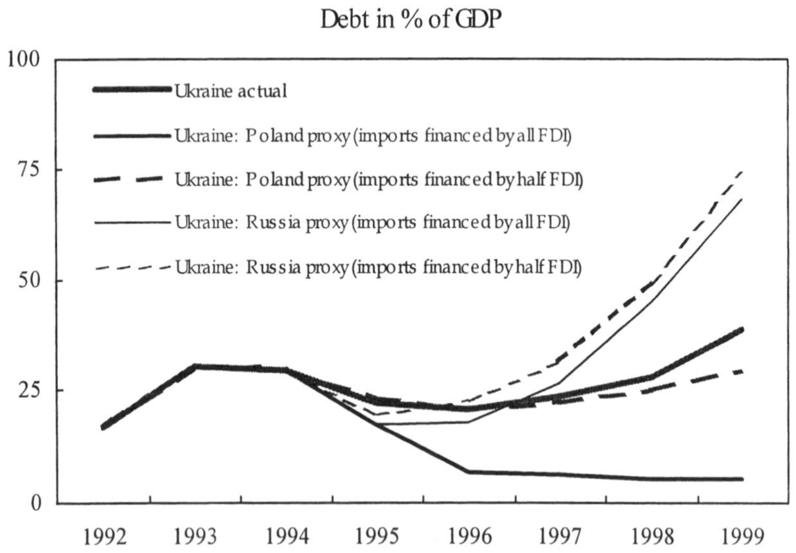

Source: National authorities; own estimates

Graph 7.9
Ukraine: Foreign direct investment, assuming start of reforms in 1994, 1992-99

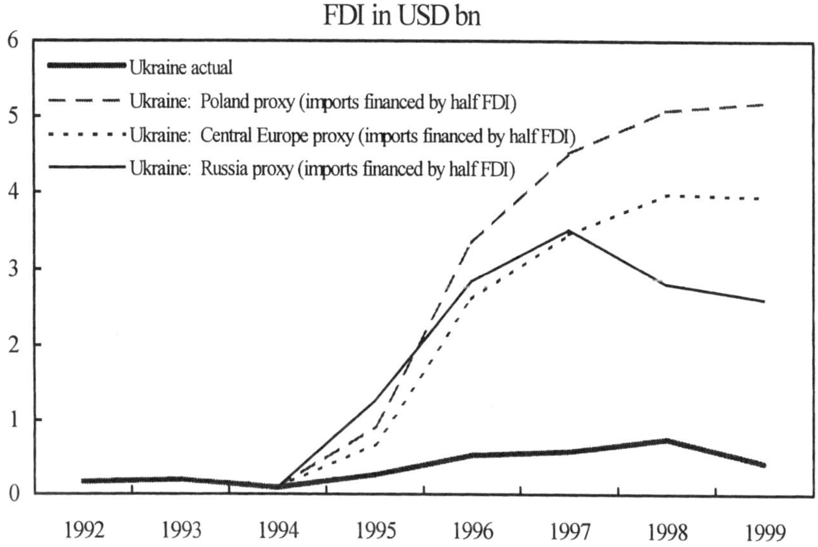

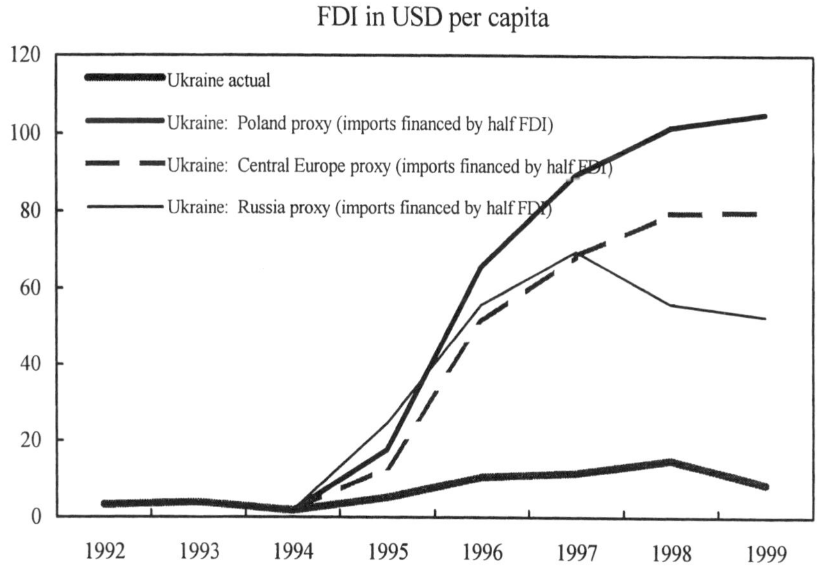

Source: National authorities; own estimates

8

Finance and Growth in Ukraine

Joachim Jahnke

1 Introduction

"Finance and Growth" is a such a fundamental and demanding subject, that – in all modesty – I need to cut it down to something practical, and fitting to my own background. I will try to describe the EBRD's experience with the subject. I will do this from the position of the specialised International Financial Institution for Eastern Europe, which at the same time is the biggest single foreign investor in the region. Our investment accounts for about 9% of all foreign direct investment in the region over the past decade, and our investor role in Ukraine is even substantially above this average share. We are also a partner in the policy dialogue with Ukraine. The Bank's President has just met with President Kuchma for another round of such dialogue and also sits on the Foreign Investment Advisory Council chaired by President Kuchma.

There is one simple relation between finance and growth: Without proper sources of finance there is surely no sustained growth, but even with such sources there may still not be sufficient and sustainable growth. Our agenda of today and tomorrow exemplifies many other engines and hurdles for growth, such as the international environment in neighbouring trading partners, competition, governance, infrastructure and the shadow economy. On all of these issues, the Bank has ample experience, but I will not duplicate what is to be said elsewhere. Let me then address, first, the availability of finance and, second, how to improve it.

2 Availability of finance for investments

If finance and growth are to be correlated, the importance is, of course, on long-term finance for investment, rather than short-term deposits or speculative portfolio transfers, and here primarily finance for private sector investment. In the wise words of the EBRD's Transition Report, private investment, entrepreneurship and innovation that drive growth cannot be sustained without well-functioning credit institutions and markets.

Looking at Ukraine's economic growth of 6% in the year 2000, strong growth that has continued into 2001, one may assume that sufficient finance was available. As we well know, this would not be the correct picture. Ukraine had a first good year of growth in 2000. It is, however, also true that Ukraine growth moves from very low levels, and also means that part of the shadow economy moves back into the official statistics. Even with the impressive growth rate of last year, Ukraine's recorded economy was only at barely 40% of the level of GDP of 1989, while neighbouring Poland is already at 130% of that starting point (Graphs 8.1 and 8.2; all Graphs in the Appendix). And gross domestic investment has fallen sharply since 1995 to below 18% of GDP in 1999 with a slight up-turn in 2000 and stronger growth in the first few months of this year. The growth in GDP, therefore, primarily suggests a better use of existing capacity, rather than a lot of new investment.

I will first deal with the status of Ukraine's internal financial market and then come to international finance. It's not a secret: There is not much of an internal market for long-term finance. Stock market capitalisation in percent of GDP is just about 6%, as compared to Hungary's more than four times or Poland's more than three times higher levels. Per capita the level is even thirty times higher for Hungary or twenty times higher for Poland (Graph 8.3). To put it into another perspective: The Ukraine low level of stock market capitalisation represents not more than 0.05% of the equity capitalisation of all Emerging Markets.

Much of the domestic credit until very recently has been focused on the government sector. Domestic credit to private enterprises is at 10% of GDP, while it is about 2.5 times higher for Hungary and Poland (Graph 8.4). Such credit, where available, is hugely expensive, even in real terms. Towards the end of last year, commercial bank credits carried an annual interest rate in the order of 40%. The spread between credits and deposits, though coming down, was still in the order of 20%. In addition, general uncertainties limit most maturities to less than six months.

This, indeed, is still an unsatisfactory picture for internal finance. However, the fortunes of Ukraine are finally changing, though realistically, it will take many more years to build a sound banking sector and to develop the whole capital market. In the absence of proper financial institutions, companies will depend more than normal on retained earnings as an important alternative source of funding.

I am now turning to international finance. In theory, there is a huge amount of private capital available for Emerging Markets. The share of private flows of capital to Eastern Europe is much larger than official flows (Graph 8.5). The most resilient to crisis part of it is Direct Foreign Investment (Graph 8.6). Total net flows to Emerging Markets were estimated at more than USD 150 bn for last year. Unfortunately, so far only a trickle of this has found its way to Ukraine. In recent years, there has virtually been no syndicated lending to Ukraine. Annual inflows of FDI have slowly increased from very low levels and are expected at around USD 800 m this year. This equates to USD 16 per capita and, therefore, still very little as compared with an average for the whole of Eastern Europe of about USD 90 (Graphs 8.7 to 8.9). We should note en passant in particular the low level of investment flowing into Ukraine from countries where there is strong regulation, good corporate governance and high standards of transparency – and this situation is not improving (Graph 8.10).

The FDI stock per capita, as accumulated since 1989, puts Ukraine into the dismal position next to Uzbekistan and Belarus. At this level FDI is only a small fraction of what Ukraine really needs for restructuring and modernising its industrial sector and thus for moving to a sustained pattern of growth. Furthermore, the privatisation programme as one of potential sources for FDI has so far not been able to attract the huge amounts of foreign investment that the Government had hoped for (Graph 8.11).

The picture would not be complete without a word on capital flight. International private lending to Eastern Europe net of deposits abroad from its own residents is to show another record deficit this year because of such deposits. The approximately USD 25 bn of deficit is almost as much as the inflow of FDI and portfolio investments together (Graph 8.12). The deficit has primarily one explanation. It largely reflects sustained capital flight, primarily from Russia, but also from Ukraine and some other CIS countries.

How likely then is a major debt repayment problem in the months to come? It is true that Ukraine achieved a large surplus on current account last year: USD 1.5 bn or almost 5% of GDP (Graphs 8.13 and 8.14). The surplus for the first quarter of this year alone is estimated at about USD 800 m. Ukraine will need some external finance to meet its external debt commitments estimated at about USD 650 m in the second half of this year, with a further amount due to the IMF. A combination of the increase in reserves and the prospect of a current account surplus this year suggest this should be possible, especially in view of the continued arrears to the Paris Club, since payments were suspended in January 2000, although it remains important to secure a satisfactory agreement with the Paris Club as soon as possible.

The consequences of these factors are rather obvious: Ukraine's main sources of external funding are likely to be for some time the International Financial Institutions and other official lenders. In this respect, it is important for Ukraine to remain on track with the IMF programme and achieve a resumption of disbursements under the Extended Fund Facility. Prime Minister Kinakh has recently confirmed that his Government will do everything possible to this end. At present, Ukraine may need the IMF money less than the credibility that comes with it. Continued lack of IMF funding, however, could affect Ukraine's ability to meet its debt obligations next year.

You will not expect me to close this chapter without mentioning the EBRD's role. We have now a portfolio of Ukraine operations of over EUR 1 bn. Last year alone we added more than EUR 300 m. We could do more, but as we go primarily with private investors – thus normally mobilising about three times our own investment – we depend heavily on the general investment climate in the country. Ukraine is increasingly becoming a key priority for the Bank as the countries of Central Europe move towards EU accession.

Here I come to my first and not so surprising conclusion. What Ukraine urgently needs is to improve the availability of internal and external finance. Only then can growth be relied on.

3 How to improve availability of finance

As indicated already, I will now not go into all the issues of the enabling environment that could attract finance, such as investment climate, tax regime, governance, etc.. Let me just touch on two issues, that we consider as important and where the EBRD is already engaged: the banking sector, including SME and microfinance support, and the privatisation programme as a potential force for expanding the capital market and attracting FDI.

Without a well functioning banking sector transition will always be a dream. Therefore, the Bank invests about one third of its resources in support of the development of sound banking sectors in Eastern Europe. The Ukraine banking sector was severely weakened in the aftermath of the Russian crisis. Both capital base and profitability of banks remain low. Special problems exist at Bank 'Ukraina', although I am aware that the government has recently proposed legislation, which could lead to the establishment of an institution, engaged in mortgage lending for the agricultural sector. Banks are still not seen by many enterprises as a reliable source of financing. Often they are viewed as convenient databases for tax inspectors rather than sources of credit. The lack of a deposit insurance system is not encouraging deposits either. In the words of the IMF Staff Report of December 2000, the health of most large banks improved somewhat, but remains worrisome. Or to quote from the German Advisory Group on Economic Reforms Report from January of this year: The danger that some banks become insolvent is increasing.

There are, however, also some recent positive developments. Over the last year, overdue loans declined from 13% to 10.5% of total bank credits. In January, the law on Banks and Bank Activity took effect, thus clarifying procedures for opening and liquidating banks and setting out differential capital requirements.

Since April, the tax authorities can no longer freeze the bank accounts of enterprises for alleged non-payment of tax. This practice contributed to the growth of non-monetary payments and constrained the use of bank accounts. In another positive development, the measures that banned barter in the energy sector have increased cash resources, and at the same time the extra demand for cash payments contributed to growth in bank lending and deposits. Furthermore, demand for credit in the agricultural sector in particular appears to be growing, with commercial banks starting to rise to the occasion and prepare themselves for the gap, which will be left by the liquidation of Bank 'Ukraina', with credits to be heavily subsidised by the Government.

The EBRD has several channels of support to the Ukraine banking sector, which include support for SMEs. Through credit lines with Ukraine banks we participate in strengthening the banking sector and at the same time provide scarce medium term finance to SME projects (so far more than 150). We have invested equity directly into three banks. We have a facility with a number of banks for up to five-year on-lending. We are participating in three equity funds. Most recently we have been a lead partner in establishing the Ukraine Microfinance Bank, where the German-Ukraine Fund is also involved. Microfinance banks are one of our success stories from Bosnia Herzegovina over Kosovo to Russia. In spite of all these efforts, much more needs to be done in order to establish a well functioning banking system as a source of finance for badly needed investment.

Privatisation of public utilities can produce another source of finance and reform at the same time. Ukraine still has a large public sector. Some major utilities, in particular in the power sector, are still to be privatised. The history of such privatisation of utilities has not always been a happy one; some needed to be aborted. It must be clear what privatisation is for. What is needed are transparently organised tenders involving bids by strategic investors, with money to spend in future on modernisation/re-structuring, and not "backdoor" forced sales of energy company assets to repay intra-sector debts.

The EBRD is closely supporting Ukraine in privatising the electricity distribution companies. In particular the energy sector, an Achilles heel of the whole economy, needs strategic investors in order to improve the efficiency and to boost investments. With support from the EBRD, Ukraine could successfully sell in April of this year further six electricity distribution companies.

Prime Minister Kinakh provided the Bank with an early confirmation of his intention to pursue this effort in the energy sector. According to a recent announcement by the State Property Fund privatisation will move on to the electricity generating companies next year. There is, nevertheless, an immediate risk that the vested interests may effect such plans, and it could also be more difficult to attract western investors in the current conditions. In addition, total privatisation receipts, of which Ukrtelecom was a major part, are projected at UAH 5.9 bn this year, equivalent to 3% of GDP, and thus also of considerable importance for the budget. Unfortunately, privatisation of Ukrtelecom is now only likely to occur next year.

Let me then conclude: Ukraine has experienced very tough conditions over the past decade, but the economy is now growing. The currency is stable and strong. Commercial debt has been rescheduled. Cash collection of utilities has increased. I would like to pay tribute to these achievements. It is clear to me that it is now possible to build on them provided that the momentum is sustained. It is extremely important that the reforms of the previous Government are consolidated, and this is indeed now part of the present Government's plans. Availability of sufficient internal and external finance will be crucial. In this respect, it is important that Ukraine continues to receive financial cooperation from its partners. The European Bank for Reconstruction and Development that I represent is ready to do its job.

Appendix

Graph 8.1
Real GDP change (1989=100)

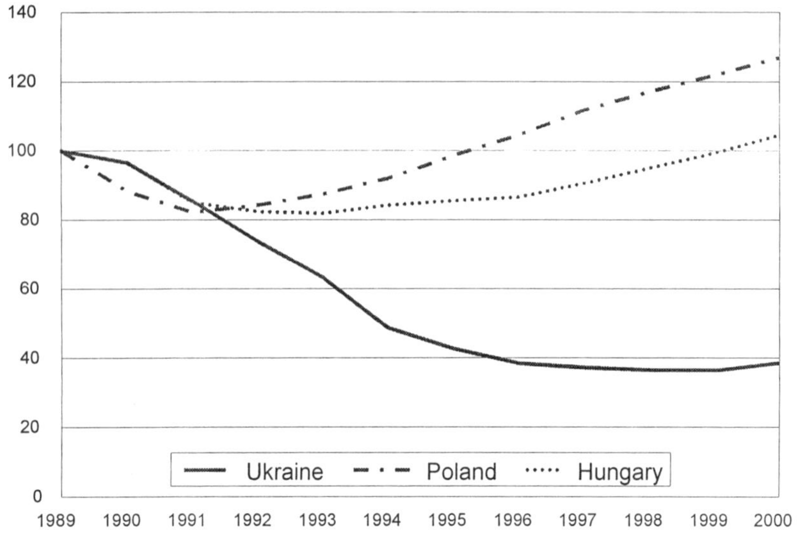

Graph 8.2
Stock market capitalisation 2000

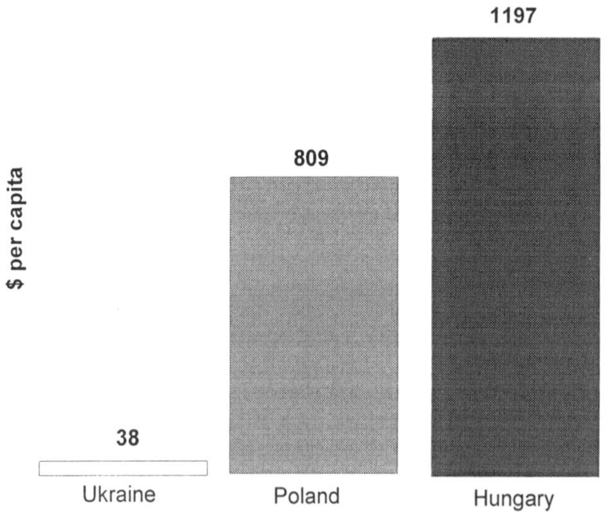

Graph 8.3
Domestic credit to enterprises 2000

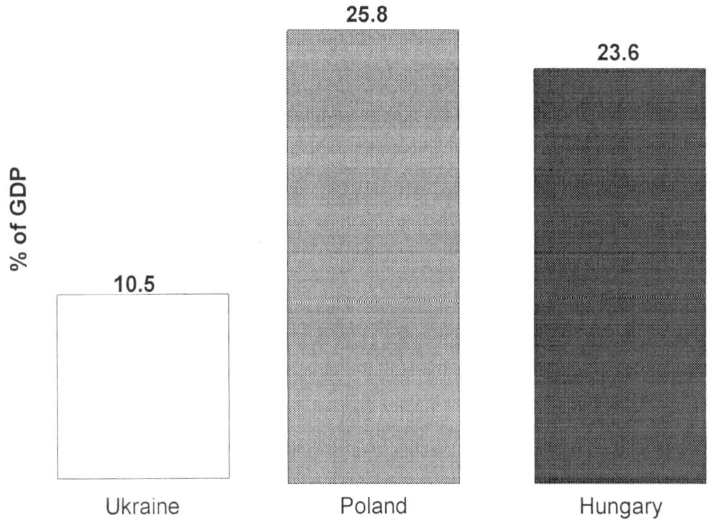

Graph 8.4
Monetary indicators Ukraine

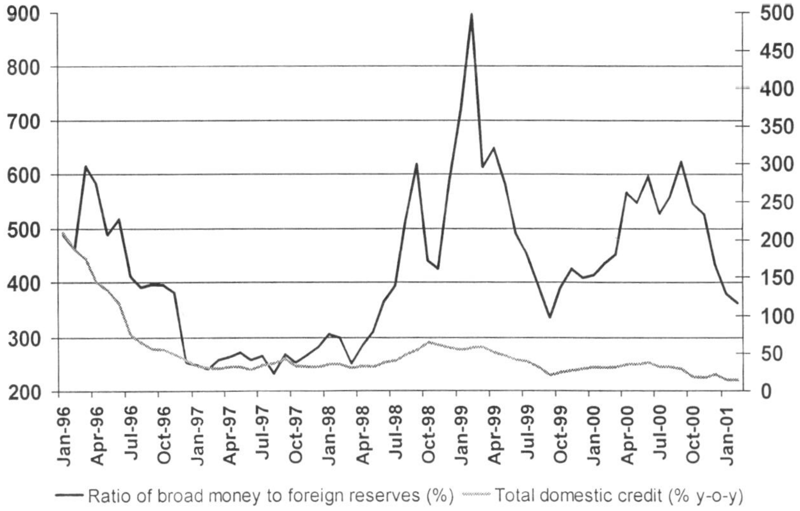

Graph 8.5
Total net and official flows to transition economies

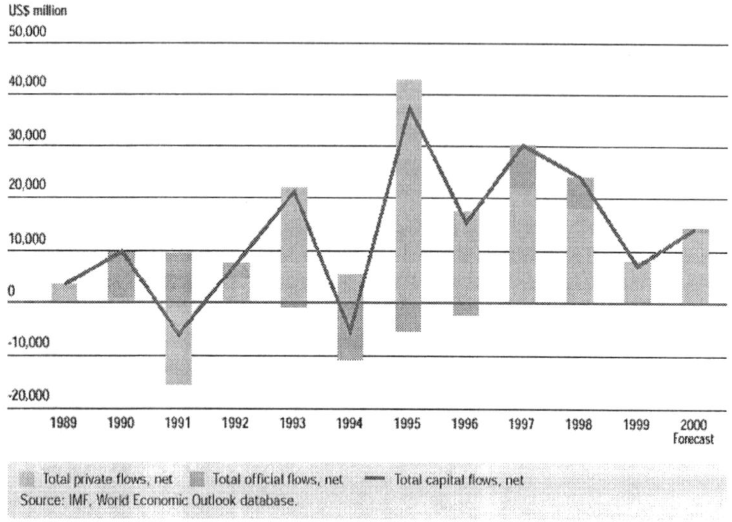

Graph 8.6
FDI is most resilient of capital inflows

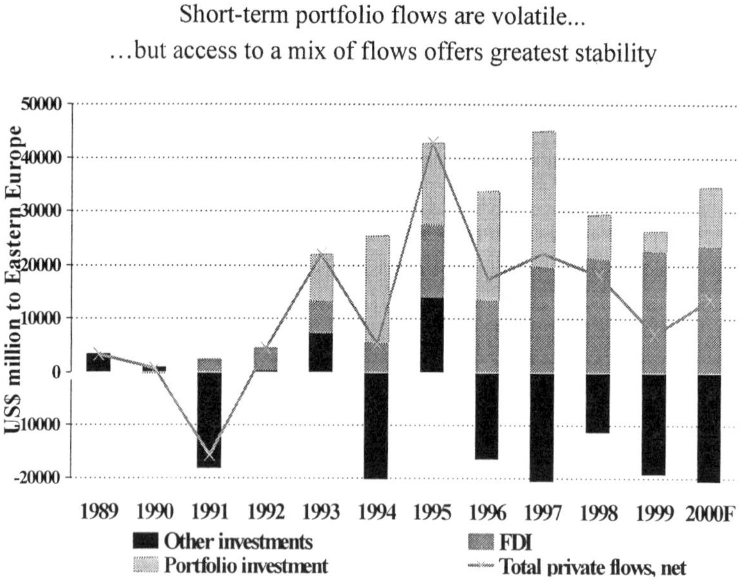

Graph 8.7
Foreign direct investment (net)

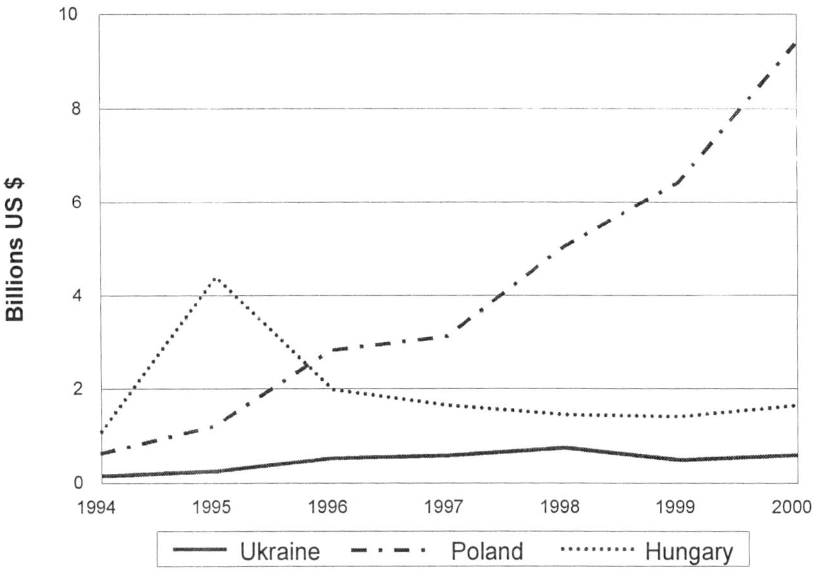

Graph 8.8
Cumulative FDI inflows 1989-2000 per capita

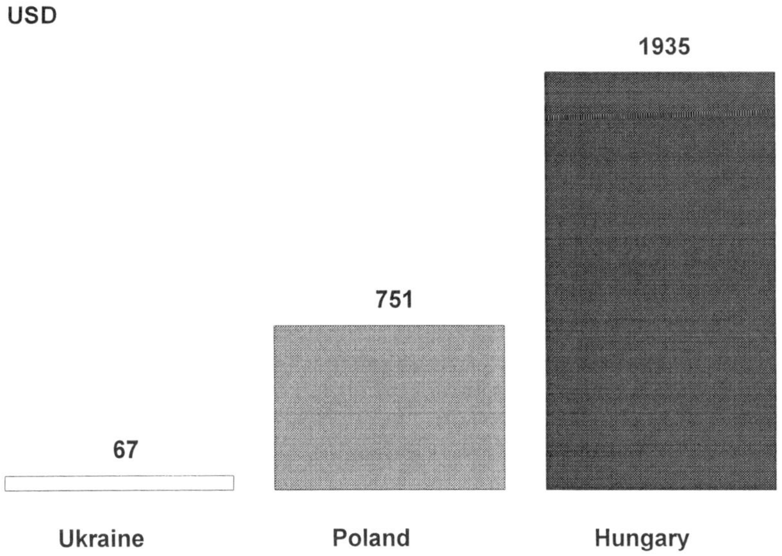

Graph 8.9
FDI attracted by sustained reform progress…

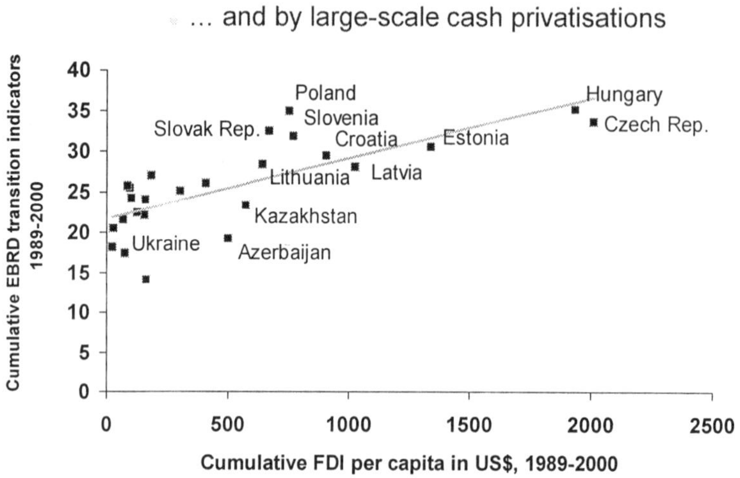

Graph 8.10
Main FDI sources cumulative 1 April 2001

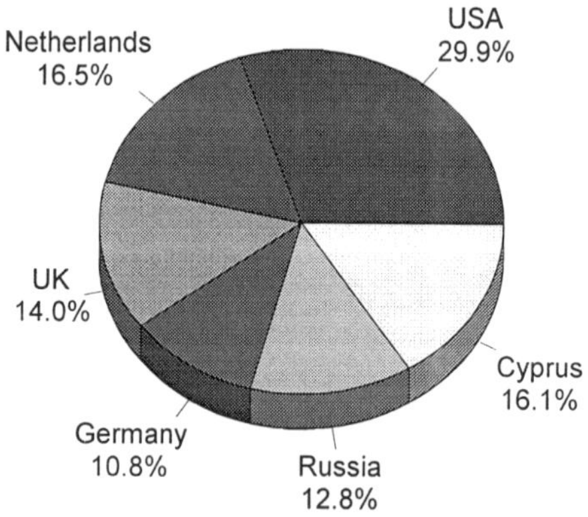

Interfax Ukraine (Foreign Investment Advisory Council)

Graph 8.11
FDI and privatisation revenues per capita

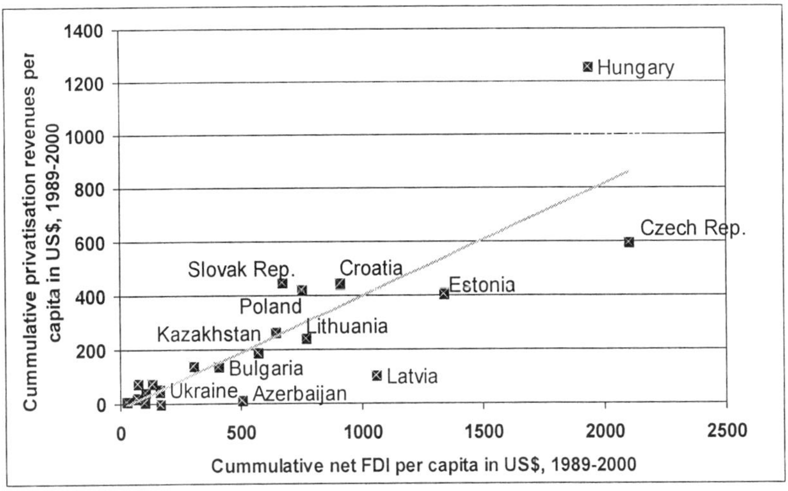

Graph 8.12
Net private capital flows to Eastern Europe, volatility, and also signs of capital flight

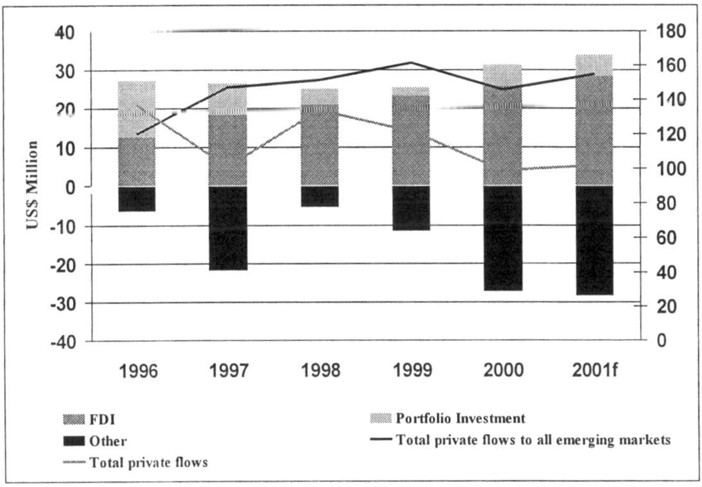

Graph 8.13
Current account in % of GDP 2000

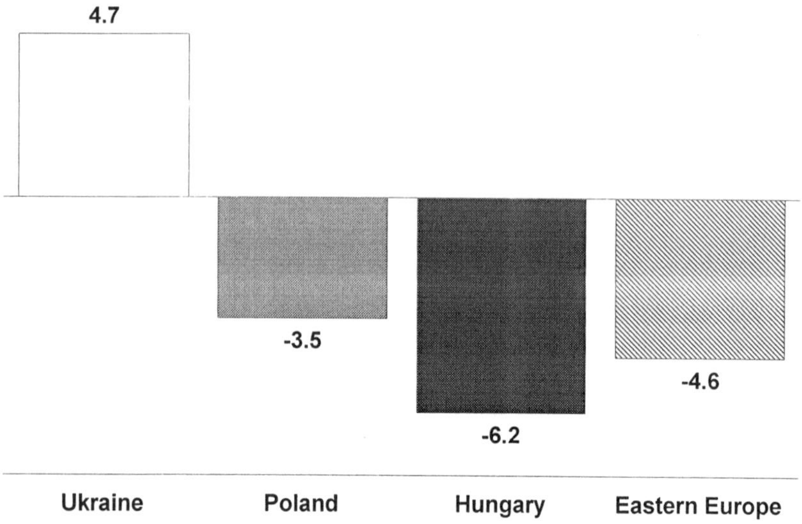

Graph 8.14
Current account and real exchange rate

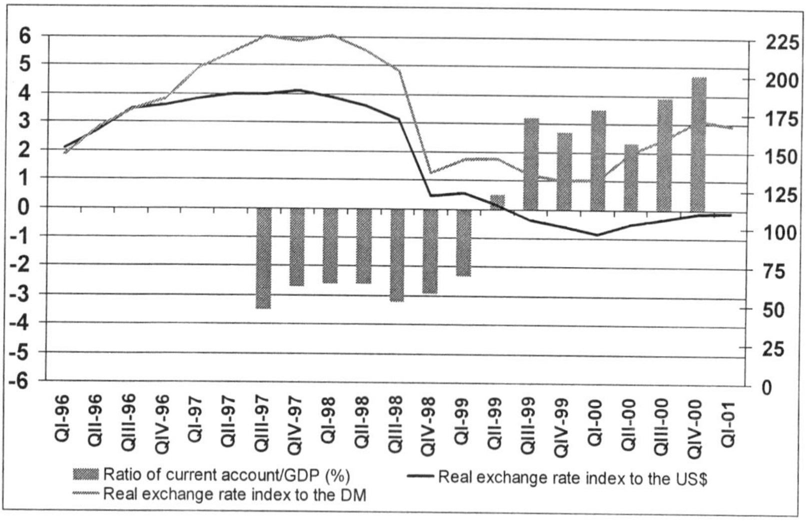

9

Fiscal and Regulatory Causes of Ukraine's Shadow Economy

Iryna Mel'ota and Ulrich Thiessen

1 Introduction

During the second half of the 1990s Ukraine has implemented considerable changes with regard to taxation, social security contributions and the regulatory regime for enterprises. Some of these measures as, for instance, the lowering of the social security contributions and the introduction of the presumptive tax for small businesses were aimed primarily at reducing the size of the shadow economy. It is therefore necessary to analyse their effects. We studied the causes of the shadow economy on the basis of an estimated demand-for-currency function. Then we also examined the dynamics of the shadow economy. Unlike other estimates of the shadow economy which are based on electricity consumption and surveys and of household expenditures, a money-demand model – extended to consider traditional and transition-specific causes for unofficial economic activity – can provide answers not only regarding the evolution of its size but also regarding the effect of particular policies.

Section 2 briefly describes the reform background, presents results from a currency-demand model and evaluates policy simulations. Section 3 compares the results with those obtained from using electricity consumption measures. Section 4 summarises the policy implications.

2 A currency-demand-for-money model to estimate the shadow economy

2.1 Methods and background

There is a substantial literature dating back to Guttmann (1977), Feige (1979) and Tanzi (1983) that uses the demand-for-money model to estimate the size and dynamics of the shadow economy. This methodology assumes that there exists an "official" demand for money in the official economy and a "shadow" demand for money in the underground economy. Subsequent authors included additional variables, such as tax complexity or regulatory burden that were presumed to cause persons and businesses to operate in the shadow (e.g. Schneider and Neck, 1993; Shabsigh, 1995; Hill and Kabir, 1996). This paper applies such a conventional model incorporating both tax and other variables to Ukrainian quarterly data for the period 1993-2000. We are not aware of a study of any transition country that uses the currency-demand method, a gap that should be closed because the monetary approach is the only method allowing causes and policy effects to be examined.

Ukraine is presumed to have a relatively large shadow economy and, when the first estimates of its size were published (see, for example, Kaufmann and Kaliberda, 1996), the government became very concerned and adopted measures in an attempt to reduce its size.

The state's first efforts were directed at the tax burden since it had been identified as the most important problem for enterprises irrespective of their size (Management Systems International et al. 2000). In 1995 the "income" tax for enterprises was replaced by a moderate corporate profit tax (30 percent rate and relatively generous depreciation allowances). Taxes and levies on exports were abolished.[1] The top marginal personal income tax rate was reduced starting from very high rates in 1993 and 1994 to 50% in late 1994 and further to 40% in the fall of 1995. Social security contributions were lowered in steps during 1997-1999 from 52% to around 40% of the gross wage. An attempt to reduce the regulatory burden on enterprises was made in 1998 by way of orders to state agencies to co-ordinate and reduce their inspections of enterprises. Also during that year a moderate and optional presumptive tax on small and medium-sized businesses was introduced. In addition, the state sought to inhibit non-monetary forms of payment, such as barter operations and inter-enterprise arrears, which facilitated

1 However transitory export taxes on livestock, oilseeds and a few other goods were, introduced in the late 1990s. These are examples of many minor and some more substantial setbacks to a consistent reform strategy that occurred in almost every policy area, making an objective assessment of the reform progress difficult.

unofficial transactions. Therefore, the state attempted to "harden" budget constraints for enterprises by reducing the share of subsidies in GDP on the expenditure side of the budget during the latter half of the 1990s (although the quantitatively more important subsidies to enterprises in the form of tax exemptions as a share of GDP remained relatively stable). Additional measures were taken in early 2000 to increase transparency and to simply forbid non-monetary transactions in the important energy sector.

These policy changes permit us to estimate a shadow demand for money that takes advantage of the considerable variation in policy variables during this period. The literature provides some guidance on the measurement of complexity and regulatory-burden variables (Wagner, 1976; Clotfelder, 1983; Schneider and Neck, 1993). Methodological notes and graphs of these variables are available in an appendix of Institute for Economic Research and Policy Consulting, IERPC, (2001) to interested readers.

2.2 Model description

We follow the demand-for-currency specifications, which have been used in estimations of the shadow economy for developed and developing countries (e.g. Tanzi, 1983; Klovland, 1984; Schneider and Neck, 1993; Shabsigh, 1995; Hill and Kabir, 1996). Specifically, our model is an equation where the ratio of currency to M2 is explained by traditional factors and by causes for unofficial transactions (a detailed explanation of our model and all variables used and constructed is contained in IERPC (2001). We use only currency and deposits denominated in Hryvnia, because a broader definition of money to include foreign currency and foreign currency deposits did not yield statistically satisfying results. Therefore, the shadow economy which is financed by using foreign currency (especially US Dollars) has to be estimated separately (IERPC, 2001).

In our model we assume the following causes for the shadow economy:

- the direct tax burden (DT), measured by a variety of variables;
- the indirect tax burden (INDT), also measured by a variety of variables;
- the social security burden (SSC), also measured by different variables;
- the effective regulatory burden (REG);
- the complexity of the tax system (REV);
- we consider in the model real overdue inter-enterprise arrears (IEAOVR), which can be assumed to represent soft budget constraints for enterprises, because in the absence of soft budget constraints the arrears would very likely be much lower. But it is not clear whether these arrears are associated with unofficial transactions. Therefore, we calculate two scenarios. In one scenario

the arrears are assumed to be associated with unofficial transactions. In the other scenario the arrears are assumed not to be related to unofficial transactions.

Finally, we consider in the model a variable that represents the influence of the introduction of the presumptive tax for small and medium-sized businesses in 1998 (DPRET) in order to test what effect it had on the shadow economy.

Given the lack of knowledge about the velocity of currency in the shadow economy, one needs to make an assumption. We use actual currency velocity. Different velocity assumptions influence the estimates of changes in the shadow economy. This does not apply to the most recent years 1999 and 2000 because the annual averages of all velocities remained nearly constant during this period. They influence the estimates for the earlier period 1993-1998 such that when using other velocities than actual currency velocity, the shadow economy would have grown more rapidly until 1997 than shown in our scenarios (see IERPC, 2001).

2.3 Results

Our estimations show that the statistically significant determinants of the currency-M2 ratio and thus the causes of the shadow economy are:

- the direct tax burden (DT), with or without social security contributions. In particular, among the tax variables, the personal income tax has always been the most significant explanatory variable;
- the effective regulatory burden on enterprises (REG);
- and the complexity of the tax system (REV).

Real overdue inter-enterprise arrears (IEAOVR) are also a significant explanatory variable. Their increase reduces the currency-M2 ratio. This effect can mean that they are a cause for the shadow economy, if arrears are used for unofficial transactions. Or it can mean that arrears replace currency and there is no relationship with the shadow economy. These two possibilities result in two scenarios.

The introduction of the presumptive tax for small and medium-sized businesses in 1998 (DPRET) had a statistically significant negative effect on the shadow economy.

The indirect tax burden (INDT) was not found to be a statistically significant explanatory variable and thus not a significant cause for shadow economic activity.

Table 9.1 provides an index of the shadow economy's share in GDP for the two scenarios concerning inter-enterprise arrears (column 2, panel A and B). We present an index of the shadow economy's share in official GDP and not its estimated levels, because we are interested in the effects of changes of economic policies and can avoid assumptions about the level of the shadow economy velocity, since only the velocity trend is needed.

The estimates in the second column suggest that the shadow economy's share reached a peak in 1997. Between 1997 and 1999 it declined considerably but rose again during 2000.

Table 9.1
Evolution of the shadow economy (estimates based on equation 2 of table 2 in IERPC (2001) and using the actual velocity of domestic currency as explained in IERPC (2001)

Year	Index of shadow economy share of GDP	Simulation 1: Tax burden at average level of 1993-94 (prior to reforms) and no presumptive tax	Simulation 2: No introduction of presumptive tax for small and medium sized enterprises	Simulation 3: Regulatory burden constant at level of 1993	Simulation 4: Complexity of tax system constant at level of 1993	Simulation 5: Regulatory burden and complexity of tax system constant at level of 1993	Simulation 6: Real overdue inter-enterprise arrears constant at level of 1993	Simulation 7: Avoidance of policy mistakes*
Panel A: Assuming inter-enterprise arrears are associated with unofficial economic activity								
1993	1.00	1.00	1.00	1.00	1.00	1.00	1.00	1.00
1994	1.06	1.06	1.06	0.86	0.99	0.79	1.06	0.80
1995	1.24	1.32	1.24	0.82	0.98	0.64	1.23	0.64
1996	1.45	1.55	1.45	0.84	1.09	0.62	1.42	0.59
1997	1.59	1.68	1.59	0.85	1.20	0.63	1.55	0.59
1998	1.55	1.69	1.55	0.85	1.10	0.59	1.52	0.55
1999	1.37	1.66	1.52	0.72	1.03	0.53	1.33	0.50
2000	1.48	1.86	1.64	0.73	1.09	0.53	1.44	0.49
Panel B: Assuming inter-enterprise arrears are not associated with unofficial economic activity								
1993	1.00	1.00	1.00	1.00	1.00	1.00	1.00	1.00
1994	1.12	1.12	1.12	0.91	1.04	0.83	1.10	0.81
1995	1.25	1.34	1.25	0.83	0.97	0.63	1.28	0.65
1996	1.36	1.46	1.36	0.78	0.97	0.55	1.49	0.60
1997	1.41	1.50	1.41	0.75	1.00	0.52	1.63	0.59
1998	1.38	1.51	1.38	0.74	0.91	0.48	1.60	0.55
1999	1.21	1.50	1.36	0.63	0.85	0.43	1.38	0.49
2000	1.31	1.70	1.47	0.64	0.90	0.43	1.48	0.48

* regulatory burden, complexity of tax system, and inter-enterprise arrears at level of 1993

Source: own calculations

The impact of various factors on the shadow economy is demonstrated by simulations (columns 3-9, Table 9.1). They show how the shadow economy would have evolved had particular policies been different while leaving the other variables unchanged. Simulation 1 shows that without the implemented tax reforms, the shadow economy would have increased nearly continuously and reached a much higher level by 2000.

The presumptive tax for small and medium-sized businesses (simulation 2) is estimated to have reduced the shadow economy's total size during 1999 and 2000 by about 11% and 12% in panel A, and by 12% and 14% in panel B.[2] Apparently, the dampening effect of the presumptive tax on the shadow economy became stronger. This may be judged to be a very respectable success. The estimate is qualified by the fact that the dummy could also capture other effects.

By contrast, had it been possible to prevent the regulatory burden from rising, the shadow economy would have declined nearly continuously (simulation 3). Had the government not increased the complexity of the tax system, the shadow economy would have remained relatively stable at its initial level (simulation 4). Had both the regulatory burden and the complexity not increased over time, the shadow economy would have declined continuously (simulation 5). Had enterprise arrears not increased, growth of the shadow economy would have been considerably dampened (simulation 6). Simulation 7 captures the effect of "avoidance of policy mistakes": Had the regulatory burden and tax system complexity not increased and had the government even hardened budget constraints for enterprises and thus prevented the rise of their overdue arrears, the shadow economy would have been reduced by more than half in 2000.

The simulations also explain shadow economy dynamics. Growth of the shadow economy's share during 1993-1997 was caused by three factors: increases of the regulatory burden, of tax system complexity and of overdue inter-enterprise arrears. Factors that reduced it since then were reduced tax system complexity during 1998-1999, the introduction of the presumptive tax, less overdue inter-enterprise arrears, and a continuation of the decrease of the tax burden, especially lower social security contributions. Despite a continued decreasing tax pressure, growing acceptance of the presumptive tax and lower real overdue inter-enterprise arrears, the shadow economy's decline appears to have been halted in 2000 due to increases in the regulatory burden and tax system complexity.[3] The results from 2000, while for one year only, should alert policy makers to the importance of consistent policies to reduce the size of the shadow economy.

---

2 To obtain these percentages, the difference between the figures in columns 4 and 2 has to be divided by the figures in column 2.

3 Does consideration of unofficial transactions financed by money substitutes and foreign currency alter the conclusions suggested by Table 9.1 that the shadow economy reached a peak in 1997 and shows a declining trend since then? To the extent that the variable overdue inter-enterprise arrears is a good proxy for money substitutes such as barter and other non-monetary transactions, our estimates shown in panel A of Table 9.1 already consider their effect on currency holdings and on the shadow economy. Regarding the use of foreign currency as a financing means, the discussion in IERPC (2001), appendix C, suggests that indicators of this type are not in conflict with concluding that there is a declining trend in the shadow economy.

Finally, the simulations reveal that the major contributors to unofficial activity in order of importance are the regulatory burden, followed by the tax system complexity, the tax burden and inter-enterprise arrears.

3 Comparison with estimates based on electricity consumption

Our results are based upon a "shadow" money demand estimation combined with actual velocity. The approach most often used in estimating shadow economies in transition countries is based on comparisons of real GDP growth with electricity consumption (e.g. Dobozi and Pohl, 1996, Kaufmann and Kaliberda, 1996, Johnson et al., 1997, Lazko, 2000).[4] We have performed such calculations using Ukraine's official data on total electricity consumption and real output growth, using two elasticity assumptions to yield two scenarios.[5]

Table 9.2 contrasts these scenarios with the results from our monetary approach scenarios. To facilitate the comparison both sets of indices are set to 100 in 1993, the first year of our data.

According to the electricity approach the shadow economy's share in GDP jumped up in 1994, grew until 1996 and then fell off very rapidly. By contrast, the monetary approach shows a relatively smooth increase until 1997 followed by a moderately declining trend, which reversed again in 2000. Another major difference between the two sets of results is that according to the first electricity scenario 1 (which reasonably argues that some energy is wasted during an economic downturn), the Ukrainian shadow economy was 3% lower than in 1993 whereas according to the monetary approach it was 30% to 50% higher!

We suggest that the money demand results are more reliable because they are based on an empirical model that yields good results, while the electricity model

---

4 All that is needed to estimate the shadow economy's evolution in this approach is the growth rate of electricity consumption, the growth rate of real official GDP and an assumption about the elasticity of electricity consumption with respect to total GDP. The gap between estimated total output and official GDP can then be taken as an indicator of the size of the unofficial economy.

5 For the first we assume that elasticity equals 0.85 during the downturn (on the assumption that much energy is wasted when output declines) to obtain a lower tending estimate for the shadow economy. This assumption is equivalent to an elasticity of 1.18, the inverse of 0.85, during an economic upswing, which occurred since 2000. The second scenario uses a unitary elasticity. Consequently, scenario 2 yields higher shadow economy estimates than scenario 1.

appears to be based on business cycle features.[6] Moreover, only the monetary method can estimate the causes of the shadow economy and identify the impact of individual policies. Unlike the electricity method, policy conclusions can be drawn, and our results show that policy reversals can have immediate negative consequences.

Table 9.2
Comparison of indices of the shadow economy

Year	Index of the shadow economy share in official GDP (1993=100%)			
	Electricity consumption approach		Monetary approach	
	Scenario 1 Assuming an output elasticity of electricity consumption of 0.85 when output falls *	Scenario 2 Assuming an output elasticity of electricity consumption of unity	Assuming inter-enterprise arrears are associated with unofficial economic activity	Assuming inter-enterprise arrears are not associated with unofficial economic activity
1993	100	100	100	100
1994	138	145	106	112
1995	154	166	124	125
1996	159	177	145	136
1997	152	173	159	141
1998	136	161	155	138
1999	125	152	137	121
2000	97	122	148	131

* This is equivalent to an elasticity of 1.18 when output increases

Source: own calculations

6 In the electricity approach the decline of the shadow economy since about 1995 is simply the result of the bottoming out of the recession which is associated with some improvement in energy efficiency. (The negative growth rates of electricity consumption declined much less than those of real GDP in absolute terms). But the improvement in energy efficiency could have been expected when considering the series of energy price shocks since about the early 1990s, which hit especially industrial consumers but lately private households, too. Soft budget constraints certainly dampened these effects but did not eliminate them. Also the substitution effects of one energy source for another may have been minor because over the longer term relative price changes among different types of energy were not pronounced and investment was relatively low, which would have been required to replace one energy type by another one.

4 Conclusions

Money-demand estimations provide new evidence on the evolution and causes of Ukraine's shadow economy and on the effectiveness of policies implemented to dampen it. The implications of this study go beyond the case of Ukraine because it suggests that an effective regulatory burden and tax system complexity appear to be quantitatively as important or even more important than the tax and social security burden. In addition, the idea of simplified taxation for small businesses should be seriously considered as a means to reduce the shadow economy.

The estimations concur with previous estimates that Ukraine's shadow economy has been attenuating in recent years. But our results suggest that this turnaround happened during 1998-1999, at least one year later than the electricity approach suggests. Moreover, growth and decline in the shadow economy have been much more modest than suggested by the electricity model. Most importantly, our approach provides specific policy reasons for the decline. The factors that contributed to the reduction of the shadow economy's share since its peak in 1997 have been the decrease of the tax burden (especially lower social security contributions and the introduction of the presumptive tax), a reduced tax system complexity (until 1998), and a decline in real overdue inter-enterprise arrears (suggesting a hardening of budget constraints). In Ukraine, the regulatory burden appears to be the prime cause. Despite efforts to reduce it, we do not find evidence of success.

Based on these findings, policies that could contribute to reducing Ukraine's shadow economy would be a tax reform that concentrates on lowering the personal income tax burden and simplifies the tax system, and reduces the number of taxes and exemptions.[7] Among the direct taxes, we found that the personal income tax is a highly significant explanatory factor for unofficial activity. This may not be surprising because there has been a continuous increase of income taxation in real terms, given that the personal income tax system has not been reformed since 1994 while inflation was high.

First and foremost, a serious reduction in the effective regulatory burden is called for. The institution of a central agency responsible for deregulation may be

7 However, there is one qualification. Those minor taxes on purchases of foreign currency, homes and jewellery that were introduced in 2000 to improve the financing of the pension fund were meant to contain the social security contribution rate while improving the credibility of the pension system at relatively low additional administrative costs. We do not want to argue that for the purpose of simplification these taxes should be withdrawn again. We believe that indeed the social security contribution rate should be contained, the credibility of the system should be improved, and there are tasks and responsibilities of the pension system, which should be financed by all taxpayers, not only by wage earners (such as pensions for former un-elected officials etc.). This may justify those special taxes.

meaningless as long as all other government institutions are not seriously co-ordinating their regulatory plans and actions with this agency.

Given that indirect taxes appear not to be a significant explanatory factor, it could be argued that the VAT rate could be raised. Considering also that income earned in the shadow economy tends to be spent in the official markets where VAT is paid, and that VAT is a tax on consumption and not on savings and investment, maintaining a relatively high VAT could be a reasonable way of taxing some unofficial income without being a major cause for it.[8] Other transition and industrial countries may want to consider these findings, too. The latter may also want to take notice of the fact that simplification of the tax system does not necessarily promote unofficial activity but may actually contribute to its reduction.

References

Clotfelter, C. T. (1983): Tax Evasion and Tax Rates: An Analysis of Individual Returns. The Review of Economics and Statistics, Vol. LXV, No. 3, pp. 362-373.

Dobozi, I. and G. Pohl (1996): Real Output Decline in Transition Economies – Forget GDP, Try Power Consumption Data. Transition Newsletter, Vol. 6, No. 1-2, World Bank, Washington, D.C., pp. 17-18.

Feige, E. L. (1979): How Big is the Irregular Economy? Challenge, Vol. 22, pp. 5-13.

Guttmann, P. M. (1997): Subterranean Economy. Financial Analysts Journal, Vol. 33, pp. 26-27.

Hill, R. and M. Kabir (1996): Tax Rates, the Tax Mix, and the Growth of the Underground Economy in Canada: What Can We Infer? Canadian Tax Journal, Vol. 44, No. 6, pp. 1552-1583.

Institute of Economic Research and Policy Consulting, IERPC (2001): Fiscal and Regulatory Causes of Shadow Economies in Transition Economies: The Case of Ukraine. Working Paper No. 9, Kyiv.

International Finance Corporation (1999): The State of Small Businesses in Ukraine. An IFC Survey of Ukrainian Small Businesses in Makeyevka, Mykolayiv, Kirovograd, Chernigiv, and Rivne, Kyiv, May.

Johnson, S., D. Kaufmann, and A. Shleifer (1997): The Unofficial Economy in Transition. Brookings Papers on Economic Activity, Vol. 2, pp. 159-239.

---

8 However, we do not want to overlook that high indirect taxes can be strong incentives for unofficial activity, especially in the services sector and with regard to goods that can be smuggled easily and are subject to high excise taxes. High excise taxes on such goods provide incentives for bribery and smuggling. Therefore, our view that though the VAT rate could be relatively high this should be tempered by the paramount goal of moderate taxation at all levels.

Kaufmann, D. and A. Kaliberda (1996): Integrating the Unofficial Economy into the Dynamics of Post-Socialist Economies: A Framework of Analysis and Evidence. Policy Research Working Paper No. 1691, World Bank, December.

Klovland, J. (1984): Tax Evasion and the Demand for Currency in Norway and Sweden. Is There a Hidden Relationship? Scandinavian Journal of Economics, Vol. 86, pp. 423-439.

Lacko, M. (2000): Hidden Economy – an Unknown Quantity? Comparative analysis of hidden economies in transition countries, 1989-1995. Economics of Transition, Vol. 8, No. 1.

Management Systems International, Development Alternatives Incorporated (2000), International Institute of Sociology, Small and Medium Enterprises Baseline Survey, Kyiv.

Schneider, F. and R. Neck (1993): Shadow Economy under Changing Tax Systems and Structures. Finanzarchiv, Band 50, pp. 344-368.

Shabsigh, G. (1995): The Underground Economy: Estimation, and Economic and Policy Implications – The Case of Pakistan. International Monetary Fund, Working Paper.

Tanzi, V. (1983): The Underground Economy in the United States: Annual Estimates, 1930-1980. International Monetary Fund Staff Papers, Vol. 30, pp. 283-305.

Wagner, R. E (1976): Revenue Structure, Fiscal Illusion and Budgetary Choice. Public Choice, Vol. 25, pp. 45-61.

Part III

INSTITUTIONS, COMPETITION, AND GROWTH

10

Enterprise Restructuring under Economic Growth in the Byelorussian Republic

Pavel Daneyko, Sergey Pukovich

1 Introduction

In Belarus there is neither macroeconomic stabilisation, nor any progress in the actual privatisation of the public sector. There are no developed financial institutions and practically zero foreign investments, and an unstable institutional environment. Prevails in spite of this, the Byelorussian Republic has been demonstrating persistent economic growth during the past several years. This country is thus a unique exception with respect to the rules and principles applied in all other transition economies.

The ten year transformation history of the Central and East European economies clearly demonstrates, that macroeconomic stabilisation and major economic growth and well-being of the people occurred in those countries, which have managed to realise large-scale privatisation and restructuring of their industrial companies. Those, who achieved most progress with liberalising prices, trade and international exchanges, achieved this by promoting the development of internal competitiveness, and creating a highly efficient banking sector, capital markets, and other financial institutions.[1]

So, how has Belarus, having rejected the conventional and proven mechanisms of transformation, been able to demonstrate, for several years now, economic growth on a scale comparable to that of the most advanced reforming economies?

This article attempts to explain this economic growth in Belarus from a microeconomic point of view.

Our investigation is based on the results of interviews with 222 managers of former socialist industrial enterprises, 300 Chief Executive Officers (CEOs) of several new private companies and individual businessmen. It consists of a study

[1] Transition Report 1999. Ten Years of Transition, EBRD, 1999.

of the process of restructuring at the enterprise and the industry levels since 1990, the starting point of transformation, of new rules about property rights and of a new market approach.

It will be shown, that economic growth in Belarus happened against a background of structural reorganisation of the economy and restructuring of enterprises, which adapted themselves both to the conditions of a new management system and to competitiveness on the internal and external markets.

2 Conditions for economic growth in the Byelorussian Republic

Drastic changes in the managing conditions resulting from changes to the economic and political system at the beginning of the 1990s, first caused a significant recession of the Byelorussian economy. Between 1992 and 1994, the GDP decreased by 27%, industrial production by 22.4%, and agricultural output by 18.8%. The investment in fixed capital fell by 46.3%. The decrease of external and internal demand and the slow adjustment by manufacturers to the new price structures caused this serious reduction of output volumes.

Crisis is the word best characterising this period of production recession, growing inflation, soaring unemployment and deteriorating living standards. Structural changes were applied: curtailing of production and a lowering of the intensity of economic activity because of markets losses. Production became unprofitable, due to the shift in the price structures and the competitiveness of foreign manufacturers. By 1994-1995, the number of products had decreased up to 10% of the 1990 level. The greatest recession occurred in the fuel industry, which depends on imported oil. Production volumes in the electric power, textile, light industry, food processing and mechanical engineering sectors had decreased too.

The enterprises were slowly adapting to the new 'rules of the game', not paying much attention to analyses of the level and structure of demand, or to prospects for sales of the products. This inattention to the new management conditions and pricing requirements by commodity producers was a major reason for the increase in mutual arrears and the development of a crisis situation in the financial and credit spheres. Another reason was the introduction of a soft budget constraint policy, and the lack of privatisation and institutional reforms.

By 1995 the GDP had fallen to 65% and industrial production to 61% of the 1990 level. In 1996 normative documents were released, creating a legal basis for a future increase in the role of government in the economy. Active interference began with new state regulations concerning pricing and foreign trade operations.

There was also a slow-down in privatisation and all other institutional transformations.

In 1997, an inflation-creating economic policy was introduced in Belarus. At the same time, the government was stimulating aggregate demand with the purpose of increasing the rate of economic growth. As objects for economic development, the government earmarked certain companies for investment support, selecting three priorities: housing construction, agriculture and export. This policy was characterised by the differentiation of exchange rates, the absence of free foreign exchange markets, administrative price controls, growth of government investment, negative interest rates, growth of barter, and stockpiling finished products in warehouses. By these means, GDP grew by 11.4% in 1997 and 8.4% in 1998, while industrial production rose by 18.8% and 12.4% respectively and investment in fixed capital by 20% and 25 % (see Table 10.1).

Thus, since 1997 economic growth in Belarus, despite high inflation, acquired a nature stable enough. From 1996 to 2000, GDP had grown by 35.8%, rising back to 88.7% of the 1990 level. The growth rates of industrial production were even higher, than the GDP growth rate. During the same period of time industrial production had risen by 64.6%, exceeding the 1990 level in 2000. This growth of production had been reached by both extensive as well intensive methods.

Table 10.1
Dynamics of some macroeconomic indicators

Years	Indicators (in % as of the previous year)				
	Gross domestic product	Industrial output	Investment into fixed capital	Exports	Consumer price index
1991	98.8	99.0	104	-	194.1
1992	90.4	90.8	71	-	1070.8
1993	92.4	90.6	85	83.5	1290.2
1994	88.3	85.4	89	85.2	2321.0
1995	89.6	88.3	69	187.5	809.3
1996	102.8	103.5	95	142.3	152.7
1997	111.4	118.8	120	123.9	163.8
1998	108.4	112.4	125	97.1	173.0
1999	103.4	110.3	92	82.9	393.7
2000	105.8	108.0	97	125.8	268.6

Source: Data of the Ministry of Statistics and Analysis of the Republic of Belarus

Extensive growth assumes either additional resources flowing into the economy, or 'spending and eating' those being available already. First of all, this concerns the fixed capital assets of industrial enterprises, which depreciated more than 60%. The share of depreciation charges in the cost of industrial production was reduced from 9.4% in 1990, down to 1.4 % in 1999.

Under high inflation and multiple exchange rates, the income of enterprises can assume a rent-seeking nature; that is, they may not be engaged in creating *new assets*, on which an enterprise's ability to continue its production depends. Up to a point, any company can finance an increase in production by mortgaging its future activities. In such cases the operation of the enterprise is based on the principle of the 'financial pyramid'. But if no assets are created, the enterprise will sooner or later go bankrupt. In 2001 more than 40% of Byelorussian enterprises became unprofitable, while in 2000 the percentage of loss-making companies amounted to 23.4%.

Economic growth proceeds under the "administrative regulation of consumer prices and administrative resource allocation in the economy", (in the public sector and in industries, which produce socially significant goods) by creating artificial consumer demand to load up the productive capacities of enterprises.

Therefore, a part of the economic growth in Belarus is explained by a distortion of the statistical indicators. There are also price and exchange rate distortions under the rigid state regulation of the economy (e.g. price increases for so-called 'socially significant goods' always grow more slowly than the Consumer Price Index (CPI) for the whole economy). The cost performance of the GDP is significantly distorted by barter deals, especially in foreign trade, when the barter price reflected in the contracts and in official statistics is higher than the price of the money market.

The administrative resource allocation also results in a serious distortion of the macroeconomic indicators, as many state-owned enterprises are compelled to acquire resources from governmental (or near-governmental) intermediaries, at prices considerably exceeding the actual price level of the Byelorussian market. Additional strains result from the administrative regulation of the foreign exchange market, by artificially maintaining an official exchange rate for the Byelorussian Rouble and by the so-called 'plurality' of exchange rates.

This extensive scenario in Belarus engages the full administrative potential of the government. All these years, the planned growth of production volumes carried not just an indicative, but a *legislatively authorised nature*. At its core, the growth is preserving the *status quo* of the CEOs: they are doing only what is required 'from the top' and tend to show minimal initiative. Only short-term interest guides the majority of enterprises. The absence of new investment makes them profitable and highly liquid. Management is motivated to pump the last resources out of their companies and maximise personal rents.

In rushing to ensure the fulfilment of their 'plans', many enterprises were compelled to employ a lot of tricks, such as distorting statistical reporting, concluding dummy deals, working 'for the warehouse' at year end, and so on. Fulfilling their plans is by far the most reliable way of securing the bosses' positions. It allows the managers (not being owners) easily to defend their own interests, they being, as a matter of fact, the only actual hosts of the privatised and state-owned companies.

And yet, the above-noted scenario cannot fully explain the growth attained, since a significant part of the production is already being exported at market prices.

Intensive economic growth envisions the increase of economic efficiency, which is achieved by a structural reorganisation of the economy and the restructuring of enterprises. This means introducing new and improving existing products and production processes, and implementing organisational changes in the companies.

Structural reorganisation of the economy assumes a redistribution of resources from less productive enterprises and industries to more productive ones. That means bringing to life new private companies and expanding existing enterprises, which have adapted as much as possible to the new market conditions, and closing old and inefficient companies, which are not capable of meeting the demand.

Tables 10.2 and 10.3 summarise certain important structural changes in the Byelorussian economy. Firstly, there was a significant (more than 50%) reduction in the share of agriculture, which had negative growth relative to GDP, as is the tradition in socialist economies. Then, there was an important increase of the share of the services sector, where in general asset creation is usually higher than in industry.

Table 10.2
GDP Production structure

	GDP change from year to year, %									
	1990	1991	1992	1993	1994	1995	1996	1997	1998	1999
Goods	69.5	68.3	68.3	54.3	47.4	50.2	50.2	50.1	48	47.5
Services	27.9	28.9	28.6	47.9	49.9	43.4	40.2	38.3	39.9	40.8
Indirect financial mediation services	0	-1.5	-1.7	-8.4	-6.7	-3.4	-1.7	-1.5	-1.5	-2
Net taxes on products and imports	2.6	4.0	4.8	6.2	9.4	9.8	11.3	13.1	13.6	13.7
GDP – Total	100	100	100	100	100	100	100	100	100	100

The relative importance of various industrial branches has changed considerably (see Table 10.4). These structural shifts in industry were caused by falling production volumes, by the loss of importance of the military defence complex, by the building materials industry, by the fuel and light industries, and by some revival and growth in production in the ferrous metallurgy, forestry, paper, and the wood and food processing industries.

Table 10.3
GDP participation by selected industries

Economic sectors	GDP change from year to year, %									
	1990	1991	1992	1993	1994	1995	1996	1997	1998	1999
Industrial production	38.2	40.3	38.5	29.0	27.9	28.3	30.7	31.6	31.1	29.6
Agriculture	22.9	20.0	22.3	16.7	13.1	15.2	13.5	11.5	10.2	10.7
Civil Engineering	7.8	7.5	7.0	7.9	5.6	5.5	4.9	6.1	6.0	6.2
Transport	5.5	4.3	7.4	11.2	10.7	10.4	9.4	9.2	8.3	10.3*
Communication	1.0	0.8	0.7	1.1	1.1	2.0	2.0	1.6	1.6	-
Trade and public services	3.5	4.6	4.9	8.8	10.1	7.7	7.8	8.0	8.7	9.9

* Total for transport and communications

Source: Data of the Ministry of Statistics and Analysis of the Republic of Belarus

Table 10.4
Production output of various industrial branches

Industrial branch	Share of the production of certain industries in total output, %									
	1990	1991	1992	1993	1994	1995	1996	1997	1998	1999
Electrical power	2.6	3.1	7.7	14.6	15.6	13.8	11.3	11.8	9	8.2
Fuel	4.6	4.2	8.1	8	6.4	4.3	3.8	3.5	3.4	3.7
Ferrous metallurgy	0.9	0.8	2	1.9	2.5	2.4	2.7	3.1	3.2	3.1
Chemical and petrochemical	9	7.2	11.6	12.4	13.8	14.3	12.9	13.3	13.5	14.5
Machine building and mechanical engineering	34.2	26.7	28	22.1	22.6	23.3	24.4	24.7	25.7	25.3
Forestry, wood processing, pulp and paper	4.4	4.8	4.6	4.5	4.6	5.3	5.6	5.7	6.2	6.4
Construction materials	3.7	3.8	4.9	5.7	4.6	5.1	4.5	4.8	4.7	4.5
Light industry	17.2	19.2	13.2	11.3	10.4	8	7.9	8.1	9.2	9.5
Food	14.9	25	13.1	13.1	13.6	17	19	17.8	18.3	18.4

Source: Data of the Ministry of Statistics and Analysis of the Republic of Belarus

The share of industries producing raw materials and semi-finished products (chemical industry, electrical power and ferrous metallurgy) has increased during the transformation period. At the same time, the share of final products (mechanical engineering and light industry) has decreased, in spite of the fact that they had higher growth in labour productivity (see Table 10.5) and that lower price increases were recorded. Thus, the structural reorganisation of the

Byelorussian industry proceeded not only under the influence of efficiency changes within certain industrial sectors, but also as a result of a shift in the price structure within the economy. In a number of industries the production growth is very extensive and is not attributable to a growth in labour productivity.

Table 10.5
Transformation and industrial growth

Industrial branches	Total output growth index in 1999, % (1990=100%)	Labour productivity index in 1999, % (1990=100%)	Price index in1999, (1992=100%)	Share of employment in the non-state-owned sector, %
Electrical power	66	45	55052	0.1
Fuel	37	21	168141	17.6
Ferrous metallurgy	139	95	65041	11.1
Chemical and petrochemical	93	98	71781	21.2
Machine building and mechanical engineering	117	187	45082	36.2
Forestry, wood processing, pulp and paper	164	155	15799	76.4
Construction materials	57	86	24683	59.4
Light industry	101	160	20199	71.9
Food	107	91	not available	63.4

Source: Data of the Ministry of Statistics and Analysis of the Republic of Belarus

In most cases the higher production growth, higher labour productivity and lower prices occur within industries having a higher ownership percentage in the non-government-owned sector. However, the structural reorganisation of the economy is of a unilateral nature.

Firstly, it proceeds without any serious development of the private sector. It is estimated that the share of the private sector in GDP does not exceed 9-12%. Businesses in Belarus amount to about 5% of the industrial production volume, 30% of retail turnover, and 4% of investment.[2] Only 20-21% of the population participates in private business activity, and more than half (57.4 %) of all private firms are located in Minsk, the capital of Belarus.

The official policy of the government is clearly anti-entrepreneurial. In Belarus today, there are more than 30,000 normative documents regulating the economic activity of companies, among them 4,500 in the field of taxation. The number of new private companies is decreasing, while prior to 1994 the number of private enterprise registrations had increased annually by 75% to 85%.

The new private sector in Belarus will have to adapt to the conditions of 'market socialism' and to 'learn' from the former socialist enterprises those strategies,

---

2 Report of the Minister of Entrepreneurship and Investment at the Board of Directors meeting on the results of 1999.

which will allow them to adapt to the new conditions. Private firms, which fail to adapt to these institutional conditions, are compelled either to leave the country or to exit the market, as former socialist enterprises did in the rest of Eastern Europe.

The actual contribution of the private sector to the GDP could be much higher, if we were to take the scope of shadow turnover in the private sector into account. Businessmen are assessing it at 45% to 50% (in private trade even up to 80 %).

Secondly, despite rather progressive legislation, the mechanism of bankruptcy is not really used in the economy. The experience of Central and East European economies proves, that in many cases resources are transferred during bankruptcies of former socialist enterprises, when the capital market is inundated by a lot of cheap fixed capital assets. This appears to be one of the conditions for the rapid development of the new private sector.

Thirdly, in Belarus there is no actual privatisation. Only 3,190 enterprises of the national and municipal property have been restructured in total during the years of transformation. Recognising, that a smaller than 25% block of shares will not give the government any actual say in the management, the majority of the 2,394 privatised enterprises in Belarus was very small.

In the course of the privatisation process 520 open joint-stock companies have been created. The government has no stake in only 84 of them. In another 81 companies the government's share is less than 25%. Thus, less than one third of all joint-stock companies became really private in the course of corporatisation. In 48.4% of the joint-stock companies the government's share exceeds 50% + 1 share, i.e. these enterprises actually remain state owned. In the other 20% of the joint-stock companies, the government owns a blocking share.

In 1991-1992, before the government had developed an ideological goal, the more efficient enterprises with a progressive enough management were rather rapidly privatised. Apart from the natural enthusiasm for reform, this group of CEOs was inspired by the possibility of removing their business activities from state interference by the prospects of attracting foreign investment and by the opening up of external markets. This is a group of companies, which are managed by CEOs with great personal motivation – some sort of 'excellent students' – who would most likely work well under any economic condition, whether it be socialism, capitalism, or transitional economy.

By 1993-1994, the privatisation of this type of 'progressive' enterprise, inspired by the enthusiasm of their CEOs, was over. It was now realised, that to work on ones own, under conditions of competition, with inexperienced personnel, and with foreign companies, required new knowledge, initiative and entrepreneurial skills that the majority of CEOs did not posses. The expectation that mass privatisation would be stimulated by initiatives 'from below' has turned into disillusionment under these conditions. Many CEOs became simply disinterested in privatising their enterprises. Some international credit organisations have demanded more privatisation and enterprise reform as preconditions for issuing loans. As a consequence, pressure from the government now began a process of privatisation 'from above'. This process is essentially of a formal nature, directed at creating an appearance of reform.

Only during the first years of the transitional period (1991-1994) did privatisation have a voluntary nature and resulted in positive changes. After 1994, the idea of privatisation was discredited, and had turned into forced corporatisation of enterprises.

The privatisation of small enterprises, i.e. in the retail trade, public catering and housing services has failed. Assessments by international financial corporations demonstrate that the share of the privatised objects reached 70% in trade, 51% in public catering and only 36% in housing service.

Another feature of privatisation in Belarus is the absence of foreign investors, without whom any active restructuring requiring larger investments is impossible. The data shows that foreign investors participate only in 9% of the privatised companies, and joint ventures are created only in 10.5% of all companies examined.

A tendency to privatise those enterprises that have an unsatisfactory financial situation and demonstrate bad business practices has recently been observed. Such 'reforming' of enterprises is accompanied by the numerous audits, and sometimes by changes of the management. The paradox of this situation is that the government already has insufficient tools and means of managing and monitoring state-owned companies. At the same time, having instituted management and monitoring at the corporatised companies, by means of Supervisory Councils, Boards, State Representatives, 'golden' shares and the like, has provided the government with many efficient and transparent enough instruments. As this investigation shows privatisation turns into a tool for increased state monitoring of enterprises under such conditions, and making it one of the incentives for the state owned enterprises to work better.

3 Restructuring of industrial enterprises in Belarus

The restructuring of enterprises requires creating organisational structures and control systems to increase both operational and administrative efficiencies. The important components of the restructuring process are investing in machinery and equipment, and in developing and introducing new products. In the intermediate and the long term, the enterprises will need capital – both their own funds and long-term loans – to finance modernisation. The process of restructuring requires hard budget constraints for industrial companies, a reduction of grants, unilateral transfers and 'soft' credits for businesses, a clear definition of exit procedures, of conditions to develop competitiveness, liberalisation of prices, etc..

We distinguish between active or operational and passive, i.e. legal and/or financial, restructuring. Active restructuring comprises among other things the replacement of out-of-date equipment, the opening up of new markets and the closing or (alternately) the expansion of enterprises. Actually, it means a specific diagnosis and 'treatment' for each individual enterprise. Passive restructuring, on the other hand, means the development of rather general approaches, applicable to all (or nearly all) enterprises, and is capable of having quick short-term effects.

Usually, active restructuring should occur after privatisation. This kind of restructuring can best be realised by a private owner, who knows what equipment must be purchased, what product lines should be abandoned or expanded, and what type of workers should be employed or if necessary dismissed. However, in the case of Belarus we often see that, when privatisation of an unprofitable enterprise is impossible, the state-owned company begins to institute some active restructuring measures under pressure from the government and from increasing competition. This often entails updating and increasing the quality of existing products and developing new ones, staff training, and improving the organisation of labour and discipline. The percentage of state-owned companies tackling such problems is higher than that of private companies (see Appendix, Table 10.10).

On the other hand, the percentage of privatised enterprises that has already implemented some active restructuring measures and is still continuing this strategy is higher than that of state-owned ones (see Appendix, Table 10.11). For privatised companies the issue of financial restructuring is still outstanding, mainly as regards selling their excessive assets and quitting unprofitable product lines. Privatised companies show more investment activity and more marketing innovations at their new markets.

It is noteworthy that almost a third of all enterprises (29.4%) had not realised any restructuring measures at all (Table 10.6). Today, more than 80% of all enterprises are realising active strategies. 83.5% of these enterprises are going to implement their active restructuring plans, and 43.6% have already done so or have taken other active measures. 55.5% of all enterprises are planning to implement passive restructuring measures, and 57.6% have already done so.

One distinguishing feature of restructuring in Belarus is that it was conducted not only in the absence of many private owners, but also under conditions of soft budget constraints, where management had no financial and legal incentives to increase the efficiency of their enterprises.

Table 10.6
Implementing enterprise restructuring, (% of sample)

Restructuring measures	All samples	Private companies	State-owned companies
No restructuring planned	7.80	6.86	8.62
No restructuring implemented	9.17	8.82	9.48
Restructuring never happened	29.36	31.37	27.59

Source: own calculations from interviews with CEOs

Our investigation has shown, that the following and other financial resources were affiliated with soft budget constraints: grants, subsidies, overdue indebtedness, state privileges and benefits, soft loans, budget financing, customs and tax privileges. They were considered important by 27.9% of all CEOs, including 33.0% of CEOs of privatised enterprises and 23.3% of CEOs of state-owned companies. As a whole, practically half of the examined enterprises (49.1%), in 1998-1999, used various privileges and benefits from the government (Table 10.7). In most cases, this type of support received from the government was larger for privatised enterprises (Table 10.8).

Table 10.7
Soft budget constraints in industries (in %)

Industries	Share of CEOs who considered soft budget constraints to be their most important source of new financial resources	Share of companies, benefiting from government privileges
Fuel	–	66.7
Chemical and petrochemical	25.0	25.0
Machine building and mechanical engineering	32.8	46.6
Forestry, wood processing, pulp and paper	19.2	44.4
Construction materials	25.0	58.3
Light industry	30.0	46.3
Food	27.6	54.2
Other industries	28.6	57.1
Total in a sampling	27.9	49.1

Source: own calculations from interviews with CEOs

The experience of Central and Eastern European economies shows, that the situation is usually reversed: state-owned enterprises usually work with softer budget conditions. In a certain sense, this testifies to higher motivation and mobility of the management of privatised companies, which tends to 'maximise the possibilities' in search for sources of additional rent.[3] On the whole, this situation characterises the majority of transition countries with 'partial' reforms.[4]

Table 10.8
Privileges and benefits received from the government (enterprises, %)

Benefits	Total sample	Privatised companies	State-owned companies
Favourable loans	32.1	30.0	33.9
Subsidies	5.5	4.0	6.8
Grants	14.7	18.0	11.9
Targeted budget funding	13.8	14.0	13.6
Customs holidays	6.4	6.0	6.8
Tax relieves	17.4	20.0	15.3
Currency surrender relieves	14.7	16.0	13.6
Write-offs or extending of budget contribution arrears	11.9	14.0	10.2
Other privileges and benefits	21.1	20.0	22.0

Source: own calculations from interviews with CEOs

The unique feature in the Belarus case is that enterprises receiving privileges carry out their restructuring more actively, than those working under conditions of hard budget constraints. Thus, among the enterprises that have already carried out some kind of restructuring, 74.8% had received privileges from the government, and 66.7% had received none at all.

As we all know, state-owned enterprises provided for many social services in the socialist economy: cultural, housing, public healthcare services, recreation, education etc.. Costs affiliated with these objects of social infrastructure negatively affect the efficiency of enterprise performance. In most Central and Eastern European countries, industrial companies quickly got rid of these excessive costs following their privatisation.[5]

However, in Belarus this process took the opposite direction (Table 10.9). The privatised enterprises reduced their social infrastructure, mainly, housing and children's pre-school establishments. However, the percentage of those that have sports objects, objects of public healthcare services, canteens, and cafes has increased among privatised enterprises. It is impossible to tell whether Byelorussian enterprises conducted a restructuring of their assets and got rid of their 'ballast' following privatisation.

---

3 Lieberman I.W., Restructuring of Enterprises in Eastern and Central Europe, in: Privatisation trough Restructuring, Ljubljana: CEEPN, 1994.

4 Gaydar E. T. After the Socialism. "Quarterly Bulletin of the Economists' Club", No. 1(5), 2000, Minsk.

5 Ellerman D.P. Restructuring for Privatisation, in: Privatisation through Restructuring, Ljubljana: CEEPN, 1994.

Table 10.9
Objects of social infrastructure (% of sample)

Social infrastructure object	Privatised companies		State-owned companies	
	in 1994	Now	in 1994	Now
Canteens, cafes	81.2	85.1	77.4	67.9
Spas	35.6	37.6	27.4	23.6
Clubs	31.7	33.7	27.4	26.4
Education objects	15.8	16.8	11.3	9.4
Living quarters	67.3	56.4	57.5	49.1
Sports objects	26.7	35.6	19.8	27.4
Healthcare objects	35.6	38.6	34.0	36.8
Kindergartens	46.5	42.6	41.5	29.2

Source: own calculations from interviews with CEOs

On the other hand, our sample also shows that there are fewer state-owned enterprises, which carry objects of social infrastructure than privatised ones. Moreover, the state-owned enterprises – whose CEOs after all have no long-term motivation – got rid of the so-called social assets more actively. Is it possible to explain this fact, which most likely is an exception in Eastern European practice?

Firstly, there is no internal competition to stimulate cost reduction.

Secondly, wages at the majority of industrial enterprises in Belarus are strictly limited and poorly differentiated, irrespective of the form of company ownership. Therefore, higher social costs can be considered an incentive for attracting more efficient labour, i.e. for 'binding' workers to their jobs.

What encourages Byelorussian enterprises – even the formally non-state-owned ones – to conduct active restructuring, though they are receiving numerous state privileges and benefits? It is possible to give some answers to this rather paradoxical phenomenon.

For many decades Byelorussian state-owned enterprises used to be part of an economic environment, which was largely closed to the competing influences of the advanced market economies. Their main incentives were to widen their capacities and increase production volumes. Minor attention was given to the problems of profitability, efficiency, productivity, or in other words, to all conditions, which determine competitiveness. At the beginning of the reforms towards a market economy, enterprise management was completely unprepared to face difficulties or discipline problems, which competitiveness imposes on enterprises.

Today the situation has radically changed. On one hand, active responses are provoked by the growing competitiveness of Russian manufacturers, who are displacing Byelorussian production not only on the Russian market, but even on the domestic Byelorussian market. On the other hand, without an active response and without going into a competition for increasing sales volumes in the Russian, Ukrainian or European markets, where market rules instead of scheduled instructions from the Byelorussian government apply, it will be impossible to increase production. Meanwhile, the Byelorussian government is trying to urge enterprises to restructure by issuing administrative orders.

Ideological support imposed for realising reforms and prescribing economic policy were not welcomed by many CEOs of state-owned enterprises (nor by privatised ones either). They understood that – though working in a new environment – if reform was continued, they might loose their positions. Therefore, the new economic policy of the day fell on fertile ground. Many relieved CEOs continued to work in the clear and familiar conditions of socialist planned economies. And, since for some time privatisation went simply on inertia, practically no enterprises had been privatised by the year 2000.

Also, many CEOs of state-owned enterprises presumably expect, that active co-operation towards improving the working of the enterprises will allow them to avoid privatisation, and thus preserve their control and status.

The situation with restructuring reflects well the general situation in the economy and proves that some enterprises, especially those, privatised right at the beginning of the 1990s, went on to 'a second round' of restructuring. If earlier on restructuring was made to adapt to market conditions, now it was necessary for enterprises again to produce the behaviour suitable to the requirements of a centralised economy.

Businesses face a problem when adapting to an external environment. On the one hand, they must change behavioural market strategy, and on the other hand they must change internal organisation variables, including the leading executives' skills, the climate (the relations culture) inside a company, the structure of power, their managerial methods and organisational structure, as well as their management staff's organisational capabilities.

It was felt that in the case of Belarus, it was not possible to use a conventional approach and to consider restructuring as the only certain process of adapting to the market economy. The Byelorussian view is that restructuring is 'the adaptation of businesses to what exists in reality'.

4 Conclusions

The investigation conducted in this article allows to reach the following conclusions concerning the reasons and the nature of economic growth in Belarus.

Despite high inflation, the economic growth in Belarus since 1997 has acquired a stable enough quality. The growth rates of industrial output appear even higher than the GDP growth rates.

In a number of cases the economic growth in Belarus bears an extensive nature, allowing economic growth partly to be explained by statistical parameter distortions, i.e. disproportionate prices and exchange rates under severe government regulation of the economy.

At the same time, the structural reorganisation of the economy of Belarus is now in progress. On the one hand, there is some reallocation of resources into more productive spheres and producing industries, and on the other hand, former socialist enterprises are now starting restructuring.

Different from other countries in Central and Eastern Europe, a powerful new private sector has yet to be established in Belarus. The key role in maintaining economic growth belongs to the restructuring of existing enterprises and some sort of 're-educating of the children of socialism'.

Maintaining production growth is the essence and remains the primary task for the CEOs of all state owned and private enterprises. Reaching this goal requires in most cases a search for new markets and expansion of existing ones. Such an expansion requires competition on the external markets mainly, where the principles and rules of an administrative economy are not valid. The influence of these external factors will also force many enterprises to conduct active pro-market restructuring.

Refusing to acknowledge the need for economic reforms, the government of Belarus had created economic and administrative conditions, essentially quite similar to the conditions of the earlier socialist administrative-and-command system. The motivations of many CEOs and the structure of management at the majority of industrial enterprises, born in socialism, was perfectly adapted to work within the framework of such a system. In that system your success as a manager did not depend on your market performance, but on plan fulfilment, on respecting all the formal conditions and procedures, on being skilful at agreeing with the ministries and governmental bodies. Thus, restructuring as a process of adapting enterprises to market requirements appeared to many enterprises as either not necessary at all or as necessary only to the degree to which they depended on external markets competitiveness.

Appendix

Table 10.10
Passive enterprise restructuring, (% of sample)

Restructuring measures	Total sample			Privatised companies			State-owned enterprises		
	planned	in process	already done	planned	in process	already done	planned	in process	already done
Measures of passive restructuring:	*55.50*	*60.09*	*57.80*	*55.88*	*64.71*	*56.86*	*55.17*	*56.03*	*58.62*
Laying-off	16.51	14.68	16.06	15.69	15.69	12.75	17.24	13.79	18.97
Change of employment structure	19.72	19.27	7.80	18.63	21.57	7.84	20.69	17.24	7.76
Changes of organisation structure	14.22	18.35	19.27	14.71	20.59	20.59	13.79	16.38	18.10
Developing structural units into independent corporate entities	11.93	6.88	9.17	13.73	7.84	5.88	10.34	6.03	12.07
Abandoning loss-making products/services	20.64	19.27	33.03	15.69	24.51	35.29	25.00	14.66	31.03
Selling off unnecessary assets	19.72	16.97	12.84	21.57	16.67	14.71	18.10	17.24	11.21
Leasing off unnecessary assets	10.09	16.51	19.72	13.73	22.55	20.59	6.90	11.21	18.97
Cutting social expenditures	16.06	13.30	9.63	16.67	14.71	8.82	15.52	12.07	10.34
Prolongation or writing off indebtedness	8.26	12.84	5.50	7.84	14.71	4.90	8.62	11.21	6.03

Source: own calculations from interviews with CEOs

Table 10.11
Active enterprise restructuring, (% of sample)

Restructuring measures	Total sample			Privatised companies			State-owned enterprises		
	planned	in process	already done	planned	in process	already done	planned	in process	already done
Measures of active restructuring:	*83.49*	*83.03*	*43.58*	*82.35*	*83.33*	*37.25*	*84.48*	*82.76*	*49.14*
New forms of products promotion	30.73	23.39	4.59	30.39	27.45	6.86	31.03	19.83	2.59
New distribution channels	24.77	19.72	4.13	27.45	18.63	4.90	22.41	20.69	3.45
Exterior investors attraction	31.65	9.17	2.29	28.43	10.78	2.94	34.48	7.76	1.72
New production technologies implementation	33.03	32.57	13.30	37.25	38.24	15.69	29.31	27.59	11.21
Increasing products/services quality	19.72	44.50	15.14	22.55	42.16	17.65	17.24	46.55	12.93
New product development	28.44	45.41	17.89	33.33	45.10	16.67	24.14	45.69	18.97
Renewing existing products	20.64	41.28	14.22	17.65	45.10	11.76	23.28	37.93	16.38
New market segments allocation	29.82	33.49	5.50	35.29	36.27	6.86	25.00	31.03	4.31
Staff training	19.72	44.50	13.30	16.67	53.92	13.73	22.41	36.21	12.93
Labour organisation improvement	19.27	38.07	8.26	17.65	44.12	6.86	20.69	32.76	9.48
Changing remuneration system and motivation	22.02	29.36	7.34	27.45	34.31	7.84	17.24	25.00	6.90
Improving labour discipline	11.93	45.41	15.60	13.73	50.98	11.76	10.34	40.52	18.97
Staff assessment system change	17.89	17.43	4.59	23.53	18.63	2.94	12.93	16.38	6.03

Source: own calculations from interviews with CEOs

11

Performance of Small and Medium Sized Manufacturing Firms in Ukraine: Does the Quality of Governance Matter?[1]

Iryna Akimova

1 Introduction

Small and medium sized enterprises (SME) represent the most dynamic firms in the transitional economies. Development of SMEs is influenced by several factors[2] among which the quality of the business environment is playing the most important role. The business environment is shaped by the quality of governance which is measured by the effectiveness of the state in providing the institutional infrastructure corresponding to the standards of a well-functioning market economy (Kaufmann et al., 1999). A low quality of governance is associated with insecure property rights, weak enforcement of contracts via legal institutions, and a non-transparent and inefficient tax and regulatory framework.

Empirical studies by Kaufmann et al. (1999), Hellman et al. (2000a, b), Johnson et al. (1999) show that countries with a better quality of governance perform better both on a country and on the firm level. However, cross-country studies, which focus on relating the differences in performance outcomes to the differences in the *absolute* level of governance indicators across these countries, do not address the question of the impact of the quality of governance on the performance results of the firms *within* the country.

---

1 This reseach was financially supported by INTAS grant N 952-280 and a Humboldt Research Fellowship.

2 Recent studies point at legal and regulatory restrictions, limited access to external financing, and the lack of managerial skills as main factors that influence the development of SMEs in transitional economies (see e.g. Brunetti et al., 1997, Hallberg, 1999, Pissarides, 1998, Tolentino, 2000, Theocharides and Tolentino, 2000).

In our chapter, we suggest that within a given country it is not only the *overall* size of the governance indicators (like the average level of corruption, regulatory burden or tax evasion) but their *variation* between firms that determines the firms' performance and future growth plans. We study the impact of the quality of governance on the firms' performance under conditions of a high corruption-and-tax-avoidance environment, using the reliability of contract enforcement by the legal system, extralegal payments, the regulatory burden and the level of tax avoidance as proxies for the quality of governance.

2 Business environment for SMEs in Ukraine

In Ukraine, the share of small enterprises in total output and total employment is not high: in 2000 it constituted 8.4% and 8% respectively. More than a half of Ukrainian small firms is involved in trade and services. Manufacturing enterprises account for 14% of the total number of small firms, producing 21% of their total output.

Real efforts in facilitating the development of SMEs started in 1997 with the establishment of the State Committee on Regulatory Policy and Entrepreneurship which focused on improving the regulatory environment by simplifying the registration procedure, clarifying the rules for conducting inspections by state agencies, and making regulatory policy more transparent. However, several surveys of Ukrainian SMEs conducted by the IFC and SIEAG in 1998 and 1999 showed that the average annual number of inspections experienced by SMEs remained the same, i.e. 9.7 (Yacoub and Senchuk, 2000).

Enforcement of economic rules constitutes a serious problem. On the country level, this is reflected in the gap between the extent and effectiveness of the legal reform, meaning that relatively comprehensive laws are not being properly implemented (EBRD, 2000). On the company level, this is reflected in distrust in the legal procedures of contract enforcement by the Arbitrage Courts. According to Johnson et al. (1999), almost 50% of Ukrainian managers held that opinion in 1998.

Weak enforcement of economic rules leads to a large shadow economy and a high level of corruption. Today, the shadow sector in Ukraine is estimated to range between 40% and 50% of GDP, with the level of tax evasion between 11% and 17% of GDP (Mel'ota, Thiessen, and Vakhnenko, 2001). About 70% of Ukrainian enterprises pay bribes to public officials. The average annual size of these bribes amounted to 6.5% of the companies' revenues (Hellman et al., 2000).

Therefore, Ukraine can be described as a country with a high level of corruption and weak property rights.

3 The quality of governance and SME development

Good governance requires the establishment of predictable, non-arbitrary rules for business activities and an effective legal enforcement of property rights and contracts. This means that *equal rules* apply to all business activities, so that enterprises compete with each other on the basis of economic efficiency, and that the allocation of productive resources favours more efficient firms. When the economic rules of business activity vary between companies, enterprises might receive advantages on the grounds other than economic efficiency.

Variations of economic rules for companies could be *systematic or non-systematic*. Both types of variations could be connected to the content of economic legislation and its practical implementation. *Systematic variations* occur if select groups of firms experience favours over time. On the *content* side, systematic variations are connected to legal privileges (e.g. direct subsidisation, tax exemption, etc.) granted to select groups of firms. On the implementational side, systematic variations are observed where favourable interpretations of economic rules are made, or/and where bias is shown by tolerating violations of the economic rules. Systematic variations in economic rules are most often associated with large firms.

Non-systematic variations are typical in the SME sector. They occur when inequalities in economic rules over time are not associated with select groups of enterprises. On the *content* side, non-systematic variations are connected with frequent changes of economic legislation, with differences in the speed of dissemination of the information about new legislation to the firms, and with differences in their adjustment costs.

Implementational non-systematic variations are due to several reasons. Firstly, poorly defined or excessively complicated economic rules allow for differences in their interpretation and implementation by public officials who use them for extracting bribes. Secondly, frequent changes of public officials produce unpredictable changes in the "rules" and in the costs of bribing. Thirdly, weak enforcement mechanisms for economic rules allow for different violations of these rules by different firms without favouring any particular group (e.g. tax avoidance).

Both, the systematic and non-systematic variations in economic rules for companies within the country have a negative impact on economic development. Systematic variations lead to reallocations of resources in favour of particular groups of firms, which are not necessarily the most effective ones. Non-systematic variations increase the risk and uncertainty of conducting business operations. They therefore dampen future investment and change the incentive structure of the firms, substituting the desire for increasing economic efficiency by a desire to receive incentives or advantages via bribing of public officials and "shadowing" the firm's operations.

Within the country, it is not only the overall level of governance indicators, but also the variation in economic rules applying to companies that is damaging for the efficient allocation of resources and for sustainable growth. For example, no matter how high the average level of the tax burden or bribes in the country, as long as they are *predictable and equally implemented* across all firms, it only means additional costs for them, but incentives for efficiency improvements are not challenged. When economic rules are badly enforced and frequently changed and vary significantly between firms, market success is connected with an ability to violate these rules, and incentives for efficiency improvements are partly substituted by incentives for extralegal activities.

Empirically this inequality in economic rules within a country could be captured by testing the existence of a significant relationship between the firm's performance and governance variables. Therefore, in our paper we test the hypothesis that there is a significant relationship between the short run performance of small Ukrainian manufacturing companies, on the one hand, and the quality of governance measured by the level of insecurity about property rights, tax avoidance, and the regulatory burden, on the other.

Property rights: Insecurity about property rights affects the performance of companies in several ways. Ill-defined and ineffectively enforced property rights, firstly, restrict the willingness of private owners to invest. Secondly they reduce the availability of external financing for enterprise development and they increase their cost (by raising the debt collecting risk). Finally they increase the firms' transaction costs and push them into developing various informal contract enforcement mechanisms and into corruption (see e.g. Hendley, Murrell, and Ryterman, 1999).

Insecurity about property rights is reflected in a general distrust in the legal system's ability to enforce contracts via the Arbitrage Courts, and a belief in systemic administrative corruption. The low trust in the Arbitrage Courts is based on the negative past personal experiences by management, and is related to the length of the court procedures, the persistence of outside influence on court judgements, and the difficulty of enforcing the judgements. Even if the effectiveness of the Arbitrage Courts increases, perceptions of the managers will not immediately improve. Management will continue to ignore legal instruments of contract enforcement till positive experiences become dominant.

We expect a negative impact of the no-trust-in-the-courts perceptions by managers on the performance results and the growth plans of their firms.

Extralegal payments for different licenses, permits and government services (administrative corruption) as well as payments for "protection" of business activities represent a portion of a company's earnings that is captured by bureaucrats and "protectors". The impact of extralegal payments on the short run performance of the firm depends on the *overall level of insecurity about property rights and on corruption in the country.* If it is relatively low, protection for the business activity and all necessary licenses and permits can normally be obtained without extralegal payments. Bribes are mostly paid by poorly performing firms that would like to continue their operations by violating some regulations. In such a case, making extralegal payments is often associated with a bad short run performance.

On the other hand, if the overall level of insecurity about property rights and corruption in the country is high, "informal" payments are the only way to obtain the protection and the licences and permits necessary to legally continue the company's activity. Those who do not bribe might face losses connected with a break in operations caused by the unavailability of the necessary permits or by a lack of "protection". Therefore, making extralegal payments minimises these types of losses and is associated with better short run performance.

The existence of a positive relationship between informal payments for licenses and protection, on the one hand, and short run performance results or growth plans of the firms, on the other, which we expect to find in our study, will indicate a high level of insecurity about property rights and corruption, making the payment of bribes a necessary precondition for the firm's growth.

Tax evasion is an anecdotal fact for transitional economies with a weak institutional framework. The impact of tax evasion on the firm's performance also depends on the overall level of tax discipline in the country, which is related to the quality of governance. In a low-tax-evasion economy the state imposes strong tax discipline, and chances to be found in violation of the tax rules as well as the costs of violation are very high. Thus, tax evaders are – on the average – worse performers. In high-tax-evasion countries, tax evasion generates substantial gains to the evading firms (since they keep larger parts of their profits) and thus has a positive impact on the short run performance.

Tax avoidance produces negative externalities to all other firms in high-tax-evasion economies. Firstly, under conditions of poor tax collection, the state has a need to increase the tax rates which negatively affects profits of all firms. Secondly, differences in the actual taxes paid by different firms provide tax-evaders with some kind of an indirect "subsidies" (uncollected share of taxes), supporting their survival and giving them better financial opportunities for growth. Productive resources are re-allocated in favour of tax-evaders, which are not necessarily the most efficient firms.

If the regulatory environment allows for a significant variation in the level of tax evasion across firms (non-systematic implementational variations are high), we will observe a significant positive relationship between the level of tax evasion and a firm's performance.

The existence of such a relationship, which we expect to find in our study, will signal a weakness of the regulatory system that provides the wrong incentives for growth and, in the long run, leads to efficiency losses at the company level.

Regulatory burden: The regulatory environment reflects the level and efficiency of state interference in the business activities of private agents. Inconsistent and non-transparent economic rules provide possibilities for excess interference by state agencies in the operations of private firms. This results in a large number of inspections imposed on business firms by different state inspection agencies. Frequent inspections impose a "time tax" (Hellman and Schankerman, 2000) and causes high penalties to those firms whose activities do not meet with full regulatory compliance, opening a door to collecting bribes. Inconsistent and non-transparent commercial legislation, as well as its frequent changes, increases the effective regulatory burden by pushing up compliance costs for the firms and enlarging "time" and "bribe" taxes.

We expect a negative impact of a high regulatory burden on the enterprise performance results and future growth plans.

4 Data

For our analysis we used the data from a survey of 265 small and medium size Ukrainian business firms (with fewer than 200 employees) that are involved in manufacturing activities. The sample was generated from the official books of these companies. The survey was conducted in the late fall of 2000 in the three regions with the highest concentration of SMEs in Ukraine (namely Kyiv, Kharkiv and Donetzk). It was carried out in the form of personal interviews with the managers/owners of the firms on the basis of a prepared questionnaire.

In this paper we use a sub-set of 151 enterprises that reported that their income derived mainly from manufacturing. The descriptive characteristics of the sample are presented in Table 11.1 in the Appendix.

5 Estimation equation and variables

The equation to be estimated is the following:

$$P = a + \sum_i b_i INDUSTRY + \sum_j c_j REGION + dSIZE + eSTARTUP + \sum_k f_k ENVIR$$

where P represents performance variables, $\sum_i b_i INDUSTRY$, $\sum_j c_j REGION$, and $dSIZE$ measure industry, region and size related effects, $eSTARTUP$ represents the "green field" effect and $\sum_k e_k ENVIR$ measures the effects of the business environment. Logistic regression is chosen as the estimation procedure, since independents are represented by dummy variables.

Performance: Performance is measured as the managers' assessment of the change in sales volume and labour productivity (sales volume per employee) in 2000 comparing to 1999. SALES and LABPROD are dummy variables that are equal to 1, if the manager reported an increase in sales volume and labour productivity respectively in 2000, compared to the previous year; otherwise they take a value of 0.

Two variables are chosen to represent the managers' expectations concerning future growth of their firms. EMPLOY is a dummy variable that equals to one if the manager reported an intention to increase the number of employees in 2001 (compared to 2000). GROWTHSL is a dummy variable that takes the value of 1 if the manager reported an expected growth of sales volume for 2001 compared to 2000. In 2000, around two-fifth of the surveyed firms experienced growth in sales volume (46.4%) and labour productivity (39.7%).

Business environment: Four proxies for the quality of the business environment are used in our analysis.

Property rights: Following the approach by Johnson et al. (1999), two dummy variables were constructed with values equal to 1 if the managers reported regular unofficial payments for licenses and government services, and for „protection", respectively. For the regressions, the two measures were combined into an index of property rights insecurity for each firm: INFPAY, ranging from 0 to 2. 0 indicates that a manager reported no unofficial payments, 1 reflects that one type of payment was common, and 2 represents the highest level of insecurity about property rights. This index is additive, meaning that a positive response of a firm to more than one question represents a greater level of insecurity than responding to only one (Johnson et al., 1999). The mean value for the index of insecurity about property rights is 0.80 (standard deviation 0.68). Our data suggests a high level of corruption and insecurity about property rights. Only about one third of the enterprises did not make any informal payments. Two thirds of the firms paid for different state services, licences, permits and other business documentation, about 16% of the enterprises paid for protection.

Contract enforcement: ARBITRAGE is a dummy variable which equals 1 if the manager stated that he would not use the Arbitrage Courts to enforce a commercial contract with bad debtors. About two thirds of the managers (63.6%) had a negative attitude towards the Arbitrage Courts as a means of contract enforcement.

Regulatory burden: The index of regulatory burden REGUL measures the total number of different inspections (by tax, fire, sanitary, ecological, standardisation and certification, antimonopoly, architecture, and other state institutions, as well as the police) experienced by the firm during first six months of 2000. For the regressions we combined nine measures of regulatory burden into one index for each firm. The index for the regulatory burden is additive, too. The mean value for the regulatory index is 4.35 (standard deviation 6.07), it ranges from 0 to 43 indicating a great variation in the total number of inspections experienced during the first half of 2000.

Tax evasion: Tax evasion is measured using a self-reported level of actual tax payment as a percentage of the total amount of taxes to be paid by the firm without being involved in tax-evasion schemes. The managers' answers were used to create a variable of actual tax payment: TAXES. Conversely, the variable TEVASION is equal to (100 - TAXES), representing the level of tax evasion. The mean value for TEVASION was 40.46 (standard deviation 27.28), it ranged from 0 to 90 suggesting that in terms of taxation the firms were treated unequally. Our data shows that one third of the firms were paying between 60% and 80% of taxes, more than 40% of the firms paid less than 60% of taxes, and only 12.9% of the enterprises were "honest tax payers".

Controls: As control variables we used regional (REGION) and industry (INDUSTRY) dummies, the firm's size (SIZE) measured by the number of employees in 2000, and the dummy STARTUP, which is equal to 1 if the company reported to have been newly created as a private firm.

6 Regression results

Table 11.2 (in the Appendix) presents the results of regressions with the short run performance indicators as dependent variables. Our dependent variables are dummy ones, therefore a positive coefficient indicates that an increase in the level of the independent variable increases the chance that a firm falls into the category of "better performers". The first set of logistic regressions with an increase in sales volume and labour productivity in 2000 as dependent variables is reported in columns 2 and 3 of Table 11.2.

Two governance variables out of four are significant, supporting our hypothesis of a weak business environment in Ukraine in providing small firms with equal possibilities to secure property rights and enforce contracts. The index for extralegal payments is significant and positive, indicating the existence of a high level of corruption where bribing increases a company's chances to become a "better performer". The measure of distrust in the Arbitrage Courts is negative and significant at the 0.05 level. This supports our hypothesis that a weak legal system of contract enforcement has a negative impact on a firm's performance. The regulatory index and the tax-evasion variable have predicted signs, but turn out to be insignificant. The dummy for start-ups is significant and positive in the labour-productivity-growth regression showing that newly created firms are more likely to show efficiency growth then enterprises with a previous state-ownership history.

Columns 4 and 5 of Table 11.2 report the results of regressions with a planned increase in the number of employees and in sales volume in 2001 as dependent variables. Again, the governance variables (two for employment regression and three for sales volume regression) turn out to be significant. It is striking that the tax-evasion variable is significant and positive in both growth plan regressions. This suggests that tax-evaders are more likely to have growth plans than honest tax-payers, or other words, tax evasion becomes a condition for growth plans of small manufacturing firms. The no-trust-in-the-courts variable is again significant and negative in both growth plan regressions indicating that a weak legal contract enforcement system erodes future growth plans of small firms. The index for extralegal payments is positive and significant in the future-sales-growth equation suggesting that firms that are involved in extralegal payments for protection and in administrative bribes are more likely to plan market growth strategies than non-payers.

We do not find any evidence that regional, industry and size criteria have any significant effect on performance results.

7 Conclusions and policy implications

This paper provides empirical evidence of the weakness of the business environment in Ukraine, which is characterised by a high level of corruption, insecurity about property rights, a weak legal system for contract enforcement, and extensive tax evasion. This reflects the lack of reforms to improve the legal system effectiveness, and a failure of attempts to improve the business climate in 2000.

Our findings suggest that the regulatory environment in Ukraine fails to establish *equal conditions* for all small firms in terms of security about property rights, enforcement of contracts, and tax burden. The empirical proof of the existence of this environmental inequality is an important warning for the policy makers: the regulatory system provides strong incentives for businesses to favour bribes and tax evasion. This leads to economic losses for the state (lost taxes) and for firms (extorted profits) and, in the long run, to the inefficient allocation of productive resources. Since the variations in the environmental variables that we have studied, are rather of an implementational than a content nature, our findings provide empirical evidence for the importance of implementation and administration mechanisms for economic rules in countries with a weak overall regulatory framework.

Our findings seem to prove that *within the group of high-corruption-and-tax-avoidance countries* negative externalities are produced *by variations in the level of corruption and tax avoidance across all firms.* This means that given similar absolute average levels of bribes and tax avoidance, *countries with a larger variation in the level of these indicators*, should show *worse performances at the enterprise level* than countries where these environmental conditions, within which firms operate, are more equal. Testing of this hypothesis on a cross-country data set is the subject of further research.

The result of our analysis shows that a lack of trust in the legal institutions like the Arbitrage Courts as the means of contract enforcement, negatively influences performance results and growth plans of SMEs.

To summarise, our findings suggest the following policy implications:

- In an economy with a weak regulatory environment and a high level of corruption, the administration and implementation of the rules is at least as important as improving the quality of the rules as such, since they shape the incentive structures of businesses. Providing equal possibilities for all firms in terms of security about property rights and enforcement of contracts, as well as insisting on their equal responsibilities for paying taxes, are basic conditions for promoting efficiency in the development of SMEs.
- New tax and regulatory acts should be assessed for their effects on corruption, using the criteria *of simplicity and stability.* Simple and transparent rules make it easier for the entrepreneurs to understand and follow them, and for the state to implement them. At the same time, simple and clear legislation offers fewer possibilities for arbitrary interpretation by lower level bureaucrats and, hence narrows the scope for administrative corruption. Once adopted, the major tax and regulatory rules should be kept stable, at least for the medium run. This will help to reduce uncertainty in decision making, positively influencing future investment and growth.
- An effective performance of the Arbitrage Courts is an essential condition for SME development.
- Reductions of the long waiting times for judgements by the Arbitrage Courts and developing effective mechanisms for implementing its decisions could increase the trust in the legal institutions as means for contract enforcement.

References

Brunetti, A., G. Kisunko, and B. Weder (1997): Institutional Obstacles to Doing Business. World Bank Policy Research Paper No. 1759.

EBRD (2000): Transition Report.

Hallberg, K. (1999): A Market Oriented Strategy for Small and Medium Scale Enterprises. IFC Discussion paper No. 40, IFC.

Hellman, J. S., G. Jones, D. Kaufmann, and M. Schankerman (2000a): Measuring Governance, Corruption, and State Capture. How Firms and Bureaucrats Shape the Business Environment in Transitional Economies. World Bank Policy Research Working Paper No. 2312, April.

Hellman, J. S., G. Jones, and D. Kaufmann (2000b): Seize the State, Seize the Day. State Capture, Corruption, and Influence in Transition. World Bank Policy Research Working Paper No. 2444, The World Bank.

Hellman, J. and M. Schankerman (2000): Intervention, Corruption and Capture: The Nexus between Enterprises and the State. Economic of Transition, Vol. 8(3), pp. 545-576.

Hendley, K., P. Murrell, and R. Ryterman (1999): Law, Relationships, and Private Enforcement: Transactional Strategies of Russian Enterprises. World Bank Policy Research Paper, January.

Johnson, S., D. Kaufmann, J. McMillan, and C. Woodruff (1999): Why Do Firms Hide? Bribes and Unofficial Activity after Communism. Working Paper, MIT, June.

Johnson, S., J. McMillan, and C. Woodruff (1999): Property Rights, Finance, and Entrepreneurship. Working Paper, MIT, June.

Kaufmann, D., A. Kraay and P. Zoido-Lobatón (1999): Governance Matters. Policy Research Working Paper No. 2196, The World Bank, October.

Mel'ota I., U. Thiessen, and T. Vakhnenko (2001): Fiscal and Regulatory Causes of the Shadow Economies in Transition Countries: The Case of Ukraine, IERPC, Kyiv.

Pissarides, F. (1998): Is Lack of Funds the Main Obstacle to Growth? EBRD Working Paper No. 33, EBRD, November.

Shleifer, A. and R. Vishny (1998): Politicians and Firms. Quarterly Journal of Economics, pp. 995-1025.

Theocharides, S. and A. Tolentino (2000): Strengthening Existing Small Enterprises. Small Enterprise Development Working paper, SED 21/3.

Tolentino, A.(2000): Guidelines for the Analysis of Policies and Programs for Small and Medium Enterprise Development. Enterprise and Management Development Working Paper, EMD 13/E.

Yacoub, M. and B. Senchuk (2000): The State of Small Business in Ukraine: The IFC Survey of Ukrainian Small Enterprises. IFC, Kyiv.

Appendix

Table 11.1
Characteristics of the sample

	Number of enterprises (% of total)
Type of ownership in 2000	
Private firm/partnership	93 (61.6%)
Joint-stock company	54 (35.8%)
State enterprise	4 (2.6%)
Size (number of employees) in 2000	
1-10	27 (18.1%)
11-25	50 (33.6%)
26-50	41 (27.5%)
51-100	25 (16.8%)
>100	8 (4%)
Industry	
Machine-building	42 (27.8%)
Food industry	20 (13.2%)
Light industry	19 (12.6%)
Wood processing	16 (10.6%)
Construction materials	13 (8.6%)
Chemical industry	9 (6.0%)
Medical industry	6 (4.0%)
Printing	6 (4.0%)
Colour metallurgy	4 (2.6%)
Others	16 (10.5%)
Region	
Kyiv	66 (43.7%)
Kharkiv	66 (43.7%)
Donetzk	19 (12.6%)

Source: own survey

Table 11.2
Determinants of the performance results and growth plans of Ukrainian SMEs

Independents	Dependent: SALES	Dependent: LABPROD	Dependent: EMPLOY	Dependent: GROWTHSL
Business environment				
REGULAT	-0.08 (0.06)	-0.08 (0.06)	-0.03 (0.05)	-0.001 (0.06)
TEVASION	0.007 (0.001)	0.015 (0.09)	0.03** (0.01)	0.02* (0.01)
INFPAY	0.84** (0.43)	0.53 (0.43)	0.38 (0.43)	1.17** (0.49)
ARBITRAGE	-1.64** (0.53)	-1.4** (0.54)	-1.35** (0.55)	-1.96** (0.56)
Controls				
START-UP	0.45 (0.68)	1.65** (0.86)	1.07 (0.75)	0.48 (0.72)
SIZE	0.008 (0.01)	0.004 (0.003)	0.009 (0.01)	0.01 (0.01)
INDUSTRY	Y	Y	Y	Y
REGION	Y	Y	Y	Y
Constant	-1.0 (1.42)	-1.50 (1.45)	-2.11 (1.59)	-1.05 (1.5)
Chi-sq.	17.5**	19.2**	21.0**	32.1**
Percent correct	87.2	87.2	90.4	89.9
Goodness of fit	70.4	68.1	76.1	76.1
N	150	150	149	149

*p<0.1; **p<0.05

Source: own calculations

12

The Investment Environment in Russia and Ukraine: Common Weaknesses in the Institutional and Policy Framework

Eva Thiel

1 FDI as an engine of growth

Virtually all countries – in particular developing and transition countries – are competing to boost inflows of FDI into their economies.

FDI provides a package of financial capital, technology, managerial skills, information, which, in combination with the resulting output of goods and services acts to make the economy more competitive in world markets, promoting growth and reducing poverty.

In the accepted parlance of today's globalised economy, FDI is a facet of advancing global integration, which will result in greater prosperity – as long as governance improves and people do not feel excluded from sharing in the benefits of the reforms.[1]

However, to benefit from FDI, a country must first receive it. It must be an attractive location for foreign investors and possess an adequate FDI enabling framework.

2 What constitutes the enabling framework?

The attractiveness and the enabling features are composed of several things:

1 See UNCTAD Foreign Direct Investment and the Challenge of Development, World Investment Report 1999 for a general overview of foreign investment/development linkages.

- one fundamental minimum condition is an adequate endowment, both with respect to natural resources and educated manpower;
- political and economic stability is also a *sine qua non;*
- in addition to providing a stable political environment and striving to ensure favourable macro-economic fundamentals, the government must also facilitate business development at the micro level;
- this includes providing an adequate physical and institutional infrastructure as well as the policies which aim to promote profitable investment activity;
- the administrative system for FDI also needs to be effective in dealing with foreign investors and their needs.

3 To what extent are Russia and Ukraine reaping the potential benefits of FDI?

In terms of investment received, Russia's poor record is well known: despite the large endowment of natural resources, highly educated labour force and potentially large market, only some USD 15 bn of cumulative FDI had been received by the start of 2001.

As for Ukraine, the picture is certainly no better: FDI remains marginal, with annual inflows reaching a peak of USD 743 m in 1998, otherwise staying at or below the half billion mark during the rest of the 1990's. As a result, the cumulative FDI stock has not reached beyond USD 4 bn, representing less than USD 80 per capita.

4 FDI flows to developing and transition countries

Graphs 12.1 and 12.2 show how Russia compares with other large emerging market economies and other European transition economies in terms of FDI/GDP, while Tables 12.1 to 12.3, based on UNCTAD data, set out absolute amounts of FDI flows to developing countries, including the Russian Federation, Ukraine and other transition countries.

Seen in the context of the significant increase of FDI flows in the global economy during the past decade, transition countries as a group still account for a relatively modest share of total world FDI stock, particularly when assessed in relation to their contribution to world GDP or world imports.

Graph 12.1
FDI in large emerging market economies

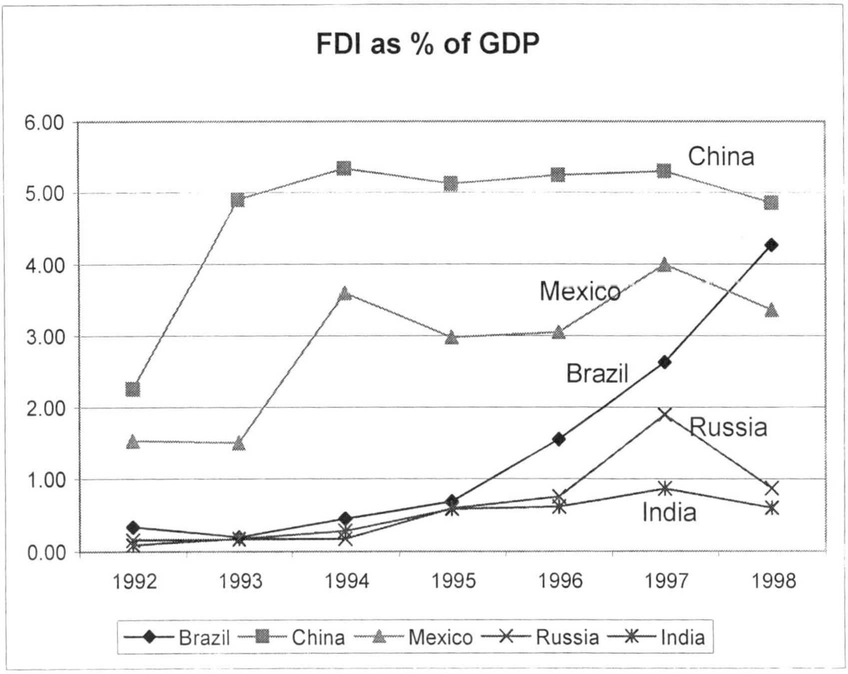

Source: IMF, International Financial Statistics; World Bank, World Development Report (2000)

Global FDI flows reached just above USD 1 trillion in 1999 and are estimated to have substantially exceeded the trillion mark in 2000. In absolute terms developing countries attracted nearly USD 200 bn, representing an all-time high and an increase by 11% over 1998. Among developing countries, Brazil continues to stand out as the main destination of FDI inflows to Latin America, followed by Argentina and Mexico. In Asia, China's still dominant position declined in relative terms with significant increases registered in newly industrialising countries such as Hong Kong China, Singapore and Taiwan (see Table 12.2).

Total FDI flows to the transition countries of Central and Eastern Europe, including Russia and Ukraine, at slightly more than USD 21 bn in 1999, still represented only 2% of the global FDI flows. As evident from Table 12.3, the transition countries currently preparing for EU accession have attracted the largest inflows in the period 1990 –1999, with Poland, Hungary and the Czech Republic as main recipients, bringing their combined FDI stocks above USD 65 bn in 1999. This compares to an estimated FDI stock in the Russian Federation of USD 17 bn in 1999 (USD 15.4 bn according to Goskomstat data). On a per capita level, inflows into Estonia, Latvia and Slovenia have also been significant – in fact placing them ahead of Poland according to this indicator. The smaller CEE countries are also those showing the highest share of FDI in terms of total fixed capital formation, with levels well above 20% for the period 1996-1998. Poland and the Czech Republic range closer to 15% in terms of this indicator, while in the Russian Federation the share of FDI in fixed capital formation remains closer to 5%, also in the period January - September 2000.

Graph 12.2
FDI in selected transition economies

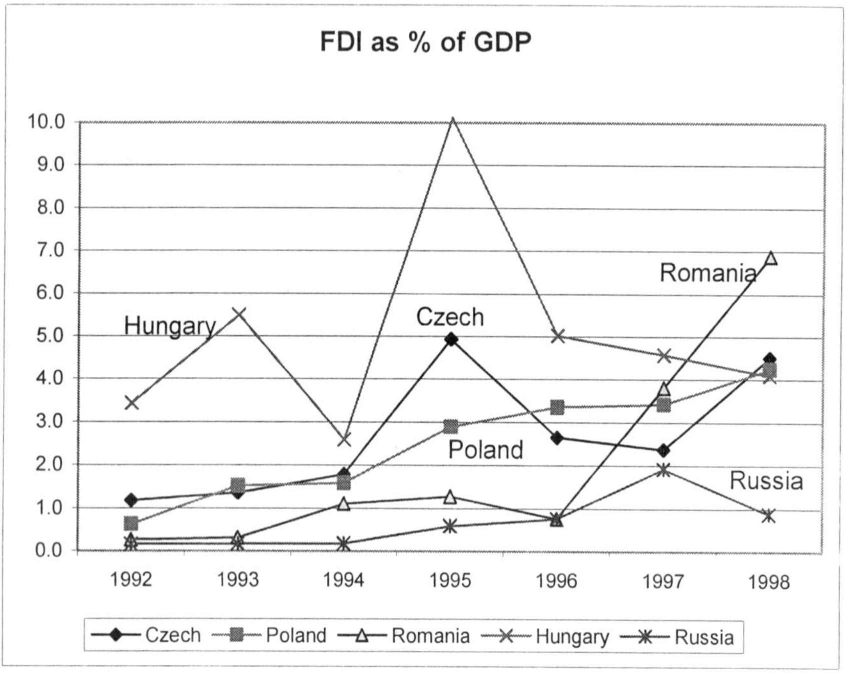

Source: IMF International Financial Statistics; World Bank World Development Report (2000)

In absolute terms, countries belonging to the former Soviet Union had negligible inflows of FDI during the transition period, with the exception of Russia, Kazakhstan and Azerbaijan. The latter group benefited from fairly substantial natural resource-related investments early in the decade but have failed to keep pace since, despite the supposedly lower sensitivity on the part of resource-seeking multinationals to economic policies and prospects of host countries. Amongst transition economies, the Russian Federation emerges as third lowest recipient of FDI over the period on a per capita basis, with Ukraine and Belarus scoring lower still, and the Russian Federation scores lowest in relation to GDP.

Table 12.1
Foreign direct investment inflows 1990–1999, by major world economic and geographical regions (USD m)

	1990	1991	1992	1993	1994	1995	1996	1997	1998	1999
World	209,220.7	160,001.9	172,111.3	226,139.7	255,785.1	331,040.5	377,231.5	473,082.0	683,304.7	1,005,957.6
Developed countries										
European Union	98,428.7	78,493.6	78,245.7	75,331.1	76,838.2	113,305.7	108,352.4	128,322.2	251,394.6	447,623.4
North America	56,005.0	25,681.0	23,945.0	55,395.0	53,302.0	68,029.0	94,091.0	117,249.0	208,752.9	300,593.2
Developing countries										
Africa	2,492.6	2,971.1	3,729.2	3,993.8	5,669.9	4,720.0	5,604.8	6,930.8	7,591.3	8,172.0
Asia	24,161.2	24,452.8	32,984.0	58,235.1	68,405.6	73,746.4	92,316.9	101,227.3	94,275.7	95,035.3
Latin America and the Caribbean	9,613.4	15,745.6	17,879.9	17,886.8	30,090.6	32,816.3	45,901.9	69,075.6	75,280.4	92,696.9

Source: UNCTAD, FDI/TNC

Table 12.2
Major recipients of World FDI Flows, selected developing countries, 1990–1999 (USD m)

	1990	1991	1992	1993	1994	1995	1996	1997	1998	1999
Africa										
Angola	- 334.8	664.5	288.0	302.1	170.1	472.4	180.6	411.7	1,113.9	1,813.8
Egypt	734.0	253.0	459.0	493.0	1,256.0	598.0	636.0	890.6	1,076.0	1,065.3
Nigeria	587.9	712.4	896.6	1,345.4	1,959.2	1,079.3	1,593.5	1,539.5	1,051.3	1,004.8
Asia										
China	3,487.0	4,366.0	11,156.0	27,515.0	33,787.0	35,849.2	40,180.0	44,237.0	43,751.0	40,319.0
Chinese Taipei	1,330.0	1,271.0	879.0	917.0	1,375.0	1,559.0	1,864.0	2,248.0	222.0	2,926.0
India	162.0	73.5	276.5	550.4	973.3	2,143.6	2,426.1	3,577.3	2,634.7	2,168.0

Table 12.2 (cont.)
Major recipients of World FDI Flows, selected developing countries, 1990–1999 (USD m)

	1990	1991	1992	1993	1994	1995	1996	1997	1998	1999
Indonesia	1,093.0	1,482.0	1,777.0	2,004.0	2,109.0	4,346.0	6,194.0	4,677.0	- 356.0	- 3,270.0
Korea	788.5	1,179.8	728.3	588.1	809.0	1,775.8	2,325.4	2,844.2	5,412.3	9,333.4
Malaysia	2,611.0	4,043.0	5,138.0	5,741.0	4,581.0	5,816.0	7,296.0	6,513.0	2,700.0	3,532.0
Singapore	5,574.7	4,887.1	2,204.3	4,686.3	8,550.2	7,206.4	8,984.3	8,085.1	5,492.8	6,984.5
Thailand	2,542.0	2,033.0	2,151.0	1,732.0	1,325.0	2,004.0	2,271.0	3,627.0	5,143.0	3,562.0
Latin America										
Argentina	1,836.0	2,439.0	4,384.0	2,763.0	3,490.0	5,315.0	6,522.0	8,755.0	6,849.0	24,131.0
Brazil	1,130.0	1,094.9	1,749.0	1,294.0	2,590.0	5,475.0	10,496.0	18,743.0	28,480.0	31,362.0
Chile	661.2	822.1	935.3	1,289.0	2,732.5	2,956.1	4,633.1	5,219.1	4,638.8	9,774.4
Colombia	500.5	456.9	728.7	959.7	1,444.5	968.3	3,111.8	5,639.3	2,961.0	1,110.0
Mexico	2,634.0	4,762.0	4,393.0	4,389.0	10,972.5	9,526.3	9,185.7	12,831.0	11,312.0	11,567.0
Peru	41.0	- 7.0	136.5	669.7	3,083.5	2,000.0	3,226.0	1,702.0	1,880.0	1,969.0
Venezuela	451.0	1,916.0	629.0	372.0	813.0	985.0	2,183.0	5,536.0	4,495.0	3,187.0

Source: UNCTAD, FDI/TNC

Table 12.3
FDI inflows to Central and Eastern Europe, Russia, Baltic and Selected Asian FSU Republics 1990-1999 (USD m)

	1992	1993	1994	1995	1996	1997	1998	1999
Albania	20.0	58.0	53.0	70.0	90.1	47.5	45.0	41.2
Azerbaijan			22.0	330.1	627.3	1,114.8	1,023.0	691.0
Belarus	7.0	17.5	10.5	14.7	72.6	200.0	149.2	225.0
Bulgaria	42.0	40.0	105.0	90.0	109.0	505.0	537.0	770.0
Croatia		120.2	117.0	115.0	506.0	517.5	893.2	1,408.0
Czech Republic	1,003.0	654.3	869.0	2,562.0	1,428.0	1,300.0	2,720.0	4,792.0
Estonia	65.0	162.2	214.4	201.5	150.5	266.7	580.6	306.4
Hungary	1,471.0	2,339.0	1,146.0	4,453.0	2,275.0	2,173.0	2,036.0	1,944.0
Kazakhstan	100.0	1,271.4	659.7	964.3	1,136.9	1,321.3	1,151.5	1,587.2
Latvia	27.0	45.1	214.5	179.6	381.7	521.1	356.7	366.2
Lithuania	10.0	30.2	31.3	72.6	152.4	354.5	925.5	486.0
Moldova	17.4	14.0	27.6	66.9	23.7	75.7	81.4	33.5

Table 12.3 (cont.)
FDI inflows to Central and Eastern Europe, Russia, Baltic and Selected Asian FSU Republics 1990-1999 (USD m)

	1992	1993	1994	1995	1996	1997	1998	1999
Poland	678.0	1,715.0	1,875.0	3,659.0	4,498.0	4,908.0	6,365.0	7,270.0
Romania	80.0	94.0	342.0	420.0	265.0	1,215.0	2,031.0	961.0
Russian Federation	700.0	1,211.0	640.0	2,016.0	2,479.0	6,638.0	2,761.3	3,309.0
Slovakia	100.0	168.0	245.0	195.0	251.0	205.6	631.1	356.0
Slovenia	111.0	112.6	128.1	175.9	185.4	320.8	165.4	181.0
Ukraine	200.0	200.0	159.0	267.0	521.0	624.0	743.0	496.0

5 What are the reasons for these low shares of FDI in Russia and Ukraine?

Delays in structural reform, suppressed competition, administrative barriers

Both countries Russia and Ukraine moved quickly with initial economic reforms, in particular price liberalisation and privatisation, although the actual privatisation pattern differed substantially in the two economies. Many structural reforms were, however, either incomplete or delayed. A genuine competitive environment for business development failed to emerge, and there was no large-scale entry of new firms to absorb productive resources freed from older, non-viable enterprises.

Similarly, in both countries, the business environment at the micro level is severely over-regulated. There are too many procedures, many of which no longer serve any legitimate governmental purpose, and these procedures are in most cases more complicated than they need to be. There is too much uncertainty, as interpretation and enforcement of laws, from registering a new company to acquiring land to paying taxes, change rapidly and are subject to official discretion. There is also too much corruption, partly engendered by this over-reliance on discretionary procedures.

Symptoms: "Missing" Investors and Capital Flight

At the macro level, this low investment, low restructuring trap is well described by data on economic growth and productivity developments during the ten years of transition. The Russian and Ukrainian economies both have been clearly under-performing in terms of both gross domestic private investment and foreign direct investment (FDI). Gross domestic investment contracted severely from 1990-1998, and has only recently started expanding again.

Not only the amounts of investment, but the activities in which it has been concentrated, can be seen as symptoms of "missing investors". A common characteristic of the Russian and Ukrainian economies is the presence of a highly educated workforce and a critical mass of world-class scientific talent in a diverse range of disciplines. Nevertheless, in Russia, FDI into the extractive sectors, plus brand-name consumer goods production has dominated, despite the comparative advantage Russia could have been expected to demonstrate in the production of R&D-intensive, high-technology goods and services.

In Ukraine, FDI has mainly gone into the food industry, retail trade and catering as well as other commercial operations. While agribusiness, food processing and packaging show potential for significant growth, delays in structural reforms including privatisation in this sector still constitute real obstacles for foreign participation. Telecommunications, computers and computer software, potentially promising in view of the highly educated labour force, has also failed to attract foreign capital in significant volumes.

Notably sparse in both countries are the export-oriented manufacturers and others involved in the new "globalised" production system, which are so prominent in other transition economies, including Central Europe, the Baltics, and China.

Another common symptom of an inadequate investment climate is the fact that capital flight has reached dramatic levels in both countries. In Ukraine it is estimated to have accumulated to some USD 20 bn overall since 1991, while in Russia, a reliable estimate for 1999-2000 puts the amount at USD 20 bn per annum, up from some USD 11 bn in the 1995-1998 period. While some of this flight capital is returned in the form of FDI inflows, as witnessed by the important position occupied by Cyprus among the sources of FDI both in Russia and Ukraine, it still represents a very substantial drain on investible resources.

6 OECD reviews of the investment environment in Russia and Ukraine – analytical approach and fundamental questions posed

Two studies recently published by the OECD, namely *"The Investment Environment in the Russian Federation – Laws Policies and Institutions"* (May 2001) and *"Investment Review of Ukraine"* (June 2001) – while different in scope and focus – share the assumption that the factors responsible for the comparatively low level of FDI inflows are on the whole the same as those depressing domestic investment. Trying to compensate for the lack of attractiveness of the FDI environment by offering special incentives or privileges to foreign investors are in neither case seen as a viable route for capturing a larger share of the growing flows of direct investment into developing and transition countries. Seeking remedies in revisions to the laws and regulatory framework relating specifically to foreign investment – as advocated in some studies – also represents an incomplete approach, as deficiencies in this respect only form a minor part of the picture in the two countries. In the OECD's view, the lags in structural reform and the policy deficiencies which have combined to produce an unfavourable climate for domestic as well as foreign investment need to be addressed as a whole.

Thus, the approach taken is to try to identify major weaknesses in the institutional framework for, and the policies towards, business activity in general, including that taking the form of FDI.

A multitude of impediments to the development of a healthy business climate exists in Russia as well as in Ukraine, and these are often linked in their origin and nature. The fundamental questions we were posing in the case of the Russian Federation can be simply stated as follows:

- Is there an adequate, rules-based legal and regulatory environment for investment?
- Does it apply consistently, for all, across the territory of the Russian Federation – without inconsistencies and regional variations?
- Are the rules being properly implemented and enforced, rather than being thwarted through corrupt behaviour and rent-seeking by economic agents?

6.1 Principal findings

There is no unified economic space, no "level playing field" for businesses in Russia, because of the multitude of administrative barriers and obstacles encountered by investors, particularly at regional level. These are often in contravention of federal legislation and regulation. As specific examples of unpredictable hurdles to be surmounted by investors at federal level could be mentioned sudden withdrawal of frequencies from telecommunication companies, or sudden unavailability of previously posted railway freight tariffs, which served as a basis for feasibility calculations. At the regional level, examples abound in the form of unforeseen licensing or permission requirements, license fees in excess of what is legally required, tax payments that are negotiable rather than statutory, "voluntary" contributions to extra-budgetary funds, etc..

In addition, the general burden of licensing and other policy-induced start-up difficulties at regional level is so onerous that firms specialising in helping new businesses to manage this process are becoming a new growth industry.

As to uniform implementation of the law, the uncertainty of proper administration and enforcement of justice by the court system and the degree of corruption throughout the economy further undermine the confidence in the existing legal and regulatory framework. There is no security of private property rights, contracts are difficult to verify and enforce and most businesses expect to pay bribes of varying levels to be able to execute claims awarded in dispute resolution.

Comparing these findings with those presented in the review of Ukraine, it is clear that many of the deficiencies in the business environment are, if not identical, at least similar in nature. A major difference is of course that the inconsistencies in the application of central government policy and legislation by regional administrative units constitute a major negative factor for the investment environment in Russia, but are of significantly smaller dimension in Ukraine.

6.2 Policy conclusions and recommendations

Although legislation at times has proceeded at very rapid pace, with little co-ordination of reforms affecting the same or related areas of economic activity, commercial legal rules are, in both countries, at present sufficiently clear, coherent and operational to support business activity in general. This being said, certain factors impacting negatively on the legislative framework include mutually exclusive provisions resulting from poor co-ordination of legislative acts, and a certain degree of devaluation or undermining of legislation due to the frequency of amendments to laws. In Russia, there is in addition the general problem of unclear balance of jurisdiction at federal and regional levels, preventing uniform implementation. Another deficiency, in both countries, is the ineffectiveness or even absence of penalties for violation of laws.

In the Russian Federation, unresolved legislative issues of major importance for all investors remain, such as:

- the adoption of a universal Land Code;
- the creation of adequate registry procedures for non-possessory pledges in line with the provisions of the Civil Code;
- harmonisation of the Tax and Customs Codes with the provisions in investment legislation, in particular as relates to grandfather clause provisions and production-sharing agreements.

In addition to the adoption of a Federal Land Code, the development of a secondary market in land should be encouraged, by privatising more land along with buildings, as allowed by Federal law.

Other issues requiring urgent attention in the legal basis for commercial activity in Russia concern primarily the foreign exchange regulations currently in force and production sharing agreements (PSAs) for extraction of mineral resources.

Foreign exchange regulation in Russia provides the basic guarantees for investors as concerns repatriation of profits and dividends, and Russia has accepted the obligations of Article VIII of the IMF Articles of Agreement, formally since June 1996. However, foreign exchange controls are, together with customs procedures, and other controls on foreign economic activity, a major source of complaints from foreign investors, and clearly constitute a significant deterrent to export-oriented FDI. The current legislation requires the prior authorisation of the Central Bank of Russia (CBR) for most capital account transfers, and the licensing system for such operations is both cumbersome to operate for the authorities and onerous and non-transparent for private sector participants. Priorities for reform are:

- the system of licensing capital account operations should be made more transparent by the issuing of guidelines (including for internal use by the control authorities) which would clarify on what grounds a license would be refused;
- the rules for the present elaborate system for non-resident rouble accounts should be rendered clearer, more systematic and user-friendly;
- the exchange control system for both current and capital account operations should be amended to permit market participants to make freely those payments and transfers which are required under contracts that have been legally entered into.

It is also the OECD view that the 1992 Foreign Exchange Law and its implementing regulations should be revised to simplify the regime and bring it into line with international practice, in particular by introducing a negative list principle for capital account operations, leaving all but a specified number of items completely free of licensing requirements.

As to the legislation and regulatory regime providing the basis for production-sharing agreements, urgent improvements are needed if the full potential of this crucial area for attracting long-term foreign capital and expertise is to be realised. Beyond the already mentioned need for reconciliation with other legislation, local content requirements should be eliminated, and a clearer and more transparent distribution of powers among different ministries and government agencies with respect to regulating and negotiating PSAs should be established.

6.3 Protection of property, shareholder and contractual rights

One major problem – perhaps *the* major one – encountered by investors relates to the perceived lack of protection and enforcement of property rights. This holds for Ukraine as well as Russia, as the resource limitations and lack of training in the judiciary, which are important factors in this context, have common origins in the Soviet legal system.

This insecurity applies in particular to the protection of shareholder/investor rights, protection of secured and unsecured creditors rights and to the balance between debtor/creditor interests in bankruptcy proceedings.

In the domain of *corporate law*, attention should be given to:

- widening the monitoring capabilities exercised by the board of directors and minority shareholders of the executive organs of companies and majority shareholders;
- developing more effective legislation prohibiting insider dealing;
- defining deals among affiliated entities, widening the concept of an affiliated party and strengthening the power of regulatory authorities to prohibit such deals when required;
- extending disclosure requirements as well as the responsibility for the content of such information disclosure;
- regulating the dilution of share capital;
- limiting cross-ownership of share capital;
- strengthening the requirements for independent audits;
- protecting good faith shareholders from effects of invalid share transactions;
- introducing personal liability and responsibility for officers, directors and controlling shareholders for the damages inflicted on their company, or on its shareholders (with outright dismissal for breaking corporate governance norms and imprisonment in graver cases).

Some of these urgent improvements were included last year in proposed amendments to the Joint Stock Company Law, the Securities Market Law, The Law on Affiliated Parties, The Bankruptcy Law and the Criminal Code – these amendments are still pending.

6.4 Financial reporting standards and disclosure

In Russia as well as in Ukraine, lack of compliance with disclosure requirements must be addressed in the joint stock company law, in the law on protection of rights and legal interests of investors, the law on securities and also through the introduction of international accounting standards and criminal liability for non-compliance.

There is by now fairly broad consensus among Russian policy-makers, regulators and the international investor community that financial reporting standards and disclosure requirements need to be substantially improved and tightened in the Russian enterprise sector. An important tool in this context, is the introduction of international accounting standards (IAS).

While the application of IAS financial statements is an important means to communicate financial information, it will not in itself eradicate fraud or prevent illicit transactions for personal gain by insiders. However, it will assist in their timely detection and also act as an important deterrent. In addition, there must be proper incentives to ensure high quality reporting. One of the key incentives is the existence of a large and sophisticated investor community.

6.5 Law enforcement and the judiciary

Weak enforcement of laws is partly a consequence of the failure of the existing judicial system to keep pace with change. Courts still need to develop expertise to deal with complex issues of the application of economic legislation. Investors are in fact often deterred from taking cases to court by the long delays due to court workloads as well as by the mistrust regarding fairness and independence of the judicial system and the likelihood of being able to obtain enforcement of a judgement. In Russia, the lack of independence of the territorial courts from the political authorities in the different subjects of the Federation is a feature of the system that many foreign investors have experience of. As a shareholder or investor plaintiff can only bring a suit against a legal entity – a company having infringed his rights – in that company's own geographical locality, foreign investors are particularly exposed to the potential interference of authorities in support of local entrepreneurs.

To deal with these problems and to create the "larger role and greater authority for the judiciary" advocated by President Putin already in a December 1999 statement, it is necessary to:

- increase the prestige of judicial power, attract qualified specialists, train currently working staff;
- guarantee real independence of the judges via substantial salary increases and via heightened risk of exposure of undue influences;
- pay special attention to the system of execution of legal rulings and other decisions so as to offer alternatives to plaintiffs faced by non-existent or inadequate market-based enforcement mechanisms.

6.6 Tax policy

Many studies and reports have pointed to the fact that the Russian tax system consistently discourages investment, both through its structure and the manner in which it has been implemented. This fact remains true for domestic as well as foreign investors, whether we discuss start-ups of new businesses or the restructuring of existing firms. The frequent changes in rules and regulations have created a degree of uncertainty that impacts negatively on business development in general.

The tax regime for business is now improving, but tax rates and tax regulations are still cited by many investment survey respondents as the most severe obstacles to investment in Russia. In addition to the complaints about high tax rates and complex tax structures (which are being addressed in the development of the new tax code), most businesses are also burdened by procedural problems in tax administration.

Tax inspectors can assess penalties regarding infractions of rules that have nothing to do with tax and even against technical errors that have no effect on calculated tax payments. It seems also widely agreed by tax inspectors and taxpayers alike that tax arrears (including penalties) can drive an otherwise healthy company into bankruptcy. This risk significantly deters new investment. Even without such risks, investors in Russia need to devote significantly more resources to accounting activities than they do in countries with less cumbersome tax structures.

We recommend that:

- the ongoing efforts to streamline the tax regime and spread the tax burden more fairly should be accelerated, including, importantly, the recognition of deductibility of business expenses in the calculation of the profit tax base;
- the tax regime for the oil and gas sector be designed to encourage new investment and provide a sufficient return to the state;
- the administrative mechanisms for implementing transfer pricing rules and double taxation treaties be improved;
- taxpayers' rights and duties be more clearly defined, with possibilities for judicial and non-judicial dispute resolution;
- the fairness and effectiveness of the tax enforcement function be improved by modernising tax administration facilities, training tax inspectors and educating judges in handling tax disputes.

6.7 Privatisation policy

Our recommendations in this area are:

- the resort to direct and competitive sales to strategic investors for the more marketable stakes;
- appropriate organisational and administrative procedures for the full privatisation of minor shareholdings and state assets requiring extensive restructuring;
- the introduction of sound management structures for property remaining in state ownership to eliminate malpractice;
- resolution of remaining disputes relating to past privatisations with the imposition of time limits for contesting past deals as well as respect of good

faith investor rights in cases where expropriation may result, giving prompt, adequate and effective compensation.

6.8 Financial sector development

Most transition countries have relied on the banking system to provide the crucial function of transforming savings into investment. Capital market structures and institutions take longer to create – not in terms of concrete operating systems but of the corporate governance systems necessary for deep and liquid markets with widespread ownership of debt and equity. Neither Russia, nor Ukraine have demonstrated any coherent policy for the development of the financial system, to form part of overall economic policy for macroeconomic stabilisation and return to growth. That the banking system in neither country as yet constitutes an important source of finance for the enterprise sector also has much to do with the aforementioned lack of information about the true financial condition of borrowers, as well as the inadequate legal basis for creditor rights. Irrespective of the financial crisis in 1998, which brought severe destruction to both banking sectors, many smaller banks in the two countries still function as banks only in name. The priorities for creating a healthier banking system are:

- opening of the banking sector to foreign competition, actively promoting the entry of foreign banks as important agents of innovation and prudent practices. This would include allowing the establishment of branches without a capitalisation requirement and removing quotas for local employees and similar forms of discrimination which still exist in Russia;
- consolidation of the banking system through the application of firm exit policies for non-viable institutions. It is vital for the attraction of medium and longer-term deposits for sustained intermediation purposes that marginal, non-profitable institutions be eliminated from the system to enhance confidence and trust on the part of the population;
- establishing an explicit scheme for deposit insurance with compulsory participation and covering fully the deposits of small and uninformed depositors. This would, in the Russian Federation, entail developing a solution for the continued role of the state-owned Sberbank, currently benefiting from a unique competitive situation in mobilising household deposits. Unless a level playing field is established for state-owned and privately-owned banks, the latter have little prospect of long-term survival.

7 Conclusions – Implementation and follow-up of reforms and the need to strengthen competition

Concluding this review of the recommendations we offer, I would like to underline two things. The first is that while in Russia determination and direction of the structural reform effort is now clearer than in Ukraine, there is still a great deal of work ahead in both countries and the pace of reform must be kept up. In addition to the legislative work, there remains the major task of developing detailed regulations to accompany the new legislation, and beyond that, a need to ensure that new procedures are implemented efficiently, consistently, and fairly throughout the territories of the two countries.

Another final comment is that one cannot enough emphasise the importance of competition in transforming the investment environment in the Russian Federation as well as in Ukraine. And the need for competition must be understood at all levels of government, not just at the centres in Moscow and Kyiv. There seems to be a lingering tendency among many bureaucrats and businessmen to consider competition as "wasteful" and unnecessary, that big companies are inherently superior to small ones, and that established firms are more trustworthy than new start-ups. This attitude in turn reinforces the problem of the un-level playing field and deters the investment that these two countries need in order to keep up with growth in the world economy.

We have emphasised that rules-based, streamlined licensing and authorisation procedures at federal, regional and local levels need to be imposed, to remove excessive administrative hurdles and arbitrary rule. Transparent guidelines and sizeable sanctions for officials who violate this rules-based system through corrupt behaviour must be put in place. The important role to be played by competition authorities in solving these problems and malpractices has also been underlined.

Even where corruption is not an issue, an outcome that treats competing companies differently should not be tolerated. The very existence of an un-level playing field deters new investors, who know they are unlikely to earn a profit in competition with firms favoured by the authorities.

Foreign investors in particular expect a regulatory regime that operates according to clear and transparent rules. This is a fundamental premise of the market economy, but is seriously lacking, throughout the Russian Federation as well as in Ukraine.

7.1 OECD's role

How can OECD help with the further advancement of the government reform programme in the directions that I have just outlined? As an organisation which for over forty years has been devoted to realising the full economic benefits of open markets for international trade, investment and capital flows, we can call on the policy experience of our members in these and many related areas developed over that time frame.

There are two avenues for making such expertise available to Russia and Ukraine.

One, which has been developed already for a number of years, is reliance on specially designed programmes in the policy areas of competition, trade, financial and corporate affairs, environment, labour and social affairs to name the major ones. Specific OECD programmes of this nature are already well developed in the Russian Federation, while in Ukraine the decision was recently taken to establish the OECD-Ukraine Forum on Investment and Enterprise Development in order to support Ukraine's reform efforts. The Forum is expected to develop dialogue and synergies among government officials, the private sector, bilateral and multilateral co-operation programmes, and above all, help identify the fundamentals of a forward-looking investment policy.

The other is for Russia and also Ukraine to take a more active part in the OECD process of analysis and policy dialogue forming the basis for developing instruments of international co-operation which are open to adherence by non-OECD members as well. I am thinking here specifically of the OECD Investment instruments, but there are also other non-binding recommendations accompanied by surveillance procedures and "peer pressure", which would be of particular relevance. Standards and benchmarking processes open to non-members are being developed in the areas of fighting corruption, corporate governance, the misuse of corporate vehicles for illicit purposes to name some important elements of the OECD work programme. Both countries are welcome to join these processes

13

Ukraine: "A Miracle in Waiting" Challenges and Reforms for an Improved Foreign Investment Environment

Mehmet Ögütçü[1]

1 Summary

Ukraine is at a crucial juncture politically and economically in its history. The fate of market-oriented reforms in this country is of concern to the OECD Member countries. Ukraine has lost a lot of time since its independence a decade ago; but it is a country with a vast potential in terms of economic and human resources. The business environment can rapidly improve if there is a strong political will to implement the long overdue reform agenda.

Ukraine urgently needs foreign direct investment (FDI) in almost every area from agriculture to telecommunications. The government has publicly stated it seeks foreign investment, but thus far it has failed to create an attractive investment climate, in spite of recent numerous but uncoordinated steps in that direction. Large parts of the country's capital stock have not been maintained or replaced during the last decade, and there has been little new investment. The likely costs of rehabilitating infrastructure alone are estimated to exceed USD 40 bn. Between 1990 and 2000, cumulative FDI inflows into Ukraine amounted to only around USD 3.9 bn, barely one tenth the amount of FDI over the same period into Poland. On a per capita basis, FDI in Ukraine is among the lowest in the region.

Although Ukraine achieved economic growth last year for the first time since 1991, largely thanks to the comprehensive reform programme launched in early 2000, the overall business climate remains unfavourable to investors. The new

---

1 This chapter is based largely on the OECD Investment Policy Review of Ukraine (OECD, 2001). The opinions expressed in the paper do not necessarily represent that of the OECD Secretariat and Member countries. The author is grateful to Mr. Rainer Geiger for his guidance and to Ms. Anna Stepanenko-Malan for her assistance.

Ukrainian government, led by Prime Minister Anatoliy Kinakh, seems to have realised the importance of building investors' confidence. But for that to happen, further crucial reforms must be achieved and vigorously implemented. OECD's recent review of Ukraine's FDI policies, conducted at the request of the Ukrainian government and published in May 2001, shows the way forward through a series of practical policy recommendations. How decisively these recommendations will be put into practice remains a key challenge for Ukraine, and might determine its future place and orientation in the world economy.

2 Overview

Ukraine has great potential for investors, domestic and foreign alike: its large landmass (604,000 square kilometres), huge domestic market of about 52 million people, highly educated labour force, rich natural resources, and strategic location, provide a solid base for sustainable economic growth and a fertile soil for investment inflows. Yet, despite its sound fundamentals, Ukraine remains one of the least advanced eastern European transition economies.

Investments needs are huge. Ukraine should raise at least an estimated USD 40 bn of investment for rehabilitating its ailing infrastructure alone. However, FDI is timid and slow to come. To a large extent, this reluctance is due to rather difficult business conditions in Ukraine, such as high and seemingly arbitrarily applied taxes, slow privatisation, over-regulation, sometimes prejudicial rules to foreign investment, and significant levels of corruption. Added to this list are the chronic political instability and the lack of a clear vision as to the country's future.

3 Major challenges

Although the major reform programme has demonstrated some encouraging achievements, the reforms remain uncompleted and the economic growth fragile. The fear that the limited reforms can be reversed is still strong. The most pressing economic priorities for Ukraine are: completing structural reforms, accelerating privatisation of many large state-owned enterprises, restructuring unwieldy governmental apparatus, broadening the tax base, combating corruption, and overhauling agricultural sector. Taxation tops the list of investment disincentives in Ukraine and drives an increasing number of businesses into the "shadow". economy. More than half of the Ukraine's economy currently operates in the informal sector.

An unfavourable environment for business has contributed to substantial capital outflows, estimated to have reached around USD 20 bn since Ukraine's independence. Investors complain of complex and often ambiguous legislation. Administrative reforms have been slow. Legislative and regulatory changes, rather than helping to establish explicit and transparent rules, have often contributed to unpredictable administration and discretionary interpretation.

Today, almost all international ratings and investment climate surveys place Ukraine among the least advanced transition economies with respect to its macroeconomic and microeconomic conditions, as well as effectiveness in affording property security and contract enforcement rights. The contribution of the private sector to GDP is quite low, at about 20% of GDP, compared to around 70% to 80% in Hungary, Poland and Russia (Sigma Bleyzer, 2001.). Estimates for the informal, "shadow", economy range from 14% (official estimates) to a more realistic 60% of total GDP. Persistent fiscal and current account deficits, even taking into account the fact that they have gradually decreased since 1994, as well as high inflation, around 20% per annum, reflect the economic decline.

Despite a vast body of law, Ukraine is still lacking a coherent, effective and transparent legal system. Complex and often ambiguous legislation invites inconsistent interpretation and unpredictable application, resulting in uncertainties and inadequate protection of business operators' property rights and contractual obligations. Thus far, all fundamental codifications, such as civil code, tax code, law on the judiciary system, are awaiting adoption by the Parliament.

In particular, the lack of a comprehensive and coherent tax code is considered to be one of the main investment disincentives in Ukraine. The reduction of tax burden (both tax rates and the number of taxes) is also required.

Public governance marked by bureaucratic interventionism and corruption remains one of the priorities of the reform. According to the Transparency International 2001 "corruption index", Ukraine ranks in 83rd position, leaving behind only 8 countries.[2]

A comprehensive re-organisation of the court system is necessary in order to improve courts' technical and financial resources as well as the competency of judges and to insure effective protection of investors' rights.

Though Ukraine has liberalised its trade regime in recent years and lowered its tariffs, considerable non-tariff barriers remain, especially through the imposition of cumbersome technical standards and certification requirements. At present, Ukraine is actively seeking WTO membership but must still implement a host of reforms in order to qualify.

---

2 The index is based on 1999, 2000 and 2001 data provided by the Economist Intelligence Unit, the Global Competitiveness Report, the World Business Environment Survey and the Freedom House.

Finally, to create a foreign investor-friendly climate, the policy agenda priorities comprise the liberalisation of capital, foreign exchange and profit expatriation controls, the lifting of restrictions on foreign ownership and control, and the minimisation of red tape. The list of required actions include further reforms of banking and capital market systems, accounting and auditing, insuring better protection of property rights, and land reform.

4 ...and first achievements

There are, however, some encouraging signs. First achievements of a comprehensive reform programme, launched in the first half of 2000, are now becoming visible. Last year, Ukraine registered a real GDP growth of 6% for the first time since its independence, and FDI flows reached USD 750 m. In January-June 2001 the country's GDP increased by 9.1% compared with the same period last year, thus surpassing the government's predictions of a 4% real GDP growth. Export revenues surged to USD 13.3 bn, while imports were at USD 14 bn.[3] These figures hold out hope for an economic reversal.

Only if the pending reform measures are implemented swiftly, foreign as well as domestic investment will be attracted to ensure a sustainable growth for the economy.[4] Under the right conditions, Ukraine could be an attractive place to invest, given its large amount of unused or underused physical and human capital and strategic location, all of which provide a solid base for sustainable economic growth. One should also acknowledge some strategically important decisions that have already been taken, such as:[5]

- approval, for the first time since independence, of a realistic budget for 2000, with a deficit of some 1.5%-2.0% of GDP;
- implementation of policies that have reduced the share of non-cash transactions in the economy, notably a ban on non-cash settlements with the budget;
- successful renegotiations of Ukraine's external debt of USD 12.5 bn;

---

3 Ukraine posted its first trade surplus in five years, exporting USD 616 m more than it imported.

4 Given the strong endowments enumerated above, private capital inflows will increase dramatically if Ukraine creates a more attractive environment for private sector development. Ukraine could increase the level of foreign direct investments from the current level of less that USD 1.0 bn per year to about USD 3.4 bn per year by year 2005 with the implementation of policy actions.

5 ICPS newsletter, No. 109, 28 May 2001

- privatisation of collective agricultural enterprises and demonopolisation of lending to the agricultural sector;
- approval of the 2000-2002 Privatisation Program[6], which sets the baseline for transparent and foreseeable sales of state property. Moreover, a Working Group to review such progress was established;
- amendments to the Law on electricity, which significantly restricted the scale of non-payments in the electricity market;
- introduction, within the framework of the administrative reform, of a new mechanism for collective decision making that prevents the approval of decisions hindering entrepreneurial activity, and publication of government decisions.

5 Foreign direct investment in Ukraine today

According to official Ukrainian data, as of the 1 January 2001, total FDI in Ukraine has accumulated to some USD 3.9 bn since independence. This translated into some USD 79 per capita, placing Ukraine the second lowest among CIS countries, ahead of Belarus only; and it is less than 10% of per capita FDI to Central and Eastern European countries, such as Poland and Hungary.

By origin of investment, the United States has been the dominant foreign investor (18% of all FDI), followed by the Netherlands with 9%, the Russian Federation (9%), Germany (7%) and the United Kingdom (7%).

From a sector perspective, as of January 2000, the main destination of FDI in Ukraine, was the domestic food industry (20% of cumulative FDI), followed by domestic commercial operations (over 17%) and mechanical engineering/metals (almost 11%).

FDI flow in Ukraine is not only insignificant, but also highly concentrated in a few regions. Kyiv and its surroundings received over one-third of all FDI; Donetsk, Zaporizhya, Poltava, Odesa and Dnipropetrovsk regions together accumulated for another third; leaving less than one-third for the remainder of the country.

---

6 The programme aims at privatising most of some 200 large enterprises holding over 80% of assets in the industrial and utilities sectors. Unlike previous privatisation rounds, the 2000-2002 programme targets primarily long-term strategic investors and foreign investors in particular. To attract them, it is envisaged to re-organise enterprises earmarked for privatisation and to restructure their debt.

Graph 13.1
Top ten FDI destinations in Central Europe, 1990-2000*

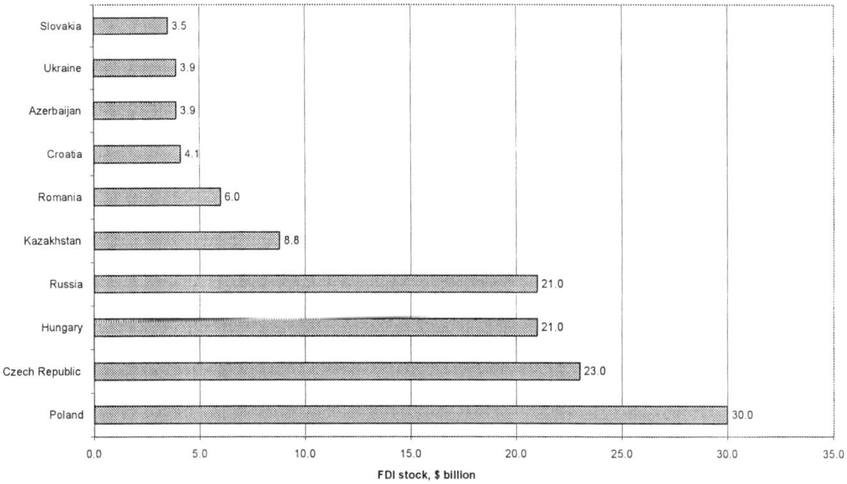

* Projection

Source: Business Central Europe, The Annual 2001

Graph 13.2
FDI inflow to Ukraine (1996-2000)

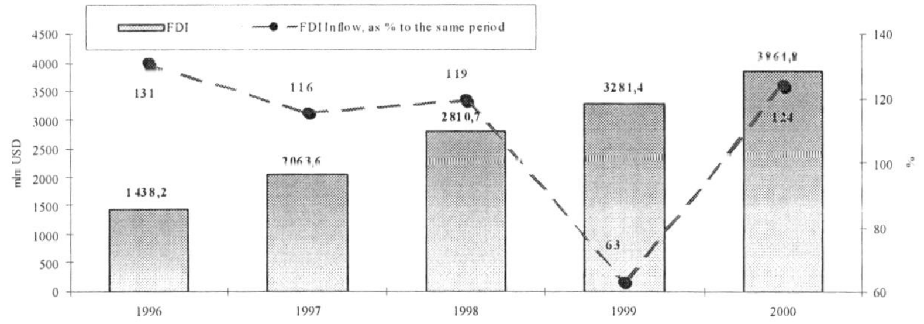

Source: Ministry of Economy, Ukraine

The legal regime specifically addressing foreign investment is set out in both Ukraine's domestic legislation and international treaties. Some domestic legislation also, while not expressly distinguishing between domestic and foreign investment, in practice applies to foreign investment only, notably the laws on production-sharing and concession agreements.

6 Legal and institutional changes

Major amendments of Ukraine's FDI legislation have been enacted during the past few years. These changes have been fundamental, as they constituted a shift from a generous, but ineffective system of specific incentives to a system of non-discriminatory legal conditions for all investors, including more extensive investment protection. Access for foreign investors to the Ukrainian market has also been considerably liberalised, though limitations remain in certain sectors.

Ukraine has also signed a significant number of bilateral investment treaties (67 treaties, 43 of which are in force), including some with OECD Member countries. The bilateral treaties, which supersede the Ukrainian Foreign Investment Law and prevail over it in case of conflict, in most cases conform to international standards. In addition, Ukraine has signed several multilateral agreements related to foreign investment, such as the 1965 ICSID Convention, the 1994 Energy Grapher Treaty and the 1998 Partnership and Co-operation Agreement with the European Union.

While foreign investment regulation appears to be compatible with that in Eastern European transition economies, implementing institutions in Ukraine are widely rated as ineffective. Until the end of 1999, several institutions were charged with the task to promote FDI but their respective assignments were not well defined. To streamline this structure, in 2000 the main central government agencies with FDI-related responsibilities were integrated into the Ministry of Economy. This concentration of FDI expertise now offers an opportunity for a coherent and consistently implemented investment promotion strategy.

Why, if the legal and institutional framework for foreign investment seems satisfactory, do FDI inflows still represent only a small fraction of Ukraine's potential? The answer is that substantive flaws in Ukraine's general legislation and especially the lack of transparency and insecurity constitute a much more important investment barrier than some insignificant lags in specific foreign investment regulation. This is due principally to the arbitrary application of legislation that is being continually modified, often with retroactive application.[7] In addition, the law enforcement mechanisms are largely underdeveloped and inefficient. Under these circumstances, there is no doubt that the factors responsible for the low level of FDI inflows are the same as those depressing domestic investment. That is why, to attract investments, the reforms should aim at addressing the shortages in structural reform and the policy deficiencies as a whole, and not be limited to the revision of foreign investment regulations.

---

7 "Report on Impediments to Foreign Investment in Ukraine" carried out by the TACIS-funded Ukrainian-European Policy and Legal Advice Centre in 1999.

7 The way ahead in reforms

FDI is one but not the only mechanism to increase economic growth. Compared to the regulatory, legal and policy environment for foreign firms, Ukraine's legal and regulatory environment for domestic private firms is highly under-developed. The emphasis in reforms should therefore be on policies that provide a favorable environment for "investment" (not just FDI) and private enterprise.

If this is done right and regulatory barriers towards FDI are eliminated, the FDI will happen and the economy will prosper with complementary developments in the foreign-owned and domestic enterprises. If policy-makers focus just on trying to attract FDI to an economy with an environment that is unfavorable to domestic investment and private enterprise, it will be rather more difficult to do and the results are likely to be less favorable with respect to the long term development of the economy.

To support Ukraine's reform efforts, the OECD and other international donors have come up with a number of policy recommendations aimed at improving the overall business environment.

8 OECD recommendations

The OECD's Investment Policy Review[8] recommends, *inter alia,* that the Ukrainian authorities:

- reorient government administration away from micro-managing the economy and in favour of the strategic formulation of framework conditions conducive to private sector development;
- develop a transparent, predictable and stable process for case-by-case privatisation, and ensure that the tender commission is independent;
- phase out non-transparent and distortive investment incentive schemes;
- open the way to international arbitration for disputes under the foreign investment law, and establish courts of appeal for economic disputes;
- align Ukraine's accounting and auditing practices with international standards, in particular for publicly-traded companies and financial institutions, so as to avoid double book-keeping and attendant costs, simplify financial reporting and ensure transparency and proper performance evaluation;

---

8 The executive summary and the recommendations are available at the OECD website (http://www.oecd.org/daf/investment/ukraine.htm).

- simplify interaction between foreign investors and Ukrainian authorities by considering the creation of a "one-stop-shop" that obtains for foreign investors all required licences, approvals and permits.

9 Conclusion

Ukraine is facing the choice either to go forward with drastic policy and institutional reforms to improve the environment for investment and enterprise development or to slip into the economic abyss. To mobilise investments now, it is necessary to build investor confidence in the reform's decisive implementation[9], persuading investors that it pays to buy into the Ukrainian economy today, when entry prices are still moderate, and reap returns tomorrow, when business conditions will be favourable.

It would not be an exaggeration to call Ukraine today a "miracle in waiting" that has all the necessary potential to become a reality.

References

OECD (2001): Investment Policy Review of Ukraine, Paris.

SigmaBleyzer (2001): Accelerating the Flow of International Private Capital to Ukraine, April 22.

ICPS (2001): Newsletter, No. 109, May 28, Kyiv.

UEPLAC (1999):Report on Impediments to Foreign Investment in Ukraine.

OECD's Investment Policy Review http://www.oecd.org/daf/investment/ukraine.htm.

---

9 To help this process, an OECD-Ukraine Forum on Investment and Enterprise Development was established by the OECD and the Government of Ukraine during a roundtable meeting on investment in Kyiv in February 2001. It is intended to help to develop dialogue and synergies among government officials, the private sector, bilateral and multilateral co-operation programmes. The Forum will also, and above all, help identify the fundamentals of a forward-looking investment policy.

Part IV

EMPIRICAL STUDIES OF THE DETERMINANTS OF GROWTH IN UKRAINE

Reserve Requirements and Implicit Taxation of Commercial Banks in Ukraine

Igor Eremenko

1 Introduction

Aside from fiscal policy, monetary policy is viewed as the major determinant of sustainable economic development in any country. Success with this policy depends on maintaining a long-term time consistent strategy, as well as on the particular ways in which it is transmitted to the economic agents, i.e. on the so-called instruments of monetary policy. In this chapter we will talk about one such aspect: reserve requirements as an instrument of monetary policy.

Reserve requirements are a powerful means of affecting money supply and credit creation, and historically this instrument was viewed as the core of monetary policy. But lately its role has significantly diminished. The main driving force behind this change was the availability of some new, more efficient instruments and the fact that reserve requirements saddle the banking sector with additional costs, lowering its profit and the level of intermediation. Eventually, as it was confirmed by empirical analyses, reserve requirements can result in diminishing investment and thus, in a drop of production.

In this investigation we will conduct a partial analysis and will concentrate on the cost side of the required reserves, i.e. their negative impact on the private sector, particularly their effect as an implicit tax on commercial banks. We will also discuss the use of this instrument in Ukraine, analysing tax effect and proposing some measures, which might improve the situation.

The chapter is structured as follows: In Section 2 we will talk about the role of reserve requirements, their pros and cons, and the major reasons why their use as an instrument of monetary policy by the central banks diminishes world-wide. The impact of reserve requirements on the private sector and on commercial banks in particular will be discussed in Section 3. Section 4 will talk about reserve requirements in Ukraine and whether their level is optimal. It also looks at possible ways of reform. Finally, in Section 5 we will summarise the main findings of the chapter.

2 The role of reserve requirements

In many countries commercial banks are obliged to comply with reserve requirements: i.e. to hold a certain fraction of their deposit liabilities in an account at their central bank or as cash in a vault.

There are four major functions of this instrument, the importance of which has changed over time, as financial intermediation and methods of using other monetary policies were developed. Firstly, reserve requirements were meant to ensure financial stability and reduce the negative effects of runs on banks. Secondly, reserve requirements are used to control bank credit creation. The third function of the reserve requirements is control over the money supply through the money multiplier. Finally, holding reserve requirements can reduce the interest rate volatility on the money market.

Traditionally, reserve requirements have been a key instrument used by central banks. They tended to rely on it heavily, to regulate the money supply or credit creation. Lately, especially during the last decade, the role of reserve requirements has considerably diminished. Table 14.1 presents legal reserve requirements in several selected countries.

Table 14.1
Legal reserve requirements, in %

United States	3.0-10.0
Canada	0.0
EU	0.0-2.0
UK	0.35
Switzerland	0.0
Japan	0.05-1.2
New Zealand	0.0
Czech Republic	2.0
Poland	4.5
Hungary	6.0
Moldova	8.0
Bulgaria	11.0
Russia	7.0-10.0
Ukraine	9.0-15.0

Source: The central banks of the respective countries

Some countries, such as Canada, the UK, Switzerland and New Zealand have drawn their reserve requirements to zero. The United States is considering this measure as well. The European Central Bank has set it at a pretty low level – from 0% to 2% of deposits – and this ratio has to be adopted by members of the EU as well as by candidate countries in the CEE region. Many other countries intend to decrease their reserve ratio as well.

Moreover, members of the European System of Central Banks and some accessing countries (Hungary for example) pay interest on the holdings of reserve requirements over the maintenance period.

In order to explain the rationale behind this change of attitude let us first consider what benefits and costs reserve requirements have for the economy.

The main advantages of reserve requirements are the following:

a) they are easy to implement and do not require a sophisticated financial market structure, which is one of the major reasons for the widespread use of this instrument in transition economies;

b) a change in the level of reserve requirements has a very powerful effect and usually just a tiny change is required;

c) reserve requirements can be a source of funds for the public sector of economy.

Disadvantages:

a) the benefit of using reserve requirements can in fact turn into a cost: As stated above, small changes have very large effects on the money supply, but this effect can be (and often actually is) too large compared to the target;

b) frequent changes in reserve requirement may cause high uncertainty for the banks, and raise difficulties with their liquidity management;

c) imposing reserve requirements at a level higher than commercial banks would normally tend to hold them is in fact an implicit taxation of these financial institutions;

d) suffering from high reserve requirements, commercial banks will try to pass as much of this cost on to their clients as they can;

e) obliging commercial banks to comply with reserve requirements can discriminate against them 1) vis-à-vis other financial institutions in the country, which do not have to meet such a regulation and 2) vis-à-vis financial intermediaries in other countries, where such regulations are lower;

f) as financial institutions develop further and use new modern financial instruments, they tend to have more possibilities for reserve avoidance. Thus, the effectiveness of reserve requirements diminishes.

Taking the experiences of central banks into account we can discern two major reasons of why reserve requirements are less used today. First of all, new monetary policy instruments have been developed. A second very important motive is the fact that reserve requirements put substantial costs on the banking sector, which are transmitted to the rest of the economy. We will analyse this question at greater length in the next section.

3 The impact of reserve requirements on the private sector

To begin with, let us consider the role of reserve requirements as an implicit tax borne by the commercial banks, and their broader impact on the private sector.

The problem of implicit taxation by reserve requirements received some discussion in the economic literature, although not a very wide one. Thus, Kuprianov (1997) analyses explicit and implicit taxes on the financial system and stresses that the reserve requirements are an implicit tax. The author builds a theoretical model defining the reserve requirement compliance costs to the banks. Further, the analysis demonstrates how these costs are transmitted to the banks' clients. The second part of the paper is devoted to empirical tests of the model using US data. In conclusion Kuprianov argues that although required reserves were diminishing in the US and have had positive effects on intermediation, further reforms and easing of requirements are needed. Repullo (1992) talks about such ways of financing budget deficits with seigniorage and implicit taxation, developing a model of the financial sector and estimating the implicit tax for Portugal and Spain. The analyses were done for the period of political instability and increased budget expenditures from the late 1970's to the early 1980's. Repullo shows that although financing budget deficits by seigniorage while simultaneously increasing reserve requirements helped the government at the moment, but it also had quite negative consequences for the banking system and the private sector. Moreover, high reserve requirements put the banks of those countries at a disadvantage to other countries, primarily the EU.

The mechanism of implicit taxation can be described as follows: Let's consider an increase in the level of reserve requirements. Now the banks have to hold a larger share of deposits, on which they have to pay interest, in the form of non-earning reserves. Also, the banks will now have fewer funds available to lend out. Taking into account the higher costs and the diminished possibilities for lending, the banks' profits will decrease. One solution for the banks would be to increase the interest rate spread, i.e. the banks would decrease the interest paid on deposits and increase the lending rate. In consequence the supply of deposits will decrease, since the consumers' supply of deposits depends directly on the interest rate paid. Firms, in turn, will demand fewer loans, in accordance with each firm's loan demand function, which has an inverse relation to the interest rate. The magnitude of the changes in deposits and loans depends on the corresponding elasticities.

An increase in the reserve requirements results in a higher lending rate, a lower deposit rate, higher costs for the banking sector and less intermediation in the economy.

The summary of the process, described above, can be represented as the follows:

$$RR\uparrow \Rightarrow Liquidity\downarrow \Rightarrow Banks\_profit\downarrow \Rightarrow (i_L - i_D)\uparrow \Rightarrow i_L \uparrow i_D \downarrow \Rightarrow L\downarrow D\downarrow \Rightarrow Intermediation\downarrow$$

It is also useful to represent the process graphically. Thus, Graph 14.1 shows the level of intermediation in the economy and the corresponding interest rates for credits and deposits.

Graph 14.1
The impact of reserve requirements on interest rates and intermedaition

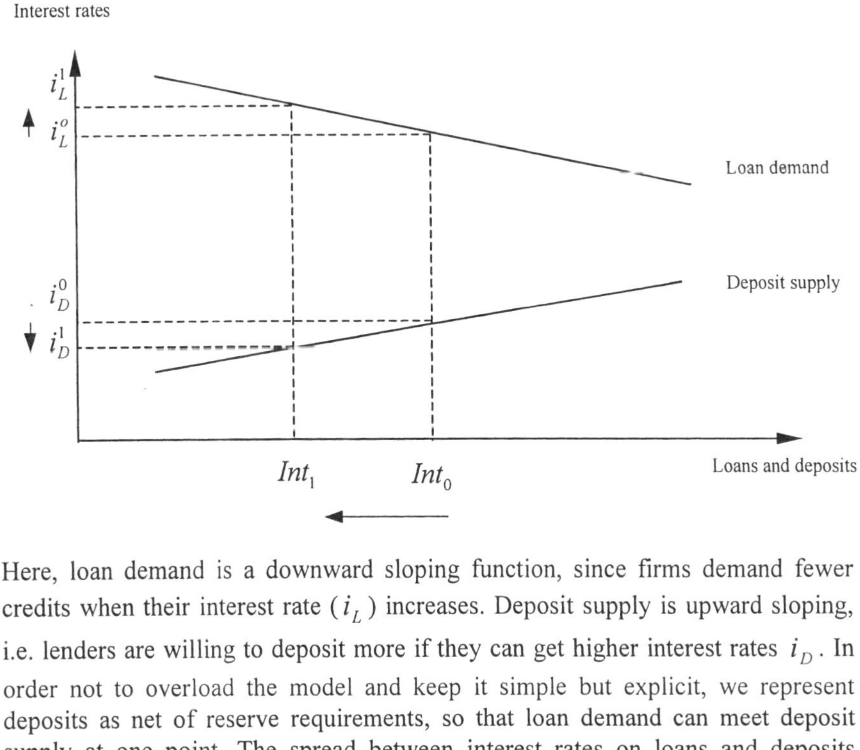

Here, loan demand is a downward sloping function, since firms demand fewer credits when their interest rate (i_L) increases. Deposit supply is upward sloping, i.e. lenders are willing to deposit more if they can get higher interest rates i_D. In order not to overload the model and keep it simple but explicit, we represent deposits as net of reserve requirements, so that loan demand can meet deposit supply at one point. The spread between interest rates on loans and deposits $(i_L - i_D)$ represents the mark-up by the banks, which covers certain profit targets and costs from various sources, including reserve requirements. The initial level of intermediation is Int^o. The corresponding interest rates are i_D^0 for deposits and i_L^0 for loans.

Now, if the central bank decides to increase the level of reserve requirements, the banks will have less liquidity and will react by widening the interest rate spread. Interest paid on deposits will come down to i_D^1, while interest for loans will go up to i_L^1. The economy will react by providing fewer deposits and demanding fewer loans, i.e. the level of the intermediation will go down to Int^1.

Thus, the new equilibrium will have a higher loan interest rate i_L^1, a lower deposit rate i_D^1 and fewer deposits supplied and loans demanded, Int^1.

Beyond that, we can say that the influence of changes to reserve requirements on the real sector is much broader yet. Economic agents will be worse off, depressing intermediation in the economy will have negative impacts on investment patterns and technological innovations, and this dynamic situation could even cause a drop in the GDP. For instance, Loungani and Rush (1995) empirically tested this hypothesis for United States, finding that raising reserve requirements had adverse effects on investment and output.

4 Reserve requirements in Ukraine

4.1 The history and role of reserve requirements in Ukraine

Reserve requirements in Ukraine were first implemented in 1989, still during the Soviet times. Thus, the State Bank of the USSR issued a decree about the creation of a fund for regulating credit resources, according to which commercial banks had to hold a certain amount of investment funds in a special account. Since its foundation in 1991 the National Bank of Ukraine started to conduct its monetary policy by using reserve requirements, changing its level in accordance with the state of the economy (see Table 14.2).

Table 14.2
The level of reserve requirements in Ukraine between 1992 and 2000, in %

Year	1992	1993	1994	1995	1996	1997	1998	1999	2000
Level	13	25	15	15	15	15	16.5	17	15

Source: NBU Bulletin

The reserve requirements were viewed as a very important instrument of National Bank policy. Thus, reserve requirements were used quite intensively during the financial crises of 1997, 1998 and 1999 for keeping money supply under control and not permitting hyperinflation. In this process, the NBU was changing the level of reserve requirements between 15% and 17%, redefining the type of liabilities on which the reserves were based, as well as the time period for complying with the requirements (from one day to several months).

Recently, reserve requirements in Ukraine have been somewhat liberalised. In 2001 they stayed at levels between 9% and 15%, and were differentiated according to the terms and types of liability, and the currency of denomination (see Table 14.3).

Table 14.3
The level of reserve requirements in Ukraine in 2001, in %

Source	Type of deposit	Short-term	Long-term
Juridical persons	National currency	14	11
	Foreign currency	14	11
Natural persons	National currency	12	9
	Foreign currency	13	13
Rest		15	

Source: NBU

4.2 An agenda for reform

Although reserve requirements have been a quite useful instrument for conducting monetary policy during last decade and their importance should not be underestimated, and although some liberalisation has taken place, the level of reserve requirements in Ukraine is still very high, which has a negative effect on the economy. As can be seen from Table 14.4, the spread between interest rates in Ukraine is one of the highest in European transition countries, while the depth of the financial system is rather low. Part of this bad situation can be associated with the costs of reserve requirements.

Table 14.4
Interest rate spread and depth of financial system in Eastern European countries, 1998*

Country	Interest rate spread, %	Credits to GDP, %
Czech Republic	5.5	79.8
Slovak Republic	5.2	71.8
Hungary	3.2	49.1
Poland	5.6	36.9
Slovenia	6.8	35.5
Bulgaria	37.1	30.0
Russia	15.3	25.9
Belarus	16.2	17.7
Ukraine	30.9	17.2

* Although the data for Ukraine do not exactly coincide with the statistics of the NBU, we give it as reported by the IMF for the purpose of comparative analysis with other countries

Source: IMF, International Financial Statistics (1999)

According to our analysis, a decrease in the required reserves in Ukraine could mean a reduction of the regulatory costs to the banking sector, and as predicted by theory and according to experience in other countries, a consequent decrease in the interest rate spread. Also, this would result in an expansion of the aggregate investment and the creation of the necessary prerequisites for output growth. Actually, during 2001, when quite substantial reforms of the reserve requirements were undertaken, credits to the Ukrainian economy for the first four months grew by 22% and deposits by 23.5%. At least part of this intermediation improvement can be attributed to the liberalisation in reserve requirements.

Moreover, a decrease in reserve requirements will be positive in the sense of equalising the costs between commercial banks and other financial intermediaries, which are not subject to reserve requirement regulations. This would reduce some of the benefits to "grey lenders" and promote the inflow of capital into the official economy. In addition, the Ukrainian commercial banks will experience more favourable competitive conditions vis-à-vis foreign financial markets.

Looking at the results of this partial analysis, the primary policy implication for Ukraine should be to bring reserve requirements down. But without first examining some other aspects of the question, we cannot be absolutely sure that a decrease in reserve requirements will entail the positive changes described above.

Firstly, the Central Bank has to be sure that it will still be able to conduct monetary policy under the new conditions, i.e. it possesses other effective and reliable instruments. For Ukraine the biggest challenge here lies in the development of open market operations and a revival of the T-bills market.

The second point is that a decrease in reserve requirements actually creates new free money in the economy. Taking into account that the planed increase in the money base for the year 2001 is UAH 2 bn, any significant change in the required reserves (which amount to about UAH 2.5 bn) could raise concerns about the stability of the national currency. Thus, the policy of liberalising reserve requirements must be part of the overall Central Bank strategy of money emission. However, following the experience of EU states and some CEE countries, issuing long-term government bonds can neutralise this negative liquidity effect.

The danger of greater interest rate volatility is another important issue. Hence, Ukraine should promote the development of the inter-bank market, which when properly functioning can help to avoid interest rate volatility.

The fourth problem lies in the conflict between private and public interests. A reduction in reserve requirements – which is like an emission of money – means that the government has fewer possibilities for direct money creation, and hence seigniorage revenues will fall as well. It should be noted here, that this issue is a matter of the government's political will to give up some easy money for the sake of long-term economic growth.

The fifth question to consider is whether liberalising the reserve requirements can actually result in a credit expansion in the economy. In cases of strongly regulated financial markets and a lack of developed legislative and institutional settings, commercial banks can accumulate considerable liquidity, but will not be able (or may not be willing) to give sound credits to the real sector (which is the actual case in Ukraine). Thus, the Central Bank should not only ease its stance vis-à-vis commercial banks through its reserve requirements, but also promote the creation of favourable conditions through effective mechanisms concerning collateral and bankruptcy, credit regulations, etc..

The final point concerns the role of reserve requirements in securing deposits in the case of a bank failure. This function was important at the early stages of implementing reserve requirements but has diminished since, mainly due to the associated high costs. The newly created deposit insurance funds should fulfil this function much more successfully. Thus, as the ratio of reserves to deposits diminishes, the need for a reliable deposit insurance fund in Ukraine becomes imperative.

Turning to the idea of reforming the reserve requirements in Ukraine and taking the above warnings into account, we can now examine how to implement the changes to the existing system.

In the first instance, we should note that a rapid decrease in reserve requirements is not desirable for any economy, since a) it creates new money, which can result in increased inflation, and b) the central bank may not have enough time for adjusting its monetary policy. Therefore, central banks pursue gradual policies of reducing reserve requirements, extending over several years. For instance, the government of Canada authorised the elimination of reserve requirements through the Bank Act of 1991, while implementation extended through mid-1994. Other countries, which also experienced substantial reforms of reserve requirements, such as the United Kingdom and New Zealand, implemented them over several years as well. CEE accessing countries, which have to meet the regulations of the European System of Central Banks, all have long-term plans for decreasing reserve requirements. For a transition economy such as Ukraine a gradual approach is especially important. Its weak financial sector and the NBU's lack of effective alternative instruments could turn a sharp decrease of reserves into volatility in the financial markets and into currency instability. This process should therefore certainly be extended over several years.

The second issue concerns the target level of the reserve requirement reform. Although bringing reserves down to a low level could bring relief to commercial banks, it also raises difficulties for the NBU with the control of the money supply. Hence again, decreasing the reserve to deposit ratio below 5% to 6% is most probably undesirable over the medium term.

The proposed speed of change and target level of the reserves should promote financial intermediation, while at the same time allowing the NBU to be confident about conducting monetary policy and controlling the money supply.

5 Conclusions

In this chapter we were talking about reserve requirements as an instrument of monetary policy and its impact on the private sector. The main point of the analysis is that although holding reserves is a suitable tool for the Central Bank, it imposes an additional burden on the commercial banks, and beyond to other agents of the economy. We argue that the commercial banks will try to pass the cost of holding reserves on to their clients, widening the interest rate spread. Eventually this process will result in distortion in aggregate investment and will have adverse effects on output.

At this time the financial system in Ukraine is pretty thin and the interest rate spread – reflecting the various bank costs – is large. Liberalising the reserve requirements could therefore be an important facilitating factor to create favourable conditions for banking sector development and for promoting credit to the real economy.

The analysis shows that a reform of the reserve requirements can be implemented without putting pressure on price stability or compromising the ability of the NBU to conduct monetary policy. We propose a program of gradually reducing reserve requirements to a 5-6% average within the next 2 to 3 years. The process of reserve reforms must be incorporated into the fiscal and monetary policies and must be co-ordinated within all government bodies. The important point here is that the NBU should accept the new funds derived from the reserve reduction into its general plan of creating money, thus avoiding inflationary pressures. In that way the financial system will experience relief of the regulatory burden and the benefits will be spread over a wider range of economic agents, promoting long-term economic growth. The NBU in turn will still be able to conduct monetary policy and have control over money supply via this instrument.

During 2001 reserve requirements underwent some reforms in Ukraine, which had a positive impact on financial intermediation. The success of further changes greatly depends on understanding the importance of the financial sector on long-term economic growth and on the commitment to pursue time consistent policies, giving up some easy-to-achieve measures for the sake of real reforms.

References

Clinton, K. (1997): Implementation of Monetary Policy in a Regime with Zero Reserve Requirements. Bank of Canada, Working paper.

Clouse A. J. and D. W. Elmendorf (1997): Declining Required Reserves and the Volatility of the Federal Funds Rate. Federal Reserve Board.

Deutsche Bundesbank (1994): The Monetary Policy of the Bundesbank, Deutsche Bundesbank.

Freidman B. M. (2000): Monetary Policy. NBER, Working paper No. w8057.

Kuprianov A. (1997): Tax Disincentives to Commercial Bank Lending. Federal Reserve Bank of Richmond, Economic Quarterly, Volume 83/2.

Loungani P. and R. Mark (1995): The Effect of Changes in Reserve Requirements on Investment and GNP Journal of Money, Credit and Banking. Volume 27, Issue 2.

National Bank of Hungary, Monetary policy in Hungary. The instruments of the monetary policy. http://www.nbh.hu.

Mishkin F. (1999): Money and Banking. Cambridge University Press.

Repullo, R. (1992): Financing Budget Deficits by Seigniorage and Implicit Taxation: the Cases of Spain and Portugal. CEPR, Working paper.

Saunders A. (1998): Financial Institutions Management. McGraw-Hill.

Sellon H. G., W. and E. Stuart (1997): Monetary Policy without Reserve Requirements: Analytical issues. Federal Reserve Bank of Kansas City, Economic Review.

Sellon H. G., W. and E. Stuart (1997): Monetary Policy without Reserve Requirements: Case studies and options for the United States. Federal Reserve Bank of Kansas City, Economic Review.

Stelmakh V., A. Epifanov, N. Grebenik, and V. Mischenko (2000): Monetary Policy in Ukraine. Kyiv, Znaniya.

15

Efficient Infrastructure Supply as a Condition for Economic Development – The Case of Ukraine

Boris Dodonov, Christian von Hirschhausen, Petra Opitz, Pavlo Sugolov

1 Introduction

Attention to the infrastructure investments as a factor of economic growth has revived after Aschauer's work. He demonstrated that in the United States the productivity down-turn was preceded by a down-turn in infrastructure investments (Aschauer, 1989). However, later aggregate production function studies and the international debate on infrastructure as a factor of economic growth have so far not brought forth any firm evidence to substantiate this contention.

Traditionally international financial institutions acknowledge the importance of infrastructure development for economic growth. At the same time they fail to provide unambiguous evidence supporting the idea. The World Bank in its review of infrastructure policies finds some correlation between infrastructure development and personal income levels. At the same time the rates of return of individual World Bank projects in different countries are found to vary significantly between different countries. After analysis of possible explanations for this fact it was concluded that the main reason of it to be weak climate of economic activity in a country (World Bank, 1994).

There is even less consensus on how specific infrastructure policies should be designed to support growth, and how they should respond to specific institutional conditions, e.g. in countries undergoing systemic transformation. A traditional neo-classical approach relates infrastructure investments to increasing total factor productivity. According to one of alternative approaches infrastructure investments influence positively through direct cost reductions and market selection effects the economic structural change and the intensity of competition (Aghion and Schankerman, 1999). Armstrong and Vickers (1996) relate the optimal speed of infrastructure liberalisation to the risks of expropriation and liberalisation.

The policy debate is mainly concerned with quantitative measures, e.g. public investments, whereas the qualitative aspects of infrastructure policy are at least equally important. The economic growth effect resulting from improved economic institutions is found to be significant. Piazolo (1999) has found government economic policy credibility to have a positive influence on economic growth in transition economies. Henisz (2000) in an extensive panel data study has shown that the political environment is an important determinant of investment in vital economic infrastructure.

Thus, there still exists substantial uncertainty about the relation between infrastructure investments and economic growth both in developed and in transitional economies. The argument that can be made so far is that the institutional environment can be a very important complement for infrastructure investments to be translated into economic growth. The ultimate objective of infrastructure reforms is to supply infrastructure services by efficient, mainly privatised companies, at tariffs close to hypothetical market levels (e.g. long-run marginal costs, complemented by a time-of-use element), and subject to an objective, transparent regulatory process. Ukraine is still far away from this ideal world, just as many other countries of the former Soviet Union. Evaluation and monitoring of the development of the current institutional framework of all infrastructure sectors are necessary preconditions for determining further policy measures to make the infrastructure sectors work more efficiently.

This chapter discusses different approaches to estimating the efficiency of infrastructure policies. Section 2 describes how infrastructure policies in transition countries are generally assessed using the EBRD methodology. Section 3 provides a more detailed assessment and applies it to six infrastructure sectors in Ukraine (telecommunications, railways, roads, power, gas and water). Finally, we provide some policy conclusions in Section 4.

2 How infrastructure development is currently monitored?

The level of infrastructure reform can be expressed qualitatively by infrastructure reform indicators. Such a policy instrument was developed by the EBRD and was aimed at comparing different approaches to reform in the infrastructure sectors of transformation countries (EBRD, 1996). The EBRD made an assessment of the infrastructure reform indicators for 26 transformation countries for 1998-2000 for the most important material infrastructure sectors: telecommunication, railways, power, roads and water/wastewater (EBRD, 2000). The evaluation was based on three criteria:

- commercialisation and privatisation, i.e. the transformation of corporate governance structures, the introduction of hard budget constraints, and eventually, assets divestment;
- tariff reform, i.e. the introduction of cost-covering and allocative efficient price structures;
- regulatory and institutional reform, i.e. the establishment of independent regulatory agencies with appropriate checks and balances within a formal institutional framework.

The scale of the evaluation ranged from 1 (no market economy oriented reforms at all) to 4.3 (full implementation of the sectoral regulation of Western European market economies), the point of reference being the degree of competition-orientation of infrastructure policies in developed market economies, in this case the countries of the European Union.

The results of the EBRD estimations of the progress of infrastructure reforms can be seen in Graph 15.1. There are three groups: Central/Eastern European market economies, Post Soviet mixed economies and Caspian state economies. A definition of these ideal type groups was done by Hirschhausen and Waelde (2001). Ukraine is in the group of Post Soviet mixed economies together with Russia and Belarus, but in the graph it is also presented separately to compare it to other economies.

Graph 15.1
Infrastructure indicators by group of countries

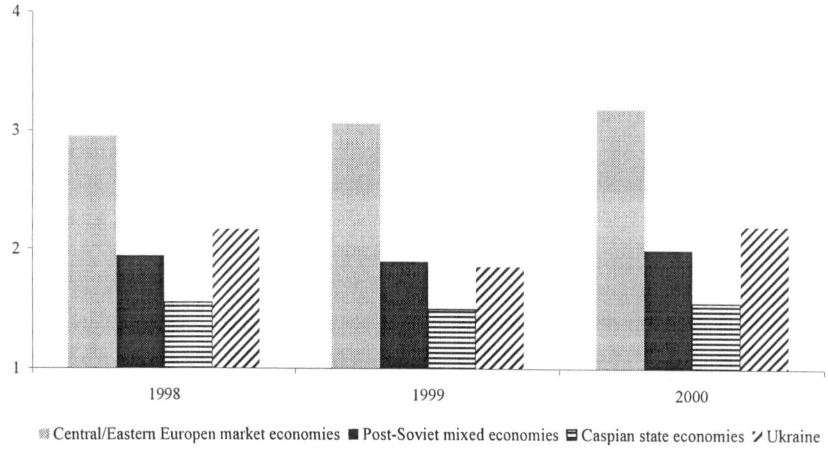

Sources: EBRD (1998, p. 44, 1999, p. 50, 2000, p. 42) and own estimates

The average results for all groups of countries decreased slightly from 1998 to 1999, which is a result of taking the average of five industries in 1999 instead of only three in 1998. The estimations for 1999 and 2000 are entirely comparable. An aggregate analysis of infrastructure sector reform in the transformation countries hints at a rather slow reform process. On average, the reform-orientation of infrastructure policies has not progressed much since 1998. Most of the countries of Eastern Europe and all CIS-countries are still far from the reference model, and some countries have carried out virtually no reforms at all (Belarus, Tajikistan, Turkmenistan). In Graph 15.1 are emerging distinctions between different groups of countries in transition shown. The *Central/East European market economies* achieved the highest degree of market-orientation, though the difference between them and the reference model is still considerable. The *post-Soviet mixed economies* carried out some reforms, but these seem to be stagnating at a low level of about 2. Finally, the *Caspian state economies* have proven to be almost totally reform-resistant (Hirschhausen, 2001).

During the initial stage of the reference period Ukraine has lagged behind the Central/Eastern European countries in infrastructure reforms. In the first decade of transformation subsequent Ukrainian governments carried out relatively little reforms in infrastructure, leading to low degrees of competition and a relatively distorted price structure. In 2000 reforms seem to have accelerated, the gap with the *Central/Eastern European market economies* has become smaller due to the adoption of new legislation on roads, a begin with restructuring the railways, and adoption of changes to power industry legislation regulating distributive accounts and increasing tariff collection ratios (Graph 15.2).

Notwithstanding the high rates of infrastructure development obtained by Ukraine, a closer study of Ukrainian infrastructure industries reveals that in fact they are still characterised by a limited involvement of the private sector, maintained monopolistic supply, had weak regulatory institutions and were oriented towards serving distributional purposes and social insurance instead of efficiency and profitability. Though over-capacities abound in many infrastructure sectors (e.g. railways and power), the quality of infrastructure services is low. Tariffs are still severely distorted. All in all, Ukraine is but at the initial stage of infrastructure reforms and needs extensive restructuring and market-oriented regulations in order to achieve efficiency and to support economic recovery and growth.

The progress in EBRD infrastructure indicators does not seem to reflect the real situation with infrastructure reforms in Ukraine. According to our estimations, only in telecommunications did the reforms substantially accelerate in the year 2000. Preparations were under way to privatise the monopolistic fixed line operator by buying out shares of the monopolistic international phone services operator and by selling shares of the largest mobile phone operator. Reforms in the power industry were directed not so much at the introduction of new regulations as at the improvement of the quality of existing regulations. The government achieved some success in fighting the non-payment problem in the power sector through the introduction of distributive accounts. Reforms in the railway industry achieved momentum only in 2001 – when restructuring of the railways by separation and corporatisation of maintenance enterprises was initiated.

Graph 15.2
Infrastructure indicators for Ukraine, EBRD

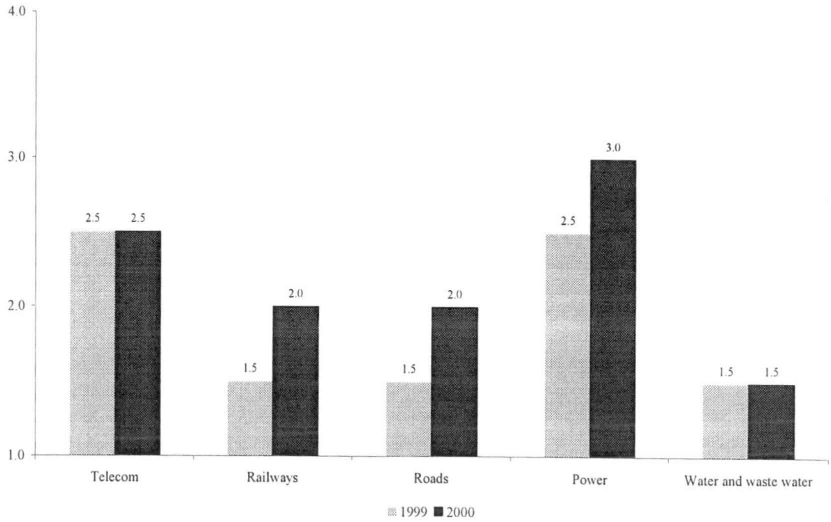

Sources: EBRD (1999, p. 50, 2000, p. 42)

Notwithstanding the adoption of progressive legislation in the road sector, it was not implemented; road tax was centralised in the state budget and was directed for other purposes. The policy towards the water supply and sewage industry did not change – tariffs are still below cost covering levels, losses in networks remain high and the payment discipline did not change.

3 Results of a more detailed assessment

3.1 Differences with EBRD methodology

In questioning the EBRD methodology we found that it could be improved when such factors as implementation of the legislation and key performance indicators were taken into account. The Institute of Economic Research and Policy Consulting (IERPC) has extended the EBRD methodology and produced its own infrastructure monitoring which evaluates the current state and the dynamics of the reform process.[1] The objective of our infrastructure monitoring is to provide a regular, in-depth analysis of policy reforms in six key infrastructure sectors: power, gas, water, telecommunication, railways, and roads.

The IERPC follows EBRD's indicators for reasons of compatibility, however it extends the methodology both through indicator dis-aggregation and through incorporation of legislation implementation issues and key performance indicators, e.g. payment arrears and mutual settlements. Both methodologies have their advantages and disadvantages. The problem with dis-aggregating indicators and producing estimations of individual aspects may result in estimation biases resulting from individual indicator selections. Nevertheless, the EBRD indicator biases related to their estimation procedures can be still higher. Here is a summary of the improvements introduced to the EBRD methodology by the IERPC:

1. The estimations scale allows for a higher level of discretion, it more closely reflects the US Grade Point Average principle, by introducing steps of 0.3 points (i.e. .3 and .7 increments are added to the straight grades 4, 3, 2 and 1). Introduction of a higher level of discretion in estimates allows more exact estimation of the progress of reforms.

2. Each EBRD indicator is derived from just one estimation, while the IERPC's indicator is a mean of 21 indicators. This dis-aggregation allows the introduction of a more objective approach to estimation. Moreover, this approach forms the basis for further development of the methodology by revision of the indicators and their weighting.

3. Key performance and legislation implementation indicators are incorporated into the IERPC's indicators. This is important for countries such as Ukraine, because an analysis of adopted legislation does not reflect the progress of reforms adequately due to problems with the implementation of the legislation. Since the indicators are qualitative, we did not incorporate such quantitative indicators as production volume, capacity extension or profitability in order to leave an opportunity to estimate the impact of these factors separately. The performance indicators reflect a quality of performance, including factors such as payments collection, barter operations, mutual indebtedness and settlements.

4. The IERPC applied universal criteria to all sectors, while the EBRD criteria are individual for each sector. Universal criteria ensure cross industry comparability of the indicators, but this implies a common ideal organisational structure for all infrastructure industries. Cross industry comparability of indicators is important for political advice. However, there is no consensus

---

[1] A definition of each indicator along with detailed description of the estimation methodology and the explanation of each score was done in Dodonov, von Hirschhausen, Opitz and Sugolov (2001).

among economists on the ideal organisational structure of most infrastructure industries.

5. We include the gas industry into the infrastructure indicator, since the gas transportation infrastructure is an important natural monopoly industry for Ukraine, the regulation of which causes heated debates.

3.2 Results of the IERPC estimations

The IERPC has produced estimations for six infrastructure sectors.[2] The IERPC and the EBRD indicators are presented in Graph 15.3. The above mentioned changes in methodology and especially the application of different reference models make the indicators not directly comparable. They are presented in one graph just for reference. Comparability was sacrificed with the introduction of the new reference model since the universal ideal reference model is a necessary innovation which makes infrastructure indicators an important policy tool. Policy makers need to be able to compare the progress of reforms in different industries. The conclusion that can be drawn so far is that the EBRD indicators tend to overestimate the pace of reforms.

Graph 15.3
Infrastructure policy evaluation in 2000

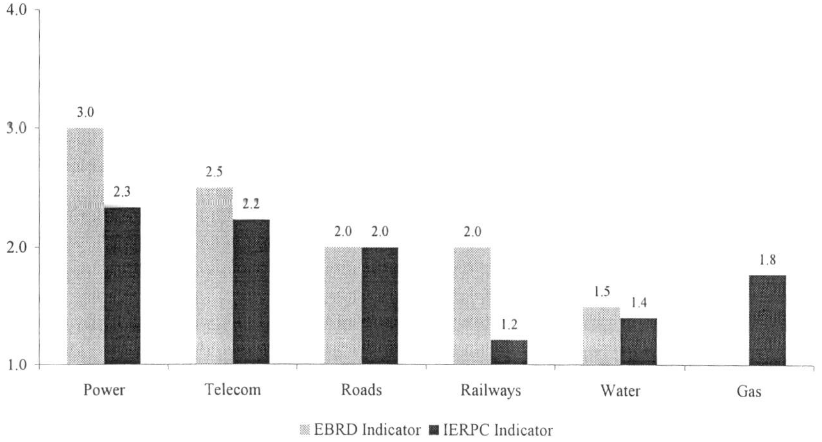

Source: EBRD, Transition Report (2000, p. 42); own estimates

2 See Appendix for dis-aggregated indicators.

3.3 Detailed assessment of infrastructure indicators in Ukraine – a case study of the railways sector

To illustrate how the evaluation of infrastructure industry indicators was produced we chose the railways industry – one of the largest infrastructure industries, which serves as an input to all the major Ukrainian industries. Currently the industry can be characterised as a monopoly serving distributional and social insurance purposes by subsidisation of other industries and the population. As a result it is constantly incurring losses and underwent a sharp deterioration of assets. Having inherited large infrastructure and rolling stock capacities from the USSR, the Ukrainian railways had not invested enough in maintenance and ended up with a 49% share of outmoded equipment in 1998.[3] The impact of reforms in this sector would be very significant; however, the industry is among the slowest reformers.

The Ukrainian railways were always operated as a government department with a strongly integrated infrastructure, freight and passenger operations, construction and maintenance services, and quite an extensive social infrastructure. Although a Ukrainian railways' restructuring program was developed and adopted in 1998, it was not implemented until now. Restructuring of the industry was only initiated in July 2000 starting with the separation of the social infrastructure, services, railway construction, rolling stock repair and maintenance from the railway infrastructure and rolling stock. The social infrastructure was planned to be transferred to communal ownership. Major reform achievements in 2000 were the reduction of payment arrears and barter payments, leading to an improvement in the financial situation in the industry. In 2000 the State Administration of Railway Transport of Ukraine reported profits for the first time in its history. The corporatisation of ancillary businesses of Ukrainian railways – seven major repair enterprises – was begun in April 2001.

These changes were reflected in our indicators shown in Graph 15.4. The IERPC indicator of institutional development of the railways industry is a mean of the commercialisation and privatisation reforms, of tariff reforms and of regulatory and institutional reforms. The overall progress of reforms achieved in 2001 due to commercialisation and separation of ancillary businesses and fighting barter payments did not significantly influence the final grade of the IERPC indicator.

The "commercialisation and privatisation" category reflects changes in the ownership structure of the industry, the extent of participation of the private sector in service contracts, and the separation of railway infrastructure and potentially competitive businesses. Ukrainian railways remain a state monopoly for infrastructure, transportation services and most construction and maintenance services. Infrastructure and transportation services are strongly integrated. The

---

[3] State Statistics Committee, 1998.

industry is still managed as a government department. The development planning and investment policies are subordinated to the production volume and to social security purposes instead of profitability and cost minimisation. Therefore, the progress achieved with construction, maintenance and service companies separation and corporatisation improved the grade for the category only by 0.2 points compared to 2000.

The "tariff reform" category monitors the procedures of tariff regulation and the extent to which tariffs cover costs, the intra-industry and final consumers' payments collection ratios, and the extent and timeliness of state subsidy provisions. The industry tariffs in 2000 were imposed administratively, they do not reflect marginal costs and are not even covering costs.

- Correct cost accounting and attribution of costs to the services provided is probably one of the major problems of the railway administration. In 2000, the Ukrainian railways reported about UAH 500 m gross profit. Since this was accompanied with a continuing steep deterioration of the rolling stock and the infrastructure, not all costs were taken into account. Cost coverage problems could be solved through tariff adjustments accompanied by adjustments of railway capacities. Almost no measures were taken to reduce the costs and adjust tariffs to achieve a cost covering level. The railway transportation volume has substantially declined during the 1990s, to 29% of the 1980 volume, while the length of rail lines has remained the same. At the same time there was no increase in real freight transportation tariffs as should have been expected.
- The other major problem with the Ukrainian railways is cross-subsidisation. A UAH 1.8 bn deficit, generated by passenger transportation in 2000, was covered by freight transportation. The problem of cross-subsidisation in the Ukrainian railway industry is worsened by a poor governmental compensations payment discipline. A significant part of the deficit generated in passengers transportation is attributed to failure of the government to compensate for transportation of privileged passengers. Ukrzaliznytsia estimates the uncompensated deficit at UAH 500 m in 2000.[4]

We have taken the success with fighting non-monetary payments and the improvement of payments collection ratios into account, but the lack of reforms in other areas of tariffs regulation in 2001 resulted in a grade point improvement of only 0.1 for the category compared to 2000.

---

4 According to Ukrainian legislation the respective costs of the Ukrainian Railways have to be compensated to the service provider by the central and by local governments depending on the authority, which made the decision on the privileges. Law "On Railway Transportation", 4 February 1996, No. 0237, article 9.

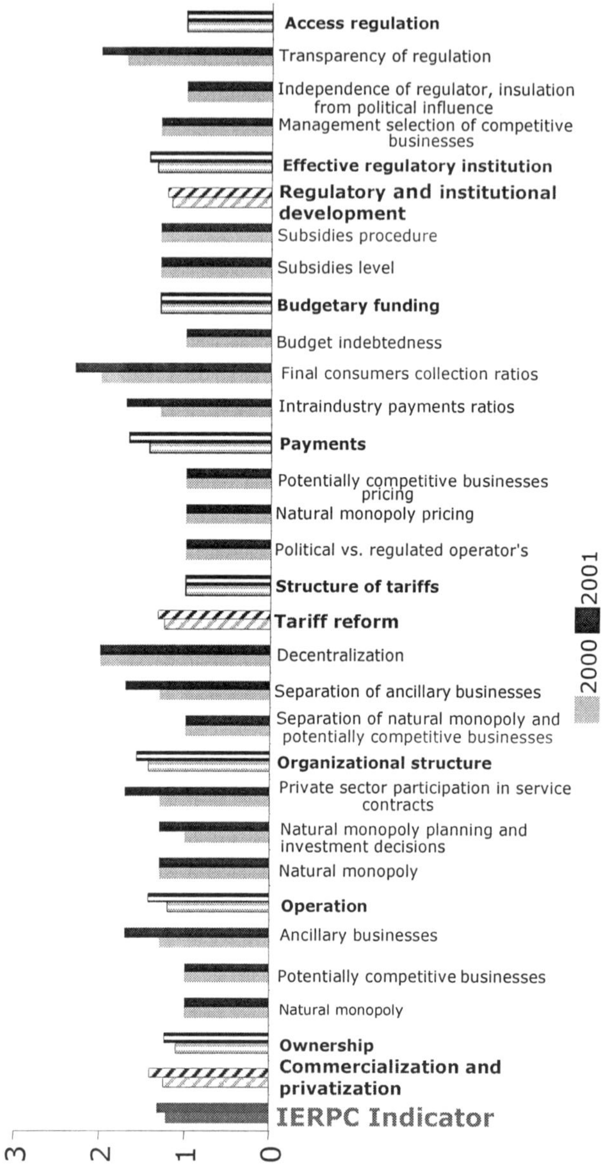

Graph 15.4
IERPC indicators for the railways industry in 2000 and 2001

Sources: own calculations

"Regulatory and institutional development" mainly reflects the independence of the regulatory body, the transparency of regulations, including regulations for access and service quality. Since the Ukrainian railways are a part of the government and there are no independent regulatory bodies, this category obtained a low grade. We have taken into account the fact that this question was openly debated within the government; however, the final grade remained unchanged.

As we can see, the categories of "ownership" and "tariff reform" remain the slowest reformers. The core businesses of railways infrastructure, and passenger and freight transportation are still untouched by reforms. Reforms concerning the corporatisation of ancillary businesses can only be regarded as supplementary. To continue to conduct only supplementary reforms has a potential danger. It may lead to substantial rent seeking and an outflow of capital through ancillary business enterprises if their owners are affiliated with the managers of core businesses and contracts are not traded in a transparent way.

4 Conclusions and policy recommendations

Infrastructure restructuring is one of the major elements of structural reforms in transition economies because of its expected large economic and social impact. Notwithstanding the fact that the relationship between infrastructure policy and economic growth still cannot be empirically tested, there are no reasons to doubt the importance of infrastructure policy. As stated above, infrastructure investments alone do not have a significant influence on economic growth. However, the argument that can be made is that an institutional environment can be a very important complement for infrastructure investments to be translated into economic growth. By enhancing competition and efficiency in infrastructure industries the government can make an indirect contribution to economic development (Hirschhausen, 2001).

Ukrainian infrastructure industries are facing the same problems as those in any other country: inefficient pricing, low cost coverage, and cross-subsidisation. International experience suggests that the solution to these problems can be to introduce the private sector into infrastructure industries and establishing effective regulatory institutions. Most attention in Ukraine should be paid to tariff regulation.

Tariff policy can play a crucial role in solving the problem of financial sustainability of most infrastructure industries. Ukraine has substantially to change its approach. Current Ukrainian tariff policy is characterised by cross-subsidisation, levying tariffs below cost covering levels, and indirect instead of direct subsidy provisions. Instead, the government should pursue a policy of commercialisation and cost reflective tariffs. The measures of tariffs adjustment to cost-covering levels should be accompanied by the provision of incentives for cost reduction. These should be supported with the introduction of built-in tariff adjustment mechanisms, the separation of infrastructure and major potentially competitive businesses, as well as by the reduction of the amount of government subsidies, an improved budget payments discipline and the elimination of cross-subsidies. This implies a need for developing quite an extensive and complex government programme.

Deregulation should be carried out simultaneously with commercialisation and tariff reform. Recent experience in both developed market economies and developing countries suggests that to start deregulation while promoting competition leads to declining prices and improved service quality. However, deregulation accompanied with a slow pace of core reforms could potentially lead to rent seeking related to distortions of incentives structures. When the separation of ancillary businesses is supported by the introduction of competition into the core businesses and the establishment of an independent regulatory body, the problem of rent seeking can be limited. Our infrastructure monitoring is designed as an instrument for keeping track of current reforms and determining necessary policy measures.[5]

References

Aschauer, D. A. (1989): Is Public Expenditures Productive. Journal of Monetary Economics, 23, pp. 177-200.

Aghion, P. and M. Schankerman (1999): Competition, Entry and the Social Returns to Infrastructure in Transition Economies. Economics of Transition, Vol. 7, No. 1, pp. 79-101.

Armstrong, M. and J. Vickers (1996): Regulatory Reform in Telecommunications in Central and Eastern Europe. Economics of Transition, Vol. 4, No. 2, pp. 295-318.

Dodonov B., C. von Hirschhausen,, P. Opitz, and P. Sugolov (2001): Infrastructure Monitoring for Ukraine (IMU). Institute for Economic Reforms and Policy Consulting, Working Paper No. 8.

EBRD (1996): Transition Report 1996, London.

EBRD (2000): Transition Report 2000, London.

5 The Infrastructure Monitoring for Ukraine (IMU) will be produced and distributed by the Institute for Economic Research and Policy Consulting (IERPC) on a bi-annual basis, see www.ier.kiev.ua. For the future we also plan additional research on an empirical estimation of the relationship between infrastructure development and economic growth for all transition countries.

German Advisory Group on Economic Reforms with the Ukrainian Government (1999): The Next 1000 Days: Economic Reform Agenda for Ukraine, Kyiv.

Henisz, W. J. (2000): The Institutional Environment for Infrastructure Investment. Mimeo, University of Pennsylvania.

Hirschhausen, C. and T. Waelde (2001): The End of "Transition" – An Institutional Interpretation of Energy Sector Reform in Eastern Europe and the CIS. MOCT-MOST Economic Policy in Transitional Economies, Vol. 11, No. 1, pp. 91-108.

Hirschhausen, C. (2001): Infrastructure Policies and Liberalisation in the East European Transition Countries. DIW-Discussion Paper.

Ministry of Economy (2001): Monthly monitor, No. 3, Kyiv.

Piazolo, D. (1999): Growth Effects of Institutional Change and European Integration. Economic Systems, Vol. 23, No. 4, pp. 305-330.

State Statistics Committee of Ukraine (1998): Transportation and Telecommunications, Kyiv.

World Bank (1994): World Development Report 1994 – Infrastructure for Development; Oxford University Press, Washington, D.C. and Oxford.

Appendix

Table 15.1
Infrastructure indicator evaluation

	Indicator	Aspect		Telecom 1999	Telecom 2000	Telecom 2001	Railroad 1999	Railroad 2000	Railroad 2001	Roads 1999	Roads 2000	Roads 2001	Power 1999	Power 2000	Power 2001	Gas 1999	Gas 2000	Gas 2001	Water 1999	Water 2000	Water 2001
	EBRD indicator			2.5	2.5		1.5	2.0		1.5	2.0		2.5	3.0					1.5	1.5	
	IERPC indicator				2.2	2.3		1.2	1.3		2.0	2.0		2.3	2.5		1.8	1.9		1.4	1.4
1	**Commercialization and privatization**		1		2.0	2.0		1.2	1.4		1.9	2.0		2.4	2.5		1.7	1.8		1.3	1.3
1.1	**Ownership**		**1.1**		**1.9**	**1.9**		**1.1**	**1.2**		**2.0**	**2.0**		**2.2**	**2.3**		**1.9**	**1.9**		**1.0**	**1.0**
1.1.1		Natural monopoly	1.1.1		1.0	1.0		1.0	1.0		1.0	1.0		3.0	3.3		1.7	1.7		1.0	1.0
1.1.2		Potentially competitive businesses	1.1.2		2.7	2.7		1.0	1.0		2.7	2.7		2.3	2.3		2.7	2.7		1.0	1.0
1.1.3		Ancillary businesses	1.1.3		2.0	2.0		1.3	1.7		2.3	2.3		1.3	1.3		1.3	1.3		1.0	1.0
1.2	**Operation**		**1.2**		**1.8**	**1.9**		**1.2**	**1.4**		**1.6**	**1.8**		**2.5**	**2.6**		**1.4**	**1.8**		**1.3**	**1.3**
1.2.1		Natural monopoly	1.2.1		1.7	2.0		1.3	1.3		1.3	1.7		3.0	3.3		2.0	2.0		2.0	2.0
1.2.2		Natural monopoly planning and investment decisions	1.2.2		2.0	2.0		1.0	1.3		1.7	1.7		2.7	2.7		1.0	2.0		1.0	1.0
1.2.3		Private sector participation in service contracts	1.2.3		1.7	1.7		1.3	1.7		1.7	2.0		1.7	1.7		1.3	1.3		1.0	1.0
1.3	**Organizational structure**		**1.3**		**2.2**	**2.2**		**1.4**	**1.6**		**2.2**	**2.2**		**2.5**	**2.5**		**1.9**	**1.9**		**1.6**	**1.6**
1.3.1		Separation of natural monopoly and potentially competitive businesses	1.3.1		2.3	2.3		1.0	1.0		3.3	3.3		3.7	3.7		2.0	2.0		1.0	1.0
1.3.2		Separation of ancillary businesses	1.3.2		2.0	2.0		1.3	1.7		2.0	2.0		1.3	1.3		1.7	1.7		1.0	1.0
1.3.3		Decentralization	1.3.3		2.3	2.3		2.0	2.0		1.3	1.3								2.7	2.7
2	**Tariff reform**		2		2.4	2.4		1.2	1.3		2.0	2.0		2.2	2.6		2.0	2.3		1.8	1.8
2.1	**Structure of tariffs**		**2.1**		**2.3**	**2.4**		**1.0**	**1.0**		**2.0**	**2.0**		**2.7**	**2.7**		**2.2**	**2.2**		**1.5**	**1.5**
2.1.1		Political vs. regulated operator's	2.1.1		2.0	2.0		1.0	1.0		1.7	1.7		3.0	3.0		2.0	2.0		1.0	1.0
2.1.2		Natural monopoly pricing	2.1.2		2.3	2.3		1.0	1.0		1.7	1.7		2.7	2.7		2.3	2.3		1.7	1.7
2.1.3		Potentially competitive businesses pricing	2.1.3		2.7	3.0		1.0	1.0		2.7	2.7		2.3	2.3		2.3	2.3		1.7	1.7
2.2	**Payments**		**2.2**		**2.8**	**2.9**		**1.4**	**1.7**		**2.4**	**2.2**		**1.9**	**3.1**		**1.9**	**2.7**		**1.8**	**2.0**
2.2.1		Intraindustry payments ratios	2.2.1		2.3	2.3		1.3	1.7		2.7	2.7		2.0	3.0		2.0	2.0		2.0	2.0
2.2.2		Final consumers collection ratios	2.2.2		3.0	3.3		2.0	2.3		2.7	2.7		2.0	3.0		2.0	2.7		1.7	1.7
2.2.3		Budget indebtedness	2.2.3		3.0	3.0		1.0	1.0		1.7	1.3		1.7	3.3		1.7	3.3		1.7	2.3
2.3	**Budgetary funding**		**2.3**		**2.0**	**2.0**		**1.3**	**1.3**		**1.7**	**1.7**		**2.0**	**2.0**		**2.0**	**2.0**		**2.0**	**2.0**
2.3.1		Subsidies level	2.3.1		2.3	2.3		1.3	1.3		2.0	2.0		2.0	2.0		2.0	2.0		2.0	2.0
2.3.2		Subsidies procedure	2.3.2		1.7	1.7		1.3	1.3		1.3	1.3		2.0	2.0		2.0	2.0		2.0	2.0
3	**Regulatory and institutional development**		3		2.4	2.4		1.2	1.2		2.0	2.0		2.4	2.4		1.5	1.6		1.2	1.2
3.1	**Effective regulatory institution**		**3.1**		**2.4**	**2.6**		**1.3**	**1.4**		**1.9**	**2.0**		**2.6**	**2.6**		**1.8**	**1.9**		**1.3**	**1.3**
3.1.1		Management selection of competitive businesses	3.1.1		2.7	2.7		1.3	1.3		2.0	2.0		2.0	2.0		2.0	2.0		2.0	2.0
3.1.2		Independence of regulator, insulation from political	3.1.2		2.3	2.7		1.0	1.0		2.0	2.0		2.7	2.7		2.0	2.0		1.0	1.0
3.1.3		Transparency of regulation	3.1.3		2.3	2.3		1.7	2.0		1.7	2.0		3.0	3.0		1.3	1.7		1.0	1.0
3.2	**Access regulation**		**3.2**		**2.3**	**2.3**		**1.0**	**1.0**		**2.0**	**2.0**		**2.3**	**2.3**		**1.3**	**1.3**		**1.0**	**1.0**

16

A Regional Agricultural Trade Model for Wheat and Sunflower Seeds in Ukraine

Alexander Kobzev

1 Introduction

Ukraine has a significant potential for agricultural production. The country enjoys a large area of agricultural land with fertile soils combined with favourable climatic conditions. All that creates the necessary environmental preconditions to cultivate many crops on a large-scale and to develop an efficient livestock production. A beneficial geographic location, and relative proximity to important markets such as the countries of the former Soviet Union and the Middle East allows Ukraine to export many agricultural commodities. And yet, agricultural production has been declining for the last decade. The agricultural output in Ukraine has decreased to almost one half of 1990 levels. Only in the last year has the situation been reversed and a slight increase in agricultural production was posted. Ineffective state agricultural policies together with excessive marketing costs have been two major reasons contributing to the decline in agricultural production.

For the last years, the Ukrainian government has repeatedly proclaimed its intention to join the world economic system and has even submitted an official application to the World Trade Organisation (WTO). However, to be fully integrated into the WTO and enjoy the advantages of membership, Ukraine must first liberalise its agricultural trade policies. Such liberalisation would apply not only to trade across external borders, but to internal trade as well. Free trade at the regional level provides for more efficient allocations of domestic resources, addresses the food security issue, and promotes the consolidation of domestic commodity markets.

The practice of the last years demonstrates than certain actions of the regional authorities in Ukraine create serious impediments to the efficiency of regional agricultural trade in Ukraine. The introduction of bans on the movement of agricultural commodities, in particular grain, between Ukrainian regions (oblasts) is a notorious example. In this situation, the losers are not only the local producers and traders, but the whole nation. Meanwhile, as the prospects for a better grain harvest in 2001 are growing, which may shift Ukraine from being a net-importer to an exporter of grain, so is the likelihood that the old practices of controlling regional commodity trade will be employed again.

In this context, the purpose of this paper is to demonstrate the negative consequences of certain state policies and established practices, and to analyse their implications both at the national and the regional levels. In section 2 the study employs a social welfare analysis and demonstrates the effects of excessive marketing costs on domestic price, on consumer and producer surpluses, and on social welfare. To simulate different state policies and practices on the wheat and sunflower seed markets in Ukraine, the author uses a GAMS model. The essentials of the model and the techniques for the calculation of regional wheat and sunflower supplies and demands as well as the regional elasticities are presented in section 3.

The results of the main model scenarios and an analysis of the distortional effects of certain policies and practices are elaborated in section 4. The study pays special attention to the changes in producer and consumer surpluses, transportation costs, and social welfare caused by high marketing costs, export taxes, and regional bans on the movement of agricultural commodities. The repercussions of such policies at the regional level are the prime focus of this section. The principal conclusions and policy implications are presented in section 5.

2 Excessive marketing costs and social welfare losses

Despite the fact that Ukraine's agricultural potential greatly exceeds the present level of agricultural production, existing ineffective mechanisms and policies are major impediments to increasing production and social welfare in the country. Excessive marketing costs combined with an undeveloped infrastructure of the agrarian market are two of the prime reasons for the decline of the national agriculture.

To analyse the effects of different policy mechanisms and practices it is useful to employ the concepts of consumer and producer surpluses and of social welfare analysis. Social welfare analysis considers costs and benefits to different socio-economic groups as well as net social welfare losses or benefits (Colman and Young, 1994).

In a broad sense, excessive marketing costs include the transportation, storage and handling costs of agricultural commodities and the costs of certain government policies on the agricultural market. Excessive marketing costs have a negative effect on domestic prices and lead to a redistribution of economic wealth between various economic agents.

To demonstrate the negative effect of excessive marketing costs on domestic prices, producer and consumer surpluses and social welfare, a graphical analysis shall be employed. Graph 16.1 represents the agricultural trade of those commodities of which Ukraine is traditionally a net-exporter, i.e. wheat and sunflower seeds. Under free trade and given that Ukraine is a small country, i.e. it cannot influence the world market price significantly, the domestic price for a given agricultural commodity is directly linked to the world price. World prices for agricultural commodities determine Ukrainian domestic prices since in general Ukrainian farmers have the choice between exporting or selling their produce domestically.

It is reasonable to assume that if domestic prices are lower than world market prices, Ukrainian producers and traders will be encouraged to export maximum volumes of the produced output. In the opposite situation where internal prices are higher than world market prices, Ukrainian farmers will not export the commodity in question but will sell it domestically. Therefore, for agricultural producers the opportunity cost of selling a commodity domestically is always the world market price (von Cramon-Taubadel, 2000).

Graph 16.1
The effects of high marketing cost on the domestic price and on social welfare

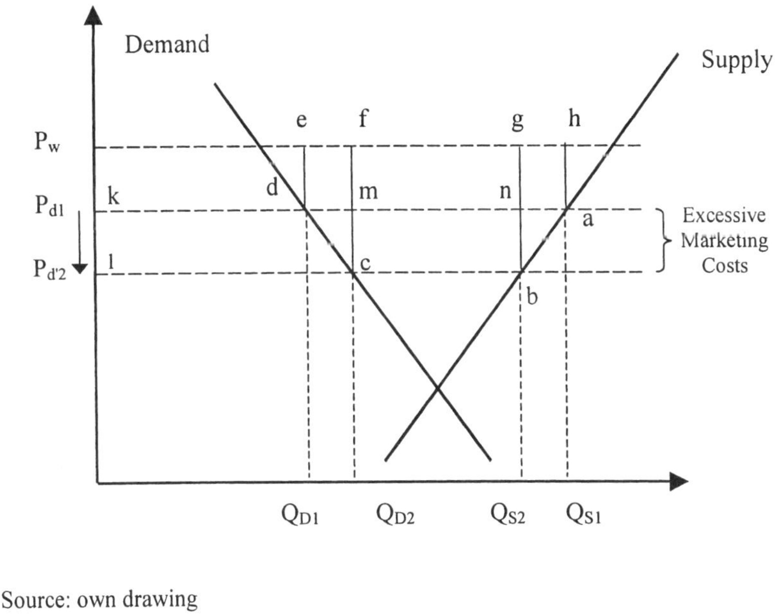

Source: own drawing

In an export situation, the price on the domestic market (P_{d1}) equals the world price (P_w) minus the costs for transportation and handling, as would be the case when marketing costs are relatively moderate and there are no interventions from the government. At the domestic price P_{d1}, producers supply the quantity Q_{S1}, out of which O_{D1} is consumed domestically and the difference (da) is exported.

Excessive marketing costs (unreasonably high transportation and handling costs combined with government intervention policies such as export tariffs and duties) depress the domestic price further, down to P_{d2}. In this situation the difference between the two domestic prices P_{d1} and P_{d2} is a wedge caused by the excessive costs. As the domestic commodity price falls, supply is shifting from Q_{S1} to Q_{S2}. The degree of supply decrease depends on a score of factors, and first of all, on supply elasticity.

The reaction of consumers to this situation of a lower domestic price P_{d2} is the opposite. Now they can purchase the commodity at a lower price, which raises domestic consumption from Q_{D1} to Q_{D2}. Thus, consumers and producers are affected differently in this situation. The lower price negatively effects local producers who receive lower revenues because of higher costs. The producer surplus is decreased by the area of $P_{d1}abP_{d2}$. Meanwhile the consumer is better off: At the lower domestic price P_{d2} the consumer surplus is increased by the area $P_{d1}dcP_{d2}$. The higher marketing costs bring additional proceeds to commodity traders and to the state budget. Their revenue rose from the rectangle *fgnm* to the rectangle *fgbc*.

Analysing the losses and gains in the graph, one can see that the area of the total losses (*kabl)* is larger than the areas of the total gains (*kdcl* plus *mnbc*). That means that the losses carried by producers outweigh the gains obtained by the consumers, the traders and the state. In this situation, the areas *efcd* and *ghab* represent the losses to society or the so-called social welfare losses. The figure *ghab* represents a net loss because $Q_{S2}Q_{S1}$ units could be sold at the price P_{d1} but are not produced after the costs have risen. The figure *efcd* is the producer surplus loss because the quantity $Q_{D1}Q_{D2}$ is sold to domestic buyers at P_{d2} rather than to foreign buyers at P_{d1}.

Marketing costs in Ukraine include elevator storage and handling, railway costs, DAF rail handling and custom costs, seaport handling weight losses, certification, financial and transaction costs, as well as certain additional expenses. Besides that, storage costs include not only the physical costs of handling an agricultural commodity at the elevators but also the opportunity costs of the capital related to the commodity stocks and the costs of quality and quantity losses in storage (von Cramon-Taubadel, 2000).

Storage costs also include a risk premium, which reflects the traders' uncertainty regarding free access to the delivered commodities. Furthermore as of last year, the State Customs Service required special export certificates from the State Grain Inspectorate to certify the quality of the grain. These policies were officially introduced "in order to eliminate defects in export-import operations with grain and to increase state control". This year the Cabinet of Ministers intends to introduce mandatory insurance for all agricultural enterprises producing grain and sugar beets (Ukragroconsult, May 2001). Such levies increase marketing costs and contribute to the declining profitability of Ukrainian farms.

Also related to excessive marketing costs is the issue of extremely high losses of agricultural crops. Along with increasing yields the gross harvest is heavily dependent on decreasing losses at the time of harvesting, during transport, procuring, and storage. Average wheat losses amount to 40 kg per hectare and total direct losses caused by repeated loading and unloading, technical deficiencies and inadequate capacities of the grain cleaning and drying equipment could reach as much as 1 m tons annually (Balabanov, 1998). One of the main reasons for losses is poorly constructed and badly maintained harvesting machinery, as well as poor conditions of rolling stock, roads, and processing machinery. Thus, under conditions of stiff world market competition excessive marketing costs are weakening Ukraine's positions as an agricultural exporter.

3 A regional agricultural trade model

3.1 Specifications of the model

To model and simulate regional agricultural production and trade, the study utilises GAMS (General Algebraic Modelling System).[1] It applies the Takayama and Judge Quadratic Programming approach with non-linear programming techniques.

Utilising existing data on marketing costs and state interventional policy instruments, the model mathematically formulates and optimises supply and demand of the agricultural commodity in question. It calculates the producer and consumer surpluses, agricultural commodity flows, and the domestic price both at the national and regional levels.

Marketing costs represent a set of exogenous variables introduced into the model. They include elevator storage and handling, railroad fees, DAF rail handling and custom costs, seaport handling, required commodity certification, harvest, storage, and transportation losses, and some additional expenditures incurred by transaction costs. As the concept of marketing costs is being considered in a very broad sense, some instruments of state agricultural policies such as export duties and import tariffs are introduced into the model as well.

---

1 The author would like to express special gratitude to Sergiy Zorya and to the Institute of Agricultural Economics at the University of Göttingen for advice and help in developing and running the model used in this investigation.

The model assesses the size of the losses to consumer and producer welfare due to excessive marketing costs and defines their distribution at the regional level. The regional specifications of the model allow determining which regions are winners and which ones are losers in this situation.

3.2 Regional supply, demand, and elasticities

At the initial stage of modelling, the author calculated regional supply and demand and determined regional elasticities for the commodities in question across all of Ukraine's oblasts.[2]

The supply of wheat and sunflower seeds was calculated on the basis of the commodity outputs in each oblast, subtracting losses. The total losses were distributed among oblasts in proportion to their harvested areas. Then the commodity opening stocks were added to the total regional supply.

Regional demand includes: produce (wheat, sunflower seeds) to be processed by the food industry, feed consumption, seed demand and commodity ending stocks. Regional food wheat consumption was calculated on the basis of each oblast's population. Regional oilseed consumption corresponds to the demand of the oil processing enterprises in the oblasts (Ukroliiaprom plants, large, middle, and small oil mills not affiliated with Ukroliiaprom). The regional seed demand was calculated on the basis of the wheat and sunflower seed sowing areas in each oblast. The regional feed demand corresponds to the oblast's share in Ukraine's livestock herd. For comparability, livestock units were converted into cattle with the following conversion coefficients: cattle = 1, pig = 0.12, and poultry = 0.01.

To assess changes in consumer and producer behaviours caused by price fluctuations, short-term supply and demand elasticities were calculated. It has been assumed that the short-term supply elasticities are rather low since agricultural commodity price fluctuations in Ukraine do not cause immediate significant changes in outputs. The nation's farmers are not able to immediately re-allocate resources and change production plans. The availability of critical agricultural inputs rather than price expectations is likely to determine future outputs. For this reason, short-term supply elasticities of 0.1 to 0.2 were assigned to the commodities in question. It was also assumed that the larger the output (or the larger the oblast's share in total production), the higher the elasticity.

The short-term demand elasticities were estimated on the basis of regional consumption. The regional wheat demand elasticities were based on the number of livestock (feed wheat) and on the population (food wheat) in each oblast. The larger the livestock and the population, the higher the elasticity. The elasticities

---

2 Ukragroconsult agricultural commodity data for the 2000/2001 and 2001/2002 marketing years were used.

vary from 0.3 (Ivano-Frankivsk and Sumy oblasts) to 0.5 (Kyiv, Odesa and Dnipropetrovsk). In the case of sunflower seed demand elasticities, a higher demand from oil mills for inputs (Luhansk, Odesa and Dnipropetrovsk) defines higher elasticities.

4 Model scenarios

4.1 Marketing cost reduction

As already discussed in section 2, high marketing costs and state intervention policies are the main reasons for the redistribution of the wealth to the economic agents, which is distortional in its very nature. In a net-export situation, high costs represent an additional tax on agricultural producers. According to a study by the German Advisory Group, farmers in Ukraine obtain around 40% of the FOB price for grain and sunflower seeds, while farmers in Western Europe receive 70% of this price (Striewe, 1998).

To demonstrate the distortional effect of excessive marketing costs, a number of simulations were run. For reasons of simplicity, all marketing costs but railroad fees were reduced by 50% and the railroad fees (set by Ukrzaliznytsia) were reduced by a third. The simulations show that at a wheat world price of 110 USD/t (FOB), the above reduction of marketing costs would lead to an increase in total social welfare by USD 64.5 m. The total producer surplus rises from USD 4,002 m to USD 4,335 m, which is offset, because of the domestic price increase, by a decrease in consumer surplus of USD 268.9 m. Thus, since the increase in producer surplus exceeds the reduction in consumer surplus, society as a whole would be better off.

The distribution of changes in producer and consumer surpluses for each region is presented in Table 16.1. The effect of eliminating excessive marketing costs is especially noticeable in the main wheat production areas of Odesa, Vinnycya, Kherson and Khmelnytsky oblasts. Producers in Odesa oblast alone would save USD 30.3 m. Concerning changes in consumer welfare, the largest losses would be suffered in the most populated oblasts (Kyiv, Donetsk, Dnipropetrovsk and Luhansk) and the oblasts with the most developed livestock production (Lviv and Ternopil). They would now have to pay the higher domestic price of 87.1 USD/t, up from 68.2 USD/t. It should also be noted that in many of these regions the changes in producer surplus would not offset those of the consumers'. Luhansk oblast is an example. The oblast is a net-loser by USD 7.3 m. Thus, along with the negative redistribution effect, excessive marketing costs also cause a redistribution of social welfare across Ukrainian regions, i.e. lower domestic prices cause the main production oblasts to indirectly subsidise the oblasts with large volumes of consumption.

Table 16.1
Changes in producer and consumer surpluses due to postulated marketing cost reductions, in USD 1,000

	Producer and consumer surpluses			
	2001/2002 marketing year* (export situation)		2000/2001 marketing year (import situation)	
	PS	CS	PS	CS
Ukraine	*333,406*	*-268,938*	*-40,536*	*43,416*
Crimea	20,599	-11,984	-2,500	2,001
Vinnycya	26,243	-13,815	-3,231	2,112
Volyn	9,171	-7,754	-1,139	1,184
Dnipropetrovsk	11,620	-14,811	-1,385	2,552
Donetsk	5,145	-16,545	-605	2,909
Zhytomyr	10,976	-10,544	-1,358	1,609
Zakarpattya	1,381	-5,443	-168	900
Zaporizhya	17,202	-11,042	-2,083	1,777
Ivano-Frankivsk	3,936	-7,316	-487	1,174
Kyiv	23,991	-18,328	-2,959	3,097
Kirovohrad	16,343	-8,182	-1,964	1,275
Luhansk	1,844	-9,188	-200	1,611
Lviv	9,727	-13,416	-1,202	2,193
Mykolayiv	16,804	-8,620	-1,999	1,362
Odesa	30,340	-15,029	-3,675	2,427
Poltava	8,858	-11,163	-1,016	1,761
Rivne	8,234	-7,673	-1,028	1,185
Sumy	10,706	-9,137	-1,294	1,426
Ternopil	13,099	-8,714	-1,622	1,328
Kharkiv	12,901	-14,451	-1,519	2,394
Kherson	22,420	-9,063	-2,698	1,425
Khmelnytsky	21,679	-11,776	-2,723	1,782
Cherkassy	18,849	-10,642	-2,314	1,640
Chernivtsi	3,658	-4,821	-449	782
Chernihiv	7,680	-9,480	-918	1,510

* The 2001/2002 marketing year data are an estimation based on Ukragroconsult agricultural commodity balances

Source: own calculations

It is worth mentioning that in the 2000/2001 marketing year when Ukraine was a net-importer of wheat, the situation concerning redistribution of consumer and producer surpluses presented the opposite picture. In that case, the elimination of excessive marketing costs would cause a decrease of the domestic price, which in turn would lead to a decrease of the producer surplus by USD 40.5 m. However, the reduction of producer surplus would now be more than offset by the increase in consumer surplus, which means that social welfare would not suffer.

4.2 Government intervention policy simulations

One of the most controversial agricultural policies implemented by the Ukrainian government remains the 23% sunflower seed export duty. The duty is a good example of a distortional policy instrument effecting production, consumption, trade, and income redistribution of several economic agents. The introduction of the duty has impaired the position of Ukraine as one of the main sunflower seed exporters and provoked a conflict situation with international financial institutions such as the IMF. Furthermore, the practice of the last years shows that the duty is unlikely to achieve some of its goals, such as to increase state revenues. Today a significant portion of sunflower seed exports is realised through a tolling scheme, which allows traders to avoid paying the duty fees.

In order to describe the possible economic impact of the duty, two scenarios were considered, one corresponding to cancellation of the export duty altogether, and another to reduce the duty down to 10%.[3]

The duty leads to a reallocation of profits on the oilseed market to the advantage of state revenues and also to processing enterprises. At the same time, the duty reduces the value of the sunflower seed production and causes financial losses to farmers. The model simulations show that in the 2001/2002 marketing year at a world price of 180 USD/t (FOB), the losses to producers could amount to as much as USD 158.2 m (the marketing costs remaining constant). In the case of a cancellation of the duty, total producer surplus would increase from USD 2,164 m to USD 2,416 m.

The duty not only puts an excessive burden on agricultural producers, but together with excessive marketing costs depresses the domestic price to 97 USD/t. This reduced domestic price can be considered as indirect subsidy to the oil processing industry represented mostly by Ukroliiaprom, which accounts for about two-third of the processed sunflower seeds. If the duty would be cancelled, oil mills would have to buy oilseeds at a higher price, which would rise to 121 USD/t. In this situation, the consumer surplus of oilseeds would reduce from USD 266.4 m to USD 171.4 m.

The introduction of the export duty has a distinct negative effect on the Ukrainian economy. It reduces the total social welfare. The farmers' losses are higher than the gains to the oil processing industry even when combined with the value of the revenue obtained from the export duty fees. As a result, the total welfare losses constitute USD 63.1 m.

As a compromise to the present situation, the model considers the reduction of the export duty down to 10%. Such a motion was proposed by the Ukrainian

---

3 The effect of the tolling scheme on exports was not considered in the scenarios being discussed.

government in March 2001, but failed to pass Parliament. The reduction would increase the total producer surplus from USD 969.6 m to USD 1,057 m, which eventually would raise the national net welfare by USD 31.8 m.

Table 16.2
Changes in regional producer and consumer surpluses due to postulated changes of the sunflower export duty in the 2001/2002 marketing year, in USD 1,000

	Producer and consumer surplus changes*			
	Export duty cancellation		10% export duty	
	PS	CS	PS	CS
Ukraine	*158,044*	*-94,950*	*87,791*	*-56,365*
Crimea	1,733	-453	961	-264
Vinnycya	3,085	-3,127	1,712	-1,841
Dnipropetrovsk	20,933	-11,602	11,613	-6,914
Donetsk	20,734	-7,396	11,605	-4,416
Zakarpattya	54	-64	30	-37
Zaporizhya	20,357	-20,249	11,291	-12,077
Kyiv	1,164	-1,187	646	-708
Kirovohrad	13,907	-9,624	7,719	-5,664
Luhansk	10,888	-5,259	6,035	-3,142
Lviv	1	-751	1	-444
Mykolayiv	11,456	-302	6,359	-180
Odesa	14,164	-10,506	7,866	-6,241
Poltava	9,222	-3,622	5,117	-2,110
Sumy	1,857	-57	1,030	-33
Kharkiv	15,652	-16,320	8,681	-9,731
Kherson	7,124	-2,582	3,953	-1,489
Khmelnytskyi	124	-6	69	-3
Cherkassy	4,914	-111	2,725	-64
Chernivtsi	274	-1,116	153	-651
Chernihiv	301	-611	168	-356

* The 2001/2002 marketing year data is an estimation based on Ukragroconsult agricultural commodity balances

Source: own calculations

The redistribution of producer and consumer surpluses at the regional level is presented in Table 16.2. The table clearly shows that the main oilseed producing oblasts – Donetsk, Dripropetrovsk, Zaporizhya, Kharkiv, Odesa and Kirovohrad – currently bear the highest losses. These oblasts, actually, subsidise a lower domestic price for the processing enterprises in the rest of the country. In this situation, the regions with large capacities to process sunflower seeds are definitely better off. This is also the case with the oblasts not producing sunflower seeds, but which have margarine and mayonnaise producing plants (Lviv, Chernihiv and Chernivtsi).

4.3 Regional commodity movement ban simulations

For the last years, a number of Ukraine's oblasts have repeatedly introduced bans on the regional movement of certain agricultural commodities, in particular so-called grain bans. Such actions are completely incompatible with the principles of a market economy and lead to substantial reductions in national welfare.

To demonstrate the negative economic effects of such intervention policies we simulated the introduction of a regional ban in the central part of Ukraine, namely Vinnycya oblast. It was assumed that the ban would only lead to an increase in transportation costs. To avoid Vinnycya oblast, the adjacent oblasts would have to use longer and more costly routes to trade their output.

Table 16.3
Producer and consumers surplus changes due to the introduction of a postulated ban on grain movement in central Ukraine (Vinnycya oblast) in the 2001/2002 marketing year; in USD 1,000

	Surplus changes	
	PS	CS
Ukraine	*-141,901*	*124,439*
Vinnycya	-112,278	94,220
Volyn	-2,265	2,062
Zhytomyr	-2,66	2,741
Zakarpattya	-571	2,446
Ivano-Frankivsk	-1,815	3,671
Kyiv	-2,002	1,702
Lviv	-2,417	3,662
Rivne	-2,026	2,029
Ternopil	-5,091	3,672
Khmelnytsky	-8,377	5,014
Cherkassy	-357	220
Chernivtsi	-2,040	3,001

* The 2001/2002 marketing year data is an estimation based on Ukragroconsult agricultural commodity balances

Source: own calculations

As can be seen from Table 16.3, the introduction of a regional oblast ban has the following effects:

- due to a lower domestic price the producer surplus is reduced by USD 141.9 m, while the consumer surplus goes up by USD 124.4;
- changes in consumer and producer surpluses would occur in twelve oblasts. The producers of Vinnycya oblast would experience the highest losses amounting to USD 112.3 m, since now they could now trade their grain only within the oblast's borders, leading to a domestic price decrease of 35 USD/t;
- the oblasts of the central and western part of Ukraine such Khmelnytsky, Ternopil and Kyiv, which are large grain producers would suffer the most. At the same time, the southern and eastern oblasts would not experience any

changes in producer and consumer surplus. They can pass around Vinnycya oblast and could increase their exports;

- the total social losses resulting from the postulated regional ban policy would amount to USD 17.5 m.

Thus, the introduction of a regional ban even in only one of Ukraine's oblasts would result in the redistribution of producer and consumer surpluses in many other regions of the nation. The reduction in producer surplus does not offset the increase in consumer surplus, leading to a substantial reduction in national welfare.

5 Conclusions

Excessive marketing costs and certain ineffective instruments of state agricultural policy negatively impact domestic agricultural production and cause distortional effects both at the national and regional levels. They lead to a redistribution of economic wealth between various economic agents and cause losses in total social welfare. Although Ukraine's agricultural potential greatly exceeds the present level of agricultural production, the described ineffective mechanisms and policies remain a bottleneck for agricultural reform in Ukraine.

The simulations of the agricultural regional model produced the following results:

1. For the 2001/2002 marketing year, the reduction of excessive marketing costs in wheat production would have lead to an increase in total social welfare by USD 64.5 m. The producer surplus would have risen from USD 4,002 m to USD 4,335 m, partially offset by a consumer surplus decrease of USD 268.9 m. This means that the society as a whole would have been better off.

2. The export duty on sunflower seeds represents another distortional instrument of agricultural policy. The duty leads to a reallocation of profits on the oilseed market to the advantage of state revenues and of processing enterprises. At the same time, the duty reduces the value of the sunflower seed production and causes financial losses to farmers. In the 2001/2002 marketing year the duty inflicted losses on producers amounting to USD 158.2 m. Had the duty been cancelled, the total producer surplus would have increased from USD 2,164 m to USD 2,416 m, and the total welfare gains would have constituted USD 63.1 m.

3. Along with the negative redistribution effect at the national level, the excessive marketing costs and the export duty cause a redistribution of social welfare across the regions. Due to lower domestic prices the main production oblasts implicitly subsidise the oblasts with large volumes of consumption. The elimination of excessive marketing costs would lead to a considerable increase in social welfare in the main wheat production areas of Odesa, Vinnycya, Kherson

and Khmelnytsky oblasts. This is true also for the main sunflower seed producing areas, i.e. the Donetsk, Dripropetrovsk, Zaporizhya, Kharkiv and Odesa oblasts. With a lower domestic price these oblasts subsidise the oil processing enterprises in the rest of the country.

4. The practice of regional bans on the movement of agricultural commodities creates a serious impediments to the efficiency of regional agricultural trade in Ukraine. The introduction of a regional ban even in only one of Ukraine's oblasts results in the redistribution of producer and consumer surpluses in many other regions of the nation. The reduction in producer surplus exceeds the increase in consumer surplus, leading to substantial losses to national welfare as a whole.

References

Balabanov, G. (1998): The Geographical Segmentation of the Grain Sector in Ukraine. CPER Occasional Papers.

Colman, D. and Y. Trevor (1993): Principles of Agricultural Economics: Markets and Prices in Less Developed Countries. Cambridge University Press.

Striewe, L. (1998): Grain and Oil Marketing and Transportaion in Ukraine. German Advisory Group, Ukraine.

Ukragroconsult, weekly issues for 2000-2001.

von Cramon-Taubadel, S. (2000): After Decree N 832: Grain Market Policy in Ukraine, unpublished.

17

The Economic Implications of Ukrainian Government Support for the Steel Industry

Nina Legeida

1 Introduction

Subsidies to the economy are characteristic for both market and transition economies. The major distinction lies in their volumes, transparency and accountability. Well-known examples are subsidies to the energy, water, transport and agricultural sectors.

The motives for government support are similar in developed and developing countries too: economic development, protection of employment and investments, protection of the domestic industry, support of the poor, etc.. The results of government support, however, vary widely in different countries. For instance, the Irish Industrial Development Authority's strategy to attract investment into the computer hardware and software industries resulted in the rapid economic development of this country in the 1990s. On the other hand, the UK government's strategy to support its coal-mining industry through grants and subsidies eventually resulted in the shutting-down of a number of mines (Downey, 2000). Usually government support is associated with negative effects such as inefficiency in resource allocation, impediments to the competition policy, trade distortions, etc..

Government support to the economy is quite wide spread in Ukraine. The government continues either directly or indirectly to interfere with market mechanisms in the domestic economy. Based on the results of previous research[1], it can be asserted that the most directly subsidised sectors are agriculture, construction, the coal industry, the energy sector and transport. The most indirectly subsidised sectors are agriculture, energy, ferrous metals and coal mining.

---

[1] See "Implicit subsidies in Ukraine: estimation, developments, policy implications", April 2001, unpublished manuscript.

One of the most widely accepted tools for studying government interventions is the partial equilibrium analysis, based on the economic surplus method which measures the efficiency benefits, the distribution of economic benefits between consumers and producers, and welfare gains or losses. This method, however, may not take into account pre-existing distortions in the industry being investigated. Another way to measure welfare effects is through general equilibrium models.

This chapter is organised as follows. Part 2 describes the role of the steel industry in the Ukrainian economy and the government support it receives. Part 3 provides the theoretical and methodological framework for the measurement of the economic impacts of such government policies in general and for the Ukrainian case in particular. Part 4 presents the measurement results for the Ukrainian case, and the resulting implications. The chapter ends with conclusions in Part 5.

2 The role of the steel industry in Ukraine's economy and the government support it receives

2.1 Government support for the steel industry throughout the world

Before talking about government support for the steel sector in Ukraine, it is interesting to look at the support steel makers receive in other regions in the world, both in developed and developing countries. This will help us to evaluate more objectively the cases of government support to the Ukrainian steel industry and their necessity. The international steel trade is distorted now by subsidies, cartels, and various trade restrictions.

Over the past two decades, US steel makers received government assistance in the form of direct grants, loan guarantees, accelerated depreciation, tax abatements, interest free loans, infrastructure grants, special electric power rates, etc. under different federal, state and local subsidy programs (AIIS, 1999).

Krugman and Obstfeld (1997) describe the strategic trade policy of Japan. In the 1950s and 1960s the government directed funds into heavy industries considering them to be essential for Japan's future competitive advantage. The steel industry was especially favoured. Between 1963 and 1970 steel production in Japan tripled, turning Japan into the largest steel exporter in the world.

Governments also support the steel sector in Europe. The commercial EU steel industry policy is ruled by the Treaty of Paris – expiring in 2002 – which created the European Coal and Steel Community (European Parliament Fact Sheets, 1998). Article 4 of the Treaty prohibits state support to steel makers under normal circumstances, but Article 95 allows granting state aid under unforeseen difficulties. These measures may be aimed at social assistance to workers who would loose their jobs, at modernisation of the economic and social infrastructure.

2.2 Government support to the steel industry in Ukraine

2.2.1 Arguments for government support in Ukraine

One can enumerate many reasons why government and parliament of Ukraine show a particular interest in the mining and metallurgical industries.

Firstly, the domestic economic structure inherited from Soviet times is one of the determinants. A large reliance on heavy industries such as metallurgy and machine-building is a historical legacy characterising the Ukrainian economy.

Secondly, these industries have a very strong sectoral lobby consisting of company managers ("red directors"), representatives of the sectoral administrative structures, big business associations, sectoral trade union leaders, who all can influence governmental and parliamentary decisions (Foreign and Security Policy of Ukraine, 2000).

Thirdly, these industries are supported for social reasons: A large percentage of the Ukrainian workforce is employed in metallurgical enterprises and enterprises of other industries whose output is used for the production of ferrous metals.

And finally, the large involvement of the government in the sector as an owner: The government has stakes in almost all plants (though almost all are now privatised). Kryvorizhstal the largest metallurgical enterprise is still fully state owned.

2.2.2 Major channels of the government support in Ukraine

1) Tax subsidies

The practice of granting tax exemptions to individual metallurgical enterprises and restructuring of their financial arrears was widespread prior to 1993.

In July 1999 the Parliament of Ukraine approved the law "On Conducting an Economic Experiment Concerning the Ore-mining and Metallurgical Enterprises of Ukraine". The Law was aimed at overcoming a crisis situation in the ore-mining and metallurgical industries, at increasing the production volumes and government revenues by granting tax privileges. The experiment is slated to be in effect from 1 July 1999 till 1 January 2002. 67 ore-mining and metallurgical enterprises participate in the experiment, among which 12 are steel mills.

Article 2 of the Law states that all fines and penalties for delays in payment of taxes, fees and other obligatory payments prior to 1 July 1999 will be written off for all participants of the experiment. New arrears accumulated during the experiment will be discounted to 50% of the existing rates.

The following tax exemptions were granted:

Enterprise profits tax (EPT): Participating enterprises will have their tax rate set at 30% of the general tax rate. Since the existing general tax rate is 30%, that means that participating enterprises pay 9% EPT. Savings resulting from the reduction of the EPT rate, are meant to be directed towards replenishment of the working capital (lack of the working capital is considered to be one of the major problems of metallurgical enterprises). These funds are not intended to be directed at other objectives such as capital investment, reconstruction or modernisation of production, etc.. As of 2001 the participants will pay 15% EPT.

Roads fund fee: 0 (Article 3).

State innovation fund fee: 50% of the exiting tax rate (Article 3).

Fee for environmental pollution: 30% of these revenues are to be directed to government revenues at different levels, 70% are to be used by the enterprises for internal environmental protection measures.

Article 4 allows the State Tax Administration of Ukraine to grant deferrals to the participants of the "experiment" on paying taxes, fees and other obligatory payments for up to 36 months, and to impose a zero payment rate for tax credits.

2) Soft budget constraints

Payables, a form of trade credit, constitute a part of the "soft budget constraints" of Ukrainian metallurgical enterprises. Arrears are means of financing enterprise operations. In market economies, debts between enterprises tend to decrease transaction costs and increase their sales. During the reviewed period of time, a significant reduction can be observed, specifically in 1999-2000, which coincides with the period of the "economic experiment" at the metallurgical enterprises (see Table 17.2 in the Appendix).

Barter transactions in export and domestic operations were quite frequently used during the last years, the greatest share occurring within the domestic market. Barter transactions significantly decreased in 2000. The share of products supplied under barter arrangements as a percent of the general volume of factory shipments for ferrous metals (total ferrous metallurgy) went down from 40.8% in 1998 to 31.4% in 1999 and to 9.5% in 2000.[2]

---

2 Source: Monitoring of macroeconomic and industry indicators. Department for Economic Strategy, Ministry of Economy of Ukraine.

3) Government guarantees on foreign credits

At the beginning of the 1990s selected metallurgical enterprises received credits under government guarantees. As of 1 March 2001, the overdue debt to the state for these credits had reached USD 1,005.7 m, of which the Makyivskiy metallurgical plant owed 9.3% and Krivorizhstal 5.7% (Interfax, 28 May 2001). These mills continue to be the state's largest debtors regarding guaranteed credits.

The following main conclusions can be drawn from reviewing the major channels of government support to the steel industry. Over time, different scenarios for providing government support were used. In the early 1990s tax subsidies in the form of individual tax privileges and credits under government guarantees were issued. In the mid-1990 and up to 1999 arrears of government revenues, extra-budgetary funds, payables between enterprises and barter transactions were permitted and used. Starting with the second half of 1999 the "economic experiment" came into force.

3 The theoretical and methodological framework for measuring the economic and welfare implications of government policies

According to the System of National Accounts definition (OECD, 1997), "subsidies on production are grants which state and private enterprises receive from the government and which represent additions to the receipts of producers of goods and services over and above what they receive from the sales of their output". In general production subsidies are given to increase the incomes of the producers of a particular industry (in many countries granted for agricultural commodities to raise the incomes of the agricultural producers) or to stimulate the production of a particular good (often granted on steel, motor vehicles, etc.).

Here the standard microeconomic approach to measuring different economic and welfare effects of governmental interventions is applied according to the application example by Rosenberg, Ruocco and Wiegard (1999) for Uzbekistan. Their approach is based on a simple partial equilibrium analysis to study the effects of exchange rate controls for the export of cotton fibre, and the effects of appreciated exchange rates for the import of capital goods.

The prime objective of the "economic experiment concerning the ore-mining and metallurgical enterprises in Ukraine" is to increase total production. Therefore, the government subsidy reducing the EPT rate to 30% of the existing tax rate can be treated as an ad-valorem production subsidy (s). However, this production subsidy is meant to be a special production subsidy, which is a kind of implicit export subsidy, since it can influence international trade. Only the effects of this specific

EPT subsidy will be looked at, holding everything else constant and assuming no other market distortions or imperfections.

Let us assume a small open economy with a perfectly competitive industry. This assumption implies a horizontal or elastic export demand function in the rest of the world.

With "small country assumption" we mean that domestic policies do not affect the world price of the commodity under investigation.

A graphical analysis of the Ukrainian steel market and of the world-wide steel market is presented in Graph 17.1.

Graph 17.1
Effects of a production tax subsidy to steel producers using a "small country assumption"

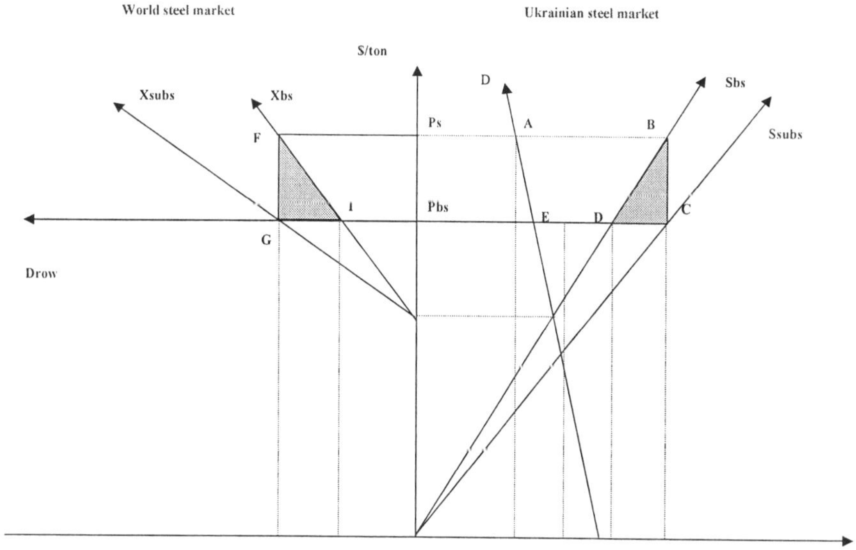

Before the subsidy the following situation is pertained at the markets: P_{bs} – world steel price, $P_{bs}D$ – quantity produced, ED = IP_{bs} – quantity exported, $P_{bs}E$ – domestic consumption.

As a result of the tax subsidy, the total supply function pivots from S^{bs} to S^{subs} by the amount of the ad-valorem subsidy s ($p_s = p_{bs}(1+s)$). The same is true for the export supply of ferrous metals. The domestic price and consumption are unaffected. As the country is small, the domestic policy will not affect the world price of the good. The price received by producers goes up from P_{bs} to P_s: $P_s=P_{bs}*(1+s)$. Exports go up from ED to AB=GP_{bs}.

The net welfare effects can be illustrated in the following way:

Δ PS (producer surplus) = $+P_{bs}P_sBD$ ⇒ producers gain as a result of the subsidy.

Δ CS (consumer surplus) does not change.

Government tax subsidy = - $P_{bs}P_sBC$.

Net welfare effect = + $P_{bs}P_sBD$ - $P_{bs}P_sBC$ = - DBC= - GFI $\Rightarrow$ deadweight losses or the so-called Harberger triangles that measure the degree of inefficiency of the government policy.

For the mathematical derivation of the net welfare loss, the log-linear export supply function for the ferrous metals is assumed:

$$P^X = B * X^\beta \text{, where } \beta>0 \tag{17.1}$$

The elasticity of the export supply function is:

$$E_X = \frac{dX}{dP_X} \times \frac{P^X}{X} = 1/\beta \tag{17.2}$$

The analytical expression for the net welfare loss is[3]:

$$NDL = \frac{\beta}{1+\beta} * P_S * X_S \left(1 - \left(\frac{1}{(1+s)^{1/\beta}}\right)^{1+\beta}\right) - s * X_s \tag{17.3}$$

Thus, as can be seen from equation (17.3), that in order to calculate the deadweight losses, the subsidy rate (s) and the price elasticity (β) are needed.

A "large country assumption" implies that exports of the country constitute a large share of the world steel market. Thus, the production subsidy will affect supply and demand, and hence welfare, both, domestically and internationally. Such a subsidy leads to an expansion of the country's exports and to an increase in the internal consumption of the good. The treatment of this case is similar to the "small country assumption".

4 Estimating the results for the Ukrainian case

4.1 Results of the experiment

There are different views with regard to the success of the "experiment concerning the ore-mining and metallurgical enterprises". The Ministry of Economy has

---

3 The derivation of the net welfare effects can be obtained from the author.

presented a brief analysis of the effects on the production and on the financial and economic activities of all enterprises participating in the "experiment" comparing the year 2000 with the year 1999 (see Table 17.3 in the Appendix). The results are presented for all participating enterprises together. Since data only for the metallurgical enterprises are not available, we have to assume that the overall results hold true for the metallurgical enterprises, too.

Enterprises managed to overcome the working capital deficit, which the give-and-take schemes and barter operations did not allow, and started to reinvest. The "experiment" added more transparency to the transactions within the ferrous metals production sector and reduced the number of intermediaries. An audit conducted by the Accounting Chamber has shown that not all enterprises made payments to the government in a timely fashion and in accordance with legal requirements. Many enterprises should not have directed the funds freed-up by the EPT rate reduction into replenishment of working capital.

4.2 Estimation of the net welfare effects

The tax exemption subsidy may not constitute a part of the market value of the output, but can help to offset a part of the production costs. The statistics available at this time about the results of the "experiment concerning the ore-mining and metallurgical enterprises" present aggregate data on the amounts of tax privileges and write-offs or restructuring of tax arrears for all enterprises participating in the "experiment". Since my investigation concentrates on the steel mills only and since dis-aggregated data is not available, the most appropriate way to calculate the subsidy amount is to take the data for the non-disposable profits of the enterprises and simply calculate the amount of the tax exemptions by reducing the EPT rate from 30% to 9%:

Subsidy amount = 21% of the non-disposable profits of the metallurgical enterprises.

In this assumption, the total amount of the government subsidy to the steel enterprises amounts to UAH 702 m, or USD 130.1 m. The ad-valorem subsidy equals $s = 2.6\%$.

To calculate the deadweight losses, formula (17.3) is now being used. The price resulting from the subsidy programme is based on the weighted average price for Ukrainian steel. Since our own estimates of the price elasticity of the export supply are not ready at the moment – mainly due to the data limitations – the price elasticities from other studies were used to check the sensitivity of the welfare losses to the export supply price elasticity. The range of elasticities allows us to reduce the measurement error for the welfare losses resulting from the difficulty of precisely estimating the supply elasticity. Here are examples of these estimations (see Table 17.1).

Table 17.1
Ukraine: Net welfare effects ("small-country assumption")

β	$1/\beta$	*Welfare losses, m, USD*
0.1[4]	10	-13.67
5.2[5]	0.2	-0.29
16.7[6]	0.1	-0.08

Thus, the deadweight losses vary from USD 0.08 m to USD 13.67 m depending upon the level of elasticity assumed.

4.3 Interpretation of the results

The costs of the subsidy is borne by the government in the form of foregone state revenues (notwithstanding the overall growth in state revenues), while the benefits are shared between domestic producers, steel mills workers and suppliers. Foreign steel consumers also benefited from the Ukrainian government's policy, while foreign steel producers are likely to have suffered.

The deadweight losses turned out to be rather low. Welfare losses rise with the elasticity of the export steel supply. The welfare effects caused by the production tax subsidy also depend on whether the country is modelled as a small or a large economy. Under a "large-country" assumption the welfare losses would be larger.

Many research studies show that subsidies failed to achieve their primary objective. In this case, the subsidy seems to have achieved its primary objective, i.e. the supply of ferrous metal, and payments to the state and to suppliers grew.

Nevertheless, one should be careful about concurring with the estimate's low welfare losses resulting from the government support. They could be much higher if other distortions in the steel market were taken into account.

A partial equilibrium analysis did not capture the effects of the subsidy on other sectors of the economy. A general equilibrium analysis may be of greater use here. There would be many points to consider: Social and environmental implications, unemployment effects, the lack of Ukraine's own energy and gas resources, etc..

---

4 Grygorenko (2001).

5 The US-Canada Free Trade Agreement.

6 Irwin (2000).

5 Conclusions and policy implications

Different approaches of governmental support to the steel industry and their consequences were reviewed in this paper. Special emphasis was laid on studying the fiscal and economic implications of the tax exemptions provided by the "economic experiment concerning the metallurgical enterprises".

To be able to differentiate between the positive effects from the "experiment" and favourable external conditions would be very useful. That would allow us to determine the true influence of the "experiment" on the industry's growth and hypothesise what the industry's development might have been without the "experiment", assuming a high world demand for the Ukrainian steel.

The investigation concentrated on the short-run effects of the subsidies, which should be contrasted with their long-run effects. The long-run effects would appear to be much more negative, especially, since the internal market for steel is not developed and dependence on external markets is predominant. The internal market for steel industry products seems to be the major determinant for future industry growth and prosperity.

The production tax subsidy is distortional in its nature and is welfare reducing. The tax burden should be reduced for the whole economy, not just for specific sectors of the economy or for specific industries. The "economic experiment" improved the financial situation of the enterprises; the threat of being excluded from the experiment stimulated them to work better. Tax reform is necessary and urgent for long-run sustainable economic growth.

References

The American Institute for International Steel (AIIS) (1999): Subsidies to the US Steel Industry: Are they "Market-Distorting" Practices that "Support Economically Unjustifiable Steel Production?" An Analysis of U.S. Federal, State and Local Assistance to Help U. Steel Companies Maintain or Add Steel Making Capacity.

Downey, M. (2000): Tax Breaks in Ukraine. The Case For and Against their Withdrawal.

Grygorenko, Y. (2001): Industry Performance under Transitional Institutions: the Case of Ukrainian Ferrous Metals Industry. EERC.

Interfax (2001) 28 May, Kyiv.

Irwin, D. A. (2000): How Did the United States Become a Net Exporter of Manufactured Goods? Department of Economics, Dartmouth College, Hanover, NH and NBER. Draft, 12 April 2000.

Krugman, P. R. and M. Obstfeld (1997): International Economics: Theory and Policy. Addison-Wesley.

Ministry of Economy of Ukraine (2001): Dzerkalo ekonomichnoi polityky, Department for Economic Strategy, March.

OECD (1997): Framework for the Measurement of Unrecorded Economic Activities in Transition Economies. OECD Working Paper 177.

Peculiarities of Lobbying External Economic Interests in the Metal Mining Complex of Ukraine. Foreign and Security Policy of Ukraine. Occasional paper 34, 2000.

Rosenberg, C., A. Ruocco, and W. Wiegard (1999): Explicit and Implicit Taxation in Uzbekistan. June, Regensburger Diskussionsbeiträge.

The U.S.-Canada Free Trade Agreement: Impact on the US Steel Industry.

UK Steel Association-Parliamentary Debate on the State of the UK Steel Industry. What Government can Do to Help the UK Steel Industry. www.uksteel.org.uk, 1998.

Appendix

Table 17.2
Ukraine: Dynamics of payables of ferrous metals enterprises (total industry), m UAH

	1998		*1999*		*2000*	
Ferrous metallurgy	Total	Overdue	Total	Overdue	Total	Overdue
Total	5,019.7	1,899.5	600.6	-2,163.1	-806.6	-929.6
1. Between enterprises	4,600.8	1,861.6	226.6	-2,137.2	-776.3	-1,073.8
Goods, works, services	2,353.3	1,290.1	-470.8	-826.8	-160.7	-601.2
Wages	114.9	44.8	-96.5	-100.4	-43.4	-93.7
On tax payments	91	14.8	-2.7	8.8	-88.3	-23.6
Budget	670.7	478	-956.8	-740	1.0	-37.3
2. With former SU countries	-165.6	-142.7	410.2	10.6	-284.9	-2.4
3. With other countries	-515.6	-347.8	875.4	50.6	39.3	1.6

Source: State Statistics Committee: form 1b of enterprises

Table 17.3
Ukraine: Results of the "economic experiment concerning the ore-mining and metallurgical enterprises"

Net profits from sales	↑ by 57.2 %
Export volumes	↑ by 1.9 times
Profitability of sold products	26.3 %
Barter operations	↓ from 36.1% in 1999 to 11.1% in 2000
Government revenue at all levels	↑ by 48.2%
Deductions to the Pension Fund	↑ by 52.2%
Wage arrears	↓ by more than 2 times
Expenses for improving production capacities	↑ by 25.4%
Working capital deficit	↓ from 3452 m UAH as of 01.01.2000 to 596 m UAH as of 01.01.2001

Source: Ministry of Economy of Ukraine (2001)

18

The Relationship between Foreign Direct Investment and Trade Flows in a Transition Economy: The Case of Ukraine[1]

Nadiya Mankovska and James W. Dean

1 Summary

This chapter examines the relationships between foreign direct investment (FDI) flows into Ukraine, and imports and exports to and from the country. Theoretically, FDI and international trade can be substitutes or complements. Empirically, the paper shows that FDI from the European Union (EU) into primary industries is mostly export-oriented and thus complements trade, whereas that into secondary, manufacturing industries tends to substitute for trade. The paper argues that primary-industry FDI from the EU is motivated by Ukraine's comparatively abundant and cheap natural resources, whereas secondary-industry FDI is motivated on the cost side by Ukraine's low wage labour and on the revenue side by its large and relatively untapped domestic market. Secondary-industry FDI thus has the potential for import-substitution, although tests of this hypothesis at aggregate levels were inconclusive.

By contrast, FDI from countries of the former Council for Mutual Economic Assistance (CMEA) complements trade in secondary products. The paper argues that FDI from the former CMEA countries is motivated by the potential for economies of scale, including those that might arise from resuming production links which existed during Soviet times. This inference is supported by evidence

---

[1] We would like to record our thanks to the EERC Research and Outreach Center, which provided financial support for this research to be conducted under Research Project "EERC RP01-02". We wish to express our sincere appreciation to those who reviewed this paper and supplied valuable comments: Roy Gardner, Charles Steele, Ghaffar Mughal, Ihor Burakovsky and Victor Goloven. Special thanks to Serhiy Kovaliov who was extremely kind and patient in supplying extensive statistical data sets that were critical for conducting this investigations, and also to Stepan Mankovsky who was of great help with processing our statistics.

of relationships between FDI from CMEA countries and intra-industry trade between CMEA countries and Ukraine.

2 Introduction

Although FDI is crucial for the Ukrainian economy, the level of FDI remains quite miserable in comparison with other transition countries.[2] Several surveys of current investors in Ukraine (Flemings/CAPS Consortium, 2000; Dean and Kudina, 1999; Moellers, 1998) show that the dominant factor motivating current FDI inflows is the possibility of expansion into the domestic market. Low wages or other potential sources of comparative advantage do not seem to be important motivators, nor does the prospect of export markets. However, survey results are often suspect and require formal testing – hence the inspiration for this paper. For example, trade barriers are still substantial in Ukraine. They may impede export-oriented FDI, and stimulate FDI inflows that lead to the production of import-substitutes.

In this paper, we analyse the relationship between FDI and trade flows within Ukraine. In particular, we ask *whether FDI into Ukraine is a complement or a substitute for trade flows.*

A large body of literature analyses both substitutability and complementarity between FDI and trade (Fontagné and Pajot, 1997; Chunlai, 1997; Razin, Yuen and Sadka, 1999). Theories that rationalise substitutability are primary based on the Heckscher-Ohlin model of international trade, where *differences in factor endowments* are the major causes of trade between countries (Mundell, 1957; Goldberg and Klein, 1999; Brainard, 1997). Dropping key assumptions of the Heckscher-Ohlin model leads to inferences of complementarity rather than substitutability. Capital may complement trade when there are *technological differences* between countries (Markusen at al, 1995; Purvis, 1972), or when countries base their trade relations on *economies of scale* (Ethier, 1982). The first might be applicable to Ukraine since we could consider differences in natural resource endowments as a proxy for differences in production technologies. The second might also apply since scale economies were widespread in the planned economies of the former CMEA countries.

Empirical evidence for transition countries like Poland, Hungary and the Czech Republic shows strong complementarity between FDI and trade (Guerriery, 1998; Kaminski, 1998). Aggregate Ukrainian data also weakly supports the

---

2 According to the State Statistics Committee (Derzhkomstat), as for 31 December 2000 the cumulative net FDI stock to Ukraine since independence (August, 1991) totalled about USD 3.3 bn.

complementarity thesis. During transition, while GDP levels decreased, the level of foreign trade as well as the share of exports in Ukrainian GDP increased substantially. We argue that these observed changes in trade might be partially explained by FDI inflows. However, our preliminary estimates with aggregate data did not reveal a strong linkage between FDI and trade. Therefore we formulated more dis-aggregation questions:

(1) *Does FDI flowing into production of primary products have a different relationship to trade than FDI destined for the production of secondary products?* We raise this question on the basis of theories of international trade that treat FDI and trade flows in primary products as potential complements, but FDI and trade in secondary products as potential substitutes (Schmitz and Helmberger, 1970). In fact, financial difficulties in transition countries often induce policies stimulating export-oriented production in order to generate foreign currency inflows. Natural resources are one of the few assets of these countries that attract foreign partners. Therefore, we suspect that FDI into primary industries in Ukraine might be a complement to trade.

(2) *Is the relationship between FDI and trade with the European Union (EU) different from that with countries of the former CMEA?* There could be different motives as well as impediments facing investors from different groups of countries. The relationship between FDI and trade seems to depend on certain similarities or differences between investing and recipient countries (Somwaru, Bolling, 1999). Cheap labour or undeveloped internal markets in Ukraine may attract investors from developed countries but not from the former CMEA since investors from transition economies have similar conditions in their own countries. At the same time the former CMEA investors may have advantages over Western investors due to their strong historical links and may be interested in recapturing the lost markets and re-establishing the former CMEA's production chains (Goloven, 2000). This last suggestion leads us to investigate the third question.

(3) *Does FDI have an impact on the level of intra-industry trade in Ukraine?* If FDI into Ukraine were oriented toward the establishment of vertical production, it would raise the level of intra-industry trade (Hoekman, Djankov, 1996) and support an inference of complementarity.

Answers to these three questions might help policy-makers to focus and fine-tune their policies concerning FDI toward particular industries from particular countries of the world. Such answers might also add to our understanding of the host country's competitiveness and long-term growth potential.

3 Peculiarities of FDI flows in Ukraine: Initial evidence

A preliminary analysis of Ukrainian data allows us to distinguish *two groups of countries* as the largest investors. The first is comprised of the EU countries, which, as of 31 December 2000 have invested about 29% of the cumulative FDI into Ukraine. The second group is comprised of transition countries, specifically former members of the CMEA, which have invested 15% of total FDI. Our evidence is that *FDI from countries of the former CMEA, mostly from Russia, is distributed differently from FDI that came from the EU.* From Table 18.1 we see that the major recipient of FDI in Ukraine is the food industry. However, this industry is mostly attractive to investors from advanced countries: some 44% of FDI from the EU was directed into food, as compared to only 4% of FDI from the former CMEA.

Table 18.1
Cumulative FDI into Ukraine, as of 31 December 2000 (constant 1996 prices)

	Total FDI inflows		FDI from EU countries		FDI from the former CMEA	
	Total, USD m	% of total	Total, USD m	% of total	Total, USD m	% of total
All sectors	3275	100	946	100	492	100
Industry	1680	51	704	74	242	49
Power sector	204	6	9	0.9	141	29
Ferrous metal	127	4	7	0.8	18	4
Non-ferrous metal	27	0.8	13	1	0.8	0.2
Chemicals	137	4	47	5	9	2
Machine-building	294	9	103	11	17	3
Wood-processing	68	2	44	5	11	2
Construction materials	49	2	14	1	10	2
Light industry	37	1	24	3	6	1
Food industry	657	20	417	44	20	4
Medical industry	19	0.6	10	1	6	1
Agriculture	67	2	18	2	4	0.9
Transport and telecommunications	196	6	54	6	28	6
Internal trade	617	19	183	19	56	11
External trade	39	1	9	0.9	0.9	0.2
Health and tourism	107	3	7	0.7	90	18
Finance sector	210	6	85	9	35	7

Source: Derzhkomstat; own calculations

Other industries of the Ukrainian economy, such as machine-building, ferrous metals, chemicals, and wood-processing, are also attractive for foreign investors, and again they attract quite different proportions of FDI from the former CMEA and from the EU. We can, in fact, hypothesise that CMEA investors have different motives for sending FDI into Ukraine than do EU investors.

The external trade line in the table above shows that substantial investments were made in the development of the trade infrastructure in Ukraine, supporting the complementarity hypothesis. At the same time, much higher figures for FDI into theinternal trade sector suggest that domestic market expansion is an important motivator for investing.

4 Main hypotheses

We hypothesise that investments from transition countries and the EU have different impacts on trade flows because the investment motives are different. In addition, we suggest that industry specifics may predetermine incentives for FDI inflows and hence the relationship between FDI and trade flows. Thus, we propose the following:

1. FDI into Ukraine from the EU:

- if it flows into industries that produce primary products, it is mostly export-oriented, and should have a positive impact on the exports of such industries (complementarity);
- if it flows into industries that produce secondary products, it is oriented towards internal market expansion and is induced either by possibilities to produce more efficiently within the country and/or by opportunities to avoid trade barriers. Such FDI acts as a substitute for trade, particularly for imports.

2. FDI from transition countries of the former CMEA:

- whether it flows into industries that produce primary products or secondary products, it is motivated by the potential for economies of scale, including those that might arise from resuming production links which existed during Soviet times. Consequently, this FDI will cause an increase in trade flows, both export and import (complementarity).

In the next section we will test the above hypotheses with Ukrainian data.

5 Empirical study

We construct export supply and import demand functions for Ukraine as functions of FDI and several control variables. The model (based on Somwaru and Bolling, 1999; Thursby and Thursby, 1987; Ethier, 1973) takes the following forms:

$$EX_{it} = a_i + \beta_1 \cdot FDI_{it} + \beta_2 \cdot DIF\_GDPPC_{it} + \beta_3 \cdot ER\_VAR_t + \beta_4 \cdot IND\_OUTPUT_t + \varepsilon_{it} \quad (18.1)$$

and

$$M_{it} = \lambda_i + \gamma_1 \cdot FDI_{it} + \gamma_2 \cdot DIF\_GDPPC_{it} + \gamma_3 \cdot ER\_VAR_t + \gamma_4 \cdot POP\_INCOME_t + \upsilon_{it} \quad (18.2)$$

where	*i*	country index
	t	index for the year, 1996-2000
	EX, M	exports, imports from Ukraine to country *i*
	FDI	FDI inflows
	DIF_GDPPC	absolute difference between GDP per capita of Ukraine and of country *i*
	IND_OUTPUT	output for industries analysed
	POP_INCOME	net real income of the Ukrainian population
	ER_VAR	exchange rate variability
	ε_{it}, υ_{it}	error terms

All data are real in thousands of US Dollar.

We ran pooled regressions on the basis of the available panel data. We used the official yearly Derzhkomstat data for FDI, trade[3], and industrial output. UEPLAC (December 2000) is the data source for net real population income. The bilateral data for per capita GDP differences between Ukraine and other countries was obtained from the IMF (2001).

Available data do not allow the use of lag variables. Not willing to ignore past FDI inflows, we tested *two types of models*: *with FDI flows* per year and *with FDI stocks*. Also, the empirical analysis of this paper was conducted for both bilateral and aggregate flows of exports and imports.

Two groups of industries were analysed: (1) industries that produce secondary manufacturing products (food and machine building) and (2) industries that mostly produce primary products (ferrous metals, chemicals, and wood).

Conclusions concerning the relationship between FDI and trade can be drawn from the estimated coefficients β_1 and γ_1 presented in Tables 18.2 and 18.3.

The coefficient estimates show that the hypothesis concerning FDI flows into primary industries from the EU is supported quite strongly. However, this

---

3 The data provided by Derzhkomstat are nominal in terms of US Dollar. We got real values through the value of USA GDP deflator (source: IMF, 2001). As for the trade data, a 4-digit level of dis-aggregation is available.

relationship is not observed on the bilateral level. Thus, this FDI cannot be explained by the relatively high demand for primary products in the investing country. Most likely, profit opportunities on world wholesale markets (especially for ferrous metals) are the reason for FDI flows into Ukrainian primary industries.

Our evidence rejects the hypothesis concerning complementarity between FDI from transition countries into Ukrainian primary industries and trade in correspondent products. This may be due to limited interest of investors from these countries in cheap natural resources, compared to investors from the EU (as can be seen from Table 18.1).

Table 18.2
Relationship between FDI and export flows

	Primary products		Secondary products		
	0.03	11.76	0.005	-0.24	FDI
European	(0.98)	(0.09)	(0.92)	(0.91)	flows
Union	-0.27	14.50	-0.01	-3.13	FDI
	(0.73)	(0.17)	(0.51)	(0.21)	stocks
	-3.30	38.77	7.28	152.95	FDI
Former	(0.30)	(0.19)	(0.37)	(0.14)	flows
CMEA	2.09	11.93	4.43	-82.40	FDI
	(0.40)	(0.38)	(0.34)	(0.25)	stocks
	Bilateral trade	Aggregate trade	Bilateral trade	Aggregate trade	

Note: p-value in parentheses

FDI inflows to Ukrainian secondary industries do not explain the export volumes of these industries' products. Rather, these investments are either induced by lower cost local production, and/or are motivated by local markets for selling final products. This finding supports the results by Dean and Kudina (1999) and by the Consortium Flemings/CAPS (2000) conducted on micro levels.

Table 18.3
Relationship between FDI and import flows into Ukraine

	Primary products		Secondary products		
	0.22	2.16	0.02	3.37	FDI
European	(0.56)	(0.61)	(0.90)	(0.17)	flows
Union	0.19	0.60	-0.04	0.95	FDI
	(0.51)	(0.80)	(0.49)	(0.39)	stocks
	0.18	-3.03	9.17	109.91	FDI
Former	(0.74)	(0.64)	(0.09)	(0.001)	flows
CMEA	-0.15	-0.92	6.31	37.87	FDI
	(0.76)	(0.75)	(0.05)	(0.19)	stocks
	Bilateral trade	Aggregate trade	Bilateral trade	Aggregate trade	

Note: p-value in parentheses

On the basis of the results for the import demand function (Table 18.3) we accept our hypothesis concerning different patterns of relationship between FDI and trade for the two groups of investing countries. Indeed, the estimated coefficients differ for the different types of investors.

However, on the basis of our estimations we cannot accept the hypothesis about substitutability between FDI from the EU into secondary industries and imports of corresponding products. The negative coefficient on the FDI variable signifies that secondary-industry FDI has the potential for import-substitution, although tests of this hypothesis are inconclusive. However, the substitutability effect is not strong enough to outweigh other effects, for example the process of external liberalisation that has simultaneously taken place in Ukraine.

The significance of our results for imports of secondary products supports the hypothesis regarding reintegration processes among former CMEA countries although it cannot be accepted with certainty since we cannot observe this for trade in primary products.

To find additional evidence for reintegration we turn to the analysis of intra-industry trade in Ukraine. This allows us to trace the impact of FDI on trade diversification, which surely should be the result of intensified bilateral economic interrelations. A positive relationship between FDI inflows and the country's intra-industry trade level for corresponding industries would support our inferences on complementarity of trade and FDI (Markusen et al, 1996).

6 Impact of FDI on trade diversification

In transition economies, FDI flowing into the production sector can be considered as a source of innovation and might lead to an increase in diversity of output and of trade. EBRD (1995) reports that countries that are more successful with reforms export and import a higher diversity of products. However, in Ukraine the Grubel-Lloyd (GL) index, which is the measure of the intra-industry trade level, has being decreasing during transition (Table 18.4).

Table 18.4
Grubel-Lloyd index calculated for Ukraine

Year	1994	1995	1996	1997	1998	1999	2000
GL Index	0.153	0.143	0.118	0.196	0.090	0.086	0.085

Source: Ministry of Economy of Ukraine, Department of Statistics; own calculations

Theory predicts that intra-industry trade arises when economies of scale are the major motivator of trade (Ethier, 1982; Helpman and Krugman, 1985). Another explanation is vertical production relations: countries may export some products for assembling or further processing and then re-import these products again (Markusen, et al., 1995).

In the empirical literature, FDI inflows are found to be highly correlated with intra-industry trade. In particular, transition countries that managed to attract the largest investment inflows rely more heavily on intra-industry trade and vertical specialisation (Hoekman and Djankov, 1996). However, taking into account the decreasing levels of intra-industry trade in Ukraine, we might suspect that FDI into Ukraine does not positively influence trade diversification.

To clarify this phenomenon we analyse the relationship between FDI and intra-industry trade between Ukraine and other countries at bilateral levels. Our evidence (presented in Graph 18.1) suggests that although the GL-index for the aggregate trade of Ukraine has decreased, it has increased at the bilateral level between Ukraine and major investing countries.

Graph 18.1
Intra-industry trade between Ukraine and other major investing countries (2000)

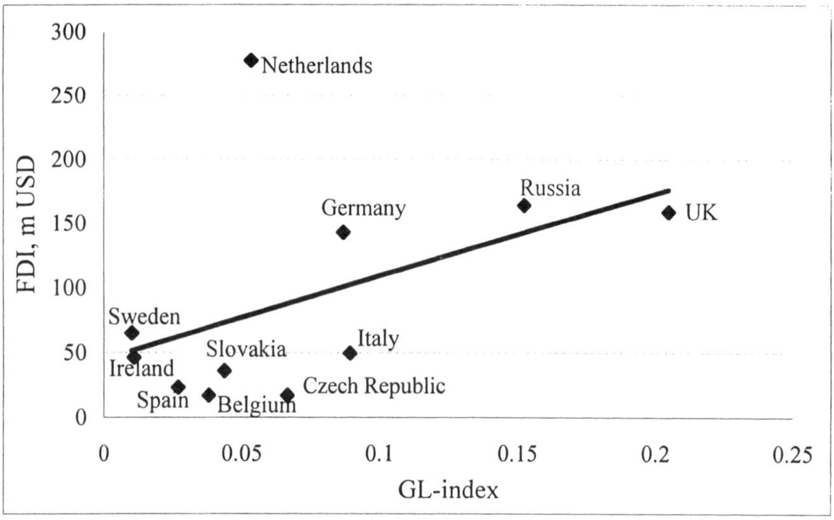

Source: State Statistics Committee and Ministry of Economy of Ukraine; own drawing

For empirical testing we use our equations of trade volumes, however, this time our dependent variable is the value of the GL index:

$$GL_{it} = \delta_i + \xi_1 \cdot FDI_{it} + \xi_2 \cdot DIF\_GDPPC_{it} + \xi_3 \cdot ER\_VAR_t + \xi_4 \cdot IND\_OUTPUT_t + \xi_5 \cdot POP\_INCOME_t + \eta_{it} \tag{18.3}$$

where all variables have the same meaning as before (η_{it} is the error term).

Table 18.5 presents the signs of coefficient ξ_1 as well as p-vales (in parentheses).

On the basis of the estimation results we conclude that FDI inflows into the Ukrainian economy positively influence the level of intra-industry trade between Ukraine and investing countries. For FDI inflows from the former CMEA this result appears to be significant for both types of industries. This finding is quite important as it supports our hypothesis about the *re-establishment of broken economic links between countries of the former CMEA* since the GL-index to some extent also measures the overall level of co-operation between countries.

As for the EU, we observe a positive impact of FDI on intra-industry trade only for secondary products.

Table 18.5
Relationship between FDI and bilateral intra-industry trade

	Primary products	Secondary products	
European Union	positive (0.9076)	positive (0.6206)	FDI flows
	negative (0.8255)	positive (0.0671)	FDI stocks
Former CMEA	positive (0.4181)	negative (0.9606)	FDI flows
	positive (0.0000)	positive (0.0758)	FDI stocks

7 Closing remarks

Studying the peculiarities of the external sector in transition economics should help to develop reform strategies and even to conduct foreign policy. External sector policy is made yet more complex by the reintegration processes taking place alongside large-scale institutional and structural changes.

Our research has shown that for Ukraine, as for other transition countries, the complementarity relationship between FDI and trade flows dominates. However, the relationship between FDI and trade flows depends on the type of investors, or more specifically on the extent of similarities between investing and recipient countries. Moreover, our research has revealed that different groups of industries, primary and secondary, show different relationships between FDI and trade.

Our results might have implications for FDI and foreign trade policies. In particular, differences between the FDI motives and trade patterns of former CMEA countries and countries of the EU suggest that optimal policies for enhancing FDI and trade with CMEA countries might differ from those designed for EU countries.

References

Brinard, L. (1997): An Empirical Assessment of the Proximity–Concentration Trade-off Between Multinational Sales and Trade. American Economic Review, 4(87).

Chunlai, C. (1997): Foreign Direct Investment and Trade: an Empirical Investigation of the Evidence from China. Chinese Economies Research Centre, University of Adelaide, Working paper No .11.

Dean, J. and A. Kudina (1999): Incentives and Disincentives for Foreign Direct Investment in Ukraine. Presented at the Academy of Business and Administrative Sciences meetings, Barcelona.

Ethier, W. (1973): International Trade and the Forward Exchange Market. American Economic Review, No. 63.

Ethier, W. (1982): National and International Returns to Scale in the Modern Theory of International Trade. American Economic Review, No. 72(3).

EBRD (1995, 1998, 1999): Transition Report.

Flemings/CAPS Consortium (2000): Determination of Interests and Abilities of Direct Foreign Investors in Ukraine. Report on survey results. Kyiv.

Fontagne, L. and M. Pajot (1997): How Foreign Direct Investments Affects International Trade and Competitiveness: an Empirical Assessment. CÉPII (Paris).

Golberg, L. and M. Klein (1999): International Trade and Factor Mobility: an Empirical Investigation. NBER, Working paper No. 7196.

Goloven, V. (2000): Determinants of Capital Flows into Ukraine from Countries of Former Soviet Union and the Rest of World and Application for Trade Diversification. Scientific Journal of NaUKMA, Kyiv.

Guerrieri, P. (1998): Trade Patterns, FDI, and Industrial Restructuring of Central and Eastern Europe. BRIE, Working paper No. 124.

Helpman, E. and P. Krugman (1985): Marker Structure and Foreign Trade. The MIT Press, Cambridge.

Hoekman, B. and S. Djankov (1996): Intra-Industry Trade, Foreign Direct Investment and the Reorientation of East European Exports. CEPR (London), Discussion paper No. 1377.

IMF, (2000): World Economic Outlook, www.imf.org/external/pubs/ft/weo.

Kaminski, B. (1990): Foreign Trade and FDI in Hungary and Slovenia: Different Paths – Different Outcomes. Transition, World Bank.

Markusen, J., J. Melvin, W. Kaempler, and K. Maskus (1995): International Trade. Theory and Evidence. McGraw-Hill, Inc.

Markusen, J., A. Venables, D. Eby Konan, and K. Zhang (1996): A Unified Treatment of Horizontal Direct Investment, Vertical Direct Investment, and the Pattern of Trade in Goods and Services. NBER, Working paper No. 5696.

Moellers, F. (1998): FDI in Ukraine – Experiences Taken from Reality. In: Siedenberg, A. and L. Hoffmann (1999): Ukraine at the Crossroads – Economic Reforms in International Perspective with Application to Ukraine, Phyisica-Verlag, Heidelberg.

Mundell, R. (1957): International Trade and Factor Mobility. American Economic Review, No. 47(3).

Purvis, D. (1972): Technology, Trade and Factor Mobility. Economic Journal, No. 82(337).

Razin, A., E. Sadka, C-W. Yuen (1999): An information-based Model of Foreign Direct Investment: the Gains from Trade Revisited. NBER, Working paper No. 6884.

Schmitz, A. and P. Helmberger (1970): Factor Mobility and International Trade: The Case of Complementarity. American Economic Review, No. 60(4).

Somwaru, A. and C. Bolling (1999): U.S. Foreign Direct Investment and Trade: Substitutes or Complements? The Case of the Food Processing Industry. AAEA.

Thursby, J. and M. Thursby (1987); Bilateral Trade Flows, the Linder Hypothesis, and Exchange Risk. Review of Economics and Statistics, 69(3).

UEPLAC (2000): Ukrainian Economic Trends. December, Kyiv.

19

The Debt Structure of Ukrainian Firms[1]

Marta Oleksiv

1 Introduction

The poor functioning of capital markets and banking systems in transition countries raises doubts about the efficiency of capital allocation in these countries. Shortages of capital as well as state interference still distort the allocation process. The financial markets in Ukraine were partially liberalised during the transition from a command to a market economy, however, state intervention such as which industries would be granted subsidies or guaranteed loans remained rather significant. Some banks were coerced to provide credits for particular enterprises or sectors (directed credits). The main economic incentives that usually define decision-making under market conditions will be distorted under such circumstances.

Imperfect financial markets, the existence of information asymmetries and moral hazards in the relations between banks and borrowers can also distort the distribution of bank loans (Cornelli and Portes, 1996). When bankers can not properly differentiate between "good" and "bad" borrowers they are forced to impose one single high interest rate for all, raising the average risk premium for the whole economy. Thus, credits become too expensive for firms with a lower than average risk. These firms will try to use available internal sources of financing. On the other hand, firms with an above average risk will take the credit offers. This leads to adverse selections and increases the risk of a banking system failure.

Another aspect of efficient credit allocation is the financial discipline that the banking system enforces on debtors once it grants credits. An effective financial system will improve the governance of the firms, and thus, improve the economy's performance (Frydman, Gray, Hessel and Rapaczynski, 1999). On the other hand, if credits are provided on a political basis, this will lead to soft budget

[1] I want to express my deep gratitude to Dr. Volkhart Vincentz for his considerable assistance, comments and support in the preparation of this chapter.

constraints and its well-known repercussions. Except for bank loans, the enterprises can use other external sources of financing such as trade credits, different forms of non-payments, tax and wage arrears, etc.. The disciplining forces of these types of credits are probably much less than in case of bank debts. In addition, the absence of the threat of bankruptcy further encourages the enterprises to use more of such types of credits due to their lower "price".

The main questions analysed in this chapter are whether there are specific differences in the allocation of different types of credits to different sectors of the economy in 1999 in Ukraine, whether distinctions between profitable and non-profitable creditors are made, and whether distortions in these allocations occurred. Attention is paid to bank loans and payables as external sources of finance. However, such sources as non-bank borrowings and prolonged tax payments are also touched on in this paper. The aggregate data of the balance sheets and income statements for 1999 for 100 different sectors[2] of the economy, divided into profitable and non-profitable firms, used in our analysis.[3]

2 The distribution of the debt stocks

2.1 Nominal debts

The external financing of companies in Ukraine is characterised by the overwhelming role of regular and overdue trade credits, while *bank loans* constitute only the small fraction of about 5% of total debt[4] (Table 19.1) for both profitable and non-profitable companies. The 1:19 ratio of bank loans to total payables, shown in our sample, is quite unique. In established market economies, with quite different regulatory and judicial systems, this ratio is more balanced. In Germany the distribution is about 60% bank credits and 40% payables; in France this ratio is about 1:2.3 (Deutsche Bundesbank, 1999). The lack of bank credits clearly demonstrates that the credit market is functioning poorly in the Ukrainian economy. Another sign of the poor financial system is the high share of short-term bank credits in total credits. In many market economies long-term bank loans normally exceed short-term loans. According to the official statistics of the National Bank of Ukraine, short-term loans at the end of 1999 constituted 77.6% of all bank credits (NBU, 2000). According to our sample this share is much lower

2 The sectors in the sample do not include small enterprises.

3 Tables in this chapter represent our own calculations based on the official statistics.

4 The total debt for particular sectors of economy is calculated as the sum of its total payables, bank loans, overdue bank loans, short-term and long-term non-bank borrowings and prolonged tax arrears.

(about 50%). This is likely due to different accounting systems used by banks and enterprises.

Table 19.1
Shares of different types of credit (stocks) in total debt, in % (external sources of financing)

Credits	All enterprises		Profitable		Non-profitable	
	1998	1999	1998	1999	1998	1999
Long-term bank loans	2.34	2.57	1.68	2.58	2.96	2.56
Short-term bank loans	2.40	2.36	2.62	2.58	2.19	2.16
Overdue bank loans	0.19	0.17	0.13	0.11	0.25	0.23
Long-run non-bank borrowings	1.53	1.73	1.61	1.93	1.46	1.56
Short-run non-bank borrowings	1.23	1.27	1.26	1.36	1.20	1.20
Prolonged tax arrears	2.24	3.07	1.52	2.44	2.93	3.60
Total payables	90.07	88.83	91.18	89.00	89.01	88.69
Trade credits	27.94	26.84	22.63	22.91	33.01	30.16
Overdue trade credits	26.11	27.72	31.58	28.98	20.88	26.65
Tax arrears	1.67	1.37	1.88	1.93	1.47	0.91
Wage arrears	3.32	2.66	2.87	2.27	3.74	2.98

Quite unexpectedly, profitable firms have a higher share of *overdue* and a lower share of *regular trade credits* than non-profitable ones. It is possible that the indebtedness of profitable firms was caused by non-payments to them. Overdue receivables of profitable firms exhibit higher shares in total assets (0.08 and 0.09 for 1998 and 1999) than the shares of their regular receivables (0.05 and 0.07). In addition, the share of overdue receivables of profitable firms is higher than for non-profitable firms. A simple correlation analysis shows that overdue receivables and overdue trade credits were highly positively correlated in 1998 and 1999 (0.54 and 0.71). In most cases (except for 1999) these correlations were higher for profitable than for non-profitable companies. This might indicate that the higher stocks of overdue receivables of profitable companies during both periods caused higher stocks of overdue trade credits.

However, these facts still require an explanation. Why are profitable firms more inclined to "accept" non-payments from their customers than non-profitable ones? In 1999 the discrepancy in the share of overdue payables between the two types of companies decreased.

It is quite natural that loss-makers have a smaller share of *tax arrears* in total debts due to their lower tax burden compared to profitable firms; profitable firms have about 60% of the total tax arrears. At the same time, prolonged tax payments – representing significantly larger shares of tax arrears than ordinary non-payments of taxes – were generated more often by non-profitable firms.

In the case of *wage arrears*, the result is just the opposite. Non-profitable firms accumulated about two-thirds of wage arrears and their share in total debt is almost one percentage point higher than that of profitable firms (Table 19.1). This shows that the more financially distressed a firm is, the more it relies on exceptional measures such as non-payment of wages.

2.2 Debts per unit of sale[5]

Total debt (the sum of bank credits and payables) in the sample constitutes about 75% of total sales. The amount of bank credits compared to total payables per sale is again less than 5%.

However, differences occur if profitable and non-profitable firms are compared (Appendix, Table 19.4, 19.5). Firstly, total debt for profitable firms is only slightly above 50% of their sales, while non-profitable ones have a debt to sales ratio of 120%. Secondly, relative to sales the percentage of bank credits is almost twice as high for loss-makers. The latter also have 2.5 times more payables than profitable firms do. The ratio of receivables to sales is also higher for non-profitable firms, however not to the extent observed for payables.

As expected, non-profitable firms are more indebted than profitable ones are. Except for tax arrears, this result holds for every single debt category.

Considering different sectors of the economy, the housing sector stands out with extremely high overdue payables and receivables (Table 19.4, 19.5). The correlation between receivables and payables is likely to be an effect of circularity. Trade credits and receivables, as well as overdue trade credits and overdue receivables are highly correlated across all sectors of the economy for both profitable and non-profitable enterprises (the correlation coefficients are 0.95 and 0.98). If the housing sector does not get paid (receivables) it will not be able to pay its suppliers (payables). In many cases high receivables cause high debts, although our data alone do not allow to infer the causality.

For the industrial sector the correlation between payables and receivables is less strong (0.42 and 0.58 for regular and overdue). Thus, liquidity constraints, which underlie the above circularity argument, are less dominant in industry.

The relationships between receivables and payables in the energy and fuel sectors (particularly gas) are particular interesting: both have more receivables relative to payables than most other sectors. This means that energy and fuel sectors are a kind of provider of credit to other sectors by accepting high (net) non-payments; thus, subsidising the rest of the economy. The energy sector seems to use "exceptional financing" through tax and wage arrears to compensate for its net credits to the rest of the economy, caused in part by state orders prohibiting it from cutting off non-payers.

---

5 Debts were divided by sales to correct for the size of the different sectors.

As expected, long-term bank credits were high in export sectors, i.e. in the non-ferrous, chemical, and textile industries. However, the bulk of long-term credits went to the non-profitable firms in these sectors, while the profitable exporting enterprises held a more or less average share of bank credits relative to sales. This could suggest that (non-profitable) exporters were supported by directed credits. A similar pattern with regard to short-term credits can be seen in the woodworking, tanning, pharmaceutical, and fruit and vegetable processing industries. Again, some of these branches have significant exports.

3 Changes in the debt structure

Due to data constraints, information about new credits (flows) is only available for one year (1999). This does not allow us to determine a trend. The changes in stock might be caused by several one-time shocks. However, it is interesting to look for effects of the crisis of 1998. The drastic depreciation of the Ukrainian currency helped the import substituting and the export industries. In addition after the default on the state obligations the banking system stopped to further invest in T-bills and had to find other business opportunities.

Table 19.2 shows that bank credits clearly surged: profitable firms were granted more long-term (investment) credits while loss-makers could improve their liquidity by short-term credits. Our estimations of the growth rates of the long-term loans coincide with the official data of the NBU, while the estimated growth rates of the short-term bank loans clearly exceed those reported in the official statistics, which do not state any real increase in this kind of credit. Hence, our estimations should be treated with care, since some discrepancies in the official statistics and in our results may exist due to possible accounting problems, as mentioned above. The improvement of the financial situation, due to higher competitiveness in the domestic economy and some relaxing of monetary policy showed itself in an overall decline of tax and wage arrears. The significant reduction of tax arrears in non-profitable firms was also due to write-offs of tax arrears in the coal sector, metallurgy and agriculture. At the same time, prolonged tax payments, especially of profitable companies, significantly increased in 1999. Trade credits and overdue trade credits did not decline, mainly because of the non-profitable firms.

Nevertheless, in general the debt structure showed some rather positive changes in the aftermath of the financial crisis.

Table 19.2
Growth of components of financing, (real terms, in %) (1999)

	All enterprises	Profitable	Non-profitable
Long-term bank loans	26.64	65.75	5.39
Short-term bank loans	13.05	6.58	20.42
Long-run non-bank borrowings	29.66	29.48	29.85
Short-run non-bank borrowings	19.38	15.88	22.92
Prolonged tax arrears	57.86	73.59	50.05
Total payables	13.57	5.43	21.54
Trade credits	10.62	9.35	11.45
Overdue trade credits	22.27	-0.88	55.73
Tax arrears	-5.34	10.66	-24.89
Wage arrears	-7.77	-14.48	-2.85

4 The skewness of indebtedness

In transition countries the debt distribution is highly skewed with a long right tail of highly indebted firms.[6] Our data confirm this observation for Ukraine too. Table 19.3 represents the skewness of different credits (and receivables) as their ratio to sales.

For all enterprises total payables (in particular overdue trade credits), total receivables (in particular regular ones) showed the highest asymmetry. For all debt categories (except wage arrears), profitable firms showed patterns that were more skewed than non-profitable ones. The former hold fewer bank loans per unit of sales than non-profitable firms do; however, even these loans were concentrated in a small number of sectors (especially the long-term loans).

The skewness of tax and wage arrears shows that specific industries could more easily accumulate these kinds of "loans". Cases of high tax arrears might partially be the result of a generous government, which preferentially supports some industries by accepting non-payments.

High bank credits were granted to both profitable and the non-profitable firms in the ferrous metallurgy sector (Appendix, Table 19.6, 19.7). The same holds true for short-term credits to the wholesale trade. It seems that in these cases profitability matters less than belonging to a specific industrial sector, either due to the dominance of the economic perspective of a given sector over specific (possibly temporary) losses or by directed credits to a specific sector.

6 In these cases the coefficient of skewness that measures the asymmetry of a distribution is positive.

Table 19.3
Skewness of different credits and receivables

Ratio of credits/receivables to sales	All enterprises		Profitable		Non-profitable	
	1998	1999	1998	1999	1998	1999
Long-term bank loans	4.65	5.71	9.03	9.14	4.35	3.65
Short-term bank loans	5.32	1.29	7.93	1.46	3.45	1.16
Total payables	9.84	9.83	4.97	4.60	9.64	9.64
Trade credits	2.31	3.24	4.00	6.38	3.49	2.74
Overdue trade credits	6.63	5.77	7.45	7.58	3.80	2.64
Tax arrears	3.96	4.47	4.55	4.92	2.67	3.74
Wage arrears	2.06	2.22	2.78	2.37	2.52	2.41
Total receivables	9.85	9.85	3.71	3.20	9.64	9.64
Receivables for commodities, etc.	9.85	9.81	5.81	3.33	9.64	9.63
Overdue receivables	4.83	3.98	4.61	4.73	3.06	2.91

The double coincidence that both profitable and non-profitable firms of the same sector belong to the highest debtors can be demonstrated for several types of debts: for the pipeline industry and the energy sector with respect to tax arrears; for ferrous metallurgy, the coal industry and machine building with respect to wage arrears. This sectoral bias in debt allocation – more or less independent of the firm-specific financial situation – might be a result of governmental influence. Due to the high concentration of debt, a strategy for debt reduction has to deal only with a few sectors, possibly only a few firms. This significantly alleviates the control and monitoring costs of any economic policy aiming at debt reduction.

5 Conclusions

This analysis suggests that the allocation of credits in Ukraine in 1999 was at least partially inefficient. For all enterprises, disregarding their financial situation, bank loans continued to play minor roles as sources of financing. Instead the enterprises turned to payables as a source of financing, dominantly short-term. Tax arrears were more concentrated within profitable enterprises. Financially distressed firms (non-profitable enterprises) relied more on exceptional measures, such as the non-payment of wages.

As expected, bank financing went mainly to the export-oriented industry sectors: non-ferrous, chemical and textile. However, the bulk of these loans went to non-profitable firms. This raises the suspicion that these were directed loans. A similar pattern of short-term loans was observed in the woodworking, tanning, pharmaceutical, and fruit and vegetable processing sectors. The indebtedness of some of the sectors, which can be explained by circularity and net crediting effects serves as evidence that weak payment discipline within the economy affects the performance of all firms, and sometimes forces them to turn to exceptional ways of financing.

In the aftermath of the currency crisis in the autumn of 1998, the debt structure showed some positive changes. Bank credits increased in 1999 owing in large extent to the increase of long-term loans to profitable firms. Payables and receivables also rose considerably with increases in overdue payables and receivables caused mainly by non-profitable firms. On the other hand, wage and tax arrears decreased, partly due to tax debt write-offs in the agricultural, coal and metallurgy sectors.

The distribution of different types of credits and receivables was significantly skewed. A few sectors obtained the largest amount of bank loans and generated large amounts of payables and receivables, regardless the firm-specific financial situation. Thus, we can assume that credits were allocated according to sector-specific priorities rather than according to the financial needs of individual firms.

References

Borenszhtein, E., J-W. Lee (1999): Credit Allocation and Financial Crisis in Korea. IMF Working Paper, No. 20.

Frydman, R., C. Gray, M. Hessel and A. Rapaczynski (1999). The Limits of Discipline: Ownership and Hard Budget Constraints in the Transition Economies. Transition Economics Series, No. 5, Institute for Advanced Studies, Vienna.

Cornelli, F.and R. Portes (1996): The Capital Structure of Firms in Central and Eastern Europe. CEPR Discussion Paper, No.1392.

Vincentz, V. (2000): A Note on External Financing of Ukrainian Firms (preliminary). Unpublished work, Osteuropa Institut in Munich and German Advisory Group with the Government of Ukraine.

Deutsche Bundesbank (1999): Zur Unternehmensfinanzierung in Deutschland and Frankreich: Eine Vergleichende Analyse. Monatsbericht Oktober, pp. 29-46.

National Bank of Ukraine (NBU) (2000): Bulletin of the National Bank of Ukraine, No 1.

Appendix

Table 19.4
Distribution of payables, bank loans and receivables as a percentage of sales (PROFITABLE enterprises) (1999)

Sectors	*Long-term bank loans*	*Short-term bank loans*	*Total payables*	*Trade credits*	*Overdue trade credits*	*Tax arrears*	*Wage arrears*	*Total receivables*	*Receivables for commodities*	*Overdue receivables*
Total (sample)	1.41	1.41	48.52	12.49	15.80	1.05	1.24	41.32	11.63	16.40
Agriculture	3.58	1.14	44.42	9.55	13.93	0.18	4.90	24.45	5.53	11.29
Transport and communication	3.62	0.61	50.54	10.05	10.06	0.78	0.92	45.76	10.82	15.33
Construction	0.24	0.66	65.90	10.93	23.14	0.95	4.12	45.91	14.77	19.29
Trade and catering	0.26	1.17	25.23	16.82	1.92	0.30	0.19	21.45	13.46	1.06
Housing	0.08	0.41	217.66	29.46	137.75	10.67	2.95	210.83	20.77	155.35
Finance	0.04	4.34	46.34	12.33	0.77	0.02	0.25	57.38	19.95	2.86
Management (Administration)	0.04	2.27	180.80	35.77	3.30	1.85	0.25	199.07	69.78	9.22
Industry	1.54	1.77	49.65	10.86	18.43	1.15	1.33	41.40	10.33	18.00
Energy sector	1.88	0.20	86.03	19.09	42.15	1.57	0.83	78.16	17.87	35.69
Gas sector	0.01	0.01	68.52	7.25	5.64	9.54	0.12	77.29	17.51	26.42
Coal sector	0.08	0.90	75.71	5.21	22.60	0.22	9.05	40.94	7.30	13.16
Ferrous metals	2.16	4.04	32.38	10.42	8.84	0.31	0.58	23.36	8.50	5.55
Non-ferrous metals	0.00	3.42	43.91	10.04	17.70	0.15	0.61	36.83	3.75	24.39
Chemical industry	0.40	1.75	38.68	13.43	9.88	0.07	1.05	17.76	6.83	3.52
Machine-building industry	1.16	3.09	46.40	8.12	6.43	0.40	3.39	29.84	9.88	8.57
Woodworking and wood-pulp industry	1.67	1.29	15.30	0.21	2.58	0.18	1.01	15.91	7.51	2.25
Textile industry	1.71	1.10	29.76	11.79	1.41	0.16	2.35	26.02	9.92	2.60
Tanning industry	2.83	2.05	35.38	21.23	4.06	0.33	1.02	17.27	7.20	1.77
Fruit and vegetable processing industry	0.16	2.50	35.93	14.01	3.63	0.01	0.88	21.05	9.13	1.83
Pharmaceutical industry	5.74	1.33	32.10	24.15	2.65	0.11	0.77	32.46	17.77	7.79

Table 19.5

Distribution of payables, bank loans and receivables as a percentage of sales (NON-PROFITABLE enterprises) (1999)

Sectors	*Long-term bank loans*	*Short-term bank loans*	*Total payables*	*Trade credits*	*Overdue trade credits*	*Tax arrears*	*Wage arrears*	*Total receivables*	*Receivables for commodities*	*Overdue receivables*
Total (sample)	3.38	2.82	115.54	39.29	34.72	1.18	3.88	70.45	29.70	22.96
Agriculture	1.68	1.89	137.00	22.19	45.83	0.29	23.74	28.10	6.03	11.20
Transport and communication	1.71	1.31	159.27	16.35	121.73	3.52	2.03	123.41	18.18	89.31
Construction	5.02	1.79	128.84	24.00	30.12	1.40	12.61	88.81	21.39	46.81
Trade and catering	1.35	2.92	85.28	55.84	12.41	0.38	0.40	52.02	33.37	5.06
Housing	0.02	0.31	251.48	28.47	167.82	9.08	4.42	181.45	23.23	126.11
Finance	32.54	5.38	247.42	43.90	1.18	0.09	0.99	222.77	43.71	7.12
Management (Administration)	0.44	0.08	123.74	72.43	4.73	1.09	0.01	107.19	82.22	5.51
Industry	7.62	4.97	112.79	24.68	31.96	0.74	4.27	52.99	12.50	21.66
Energy sector	0.00	0.51	146.15	37.30	51.49	2.40	0.76	114.97	23.66	66.75
Gas sector	-	-	-	-	-	-	-	-	-	-
Coal sector	0.12	1.88	249.70	9.69	97.36	0.11	34.88	55.31	3.90	19.43
Ferrous metals	8.03	8.12	90.36	21.55	24.87	0.15	2.50	31.44	11.09	8.58
Non-ferrous metals	27.26	5.11	62.27	13.99	14.97	0.00	1.50	17.46	4.87	3.63
Chemical industry	44.44	9.19	228.76	46.28	58.77	0.30	4.26	91.71	9.47	10.31
Machine-building industry	7.69	6.35	114.28	16.02	28.68	0.39	7.79	45.36	11.74	18.43
Woodworking and wood-pulp industry	11.86	9.48	112.05	32.39	16.76	0.31	6.68	49.49	16.57	7.99
Textile industry	60.15	9.23	176.59	24.33	14.46	0.49	9.73	43.18	10.30	12.32
Tanning industry	1.88	14.97	57.62	18.22	9.39	0.38	4.23	35.18	16.15	5.63
Fruit and vegetable processing industry	0.15	11.21	84.15	32.08	11.33	1.07	3.00	34.66	15.89	8.19
Pharmaceutical industry	2.38	14.39	74.03	53.79	8.19	0.01	1.01	36.21	14.73	8.83

Table 19.6

Distribution of different credits and receivables across the whole economy, in % (PROFITABLE enterprises) (1999)

	Percentages obtained by the largest 5 indebted sectors	*Sales percentage of the largest 5 indebted sectors*	*The largest 5 indebted sectors*
Profits	41.50	44.7	Ferrous metals, Gas sector, Energy sector, Wholesale trade, Pipeline transportation
Long-term bank credits	66.4	26.1	Ferrous metals, Communication industry, Energy sector, Food sector (other), Air transport
Short-term bank credits	63.4	38.0	Ferrous metals, Wholesale trade, Machine-building, Oil refinery sector, Food sector (other)
Total payables	47.1	45.0	Municipal economy, Wholesale trade, Other industries, Ferrous metals, Energy sector
Trade credits	55.2	45.0	Ferrous metals, Pipeline transportation, Other industries, Wholesale trade, Energy sector
Overdue trade credits	72.6	33.8	Municipal economy, Pipeline transportation, Ferrous metals, Other industries, Energy sector
Tax arrears	73.4	32.1	Gas sector, Pipeline transportation, Oil extracting industry, Municipal economy, Energy sector
Wage arrears	55.2	31.1	Ferrous metals, Coal industry, Machine-building, Energy sector, Contracting organisations
Total receivables	50.8	45.0	Pipeline transportation, Wholesale trade, Other industries, Municipal economy, Energy sector
Receivables for commodities	51.7	46.2	Pipeline transportation, Wholesale trade, Other industries, Ferrous metals, Energy sector
Overdue receivables for commodities	68.1	33.8	Municipal economy, Other industries, Pipeline transportation, Gas sector, Energy sector

Table 19.7
Distribution of different credits and receivables across the whole economy, in % (NON-PROFITABLE enterprises) (1999)

	Percentages obtained by the largest 5 indebted sectors	*Sales percentage of the largest 5 indebted sectors*	*The largest 5 indebted sectors*
Losses	46.0	53.3	Plant cultivating sector, Wholesale trade, Machine-building, Stock-raising industry, Management
Long-term bank credits	63.2	35.1	Ferrous metals, Chemical industry, Machine-building, Wholesale trade, Non-ferrous metals
Short-term bank credits	61.2	39.9	Ferrous metals, Wholesale trade, Machine-building, Retail trade, Food (other)
Total payables	54.9	54.8	Municipal economy, Wholesale trade, Management, Pipeline transportation, Energy sector
Trade credits	74.5	57.3	Ferrous metals, Energy sector, Plant cultivating, Management, Wholesale trade
Overdue trade credits	63.0	26.2	External trade, Municipal economy, Plant cultivating, Pipeline transportation, Energy sector
Tax arrears	81.0	50.5	Municipal economy, Wholesale trade, Management, Pipeline transportation, Energy sector
Wage arrears	69.5	21.5	Plant cultivating, Coal sector, Machine-building, Stock-raising industry, Ferrous metals
Total receivables	70.1	55.1	Pipeline transportation, Wholesale trade, Management, Municipal economy, Energy sector
Receivables for commodities	81.4	56.6	Pipeline transportation, Wholesale trade, Management, Logistics, Energy sector
Overdue receivables for commodities	73.0	36.0	Municipal economy, Management, Machine-building, Pipeline transportation, Energy sector

20

A Restructuring Trap in Transition Economies: Where Does it Lead?

Alexander Scherbakov

1 Introduction

Transition economies have become "the topic number one" in the recent economic literature. The very opportunity to observe economies in different kinds of disequilibria with high variations of key indicators represents a kind of test laboratory for economic concepts and theories. At the same time the research accents have changed dramatically. Previously popular macroeconomic studies receded into the background because most have failed to explain differences between successes and failures in different transition countries. Instead, greater attention is now paid to microeconomics and institutional arrangements that seem to have more appropriate instruments, and thus, a potentially higher explanatory power.

One of these topics is restructuring of state owned enterprises. In order to avoid confusion, let me first define the term "restructuring". According to Ericson (1998), restructuring is "changes in operations, interactions, and motivation [leading] towards success in a changing market environment". Restructuring of large and medium sized enterprises was extensively discussed by a number of economists (see e.g. Akimova and Schwödiauer (1999), Boycko et al, 1995; Shleifer and Vishny, 1994, 1996; Earle and Estrin, 1996, 1997, 1998; Barberis et al 1996; Frydman at al, 1997; Claessens, Djankov and Pohl, 1997; Djankov and Pohl, 1997, 1998). Major instruments that provide the necessary background for successful restructuring are (1) liberalisation, which leads to enhanced competition and as a result to better enterprise performance, and (2) privatisation, which leads to significant improvements in corporate governance of the enterprises. Brown and Earle (2001), for example, investigate co-interaction between these instruments in great details. At the same time, the question whether these policies also provide a sufficient condition for effective enterprise restructuring is an open one. In this chapter the author concentrated mainly on the microeconomic institutional heritage, which might be of the same importance as privatisation and liberalisation themselves. The chapter especially emphasises the dynamics of market competition and the potential obstacles in its way.

2 Theoretical background

According to general economic theory, in the long-run firms should produce at the minimum efficient scale (MES) point where average costs are lowest (point B on Graph 20.1). Thus, one of the main targets of government competition policy should be to "(1) encourage firms to reach that size [MES] – and (2) discourage them from substantially exceeding it" (Mueller, 1996. p. 3). Usually (in market economies), the movement of a firm along LRAC is defined by increased efficiency, which in turn defines the industry's structure (there are also arguments of bi-directional causality, which will not be followed up here) In the case of transition economies the situation is rather different. First of all, the market structure for soviet-style enterprises was not primarily based on efficiency considerations (see for example, Brown and Earle, 2000. p. 6.).

Graph 20.1
Minimum efficient scale and initial conditions for SOE

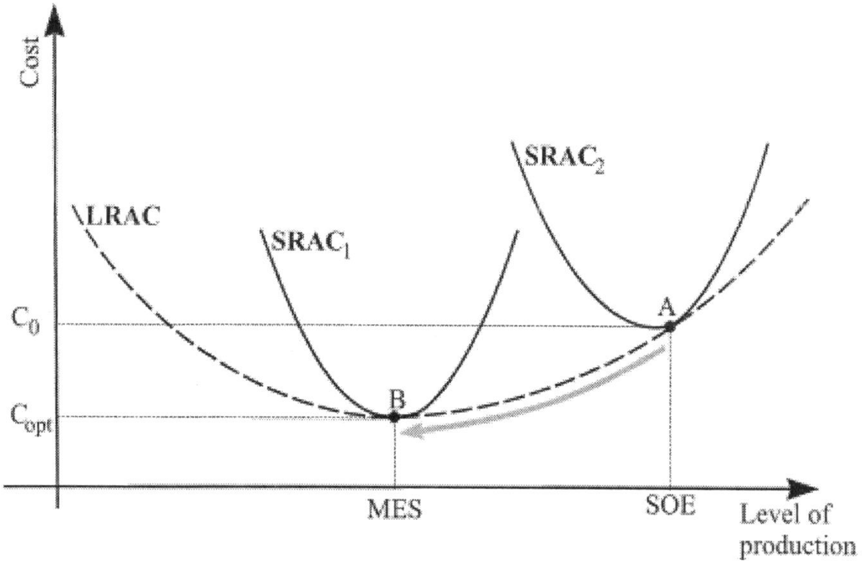

Source: own drawing

That is why the initial market structure in transition economies was in some sense exogenous to the firms' efficiencies. In Graph 20.1 this situation is depicted as point A. Moreover, we have good reasons to expect extremely high concentrations in certain key industries because of market size shrinkage after the collapse of the USSR and the dramatic fall in demand for industrial products. Thus, it is theoretically possible that a number of former state-owned enterprises (SOE) produce currently at the "size-inefficient" level (point A on Graph 20.1). The loss caused by this inefficiency is (C_0 - C_{Opt}) per unit of output. Under these conditions it seems rational to squeeze the firm down to an efficient size. However, we consider this "squeezing" not to be a very likely outcome in transition economies, or at least to be a more problematic undertaking than a simple move from the left part of LRAC to MES. The a-priori hypothesis is as follows: The larger the enterprise, the more reluctant it will be to be squeezed toward MES. There are several arguments for this "reluctance". The most important ones from the author's point of view are included into the theoretical model presented below.

3 A game theory approach

Let me suppose that initially only one firm of size *IS* operates in the industry, which produces some sort of homogenous product (oil, cement, steel, etc.). The technology of the industry is such that it allows achievement of the minimal efficient scale at the level of *IS*/2. This simply means that there might coexist at least two plants in the industry. For simplicity in our model we assume Cournot's quantity competition.

If there is only one plant in the industry, its profit is π^M. If there are two plants in the industry, each of them receives $\pi^O < \pi^M$. Thus, the incumbent firm is interested in maintaining its monopolistic power. To retain this power, the monopolist is ready to spend up to $\sum_{i=0}^{\infty} \frac{\pi^M - \pi^O}{(1+R)^i}$. Let me define this term as resistance cost (RC).

In addition, there is the cost of restructuring itself (RS): compensation to and training of laid-off workers, regulatory measures that should enforce restructuring, costs associated with capital transfers, new contracts creation, etc.. These costs can be approximated as (*IS* – *MES*)*c, where c is the cost per unit of restructuring (disregarding one of the basic assumptions of the neo-classical theory, that is, zero transaction cost). To summarise, we have two costs of restructuring: RC and RS. The incumbent firm can manage only RC.

3.1 Definitions

- π^M – Monopolistic profit
- π^O – Oligopolistic (in our case duopolistic) profit

- NR – Normal return, can be estimated as an alternative investment or the cost of raising funds
- RC – Resistance cost (Cost that an incumbent firm can pay for retaining its monopolistic power. It can be approximated by $\sum_{i=0}^{\infty}\frac{\pi^M - \pi^O}{(1+R)^i}$)
- RS – Restructuring cost (A cost that arises as a result of restructuring. It can be approximated as c*(*IS* – *MES*), where c is the transaction cost per unit of restructuring)
- $\overline{RC}$ – The resistance cost, which a new entrant faces.

3.2 Players

Let me assume that there are only three players on the market: (1) the government, (2) the entrant firm, and (3) the incumbent firm. Each of these players has its own objective. The entrant firm and the incumbent firm are rationally assumed to be profit-maximisers. The government is assumed to care about net benefits for society while simultaneously minimising its costs. To simplify the model, let me assume that each of the players has a final set of strategies.

3.2.1 The government's options

Government can fully support restructuring. This means that it is ready to subsidise the entrant up to the amount of RC. In addition, government will fully cover the RS costs: retraining programs for the workers, purchasing of capital in case of a low development of capital markets, etc., that is, it covers all costs associated with transformation of the one-firm industry into a duopoly. In the extreme case the government can completely open the industry to importers to reduce the monopolistic power of the incumbent firm. However, this is not likely to be the case: any government wants to intervene as little as possible, and usually leaves this job to the market.

A second possible solution is to behave neutrally, which means a simple elimination of the market failures. This means that the government will cover RS, but not subsidise RC. This case represents the most likely strategy of the government. Thus, the entrant faces RC and enters if $\sum_{i=0}^{\infty}\frac{\pi^O - RC}{(1+R)^i} > NR$, where NR is the normal return.

The third strategy for the government is to "stay out", which means in some sense a resistance to restructuring. The government switches RS to the entrant (in addition to RC). This can be done through a system of expensive licenses, which include the costs necessary to cover RS. The government can also simply reject the entrant during registration to minimise RS. However, this strategy is not likely to be pursued. If the government chooses to "stay out" and there will be no entry, it would be likely that international organisations would berate the government for slow reforms and impose some costs. Furthermore, domestic economic agents also can impose political costs on the government. Let me define these costs as SOC. Formally the Government's objective function is $\max U\left(B^R - C^R\right)$. The complete list of possible strategies is:

- Support restructuring by bearing RC and RS,
- Take a neutral position by bearing only RS in case of an entry,
- Stay out and switch both RS and RC to the entrant.

3.2.2 The entrant's options

The entrant observes profit opportunities in the industry and compares them with, say, normal returns in the economy, which according to the efficiency market theory, can be represented by the yield of alternative investments or simply by interest rates. Let me assume that the decision rule is as follows: Enter if $E\pi >$ NR, where $E\pi$ is expected profit from entering the market. Thus, the entrant can choose to either enter or not. Formally the entrant firm's objective function is $\max U\left(\sum_{i=0}^{\infty}\frac{\pi^O - \overline{RC}}{(1+R)^i}, NR\right)$. The complete list of possible strategies is:

- Enter,
- Stay out.

3.2.3 The incumbent firm's options

(1) The incumbent firm could impose RC on the entrant. This part is common for the conventional industrial organisation theory. For example, the incumbent firm could invest into R&D activity to decrease the costs of production, and/or to differentiate the homogenous product (through services provided). In addition, the incumbent firm could heavily invest in advertising, in the development of a client network, in other types of vertical or horizontal integration, or in building excess capacities to make a credible threat. In the recent economic literature this process has been defined as the creation of endogenous barriers to entry.

(2) Alternatively, the incumbent firm could impose RC on the government. This issue has much in common with the literature on rent-seeking activities. Roughly speaking, the incumbent firm could pay bribes to the authorities, engage judges

into training activity with special economics thought study[1], lobby the legislature, etc.. Of course, in some circumstances a combination of (1) and (2) might be used.

The incumbent firm's objective function is $\max U\left(\sum_{i=0}^{\infty}\frac{\pi^{M}-RC}{(1+R)^{i}},\sum_{i=0}^{\infty}\frac{\pi^{O}}{(1+R)^{i}}\right)$. The complete list of possible strategies is:

- Impose RC on the government if it chooses a neutral or supportive strategy,
- Impose RC on the entrant firm.

3.2.4 Assumptions

- A1: $PV\pi^{O}$-RC > NR > $PV\pi^{O}$-RC-RS
- A2: SOC, i.e. the cost imposed on the government in case if it does not support reforms < RC
- A3: Similar technology levels used by the incumbent and the entrant firms

3.3 The game*

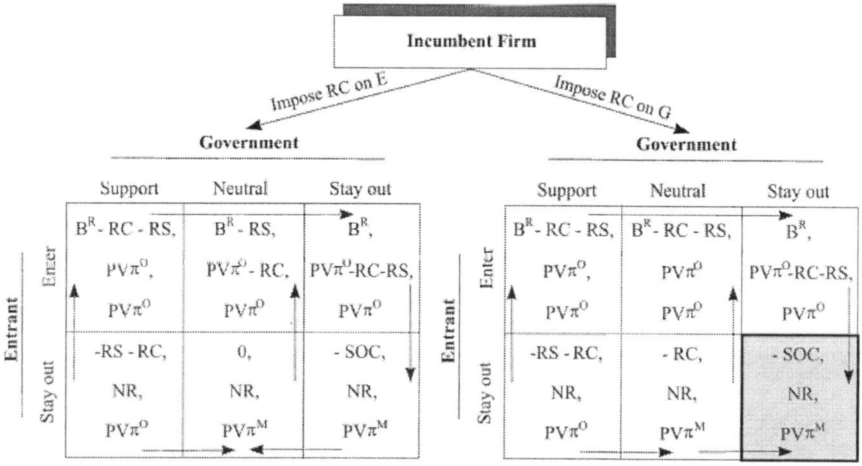

- Payoffs in the cells are arranged in the following way: (1) Government, (2) Entrant, and (3) Incumbent firm.

Source: own drawing

---

[1] See, for example, Mueller C. (1996) (http://home.mpinet.net/cmueller/i-overvw.html?)

The RHS sub-game has a unique Nash equilibrium: Stay out, Stay out. The LHS sub-game also has one mixed-strategy equilibrium. Incumbent firm observes these opportunities and chooses to impose RC on the government because the mixed strategy equilibrium yields less than the Nash equilibrium on the RHS. The game has a unique Nash equilibrium: Stay out, Stay out, Impose RC on the Government. The specificity of the above described game is in existence for substantial RS, which makes the outcome quite different from what can be seen in economies, where firm sizes are endogenously determined. The following game represents a similar case without RS.

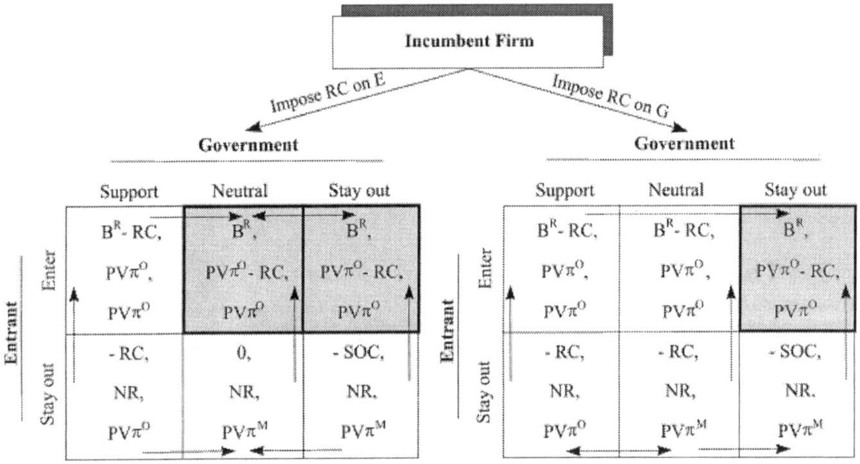

Source: own drawing

This game has three possible Nash equilibria:

	GOVERNMENT	ENTRANT	INCUMBENT FIRM
1	Neutral	Enter	Impose RC on Entrant
2	Stay out	Enter	Impose RC on Entrant
3	Stay out	Enter	Impose RC on Government

It can easily be seen that entry occurs in each of the cases. The inference of the model is that economies where firm sizes are exogenously defined may experience a restructuring trap that is primarily caused by a sufficiently high RS.

Now, let me specify the parameters that determine this approach to industrial development. Restructuring Trap = $f(\overset{+}{RC},\overset{+}{RS},\overset{-}{PV\pi^O},\overset{+}{\pi^M},\overset{+}{NR},\overset{-}{B^R},\overset{-}{SOC})$.

It can be supposed that there is some critical level of concentration in the industry when a leading firm (or firms) can retain monopolistic power for a substantial period of time. Restructuring (in terms of optimal size) might be even negative because of increased monopolisation.

Up until now we have said nothing about vertical and horizontal integration of the incumbent firm(s). But the results seem to be even more solid: with an increase in the incumbent firm's vertical or horizontal integration, both RC and RS should rise sharply.

4 Empirical testing

4.1 The data

The data used in our empirical analysis are firm-level balance sheet information, collected by the State Statistics Committee. The time series covers all of 1998. The cross-section part includes over 11000 firms with over 2000 product groups including services. At the same time several points are worth noting.

Firstly, as it is well known, firm-level data in transition economies should be treated with caution. Statistical measurements remain poor in many cases, especially when dealing with the private sector, substantial parts of which are operating in the informal economy. In this chapter we use the official data, since no other satisfactory information is available.

Secondly, for the reasons mentioned above we can also expect small firms to understate their key parameters. However, since we only use information for large firms – the leaders and most the efficient actors within a given product group – the level of data reliability is expected to be sufficiently high.

Thirdly, the information used is at the highest possible degree of dis-aggregation across different product groups. That is why the substitutability question is urgent. To partially resolve the problem, we introduce a control variable for product differentiation of the enterprise.

Fourthly, the market shares of enterprises are calculated without correction for import/export volumes, that is, assuming that the total production of the domestic enterprises equals the total domestic supply. Despite the fact that such an assumption is quite improbable it is unlikely to damage the econometric results. In our specification, only relevant but not absolute market shares are important.

4.2 The model

Data constraints do not allow us to perform time series analyses of concentration indexes or market shares. For this reason we use a methodology based on a comparison of the leader's efficiency with the efficiencies of the other firms within the product group. In other words, we use a cross-industry analysis comparing the number of firms that outperform the leader. The dependent variable in this case is $PEF = \dfrac{NumEff}{TotFirmNum - 1}$, where *NumEff* is the number of firms that outperform the leader on the PCM basis and *TotFirmNum* is the total number of firms within the industry. The null hypothesis is as follows: If a restructuring trap exists, the leading firms will differ significantly in a set of parameters as mentioned above. The following table represents the list of explanatory variables.

Table 20.1
Explanatory variables

Variable	Calculation	Explanation	Sign
MS_E	Level variable	Market share of the most efficient firm serves as a proxy for the MES. An increase in MES causes size-inefficiencies to fall	–
MS_Dif	$MS^{Lead} - MS^{Eft}$	The difference between market sizes of the leader and the most efficient firm. Greater probability of "size-inefficiency"	+
Lab_Dif	$\dfrac{Lab^{Lead} - Lab^{Eff}}{Lab^{Eff}}$	The difference in the labour employed by the leader and the most efficient firm. An increase in this variable means a decrease in the leader's efficiency	+
Cap_Dif	$\dfrac{Cap^{Lead} - Cap^{Eff}}{Cap^{Eff}}$	Difference in capital used by the leader and the most efficient firm. Possibility of "no-purpose" capital usage, excess capacities strategy	–
Lead_Prof	Level variable	Resistance costs are greater. Lesser opportunities for successful entry	–
Eff_Prof	Level variable	More attractive industry. Greater incentives to enter and, thus, probability of entry.	+
PCM_Dif	$\left\lvert \dfrac{PCM^{Lead} - PCM^{Eff}}{PCM^{Eff}} \right\rvert$	Difference in technology level. The greater, the better the opportunity to compete successfully	+
L_E_D	1 if leader is an exporter, 0 otherwise	Exporting leader is more likely to be efficient. Less opportunity to outperform	–
E_E_D	1 if efficient firm is an exporter, 0 otherwise	If efficient firm is an exporter, then the overall industry technological level is high, giving a possibility to penetrate into foreign markets and avoiding competition at the domestic one	+
Integr_Dif	Number of products produced by the leader	The greater the leader's production differentiation, the greater the opportunities to deter entry successfully	+

4.3 Results

The econometric estimation uses the OLS cross-section specification. Below we present an E-Views 3.0 estimation output. As can be seen from the estimation output table, all coefficients have a-priori expected signs. Only the Lead_Integr variable is not statistically significant, the other variables are significant at a 99% confidence interval. The explanatory power of the model is not outstanding.

However, if we take the cross-sectional specification into account, R-squared seems to be sufficiently large. Now let us discuss the model in greater detail.

As we expected, the MS_E variable, which stands for the minimal efficient scale has a negative correlation with the percentage of firms that outperform the industry leader. Simple logic dictates that an increase in the MES reduces the probability of the leader's size-inefficiency. The MS_Dif variable in turn measures the difference between the leader's size and MES. The greater this difference, the more leaders are likely to be inefficient. In our model we have found a strongly positive correlation between this difference and the quantity of firms in the industry that perform better than the leader.

Table 20.2
Econometric results

Variable	Coefficient	Std. Error	t-Statistic	Prob.
C	0.167924	0.022397	7.497596	0.0000
MS_E	-0.103050	0.031028	-3.321224	0.0009
MS_DIF	0.564418	0.025642	22.01185	0.0000
LAB_DIF	0.000517	0.000180	2.870145	0.0041
CAP_DIF	-4.11E-05	1.45E-05	-2.845085	0.0045
LEAD_PROF	-8.48E-07	1.29E-07	-6.589467	0.0000
PCM_DIF	0.280780	0.024150	11.62671	0.0000
EFF_PROF	3.65E-07	8.75E-08	4.173975	0.0000
L_E_D	-0.074484	0.016331	-4.560849	0.0000
E_E_D	0.085356	0.013922	6.131056	0.0000
LEAD_INTEGR	-0.000413	0.000897	-0.460708	0.6451

R-squared	0.422727	Mean dependent var	0.402169
Adjusted R-squared	0.419975	S.D. dependent var	0.350762
S.E. of regression	0.267138	Akaike info criterion	0.203099
Sum squared resid	149.7189	Schwarz criterion	0.232589
Log likelihood	-203.1680	F-statistic	153.6328
Durbin-Watson stat	1.898573	Prob(F-statistic)	0.000000

Another explanation might be: the leader can be X-inefficient. However, it is not the purpose of this paper to discuss which effect is more important. The fact that larger firms are less efficient is sufficient to raise a question about reasons of their leadership. Now let us switch to the next variable Lab_Dif. According to our model, excess employment substantially reduces the efficiency of the leading firms. But why does this excess employment exist? One of the possible answers comes from the theoretical framework presented above. A large labour force gives greater political power to the industry leaders when lobbying for direct and indirect subsidies. Since these subsidies are not reported on the balance sheets, we can observe overwhelming inefficiency. But in reality the subsidy volumes may be sufficient to retain market share and continue production. The next variable is Cap_Dif, which has a negative sign. In real life excess capacities may significantly reduce an industry's attractiveness for newcomers especially if their maintenance is not a question of extra and non-productive investments, but simply a heritage that has no better use. The Leader_Prof variable is directly drawn from the model presented in the previous section. The greater the profitability of the leader, the greater is his opportunity to deter entry or to fight off efficient newcomers. There is also is a second type of causality. If the leader has greater profits he is likely to be more efficient and fewer firms are likely to outperform him. At this stage we cannot distinguish between these two effects and thus leave this topic for further investigations. The PCM_Dif variable stands for the difference between the leader and other efficient firms in the technology levels employed. Obviously, the smaller this difference is, the smaller are the chances for entrants to be competitive vis-à-vis incumbent firms. The Eff_Prof variable defines the potential attractiveness of the industry for entrants. The greater the profit opportunities in the industry are, the greater is the number of firms wanting to enter. The L_E_D variable shows that the exporting leader is likely to be more efficient, and thus, more successful in competition. At the same time if the most efficient firm is also an exporter, there is a possibility to avoid hard competition in the domestic market and penetrate new regions. That is why, the variable E_E_D has a positive sign. The Lead_Integr variable is statistically insignificant in our specification. However, it has the a-priori expected sign, which says that greater integration is one of the strategies to prevent entry. The second possible effect is the so-called economy of scope. The leader may benefit from product differentiation directly, that is, by reducing his production costs. A reasonable explanation for the low statistical significance is that disintegration remained a major tendency in 1998 and that it was caused by the privatisation process rather than by cost efficiency considerations.

4.4 Weak points of the model

The hypothesis developed in the theoretical section suggests that large enterprises derive benefits from their sizes, which allows them to retain monopolistic power. At the same time data constraints do not allow us to perform a panel analysis. Instead we use a specification, which relates the number of more efficient enterprises to their market shares, labour, capital differences, etc.. Thus, though affirmative, our findings do not prove the theory directly.

5 Conclusions

This chapter developed a theoretical model that raises the question about the most appropriate competition policy for transition economies. The key message is that there is at least a theoretical possibility for large and inefficient enterprises to resist competition using their status of being "too big to fail". Following Sutton's tradition, this may be expressed as endogenizing of the exogenous sunk costs previously paid by the Soviet government. The benefits from having a restructuring trap can be expressed in terms of direct and indirect subsidies.

The empirical testing of the model assumes a time series analysis. The indirect hypothesis testing performed in this paper relates the number firms more efficient than the leader firm to the restructuring trap parameters. The key parameters that indirectly test the existence of the restructuring trap turn out to be significant with expected signs. This chapter should be followed by development of a time series analysis testing the dynamics of market leader development. In particular, if a restructuring trap exists, excess labour shedding, market share decreases for inefficient leaders, and other measures of restructuring will be comparatively slow for leading firms.

References

Akimova, I. and G. Schwödiauer (1999): Restructuring of Ukrainian Enterprises after Privatisation: Does Ownership Structure Matter? Otto-von-Guericke Universität Magdeburg, Fakultät für Wirtschaftswissenchaft, Discussion Paper.

Amess, K. and A. Gourlay (2000): The Dynamics of UK Industrial Concentration, 1993-1997. Department of Economics, Loughborough University.

Asplund, M. and V. Nocke (2000): Imperfect Competition, Market Size and Firm Turnover. Nuffield College, Oxford, 17 October.

Brown A. and D. Brown (1998): Does Market Structure Matter? New Evidence from Russia. Stockholm Institute of Transition Economics, Stockholm School of Economics, Working Paper, January 30.

Brown D. and J. Earle (2000): Competition and Firm Performance: Lessons from Russia. Stockholm Institute of Transition Economics, Stockholm School of Economics, Working Paper 154.

Caves R. E. (1998): Industrial Organisation and New Findings on the Turnover and Mobility of Firms. Journal of Economic Literature, No. 36(4), 1947-1982.

Claessens S. and S. Djankov (1998): Politicians and Firms in Seven Central and Eastern European Countries. World Bank, Working Paper.

Djankov S. (1998): Restructuring of Insider-Dominated Firms: A Comparative Analysis. World Bank, Working Paper.

Djankov S. (1999): Ownership Structure and Enterprise Restructuring in Six Newly Independent States. World Bank, Working Paper.

Dutz M. and M. Vagliasindi (1999): Competition Policy Implementation in Transition Ecanomies: An Empirical Assessment. European Bank for Reconstruction and Development, Working Paper 47.

Dutz M. and A. Hayri (2000): Does More Intense Competition Lead to Higher Growth? World Bank Research Project, RPO-682-47.

EBRD (1998): Transition Report 1998. European Bank for Reconstruction and Development, London.

Grigorian D. and A. Martinez (1998): Industrial Growth and Quality of Institutions: What Do (Transition) Economies Have to Gain from the Rule of Law? Private and Financial Sector Development Unit, Europe and Central Asia Region World Bank, Working Paper.

Hackett S. (2000): Cost Analysis. Lecture notes. http://www.humboldt.edu/~microeco/note/cost.htm.

International Institute for Applied System Analysis (1996): 3 Competition Measures and Policy. IIASA WP-96-049, http://www.iiasa.ac.at/Publications/Documents/WP-96-049.html/node3.html.

Kennedy D. (1999): Competition in the Power Sectors of Transition Economies. European Bank for Reconstruction and Development, Working Paper 41.

Mueller C. (1996): Antitrust Law and Economic Review. Antitrust Law and Economic Review Inc..

Nocke, V. (2000): Monopolisation and Industry Structure. Nuffield College, Oxford, 20 October.

Recanatini F., S. Wallsten, and L Xu (2000): Surveying Surveys and Questioning Questions: Learning from The World Bank Experience. World Bank, Working Paper.

Richards T. (1996): Positioning Your Dairy Farm Business for a Profitable Future – A Western Canadian Perspective. Center for Agribusiness Policy Studies, Arizona State University. http://www.afns.ualberta.ca/wcds/wcd96/wcd96175.htm

21

The Feasibility of Monetary Targeting in Ukraine

Vadim Volosovych

1 Introduction

Faced with considerable inflation in 2000 (25.8% yoy), the National Bank of Ukraine (NBU) and the government became more and more concerned about controlling the inflation rate. In 2001, the NBU adopted a more restrictive monetary policy aiming at a substantial reduction of the inflation rate.

Under the assumption that the ultimate long-term goal for the NBU is price stability, this investigation looks at the optimal intermediate target through which to perform this task effectively. In particular, the paper studies the important central bank strategy of *monetary targeting*. Monetary targeting is one of the options for assuring price stability, influencing inflationary expectations, and improving the transparency of monetary policy.

2 Review of the strategies for monetary policy

2.1 The transmission mechanism of monetary policy: goals and targets

It is necessary to stress that several of the ultimate goals of monetary policy are in conflict with each other. For example, in the short run the goals of price and of interest rate stability are seen to be incompatible, which may not be true in the longer prospective. Given the general consensus on the high cost of inflation and the National Bank's concern over high inflation rates in Ukraine in 2000, we postulate that price stability is the ultimate goal of Ukrainian monetary policy.

Central banks do not affect their ultimate goals directly. Every central bank has in its arsenal a set of *tools* (or *instruments*) that can affect the chosen goal indirectly after a certain time lag. When a central bank chooses its monetary strategy it concentrates on variables that lie somewhere between its instruments and the ultimate goal. The strategy is designed in the following way: After deciding on its ultimate goal, the central bank chooses the set of variables, so called intermediate *targets*, to aim for which will have a direct effect on the goal. Intermediate targets are in their turn affected directly by another set of variables, the so called *operating targets*, which are more closely linked to the bank's *instruments*. The central bank proceeds in this way when formulating monetary policy because it is easier to attain the ultimate goal by aiming at targets than by aiming at the final goal directly. By using operating and intermediate targets the central bank can more quickly monitor whether its policies are producing the right results and make any necessary corrections, rather than waiting until the final outcome of its policies on the ultimate goal materialises. Graph 21.1 presents the contemporary approach to the monetary policy via instruments and targets.

Graph 21.1
General principle of the transmission mechanism for monetary policy

Tools (instruments)	⇒	Operating targets	⇒	Intermediate targets	⇒	Ultimate goal

There are three major criteria that should be considered when choosing *any* intermediate target: measurability, controllability and a predictable effect on the goal. In the broad sense, *measurability* means how quickly and accurately the central bank can measure the intermediate target variable. The central bank must be able to *control* a variable effectively once it is chosen as a useful target. The reason is that the target may have to be altered quickly should it go off track. For example, while the central bank may set interest rates directly, it often has difficulties with affecting inflationary expectations and thus fails to control the development of the real interest rates. *Predictability* of the target's effect on the final goal is of equal importance. In the context of this chapter 'predictability' implies the stability of the ties between the various candidates for intermediate targets and the ultimate goal. This aspect is the key question studied here.

2.2 International experience with choosing monetary strategies

One of the possible intermediate targets is the *amount of money* available in the entire economy and its growth rate. According to classical economics, there is an unambiguous congruence between the money supply and the price level; hence the central bank is able to control the price level by influencing the money supply.

The history of the monetary policy conduct of *advanced economies such as the USA, Canada, UK, Germany and Japan* (Mishkin, 1998, pp.483-500) shows that the use of the money supply as an intermediate target was a popular instrument among central banks since the 1970s. However, the use of this strategy has seriously declined since the second half of the 1980s. Yet, the following facts are worth emphasising. First, to successfully use monetary targeting requires the central bank to follow this strategy in a very consistent manner as has been shown by the failure of monetary targeting in the USA, UK, and Canada, and its relative success in Germany and Japan. Another interesting lesson from the Japanese experience is the possibility to use the interest rate operating target (interbank interest rates) to control the intermediate monetary target. The breakdown of the close ties between money aggregates and goal variables (nominal GDP, inflation) – experienced during the second half of the 1980s – eventually made monetary targeting in many advanced economies unfeasible. At that time central banks noticed that the causal relationship between growth in the money supply and inflation, which used to function so well previously, was broken, and that they were now unable to control the price level through the money supply. The most likely cause for this change was the rapid development of financial innovations. Paying interest on sight deposits and the increasingly intensive use of the many means of cashless payment (e.g. credit cards) led to an erosion of the boundaries between cash and non-cash type instruments. This has complicated the definition and measurement of money and broke the link between money aggregates and economic activity rendering instability to money demand. Consequently, central banks in several countries (including the United States and the United Kingdom) gave up the system of monetary control based on the money supply.

After the highly inflationary years at the beginning of transition, the central banks in the economies of *Central and Eastern Europe (CEE)* also tend to look closely at price stability. They decided to choose different intermediate targets as nominal anchors in pursuing their monetary policies. Many of them use the exchange rate as the nominal anchor to control inflationary expectations. Exchange rate targeting is not synonymous with maintaining a fixed-type exchange rate regime. Several countries – and *Ukraine* among them – pursue an exchange rate target. Others use formally more flexible exchange rate regimes (floating, wide-band exchange rate regimes) or limit the actual movement of the exchange rate through managed floats.

If one assumes the ultimate long-term goal for the NBU to be price stability, one should also consider such an important central bank strategy as *monetary targeting*. Control over the money supply remains a major means of ensuring external and internal stability of the domestic currency and a basis for gradual and predictable variations of the exchange rate. Additionally any central bank, which has proclaimed a flexible exchange rate policy, has to think about how it raises the credibility of its commitment to fight inflation. Therefore, the first important question raised in this paper is whether monetary targeting is feasible in Ukraine.

If so, the next question becomes quite naturally "What is the best monetary aggregate as the NBU's intermediate target to achieve the final goal of price stability"? To answer that question it is first necessary to determine the monetary aggregate, whose volatility causes the greatest fluctuations in the price level. Then one needs to check whether this relationship would be the most stable over time.

3 Theoretical background

The development of Hryvnia exchange rate and its links to the money supply and to prices are omitted from this investigation.

The monetary approach to the relationship between the money supply and the price level (i.e. the quantity theory of money) as described by Krugman and Obstfeld (1997) is used here. The monetary approach assumes that prices in an economy change only because of changes in the money supply (the quantity of money) and of money demand. This long run theory assumes no price rigidities occur over the short-run. The equilibrium condition can be expressed as follows:

$$P = \frac{M^S}{L(i, Y)} \tag{21.1}$$

where P is the domestic price level, M^S is the money supply in Ukraine, and L(.) is the money demand, depending on the domestic interest rate i and real output Y.

One of the most important predictions of this theory concerns the relationship between a country's price level and its money supply: *All else being equal, an increase of the (level of) money supply in an economy causes a proportional increase in its price level.* This claim is justified by the fact that money demand L(.) is the demand for real money balances. There is virtually unanimous consensus among monetary economists regarding the long-term of monetary policy. The idea that *monetary policy is unable to influence real economic variables in the long run* is widely shared by economists. Since M^S has no effect on the long-run economic variables (i, Y), an increase in the level of the money supply has no effect on the real money demand and manifests itself in a price level increase.

Evidence concerning this relationship between money supply and prices for transition economies of Central Europe and of the FSU is presented in Graph 21.2. Here the vertical axis measures the average CPI inflation for the years 1996 to

1999, and the horizontal axis the average growth in money aggregate M1 as defined by the IMF International Financial Statistics.[1]

Graph 21.2
Average growth rate of M1 and CPI in CEE and FSU countries, 1996-1999

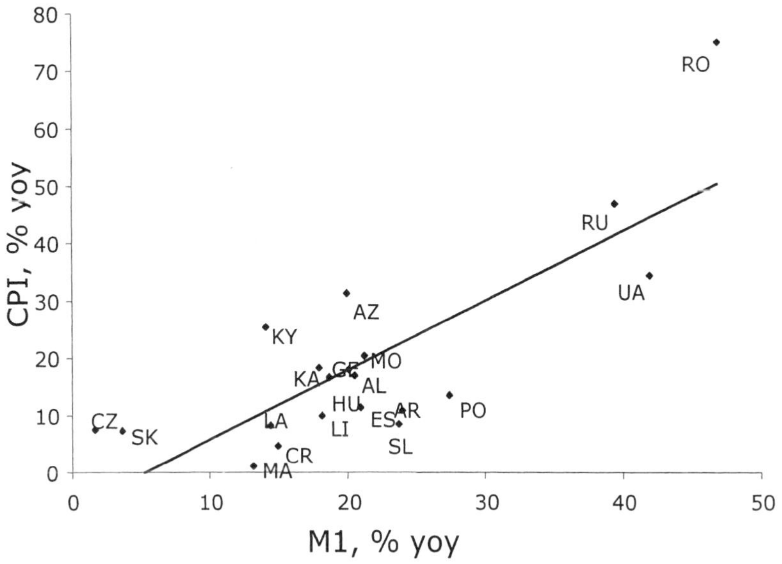

Source: IMF (2000)

Clearly, a positive relationship between money supply and prices exists in this group of countries as predicted by the monetary approach. While the assumptions of the approach may be very limiting and do not hold in the short run, predictions based on that are useful to study the development of macroeconomic variables over longer time periods. Hence, applying these assumptions of monetary theory here is justified because we seek for the most stable relationship between an aggregate and the price level in Ukraine. Additionally, when applying a monetary targeting strategy a central bank usually sets the parameters of its target variables (level or growth rate) for a rather long period. Also, when choosing a given aggregate from several options it should be interested in the variable that has the *strongest* link to the price level and behaves *predictably*, i.e. according to the economic theory, over a reasonable forecasting horizon.

---

[1] The International Financial Statistics database employs the national definitions of monetary aggregates, reported by the corresponding central banks. The aggregates are measured in domestic currency.

Due to estimation limitations, which will be discussed later, some additional assumptions need to be made. Fortunately, they are justified by the monetary theory. In particular, a contemporaneous reaction in prices and an absence of immediate adjustments of monetary aggregates to price changes are assumed. The rationale behind price flexibility is that during the period under study (1996 to early 2001) consumer prices were mostly liberalised (the major state regulation concerned some producer prices). Additionally, the market actors could easily observe an increase of money in circulation (when the NBU directly of indirectly financed a budget deficit and/or purchased foreign exchange) and adjusted prices rather quickly. On the other hand the money supply (especially the broad aggregates) can only be changed with a certain lag – this implies some stickiness in the monetary adjustment.

4 Methodology

4.1 Data

To study the relationship between money and prices over time it is natural to use time series data. To assure a sufficient sample size, official monthly data on CPI and money aggregates were used. Consumer Price Index (CPI) series are available from the Derzhkomstat (State Statistics Committee of Ukraine) with the lag of one week. The money aggregates are calculated and published by the NBU with a considerable time lag, normally 45 days (however some preliminary estimations became available on-line from the NBU recently).

Since many definitions of "money supply" are in general use it is important to define the NBU definitions of money aggregates (national definition of money) that are used in this investigation (Table 21.1).

Table 21.1
NBU definitions of the money aggregates.[2]

M0 =	currency outside banks;
M1 =	M0 + funds in current accounts in domestic currency;
M2 =	M1 + time deposits in domestic currency and foreign currency deposits;
M3 =	M2 + client funds under banks' trust operations and banks' own liabilities (before 1998 M3 = M2 + client funds in banks' trust operations).

Source: NBU

[2] No formal definition of Monetary Base is presented in the official NBU sources.

The data are presented in logarithmic form in order to reduce possible heteroskedasticity and to make the interpretation of estimated coefficients easier. The sample covers monthly data from January 1996 to March 2001, i.e. 63 observations.

4.2 Statistical estimation of the relationship between money supply and prices

For the purpose of statistical estimations one should take into consideration both short-term interdependence between inflation and money supply and long-term links. Vector-autoregressive (VAR) models are commonly used for systems of interrelated time series and for analysing the dynamic impact of random disturbances on the system of variables. Failure of large statistical models of the 1950s and 1960s, which were based on theoretical grounds, to describe reality and better forecast performance of VARs led researchers to the conclusion that simple small-scale VARs without sophisticated theoretical foundations prove to be better than large structural equation systems. The VAR approach avoids the need for structural modelling by modelling every endogenous variable in the system as a function of the lagged values of all of the endogenous variables in the system. As pointed out by Greene (2000), one of the virtues of the VAR is that there is no need to define a-priori what variables in the model are exogenous; it has only lagged (pre-determined) variables on the right-hand side and all variables are treated as endogenous.

In this paper the interdependence of two variables: money supply (M) and consumer price index (P) is studied. The VAR model constructed in this paper has the following form:

$$\underbrace{\begin{vmatrix} a_{pp} & a_{pm} \\ a_{mp} & a_{mm} \end{vmatrix}}_{A} \cdot \underbrace{\begin{vmatrix} P_t \\ M_t \end{vmatrix}}_{y_t} = \underbrace{\begin{vmatrix} \alpha_p \\ \alpha_m \end{vmatrix}}_{\alpha} + \underbrace{\begin{vmatrix} b_{pp} & b_{pm} \\ b_{mp} & b_{mm} \end{vmatrix}}_{B} \cdot \underbrace{\begin{vmatrix} P_{t-1} \\ M_{t-1} \end{vmatrix}}_{y_{t-1}} + \underbrace{\begin{vmatrix} e_{pt} \\ e_{mt} \end{vmatrix}}_{\varepsilon_t} \tag{21.2}$$

Only one lag of right-hand side variables is included for simplicity of presentation. Despite its merits for forecasting, this method was criticised for it's a-theoretical (non-structural) approach. The model does however include some structure if we treat it as a reduced form of some dynamic structural model (a structural vector-autoregressive (SVAR) model). The most important decision to be made was what type of restrictions should be placed on matrix **A** so that they correspond to the theory and the system of equations is exactly identified. This can be done if matrix *A* has an upper triangular form (i.e. all the zeros below diagonal). This implies that the SVAR representation in (1) must be recursive to be identified. One has to bear in mind the following restrictions to interpret the obtained results in a meaningful way.

The *impulse response function* (IRF) analysis is the most interesting application of the VAR approach for this paper. An IRF traces the effect of a shock to one of the disturbances on current and future values of the endogenous variables. Simply put, an IRF is a graph of the impact of an innovation over time (Kennedy, 1998). For example, in model (1) a monetary shock e_{mt} directly affects money M_t, and is also transmitted to the endogenous variable P_t through the dynamic structure of the VAR. By constructing an IRF one can show how monetary shocks affect inflation, and how price shocks influence the behaviour of money. Then by constructing various VARs with different monetary aggregates and analysing corresponding IRFs of prices to monetary shocks, it is possible to decide what monetary aggregate has the greatest and longest impact on inflation. This aggregate may then be suggested as an intermediate target for the monetary policy aiming at price stability. At this time, the simple pair-wise correlation coefficients will be constructed to check the stability of this link over time. In the next section some technical issues connected with estimation of VAR models are discussed.

4.3 Some aspects of time-series estimation

Firstly, the number of lags to be included in the model is defined. For this purpose the series of unrestricted VAR models are run for (logarithms of) CPI, and various money aggregates and information criteria are analysed. An economic judgement supplements the formal statistical approach.

Secondly, the time series data used in the VAR system should be *stationary*. When the data are expressed in levels, it turns out that there are clear trends present. Use of non-stationary time series in regressions gives spurious results about non-existent relationships. Therefore, the test for stationarity is essential in any time-series analysis. The most popular test for stationarity is the so-called unit root test. Here the well-known Augmented Dickey-Fuller (ADF) test without trend will be used to test the null hypothesis that there is a unit root in the series. If the hypothesis of unit root is rejected the data in levels can be used; otherwise the series are first-differenced and the ADF test performed again on the transformed data.[3] If the hypothesis of unit root is not rejected a further analysis of the series is required. The major critique of all such tests is their low power: they are unable to reject the unit root if it is actually absent from the data.

---

3 In general, the variable is called integrated of order d (written I(d)) if it must be differenced d times to become stationary. Economic variables are seldom integrated of order greater than two; and if non-stationary are usually I(1) (Kennedy, 1998).

Thirdly, some non-stationary economic series may vary but not drift too far apart due to some dis-equilibrium forces that tend to keep them together. Such series are characterised by long-run equilibrium relationships. By definition, if two series are integrated of the same order (say, having unit roots) but their linear combination is stationary (I(0) in this notation) they are said to be *co-integrated*. Their entry into the estimating equation will not create spurious results. If the series are co-integrated and this "long-run relationship" is found, in the short-run there can still be dis-equilibrium. As Kennedy (1998) points out "if a co-integrating relationship can be found, this should be exploited by undertaking the estimation in an ECM (error-correction mechanism) framework". In a VAR context a VAR incorporating co-integration is called a vector error correction (VEC) model. The VEC specification restricts the long-run behaviour of the endogenous variables to converge to their co-integrating relationships while allowing a wide range of short-run dynamics. It is common that such data like price level and money supply have the long-run association, therefore testing for co-integration is an important step in the analysis. Johansen tests for co-integration will be used for this purpose.

5 Empirical results and interpretation

Following the steps outlined in Section 4.3, first the number of lags to be included in the model is defined. To this end the series of unrestricted VAR models is run for (logarithms of) CPI and various money aggregates and the information criteria are analysed. Then the data are tested for stationarity by an ADF test. Deterministic trends were not included into the regressions, given the imperfection of this kind of de-trending. It turns out that for all the series of levels the hypothesis of unit roots cannot be rejected even at the 10% significance level, implying that they are non-stationary. The results of the ADF test for first differences of series imply that all the series become stationary when first-differenced; or, put differently, they are I(1). Consequently, for all monetary aggregates the VAR model will be run in first differences of the raw data to remove the non-stationarity problem. An additional benefit derived from this formulation is the interpretation of results. As the raw data are taken in logarithms, the first difference is interpreted as a growth rate. For example, a difference in log(CPI) equals to the monthly inflation rate, etc.. The results of the Johansen co-integration tests imply that one cannot reject the existence of co-integrating equations at a 5% significance level for all monetary aggregates. These equations can be easily incorporated into VAR models in the form of an error-correction term.

Summarising all the statistical tests and judgements, the following models are suggested: all the models include a time series in first differences with three lags; all monetary aggregates are modelled by VEC models with one co-integrating equation incorporated. The major interest for this paper lies in the analysis of impulse response functions. Therefore, the interpretation of the particular coefficients is of minor interest here. The goodness-of-fit measure R^2 of the price equation implies that a rather big proportion (up to 50%) of variation in prices is explained by money growth. For the money supply equation the goodness-of-fit is smaller (18-27%) with higher R^2 for the aggregates M1 and M2. This may imply that the monetary authority reacts little to inflation changes by means of altering the money supply. Another reason of the small R^2 is the omission of other important explanatory variables (the exchange rate, for example).

The impulse response functions obtained from the VEC models estimated in this paper are presented in Graph 21.3. They trace the effect of a shock in the corresponding monetary aggregate on current and future values of the price level. Each graph represents the response of 36 periods forward from the initial shock, which corresponds to three years (1 period = 1 month).

Quite in line with the theory, the price level increases after the monetary shock for all aggregates, and this increase is preserved in the long run. A shock in the monetary aggregates has a positive impact on inflation only in the first year with some volatility in the first quarter following the shock. In the subsequent periods (after a year) the CPI stabilises at the higher level.

Instability in M1 and M2 may cause the biggest increase in inflation rate (captured by the slope of the IRF line) within a time period of 6 to 10 months. *Therefore, it is better to control these aggregates to prevent rapid price hikes.* Unfortunately, at this stage one cannot discriminate between the two because they have almost identical standard errors and IRFs for the CPI.

Co-integrating equations in VEC estimates present the long-term relationship between inflation and changes in the monetary aggregates. The long-run elasticity of consumer price inflation with regard to a change in money supply can be revealed from these equations (Table 21.2).

Table 21.2
Long-run elasticity of the inflation rate with regard to a change in money supply

M0	MB	M1	M2	M3
0.683 (0.070)* (9.716)**	0.588 (0.033) (18.066)	0.638 (0.030) (21.026)	0.575 (0.025) (22.912)	0.567 (0.030) (19.247)

* standard error; ** t-statistics
Source: own calculations

Table 21.2 reveals that the long-run relationship between changes in M2 and inflation can be most precisely estimated during the period of study (lowest standard error). A 10% increase in M2 causes an average growth in inflation rate of 5.75% (±0.25%) in the long run.

Graph 21.3
Responses of CPI to shocks in monetary aggregates

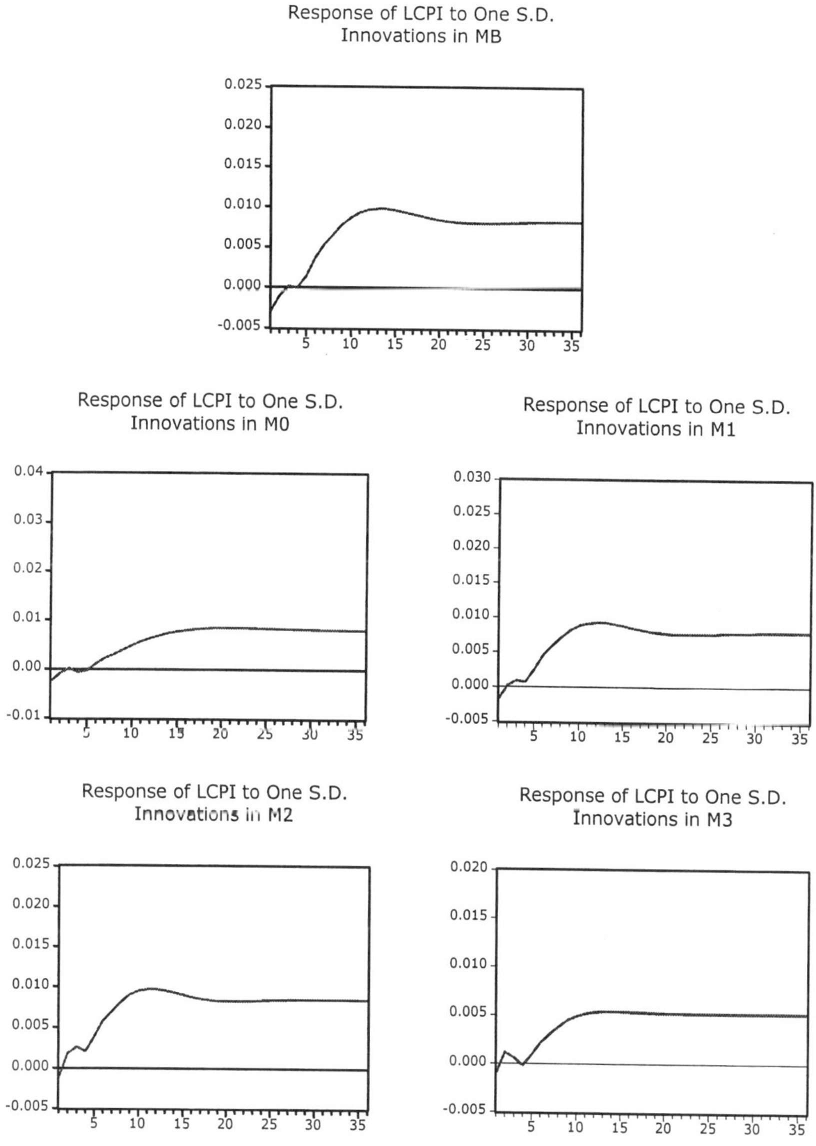

Source: own calculations

To permit us to choose the major criterion for the intermediate target, i.e. predictability, it is necessary to assure that the link between the candidate aggregate and the price level remains stable over time. Pair-wise correlation coefficients were constructed to check the stability of the link between the candidate aggregate and the inflation rate over time for various aggregates.

Table 21.3
Pair-wise correlation coefficients between the changes in monetary aggregates and the inflation rate

	dM0	dMB	dM1	dM2	dM3
1 month lag	0.100	0.086	0.080	0.089	-0.040
3 months lag	-0.111	-0.137	-0.162	-0.224	-0.163
6 months lag	0.231	0.230	0.275	0.298	0.216
8 months lag	0.179	0.233	0.299	0.336	-0.058
10 months lag	0.266	0.247	0.301	0.166	0.031

Source: own calculations

The correlation between the monthly change in M2 and the inflation rate was highest taking into account reasonably long lag length (6 to 8 months). While the correlation is not very high for shorter lag length, it reaches its maximum of approximately 34% with an eight-month lag. This implies that the impact of a change in money supply on inflation reaches its maximum in eight months. It is necessary to note that this finding is quite in accordance with the results of the VEC analysis. If one looks again at Graph 21.3 one can notice that the slope of the IRF reaches its biggest value just at the eighth month point for M2. For the M1 aggregate the correlation coefficient is lower for the majority of lag lengths, but not by very much.

6 Conclusions and policy implications

This paper is devoted to the study of an important question concerning the feasibility of monetary targeting in Ukraine. A search for an alternative strategy for monetary policy is necessitated by the commitment of the National Bank of Ukraine to price stability. The general conclusion of the paper is that use of monetary targeting in Ukraine is possible. The answer to the question what aggregate should play the role of the intermediate target is not so obvious. Comprehensive statistical tests where performed to resolve this problem.

Summarising the results of the statistical analysis one can claim that shocks to M1 and M2 cause the biggest and most rapid increases in the inflation rate among all monetary aggregates. The long-term money-price relationship can be estimated most precisely for M2, for which the link of variation between M2 and CPI inflation is also the most stable. Therefore, the empirical analysis shows that if there is a decision to use a money aggregate as the intermediate target of a monetary policy aimed at curbing inflation the best candidate is M2.

However this finding should be supplemented by some other considerations that can add a 'grain of salt' to the above conclusion. While the M2 aggregate is superior to M1 based on the predictability criterion, some additional problems may arise in connection with M2. The M1 aggregate is "transaction money" and due to its higher liquidity has a direct impact on consumer prices. The biggest part of fluctuations in M2 can be attributed to M1. Also, M2 is possibly inferior to M1 regarding the measurability criterion because it includes deposits in foreign currency whose valuation depends on the current exchange rate. For the predictability of the M2 developments it is necessary to assume a more or less predictable behaviour of the exchange rate. If the NBU is also concerned about measurability and predictability problems that might arise from unstable exchange rates, priority may have to be given to the narrower aggregate M1.

References

Anatliev, S. (2001): Time series analysis. Materials of the Methodological seminar, Moscow, April.

EBRD (2000): Transition Report. European Bank for Reconstruction and Development, London.

Fischer (1993): The Role of Macroeconomic Factors in Growth. Journal of Monetary Economics, No. 32, pp. 485-512.

Holod, D. (2000): The Relationship Between Price Level, Money Supply and Exchange Rate in Ukraine. A thesis submitted in partial fulfilment of the requirements for the degree of Master of Arts, National University of Kyiv-Mohyla Academy, Kyiv, Unpublished.

IMF (2000): International Financial Statistics CD. Washington, D.C.

Greene, W. H. (2000): Econometric Analysis. 4th edition, Prentice Hall, Upper Side River, New Jersey, USA.

Hamilton, J. D. (1994): Time Series Analysis. Princeton University Press.

Kennedy, P. (1998): A Guide to Econometrics. 4th edition, The MIT Press, Cambridge, Massachusetts.

Krugman, P. R. and M. Obstfeld (1997): International Economics: Theory and Policy. 4th edition, Addison-Wesley.

Mishkin, F. S. (1998): The Economics of Money, Banking, and Financial Markets. 5th edition, Addison Wesley Longman, Inc.

National Bank of Hungary (2000): Monetary Policy in Hungary.

Russian Central Bank (Tsentralniy Bank Rossii) (2000): Monetary Policy Aims by RCB. http://www.cbr.ru/analytics/standart_system/policy_e.html

The Authors

Iryna Akimova, Ph.D.: Director of the Institute for Economic Research and Policy Consulting, Kyiv, founded by the Ukrainian Government and the German Advisory Group on Economic Reform with the Government of Ukraine (Kyiv). Associate Professor of Economics at the Kharkiv State Polytechnic University. Alexander von Humboldt Research Fellow at the University of Magdeburg. Teaching and research in macroeconomics and economic reforms in transition countries. Particular focus on corporate restructuring and the development of the small business sector in Eastern Europe.

Yilmaz Akyuz, Ph.D.: Acting Director, Division on Globalisation and Development Strategies, UNCTAD. The principal author and head of the team preparing the *Trade and Development Report*; and UNCTAD coordinator of substantive support to the Group-of-24 in the IMF and World Bank on International Monetary and Financial Issues. Author of books on "Money and Inflation in Turkey", "Capital, Distribution and Growth", "Macroeconomic Disequilibrium", "Financial Structure and Flow of Funds", and "East Asian Development". Acted as referee for various academic journals, as the editor of *UNCTAD Review* and guest editor of *Revue Tiers-Monde, Journal of Development Studies, Cambridge Journal of Economics.*

Marek Dabrowski: Professor of Economics, Chairman of the Council of the CASE-Center for Social and Economic Research in Warsaw. Chairman of the Supervisory Board of CASE-Ukraine in Kyiv, member of the Monetary Policy Council of the National Bank of Poland. In the last decade has been involved in policy advising to the governments of Ukraine, Russia, Kyrgyzstan, Kazakhstan, Uzbekistan, Mongolia, Moldova, Romania, Bulgaria, Macedonia and Yugoslavia.

Pavel Daneyko: Chairman of the Supervisory Council of the Institute for Privatisation and Management (IPM) Business School in Minsk. Research on macro-, microeconomic and institutional aspects of transformation, the political economy of transformation, and stock markets. Participation in the Economic Forum funded by the German Government's TRANSFORM Program, the IPM, the Polish Know-How Fund and the joint IPM-CASE project on a Concept for Economic and Institutional Reforms in Belorus. Author of more than 40 works on economic transformation in Belorus, Russia, and Poland.

James W. Dean, Ph.D: Kaiser Distinguished Professor of International Business, Western Washington University and Professor of Economics, Simon Fraser University, Vancouver, Canada. Extensively published in international economic journals. Visiting appointments at 24 universities and research institutes world-wide. Currently Citibank Visiting Professor, EERC MA Program, "Kyiv-Mohyla Academy".

Rumen Dobrinsky: Senior Economic Affairs Officer at the United Nations Economic Commission for Europe (UNECE) in Geneva. Research on current macroeconomic developments and policies in Central and Eastern Europe and the successor states of the former USSR. Before joining the UNECE was President of the Centre for Economic and Strategic Research in Sofia, where he conducted and directed research on the process of economic transformation in Bulgaria.

Boris Dodonov: Research Associate at the Institute for Economic Research and Policy Consulting. Particular concentration on the performance of the Ukrainian energy sector. Education at the National University of "Kyiv-Mohyla Academy" (MA in Economics) and the Kyiv National Taras Shevchenko University (Specialist's Degree in Applied Mathematics).

Igor Eremenko: Research Associate at the Institute for Economic Research and Policy Consulting. Particular interest in financial markets, monetary policy and international trade. Internship at the Ministry of Finance of Ukraine and the Harvard Institute for International Development. Education at the National University of "Kyiv-Mohyla Academy" (MA in Economics) and the Tavria Institute of Entrepreneurship and Law (Bachelor's and Specialist's Degrees with Honours in Finance and Credit). Post-graduate student at the National University of "Kyiv-Mohyla Academy".

Evgeny E. Gavrilenkov: Acting General Director of the Economic Analysis Bureau Fund. Deputy Rector and Chairman of the Department of Applied Macroeconomics, State University - Higher Economics School (HES) in Moscow, Director of the Institute of Macroeconomic Research and Forecasting. Editor-in-Chief of "HES Journal of Economics". Co-author of the Economic Program of Mr. German Gref (Government Minister of the Russian Federation). Main area of scientific interest - transition macroeconomics and macroeconomic policy.

Valeriy Heyets: Member of the National Academy of Science of Ukraine (NANU), Academician-Secretary of the NANU Economics Department, Director of the Institute for Economic Forecasting of the National Academy of Science, member of the Council on Science, Scientific and Technical Policy under the President of Ukraine. Since 1991 Mr. Geyetz represents Ukraine's economic forecasts in the UN LINK Project. He is an expert on macroeconomic, economic and mathematical modelling and forecasting economic development. Has published 162 works, among them 22 individual and collective monographs.

Thorvaldur Gylfason: Research Professor of Economics at the University of Iceland and Research Fellow at CEPR, SNS in Stockholm, CESifo in Munich, and the Center for US-Japan Business and Economic Studies at New York University. Has published over 100 scholarly articles and 14 books, including *Understanding the Market Economy* (with Isachsen and Hamilton, Oxford, 1992), which has appeared in 17 languages, and *Principles of Economic Growth* (Oxford, 1999).

Oleh Havrylyshyn, Ph.D.: Senior Advisor in the IMF's European II Department, dealing with Fund operations in the Baltic countries, Russia, Ukraine and other former Soviet Union countries. Special Advisor/Deputy Minister of Finance in the Government of Ukraine in 1992. Alternate Executive Director in the IMF's Executive Board, 1993-96. Joined the staff of the IMF in 1996 as Assistant Director in the Policy Development and Review Department. Ph.D. from the Massachusetts Institute of Technology in 1972.

Gábor Hunya, Dr.: Senior economist at the Vienna Institute for International Economic Studies (WIIW) in Vienna, Austria. Specialises in the macroeconomic analysis of Romania and Bulgaria and does comparative research on foreign direct investment and privatisation in transformation economies. In the 1980s staff member of the Institute for World Economics of the Hungarian Academy of Sciences. Education in Budapest.

Joachim Jahnke, Dr.: Vice President of the European Bank for Reconstruction and Development (EBRD), London. The EBRD is actively engaged in supporting economic transition in Ukraine as its second largest client country, with priority areas in the financial sector, SME support, energy sector reform and nuclear safety (Chernobyl related project volume of close to EUR 1 bn in grant financed projects). The EBRD is also represented by its President in the Foreign Investment Advisory Council chaired by the President of Ukraine.

Alexander Kobzev: Economist with the IFC Agribusiness Development Project. Specialises in regional and agricultural economics, institutional reforms. Previous employment with the US Agency for International Development and the Institute for Social and Economic Problems, Institute for Economic Research and Policy Consulting. Educated at Ohio State University (Master's Degree in Public Policy and Management) and the Kyiv National Taras Shevchenko University (Degree with Honours in Economic Geography and Regional Development).

Nina Legeida: Research Associate at the Institute for Economic Research and Policy Consulting. Focuses on fiscal policy analysis, in particular, public deficit, debt and budget issues. Yearly internship at the Macroeconomic Indicators and Monetary Policy Department of the Ministry of Finance of Ukraine. Education at the National University of "Kyiv-Mohyla Academy" (MA in Economics) and the Nyzhin State Pedagogical University (Specialist's Degree in Foreign Languages).

Bogdan Lissovolik: PhD in economics from the European University Institute, Florence, Italy. Currently IMF Resident Representative in Kyiv. Has worked as an IMF desk economist in Eastern Europe, Africa and Latin America. Research interests are mainly concentrated in the area of the economics of the transition process.

Nadiya Mankovska: Research Associate at the Institute for Economic Research and Policy Consulting in Ukraine. Research on investment policy, foreign exchange markets and international trade development in transition economies.

Education at the National University of "Kyiv-Mohyla Academy" (MA in Economics). Previous position in the Office of the Vice Prime Minister of Ukraine (Serhiy Tihipko) where she was involved in the implementation of the Administrative Reform Program in Ukraine.

Iryna Mel'ota: Research Associate at the Institute for Economic Research and Policy Consulting. Particular concentration on fiscal policy, social policy and the shadow economy. Education at the National University of "Kyiv-Mohyla Academy" (MA in Economics) and the Lviv National University (Diploma in Mathematics).

Mehmet Ögütçü: Principal Administrator, responsible for the OECD's relations with non-member economies and other stakeholders in the field of international investment and multinational enterprises. He is also the program manager for the recently established OECD Global Forum on International Investment. Has written extensively on Turkey, China, South East Europe, Asia-Pacific and Eurasian countries, with a focus on foreign investment, energy security and geo-politics, economic and trade diplomacy. Prior to joining the OECD in 1994, Mr. Ögütçü was with the Turkish diplomatic service in Ankara, Beijing, Brussels and Paris.

Marta Oleksiv: Research Associate at the Institute for Economic Research and Policy Consulting. Focuses on corporate sector reform (privatisation, enterprise restructuring, state corporate governance) and the development of small and medium-sized business. Education at the National University of "Kyiv-Mohyla Academy" (MA in Economics) and the National University "Lviv Polytechnik" (Bachelor's and Specialist's Degrees in International Business Management).

Petra Opitz, Dr.rer.oec.: Research Associate at the German Institute for Economic Research (DIW), Berlin, and member of the German Advisory Group on Economic Reform with the Government of Ukraine (Kyiv). Particular concentration on deregulation and corporate restructuring in Eastern Europe. Formerly with the Institute for Economics at the University of Oldenburg, the International Centre for Conversion (Bonn), the Free University of Berlin and the Academy of Sciences (Berlin).

Serguey Pukovich: Deputy Director of the Research Center of the Institute for Privatisation and Management (IPM) Business School in Minsk. Scientific interest: enterprise restructuring and strategic management. Participation in an IPM Business School project on increasing the export potential of the agricultural rayons of Minsk oblast (1999-2000) as well as a joint IPM Business School-CASE project on a Concept for Economic and Institutional Reforms in Belorus (2000). Teaches seminars and courses at the IPM Business School on problems of strategic management and enterprise competitiveness, marketing, and business planning.

Alexander Scherbakov: Research Associate at the Institute for Economic Research and Policy Consulting. Focuses on industrial organisation issues with a special emphasis on structural reforms (in particular, restructuring medium and large-size enterprises) and competition policy. Education at the National University of "Kyiv-Mohyla Academy" (MA in Economics and Bachelor's Degree in Social Sciences). Post-graduate student at the National University of "Kyiv-Mohyla Academy".

Pavlo Sugolov: Research Associate at the Institute for Economic Research and Policy Consulting. Focuses on infrastructure development and regulation, in particular tariff reform, the development of regulatory institutions and the relationship between infrastructure policies and economic growth. Work experience with the Parliament of Ukraine. Education at the National University of "Kyiv-Mohyla Academy" (MA in Economics and Bachelor's Degree in Social Sciences).

Eva Thiel: Senior economist at the OECD, Directorate for Financial, Fiscal and Enterprise Affairs, presently engaged in research and analysis for the Committee on Capital Movements and Invisible Transactions. Her previous working experience with the OECD and the European Bank for Reconstruction and Development includes research on transition economies. Eva Thiel is a Swedish national and has graduated from the University of Lund, Sweden and Princeton University, USA.

Ulrich Thiessen, Dr.rer.pol.: Research Associate at the German Institute for Economic Research (DIW), Berlin, and member of the German Advisory Group on Economic Reform with the Government of Ukraine (Kyiv). His work concentrates mainly on macroeconomic analysis, especially on monetary, fiscal and external economic policy. Formerly economist with the IMF in Washington D.C.

Vadym Volosovych: Research Associate at the Institute for Economic Research and Policy Consulting. Particular concentration on macroeconomic analysis and forecasting as well as monetary, exchange rate and investment policy. Education at the National University of "Kyiv-Mohyla Academy" (MA in Economics) and the Dnipropetrovsk State University (Specialist's Degree in Economics with specialisation in International Law).

Stephan von Cramon-Taubadel: Professor of Agricultural Policy at the University of Göttingen, and member of the German Advisory Group on Economic Reform with the Government of Ukraine (Kyiv). Editor-in-Chief of Agricultural Economics, the official journal of the International Association of Agricultural Economists. Research on agricultural policy analysis, and quantitative methods of agricultural market and price analysis. Education at McGill University, the University of Manitoba, and the University of Kiel.

Christian von Hirschhausen, Dr.rer.oec.: Research Associate at the German Institute for Economic Research (DIW), Berlin, and member of the German Advisory Group on Economic Reform with the Government of Ukraine (Kyiv). Specialises in structural and competition policy and enterprise reform. Previous positions at the United Nations (New York), École des Mines de Paris, the University of Colorado (Boulder), and the Technical University of Berlin.

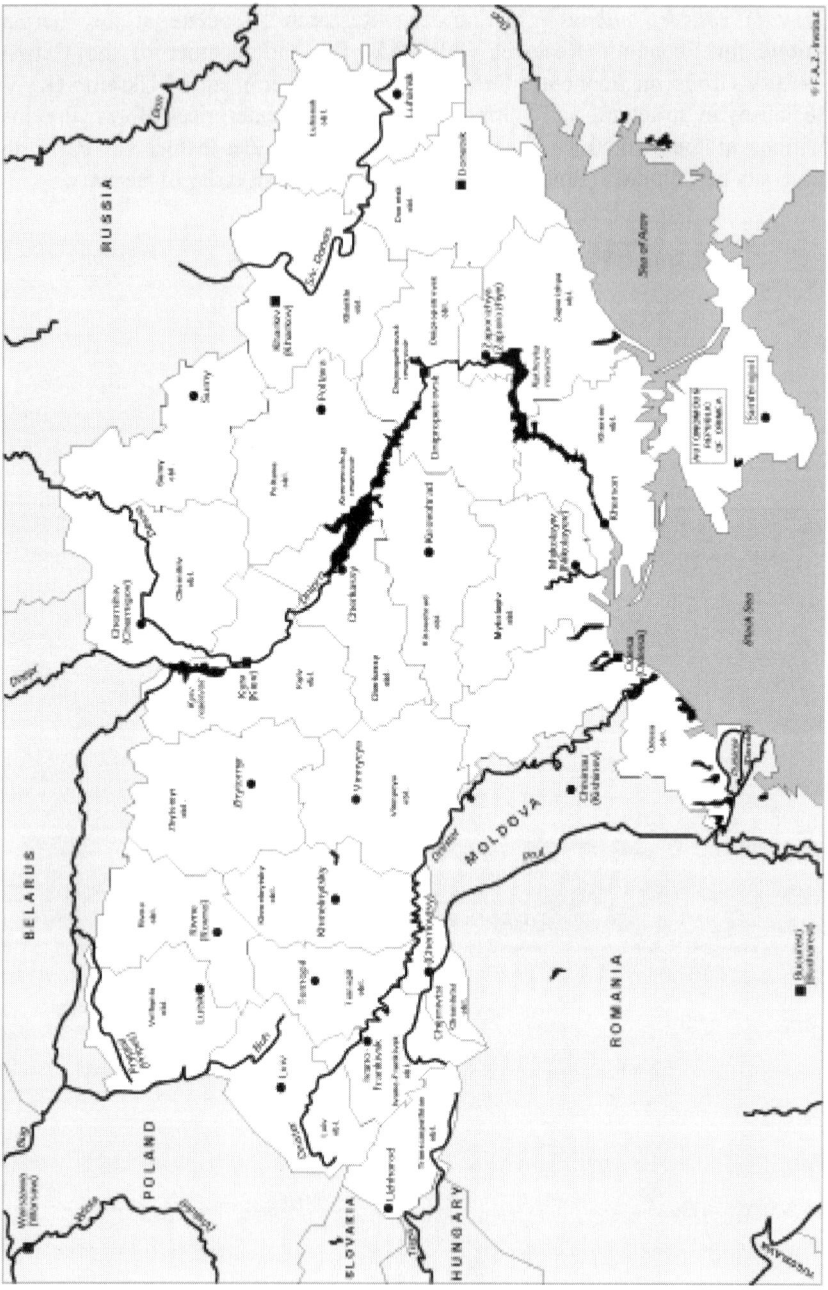

Ukraine: Administrative map

Ukraine: Economic map

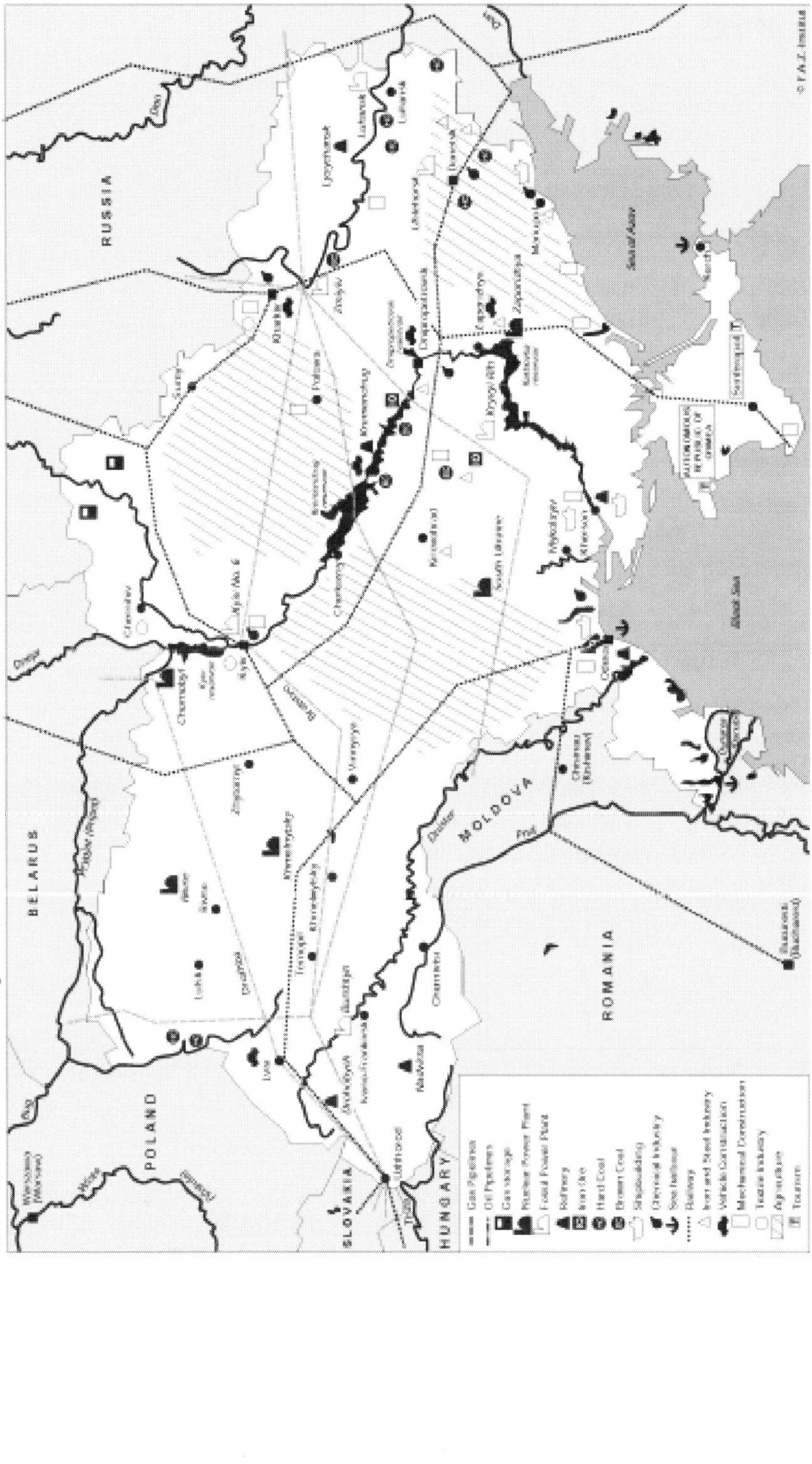

Tables

Graphs

Abbreviations

CASE	Center for Social and Economic Research in Warsaw
CBR	Central Bank of Russia
CEB	Central European and Baltic
CEE	Central and Eastern Europe
CEO	Chief Executive Officer
CIS	Commonwealth of Independent States
CMEA	Council for Mutual Economic Assistance
CPI	Consumer Price Index
EBRD	European Bank for Reconstruction and Development
EPT	Enterprise profits tax
EU	European Union
EUR	Euro
FDI	Foreign direct investment
FOB	Free on Board
FSU	Former Soviet Union
GDP	Gross domestic product
GNP	Gross national product
IAS	International Accounting Standards
ICPS	International Centre for Policy Studies
IERPC	Institute for Economic Research and Policy Consulting
IFC	International Finance Corporation
IMF	International Monetary Fund
NBU	National Bank of Ukraine
OECD	Organisation for Economic Cooperation and Development
OPT	Outward processing trade
PPI	Producer Price Index
RAO UES	Russian Joint Stock Company United Energy System of Russia

RUR	Russian Rouble
SME	Small and medium-sized enterprises
SOE	State-owned enterprises
TACIS	Technical Assistance to the Commonwealth of Independent States
TNC	Transnational companies
UAH	Ukrainian Hryvnia
UEPLAC	Ukrainian-European Policy and Legal Advice Centre
UNCTAD	United Nations Conference on Trade and Development
USAID	United States Agency for International Development
USD	US Dollar
USSR	Union of Soviet Socialist Republics
VAT	Value-added tax
WTO	World Trade Organisation

Index

Druck: Strauss Offsetdruck, Mörlenbach
Verarbeitung: Schäffer, Grünstadt